LANGUAGE IN USE

Readings in Sociolinguistics

Edited by
JOHN BAUGH and JOEL SHERZER
University of Texas

PRENTICE-HALL, INC., ENGLEWOOD CLIFFS, NEW JERSEY 07632

Library of Congress Cataloging in Publication Data
Main entry under title:

Language in use.

   Includes bibliographies.
    1. Sociolinguistics—Addresses, essays, lectures.
I. Baugh, John (date)   .   II. Sherzer, Joel.
P40.L297 1984   401'.9   83-27046
ISBN 0-13-522996-0 (pbk.)

Editorial/production supervision and
   interior design: *Hilda Tauber*
Cover design: *Diane Saxe*
Manufacturing buyer: *Harry P. Baisley*

Printed in the United States of America

10 9 8 7 6 5 4 3 2 1

ISBN 0-13-522996-0

PRENTICE-HALL INTERNATIONAL, INC., *London*
PRENTICE-HALL OF AUSTRALIA PTY. LIMITED, *Sydney*
EDITORA PRENTICE-HALL DO BRASIL, LTDA., *Rio de Janeiro*
PRENTICE-HALL CANADA INC., *Toronto*
PRENTICE-HALL OF INDIA PRIVATE LIMITED, *New Delhi*
PRENTICE-HALL OF JAPAN, INC., *Tokyo*
PRENTICE-HALL OF SOUTHEAST ASIA PTE. LTD., *Singapore*
WHITEHALL BOOKS LIMITED, *Wellington, New Zealand*

CONTENTS

LANGUAGE AND SPEECH
IN ETHNOGRAPHIC PERSPECTIVE   165

SOCIAL BASES OF LANGUAGE CHANGE   245

INTRODUCTION

In the 1960s and 1970s a series of edited collections were published, calling for research dealing with the intersection of language, culture, and society, and reporting on research that had been carried out to that time. Since then sociolinguistics has become a recognized and established perspective on the study of language and language use. This book represents a selection of developments in the field of sociolinguistics since the formative period.

One aspect of the development of sociolinguistics has been its tremendous growth in a wide variety of directions. We have thus found it necessary to select and to focus our choice of papers according to a particular set of orientations. Our focus can best be stated in terms of two key concepts—empirical and ethnographic. The papers in this collection are empirical in that they deal with real language usage, recorded in and analyzed in terms of actual social and cultural contexts. These contexts vary from whole societies (the Kuna Indians of Panama) to urban centers (Philadelphia), to particular public places (urban streets) or institutions (convenience stores). The papers are ethnographic in that they relate to social and cultural context in two distinct but integrated senses: first, the social and cultural backdrop, the ground rules and assumptions of language usage; and second, the immediate, actual, ongoing, and emerging social and cultural contexts of speech events. The authors are also committed to the need for cross-cultural comparisons, both within our own quite complex and heterogeneous society and in the larger world.

Certain basic assumptions of sociolinguistics that emerged from its formative period are reflected in this book. These include the fact that language use is heterogeneous (whether studied from the point of view of single individuals, networks, or whole communities) and that this heterogeneity may occur at any level of language, from phonetic and phonological variation to choices between or among entire languages; that utterances can mean more than they say on the surface, and attention to social and cultural context in relation to actual language use is necessary for the analysis of language in general; that patterns and processes of language use are intimately related to both language change and to language acquisition and development. This collection also views communicative competence as a fundamental concept in sociolinguistics. While all of the papers share certain theoretical bases and are empirical and ethnographic in orientation, the authors employ a wide variety of methods of data collection and analysis. There are statistical surveys as well as qualitative analyses; and there are ethnographic, interactional, and symbolic interpretations.

The topics represented in this volume, which are reflected in part by our section titles, are the nature and proper description of linguistic variation; multilingualism, including code-switching; the analysis of discourse, including narrative; a fine-grained approach to everyday language, especially conversational; ethnography of speaking; language change in social context; and the acquisition and development of communicative competence. This collection demonstrates certain significant directions of current work in sociolinguistics, in particular the growing convergence of three separate traditions: the linguistic, the sociological, and the ethnographic.

While they reflect the empirical thrust of research in sociolinguistics, as well as the editors' own orientations, the papers collected here also offer important theoretical contributions. These theoretical contributions can be viewed either in terms of the parent disciplines—anthropology, linguistics, and sociology—or in terms of a set of concerns inherent in sociolinguistics itself. Thus advances have been made in our understanding of linguistic diversity, and concepts like the speech community, social networks, and variable rules have been considerably refined. The study of the dynamic intersection of linguistic and social factors in language change has added sophistication to our conceptions of the nature of language history. With regard to the study of discourse, speech acts, events, and situations, analysis has achieved fine-grained precision in the description of the way in which context—social, cultural, and personal—relates to verbal patterning at every level. Rules of communication along with causes of miscommunication have been better understood. Although much analysis in language has focused on particular cases, certain universals have also emerged. Some of these have to do with units of discourse, such as greetings and leave-takings. Others involve general dimensions of language use, such as formality and politeness.

The sections of this book are but one organization of the various theoretical, methodological, and empirical directions of sociolinguistics. We find them a convenient way to conceive of the field. Section One deals with various types of diversity, including multilingualism and variation within a single language. Attention is paid to social units, such as the tribe, which have direct implications for understanding speech communities, and to theories and methods in the study of linguistic heterogeneity. Section Two includes papers that view language both as a reflection of, and a contributor to, social interactions between individuals. These papers demonstrate the complicated underpinnings of seemingly simple, routine, and ordinary talk. They also contribute to the understanding and analysis of units of discourse—conversations, statements, questions, promises, directives, greetings, leave-takings, and turns at talk. The study of discourse has involved an interesting intersection of perspectives from philosophy, linguistics, and sociology; this section reflects some of this development. Section Three contains recent research in the ethnography of speaking. These papers are the most cross-culturally varied of the collection, including South America, Papua New Guinea, and Africa, as well as Anglo Texas. Ethnographers of speaking are concerned with a variety of topics involving the social and cultural dimensions of language, such as narrative, oratory, and metaphor, along with the acquisition and development of communicative competence. The papers in Section Four share a concern with the relationship between social change and language change. They deal with a variety of areas of language—pidginization and creolization, linguistic variation, vocabulary, pronominal usage, and bilingual choice. All of the papers in this volume, whether dealing with American society or other societies, stress both universal and cross-cultural differences, continuities through time and space, and the particularities of individual cases.

A number of themes and issues cut across the organization of these sections. One is the close connection between linguistic variation in social context and language change over time, which relates sections One and Four. Another is the interplay of social interactional and sociocultural factors in discourse, which relates sections Two and Three. Still another is the fact that acquisition of communicative competence involves the learning and teaching of all aspects of language, including variation and discourse patterning, social interactional and cultural norms, and even aspects of language change in progress.

When viewed collectively, the salient theme of social relevance represents a common denominator for these papers, as it has been since the inception of sociolinguistics. Because of its empirical focus and its concern with the relationship of language to actual social and cultural contexts, sociolinguistics by its very nature involves the analysis of social conflicts and social issues, in a range of areas including language and sex roles, language and ethnicity, language and social class, and language and institutions. While the papers in this volume do not make explicit recommendations for change, they provide empirical, analytical bases for better understanding of these areas of language use.

SELECTED BIBLIOGRAPHY

BRIGHT, W. (ed.). 1966. *Sociolinguistics*. The Hague: Mouton.
GIGLIOLI, P.P. (ed). 1972. *Language in Social Context*. Harmondsworth: Penguin.
GUMPERZ, J.J. 1971. *Language in Social Groups*. Stanford: Stanford University Press.
GUMPERZ, J.J. and HYMES D.H. (eds.). 1972. *Directions in Sociolinguistics: The Ethnography of Communication*. New York: Holt, Rinehart, & Winston.

HUDSON, R.A. 1980.   *Sociolinguistics*. New York: Cambridge University Press.
HYMES, D.H. (ed). 1964.   *Language in Culture and Society.* New York: Harper & Row.
———. 1974.   *Foundations of Sociolinguistics: An Ethnographic Approach.* Philadelphia: University of Pennsylvania Press.
LABOV, W. 1972.   *Sociolinguistic Patterns*. Philadelphia: University of Pennsylvania Press.
PRIDE, J.B. and HOLMES, J. (eds.). 1972.   *Sociolinguistics*. Harmondsworth: Penguin.
TRUDGILL, P. 1974.   *Sociolinguistics: An Introduction*. Harmondsworth: Penguin.

LINGUISTIC DIVERSITY IN SOCIAL AND CULTURAL CONTEXT

The papers in this section consider some of the most basic issues in sociolinguistics. DELL HYMES reviews aspects of the concept of tribe, which are pertinent to definitions of speech communities; he stresses communicative relationships among persons and groups, and the lack of a necessary isomorphic relationship among language, culture, and society. The result is a most significant contribution to the anthropological notion of tribe, with strong interdisciplinary implications. WILLIAM LABOV provides insights into quantitative studies of linguistic change and variation, which grew out of extensive research in the greater Philadelphia speech community. He offers alternative methodological strategies for approaching studies of language in community settings generally, and urban areas in particular. PETER TRUDGILL builds on the concept of linguistic variation, with specific attention to language change. He examines change in contemporary terms in an urban setting.

When viewed collectively, these papers share the observation that social and linguistic diversity is characteristic of speech communities. Sociolinguists analyze the relationship between this social and linguistic diversity. In spite of their different perspectives, these papers jointly offer insights that can only be gained through careful study of the social and cultural contexts in which language is used. The themes that are raised in these papers are also echoed in others in this volume. JUDITH T. IRVINE's observations about formality and informality (Section Three) complement Hymes's discussion of communicative relationships, and Labov's paper raises issues of linguistic change that are pertinent to JOHN BAUGH's analysis of the Black English copula (Section Four), and hints at the pidginization and creolization processes that are examined by GILLIAN SANKOFF and SUZANNE LABERGE for Tok Pisin in urban New Guinea (Section Four). Trudgill's paper offers

5

insights that enhance the observations that CAROL BROOKS GARDNER makes about urban females in public settings (Section Two). The essential shared goal for these papers is to examine the dynamic nature of language, along with a firm commitment to empirical verification in social and cultural context.

SELECTED BIBLIOGRAPHY

LABOV, W. (ed).) 1980. *Locating Language in Time and Space*. New York: Academic Press.
SANKOFF, D. (ed.). 1978. *Linguistic Variation: Models and Methods*. New York: Academic Press.
SANKOFF, G. 1980. *The Social Life of Language*. Philadelphia: University of Pennsylvania Press.
TRUDGILL, P. 1983. *On Dialect*. New York: New York University Press.

DELL HYMES

Linguistic Problems in Defining the Concept of "Tribe"

INTRODUCTION

To consider the concept of "tribe" from the standpoint of language, I must consider the relation of language to social units generally. I shall argue that current anthropological practice often reflects, perhaps unwittingly, a view of the relation that is untenable.

A direct way to put the matter is this: Do tribes have linguistic correlates? If they do, can these correlates be used as diagnostic markers of units that are culturally distinct for purposes of analysis and cross-cultural comparison? In principle, the answer is yes. The question of linguistic correlates for tribes is a question of ethnolinguistic (or sociolinguistic) theory, and such a theory, if adequate, must include a fundamental assumption of some such sort as this:

> ...each enduring social relationship entails the selection and/or creation of com-
> municative means considered specific to it by its participants (Hymes 1967, 1971).

If there exists a set of social relationships, then there will exist communicative (and, by extension, linguistic) features considered specific to the relationships by their participants. It will be possible in principle to identify the features, and to use them to identify the group.

In short, it follows from the place of language in social life that for any set of social relationships one may wish to call a tribe, some set of corresponding linguistic features may be found. (Moreover, the features in themselves are cultural, so that with respect to them, if nothing else, the tribe is distinctively a culture-bearing unit.) This answer holds, whatever one's definition of "tribe," and for whatever "cultunit" is of concern.

This general answer is of small help to one who wishes to state the number and boundaries of units in a region or sample now. For one thing, the linguistic features that serve as correlates of a given type of social unit may vary greatly in number, kind, and salience from one case to another. Perhaps but a single "shibboleth" of pronunciation may be involved; or a pattern that emerges only from the differential frequency across a series of situations of certain common traits (Labov 1966). In general, the linguistic correlates of social relationships, the sociolinguistic structure present in a group, can only occasionally and partially be recovered from the literature. Ethnographers and linguists have usually not done the

From the *American Ethnological Society Proceedings*, 1967. Reproduced by permission of the American Ethnological Society and Dell Hymes.

necessary work. (Indeed, the idea of sociolinguistic description as an explicit goal, theoretically motivated, has only recently come to the fore.)

To be sure, ethnologists wish usually to deal just with those social units that bear, not just some cultural features, but such masses of them as are commonly called "cultures." To this purpose, one usually wishes information as to not just some linguistic features, but as to sets considered to be of the same scale as "cultures," namely, whole dialects or languages. Typically one inquires as to the relation between cultures and languages (or dialects) as wholes. One wants an enumeration of language units, together with their full genetic classification (facts of relationship, subgrouping of dialects, mapping).

Scholars have been usefully at the business of genetic classification, as a guide to ethnic identity and origin, since at least the early eighteenth century,[1] and it is a task that is more clearly understood and more limited than that of sociolinguistic description; but it is not the answer to the problem in hand. The reason is theoretical, rather than practical. To be sure, we are far from adequate knowledge of the genetic connections for all the world's languages. There are methodological questions as to delimitation of units within complexes of dialects, as to proof of remote relationship, and as to determination of subgroups (languages with specially shared history subsequent to the breakup of a larger group to which they belong). There is sheer need for information from field work, philology, reconstruction. Even perfect knowledge of this sort, however, would not suffice.

Perfect knowledge would not suffice because it is a mistake to put the matter so. One must ask, not about genetic relationships among languages and objective linguistic demarcation of dialects, but about *communicative relationships among persons and groups*. What count for the establishment of "culture-bearing" units, and the transmission of cultural phenomena, are boundaries of communication.

In one sense, we all know this. If anthropologists continue to ask for information as to genetic classification of languages, and purely linguistic demarcation of dialects, then, it must be because such classification and demarcation are thought to stand in some diagnostic relationship to boundaries of communication. But just this assumption must be abandoned. The relation of languages and dialects to communicative relationships among persons and groups is problematic. It is a relationship that needs desperately to be investigated, both in ethnographic depth and in comparative perspective.

Naroll (1964:291a) reports that for many anthropologists "the criterion of language is considered essential," the one reservation being that "there are serious practical difficulties in applying it." The fact of the matter is that the difficulties are not just of application, but of empirical and theoretical adequacy.

Let me consider more fully the assumptions made as to language in much recent ethnological work; indicate why they cannot be part of a theory of the relation of language to cultural units; and sketch the sort of perspective that may serve instead. (Consideration of the general relation of language to ethnic units applies a fortiori to the case of the "tribe.")

LANGUAGES AS BOUNDARY MARKERS
IN RECENT ETHNOLOGY

Recent discussions of "cultunit" and comparative ethnology in *Current Anthropology* provide a reference point,[2] but my argument is directed at widespread assumptions, not at particular authors of recent articles. Naroll's formulation will be focussed upon here because he has recently wrestled with the many grave difficulties that the widespread assumptions entail (1964:287-288, 289a, 290b, 291a, 306a-b). He carries the effort about as far as it can go. I hope to show that if the formulation is unsatisfactory, it is because it cannot be made satisfactory.

Let me stress also that I do not argue the necessary invalidity of the sort of cross-cultural research pursued by Naroll, Driver, and others. It may well be that much research often does not depend upon the use of a fine-grained criterion for ethnic identity, linguistic or otherwise. The inevitable scatter of adequately documented cases (cf. Naroll 1964:290b), and statistical and other controls may obviate the problem.

It remains that much attention is lavished on language (and dialect) boundaries, that indeed, field workers are urged to report in terms of them (Naroll 1964:309c). Even if cross-cultural research should not need to rely on such boundaries, then, the present concern reinforces the mistaken assumptions on which the reliance is based. For some research, moreover, the validity of the assumption is of direct concern (for example, controlled co-variation within an area to determine causal relationships); and the validity is of central concern to anthropological theory of language.

Nature of Assumptions

The assumptions underlying the use of language as a criterion in recent cross-cultural research would seem roughly to be as follows:

(1) "One language—one culture"; that is, the ethnographic world can be divided into "ethnolinguistic" units, each associating a language with a culture.

(2) When the units are demarcated in space (mapped), the demarcation implies a break in mutual intelligibility in virtue of the language, and hence in communication in virtue of the culture.

(3) The language in question is the medium of communication for the content of interest with regard to the culture in question.

(4) These boundary relationships (language, culture, communication) have persisted in time.

A practical problem arises with regard to (2): it is one of finding an objective measure of the demarcation of language units. From such a measure, demarcation of communicative units is thought to follow. (I shall comment later on the failure to treat the practical problems arising with regard to [4].)

Persistence of Assumptions

Some or all of this set of assumptions is very old (as note 1 indicates). The outlook is one which I have labelled "Herderian" (ms. c), after the great German pioneer of modern anthropology, whose view of the integral relation of language to cultural identity did so much to shape subsequent thought for both good and ill. The hold of the outlook has been reinforced in American work by the dominant neogrammarian approach to genetic relationship and the reconstruction of language history on a family-tree (*Stammbaum*) model, at the expense of the perspective of wave-theory (*Wellentheorie*) or mesh principle (Swadesh 1959); and by the structuralist practice of abstracting grammar from ethnographic context, and of positing a homogeneous speech-community as object of description.

In recent ethnological literature one finds Driver (1966:158) writing of the troubles over ethnic units:

> If we had a more accurate classification of languages with quantitative guides for such labels as dialect, language, subfamily, family, and phylum, *we could accurately group all ethnic units according to their position in such a scheme* [my emphasis] ...because neither classification [language, culture area] is sufficiently refined, there is no immediate solution to the ethnic unit problem.

Later Driver observes (1966:160b): "As is apparent, I prefer to regard all mutually unintelligible languages as separate ethnic units" (citing another study [1965:328-29]).

In his review of discussions of the culture-bearing unit, Naroll singles out as a common thread the conception of the unit as one in which a common language is spoken, and himself repeatedly points out this agreement on the importance of languages (e.g., 291a in his Summary, and in his Abstract). At the same time Naroll adds that none of the writers he reviews thinks that speech community alone can be relied on to define the basic culture-bearing unit, although they do not agree on what else needs to be considered. (Notice the implicit equation of common language with speech community.) Naroll stresses the serious practical difficulties of defining and measuring the intelligibility of dialects, of marking boundaries along linguistic continua, and of classifying multilingual speakers; at one point, indeed, he writes of his own concept:

> The cultunit, I submit, generally resembles fairly closely at least *some* operating social unit within the society wherever these units have sharp boundaries. Its most arbitrary element is its delineation of boundaries along linguistic continuums from a bibliographic vantage point... (289a).

His final definition of the basic culture-bearing unit to be used in cross-cultural studies, however, selects language as one of three criteria, together with political organization and territorial contiguity. And it must be noticed that the four cultunit types are introduced as emerging when one considers the interrelations of two kinds of boundaries, a linguistic boundary and a communication-link (state or contact group) boundary, a cultunit boundary being formed by either of these two boundaries. The communication-link boundary is thus in effect a linguistic boundary too, being defined by a common *lingua franca* (state) or common distinct language (contact group). Where there is no state ("a territorially ramified territorial team whose leaders assert and wield the exclusive right to declare and conduct warfare" [286]), then

> *linguistic boundaries only* [my emphasis] are followed unless contact gaps occur which break up speech communities into cultunits within which speech communication presumably flows freely but between which speech communication presumably is rare and unimportant; [later, reference is made to]...the speech communication groups thus defined... (288a).

My purpose here is not to exposit or discuss Naroll's classification of types of units, but to indicate the way in which linguistic terms and criteria enter into it. The passages just cited make clear that linguistic boundaries and boundaries of speech communication are equated. That in general Naroll intends his criterion of linguistic boundaries to demarcate communication boundaries is indeed made explicit:

> My approach has been rather to identify communication units (*assuming* [sic] that, since culture is constantly changing, these units will tend to be culturally distinct) (307b).

This passage recalls an earlier statement that

> The communication nets through which these [cultural] changes are passed from "mouth to mouth"—i.e., from mind to mind—are obviously key elements in defining the culture-bearing group. A speech community tends to form such a communication net, even though its boundaries may be blurry... [problems of translation, political states, distance are then alluded to] (289a-b).

Such concepts as communication net, communication unit, speech community, speech communication group, linguistic boundary, common distinct language, communication-link boundary, mutual intelligibility (interintelligibility) unit within which cultural changes accumulate—all these appear to be regarded as pretty much equivalent in delimiting what is wanted.

The operational test for delimitation is discussed in terms of the measurement of mutual intelligibility by objective criteria of lexical similarity between dialects. *Percentage of lexical similarity, mutual intelligibility, language boundary, communication boundary thus are effectively equated.*

In keeping with this equation, several comments indicate that the problem with the use of language as a criterion in ethnology is not after all empirical or theoretical, but one of application. The problem is not one of the relation between lexical percentages and mutual intelligibility; of the relation between mutual intelligibility and language boundary; or of the relation between language boundary and communication boundary. Rather, the problem is one of obtaining sufficient information to make the objective measurement of all of these at once that in principle is possible. In its reference to a "bibliographic vantage point," the comment quoted above on delineation of boundaries within linguistic continua implies lack of reported information as the difficulty (cf. 209b). In an itemization of eleven serious linguistic classification problems (284a-b, 285), the stress is upon the extremely technical and difficult nature of defining mutual intelligibility operationally; existing ethnographic materials are found to make the definition often sheer guess work. When a practical working method for comparative ethnologists is proposed (287), it is in terms of percentages of "recognizable cognates" on word lists (80% or more implying mutual intelligibility, less than 80% lack of it [286a-b]). Where comparative word lists are not available, statements by informants or ethnographers about intelligibility can be followed; the primacy of the objective lexical measurement is implied in the comment that such judgments can probably be trusted to agree with the "recognizable cognate" word-list method, except when the dialects concerned are in the "partially intelligible" class.

In sum, while there is frank recognition of difficulties posed by the notion of language as boundary-marker, and by the testing of boundaries by lexical percentages, it is on this package that one falls back.

The attention to lexical percentages probably is an American, rather than international, propensity, because of the greater attention given lexicostatistics here. It is worth pointing out, therefore, that even if one does not rely on lexical measures of boundary and subgrouping, the considerations to be presented still apply. Use of phonological isoglosses, grammatical criteria, shared innovations of whatever sort, combinations of linguistic features of diverse sorts, all have in common the fact that they are diacritics whose relation, as markers of language boundaries, to mutual intelligibility and communication boundaries remains problematic, as will be shown.

CRITIQUE (I): EXCEPTIONS

The commentators in *Current Anthropology* themselves provide something of a running series of empirical illustrations of the failure of linguistic unity and separateness to coincide with cultural units in various parts of the world: Western desert of Australia (Berndt, 292b), northeast Arnhem Land (Berndt, 292b), Chinese Moslems (Bessac, 293b), Tumet Mongols (Bessac, 293b), Northern Cayapó (Dole, 294b), Nyul-Nyul and Bard of northwestern Australia (Dole, 294b), Upper Xingu region of Brazil (Dole, 294c), China (Sjoberg, 303c), together with flat objection (Moore, 300c) and some criticism of the operational criteria (Driver, 294b).

Nuba: Ethnolinguistic Mosaic

To these examples others, well-known, can be added. Nadel on the Nuba has already been cited in connection with this problem by Moerman (1965:1220):

> We shall meet with groups which, though they are close neighbours and possess an almost identical language and culture, do not regard themselves as one tribe...; and we shall also meet with tribes which claim this unity regardless of internal cultural differentiation. Cultural and linguistic uniformity, then, does not imply, and cultural and linguistic diversity—at least within certain limits—not preclude, the recognition of tribal unity (Nadel 1947:13).

Yir Yoront: Personal Network

Lauriston Sharp's portrait of the Yir Yoront, Koko Bera, and Kut Taiori, three language groups of Australia, is well known for its conclusion that there does not exist among them a "tribe" as an organized society or community which holds territory; that clan membership, not speech affiliation, is the basic element in determining a person's geographic associations and social relations; and that the language community, such as Yir Yoront, is purely a linguistic category, comprising people who in no sense constitute a corporate or organized entity. There is Yoront speech (or Koko Bera speech, or Kut Taiori speech), but not such a thing as Yoront country or Yoront customs. The Yir Yoront form of social organization is one in which three speakers of the same language based in the same language area may each have an essentially different interaction network along a geographically different circuit. The situation is representative of the organization of more than one hundred different named speech communities investigated by Sharp throughout all north Queensland.

Eastern Niger Delta:
Ethnic, Linguistic, Intelligibility Boundaries

A particularly cogent example of the non-identity of ethnic group, language group, and mutual intelligibility—all three—is provided by Wolff (1967). In the Eastern Niger Delta ("Rivers" area) hinterland several languages have diverged from a common ancestor in a contiguous territory. The result is that ethnically, from west to east, there are found three groups, the Ogbia, Odual, and Abua. Linguistically, from west to east, there are found three groups, but not the same three: Ogbia, Kugbo, and Odual-Abua. Kugbo is the language of a group of four villages among the Odual; the language while closely related to Odual, is distinct. Odual proper and Abua, on the other hand, are divergent dialects of the same language. With regard to mutual intelligibility in terms of language, from west to east, there are three groups again, but again not the same three: the western Ogbia dialects; the eastern Ogbia dialects and Kugbo; and Abua, with mutual intelligibility that is less than satisfactory, with Odual. Schematically, one has:

Type of Unit:				
Ethnic	Ogbia		Odual	Abua
Linguistic	Ogbia	Kugbo	(Odual — Abua)	
Intelligibility	W. Ogbia	(E. Ogbia-Kugbo)	(Odual ?—? Abua)	

The example shows that there may be mutual intelligibility, despite difference of language (E. Ogbia-Kugbo), and mutual non-intelligibility, despite oneness of language (W. Ogbia-E. Ogbia) (cf. discussion of intelligibility below).

Such examples might be thought to dispose of the question. Clearly language classification cannot be taken for granted as boundary marker of units at once ethnic and communicative in nature. Clearly the relations between the units classified by linguists as languages, and the communicative units of ethnology, are problematic. Apparently the examples do not suffice. The felt need for an ethnological criterion, and the underlying, persistent assumptions about the isomorphic relation of languages to cultures seem to withstand citation of exceptions, however numerous. Let me come at the matter in a different way.

From a theoretical standpoint, *each language-involving term in the proposed definition of cultunit—and any language-involving term in any definition of ethnic or cultural unit—is to be regarded, not as a constant, but as a variable.* No such term can be taken for granted as having fixed value with regard to communicative boundaries. Each such term can be realized by more than one kind of circumstance, entailing more than one kind of consequence for the boundaries of communication.

CRITIQUE (II): COMPONENTS OF CULTUNIT

The definition of cultunit enumerates "domestic$_1$ speakers$_2$ of a common$_3$ distinct$_4$ language$_5$," (numerals supplied). I shall consider each in turn.

(1) *Domestic:* There may be more than one language of the home, each linking the family in a different direction. Voegelin (1964:304a) raises the question of situations in which the language of the parents is not that of the child. The code relevant for communicative boundary with respect to certain cultural features may not be definable in terms of domestic use, but may be an "argot" (Gumperz 1962) specialized to use outside the home. In general, in a world of multilingual societies, codes are specialized in use, and choice of code is governed by rules, these rules depending upon features such as scene, participants, end in view, topic, channel, and the like—in sum, upon different opportunities, and contents of communication. (Cf. discussion in Hymes 1967a.) Which of a group's codes is relevant as defining its communicative boundary may vary with the cultural or social content of one's problem.

A very striking and interesting case in point is reported by Arthur F. Sorensen. The central northwest Amazon, straddling the Brazilian-Colombian border, is an area homogeneous in culture. One level of social organization of the peoples within the area may be termed the tribe. Such a tribe is a politico-ceremonial unit, consisting of certain sibs, and associated with other tribes within an exogamous phratry (that has no function other than exogamy). The tribe has a unique history and is identifiable with a discrete language. Its members are expected to have used the language as principal language in their childhood nuclear family. That language of tribe and longhouse, however, is a "father-tongue." The mothers (each from a different tribe, due to exogamy) retain their separate tribal identity, and while using the husband's language when talking directly with their children, usually have several other women from their own tribe in the longhouse with whom to use their own "father-tongue." Each longhouse may have a characteristic repertoire of languages, determined by the origins of its wives. All individuals of the longhouse will control the repertoire, amounting commonly to at least four languages. Multilingualism is the norm and expectation. There is a spurt in active command of languages during adolescence; augmentation of the repertoire and of competence in it continues throughout life. These languages are mutually unintelligible, and often quite different in character. Persons are unselfconsçious about their multilingualism, using it purely instrumentally with regard to the language of their interlocutors and locale. One of the languages, Tukano, serves as a *lingua franca* throughout much of the area. The commonalty of patterns of speaking, as in greeting conversation, is such that Sorensen has witnessed and participated in many occasions in which the language of a longhouse was unknown either to him or to some of his Indian travelling companions, yet it was perfectly clear to all what the content was of the sequence of bilingual statements being made (cf. mention below of *Sprechbund*, or speech area).

In sum, we have here a striking case in which cultural unity is independent of both political and linguistic hegemony. Communicative unity extends throughout the region through a cultural pattern of multilingualism, and areal patterns of speaking. The patterns are supported by attitudes toward the acquisition and use of languages that extend multilingualism into the domestic residence in a patterned way, and link longhouses along the rivers in continua, not of dialect, but of overlapping code-repertoires. With regard to tribe and language, there is complete correlation between tribal identity and a given language, yet the fact in isolation would be quite misleading as to the actual communicative and cultural relationships.

(2) *Speakers:* The term "speakers" is usable only as a surrogate for the set of possible relationships to use of a code that permit intercommunication. As a general term, *users* may be preferable. One may find speakers, hearers, writers, readers, and all possible combinations. Which mode of use, or which set of modes

of use, is pertinent in defining a communicative boundary will vary with one's problem. (I do not understand why Naroll [1964:309c] wishes to ignore both the use of written Chinese as a lingua franca, and its former wider distribution as such; both facts would seem pertinent to communicative links and boundaries.)

In north Queensland (Sharp 1958) one finds communicative and cultural unity based on shared understandings, shared hearer's rules of interpretation. Such unity of understanding is compatible with diverse overt forms for signalling. Sharp writes:

> While most of the six hundred people of these three language groups (Yir Yoront, Koko Bera, Kut Taiori) speak only one of the languages mentioned, a majority of them also understand or "hear" a second language, and many, a third. The "network . . . of understandings" thus exists which might serve, regardless of language differences, as a basis for a society or for a community of interests. . . . everywhere there is flux or overlap of people with their mutually understood but different behaviors. (Sharp cites these facts in the context of making the point that such communicative understanding is not associated with any boundedness of territory, or political or other social demarcation into fixed units of the "nation" or "tribe" sort.)

(3) *Of a commmon:* The remarks under (1) *domestic* as to specialization of codes, and the remarks just made about shared understanding in the absence of shared speaking, apply here. Note that specialized codes may determine a communicative boundary without being common to a group as a whole. A certain number of users of a given code may be both necessary and sufficient to ensure the communication into a group and spread throughout it of some cultural features of interest. (The fact that the distribution of myths in North America does not correlate with language boundaries implies a series of bilingual links leading to the common sharing of narratives among tribes most of whose members did not know each other's language.)

(4) *Distinct* (i.e., mutually intelligible to speakers of a stated dialect). The concern here is to make boundaries of mutual intelligibility demarcate distinct languages.

The Niger Delta example has already shown that equating "interintelligibility" with a fixed degree of linguistic difference is in error. I must stress this point. An enumeration and classification of languages will not suffice as an index of communicative boundaries, quite apart from any question of correlation with ethnic units, recent shifts of language or ethnicity, and the like. Even if one could demarcate all languages objectively, one to a group, there is no univocal relation between the linguistic facts and facts of communication.

One might think that the more closely related two dialects, or two languages, the easier would be communication through their use; or, the more recently it would have lapsed, and hence the more commonalty of culture through communication ought there to be. It is impossible, however, to identify mutual intelligibility and the existence of communication by means of any measure of linguistic distance alone (cf. Wolff 1959:559). The most common index (that considered by Naroll) is one in terms of percentage of lexical cognates. Such an index may be useful for tracing the past connections of languages in and of themselves; no such measure can be guaranteed as a measure of communicative boundary.

There are several intersecting reasons. First, objectivity is not possible without attention to "subjective" factors of attitude. Depending on attitude, users of closely related codes may refuse or disdain to understand each other (Wolff 1959); users of distantly related or unrelated codes may make special effort and succeed in understanding. Haugen (1966) has discussed the way in which attitudes incorporating aesthetic evaluations of related languages (Danish, Norwegian, Swedish) may affect the degree of communication through them.

Second, the patterns as to the organization and content of speech must be taken into account. Just as adjacent languages may belong to a common linguistic area (*Sprachbund*) through sharing of common features irrespective of genetic relationship, so adjacent communities may belong to a common speech area (*Sprechbund*) through sharing of common patterns of speaking, irrespective of code relationships. Presumably where retention of features is not the explanation, such areas come about through the mediation of bilinguals; but they extend to monolinguals. Where speech areas exist, speakers of different dialects or languages share understandings as to what is to be said, as to what to say or expect to be said next. One and the same degree of objective linguistic distance thus may be associated with quite different degrees of mutual intelligibility, depending on the degree to which the patterns of speaking differ. Some speakers of Czech feel themselves to share a common "speech area" with Hungarians, Poles, and Germans, but not with the English, quite apart from knowledge of the respective national codes. (I owe the example, concept and term to Jiři Neustupný.) Recall also the northwest Amazon case cited earlier.

Third, the different sectors of a language need not sort identically as between groups. There may, for example, be shared phonology and syntax; and only lexicon may differentiate two languages in a community, as shown by recent work of John Gumperz on the Marathi and Kannada in certain Indian villages. There may be shared semantic systems expressed through different grammars, as between the Algonkian Yurok and the Athapaskan Hupa of northern California (Bright and Bright 1965). In general there may be likeness in one sector and not in others; likeness in two and not in a third; etc. Phenomena investigated under the too much neglected leading of "linguistic area," or "areal linguistics," attest to this. A striking example is that of Australia. Voegelin et al. (1963:24) observe:

> Something special is going on in Australia. To draw attention to this we use the term FAMILY-LIKE LANGUAGE for Australian languages having neighbor intelligibility but otherwise having as low a cognate density as exists between languages in the usual language families of the world.

The languages are so similar in phonology and grammar as to be considered closely related dialects of one language, yet so diverse in vocabulary as to suggest distinct languages. This phenomenon has been reported in many parts of Australia by several observers (Miller 1966). (The interintelligibility probably depends not only upon the phonological and grammatical resemblance, but also upon attitudes of acceptance toward differences of dialect, and great commonalty of what is said, when, to whom, etc., permitting predictability of content despite lexical differences [recall Sharp on north Queensland].)

One may compare to this the situation in parts of India (mentioned above) wherein switching from one language to another is a switch from one lexicon to another, retaining common patterns of syntax and pronunciation.

Fourth, the linguistic changes separating dialects or languages may be asymmetrical in their effect on communication. The distance is objectively the same in either direction; but users of one may be better able to understand users of the other than the converse. (The phenomenon has become known as non-reciprocal intelligibility; cf. Olmsted [1954] for a review.) The effect of change is perhaps always complicated by attitudes, patterns of speaking, and metalinguistic practices: the differences may be valued or disvalued (cf. Haugen 1966 on semicommunication in Scandinavia); folk equations between cognates may be developed that facilitate understanding (Garde 1961 on Slavic dialects) or not.

Fifth, language learning is not merely a question that poses difficulty for classifying speakers. It is a universal consideration, whether the differences between communities are in terms of dialects, related languages, or unrelated languages. Voegelin (1964:304b) calls attention to the question of the length of time needed to learn the form of language across a language barrier. Among the Zapotec there is a folk taxonomy of dialects in terms of the number of days required to learn them. Such a question must of course be investigated in terms of what is regarded as an acceptable criterion of knowledge and use of the languages or dialects concerned. The Zapotec conception implies that one must deal not only with continua of dialects, but also with continua of acquisition and competence.

In general, then, given pairs of dialects or languages, equally distant, there may be special learning (some degree of bilingualism) in one case, and not in another; and where learning occurs, it may be in one direction only. For any case of language or dialect distance, then, there are four possible cases of communicative relationship with respect to just this fact alone:

(a)   no learning in either direction;
(b)   learning in one direction;
(c)   learning in the other direction;
(d)   learning in both directions.

The cases may be complicated by differential degree and specialization of learning in one or both directions. The topics and circumstances to which a language is specialized within a multilingual situation may differentiate cases otherwise alike with regard to the linguistic distance between dialects or languages. There may be free communication of whatever there is to talk about to the extent that it can be talked about; or, there may be no communication with regard to one or more aspects of culture, discourse on such aspects being restricted to another code, on one or both sides.

It has been cited as one problem of demarcation that "although Yahgan dialects are said to be mutually intelligible, they are also said *contradictorily* [my emphasis] to differ as much as Scotch and Cockney" (Naroll 1964:285a). It should be clear that there is nothing contradictory in such a situation. The cases cited from Australia, the Niger Delta, and elsewhere, together with the theoretical considerations, show as much. Mutual intelligibility depends upon a complex of factors, including lexical relationship, phonological relationship, grammatical relationship, relationship of patterns of speaking, and social attitudes toward such differences as exist.

It is not surprising that efforts to measure mutual intelligibility by a single device, such as percentage of lexical difference, have failed. Even efforts to measure dialect distance by the so-called "test the informant" method, wherein ability to translate tapes of other dialects is assessed in terms of percentages, can be vitiated, if such factors as learning and the patterns of the content and use of speech, are not controlled. The "ask the informant" method does not give a measure, only a judgment, to be sure, and such judgments can be biased as well as inexact; but such judgments are likely to reveal with rough accuracy the resultant in actual communication of all the impinging factors. I would trust an informant's judgment in preference to any one objective measure, and would take such a judgment as starting point for analysis of the situation.

In sum, facts of language condition communication across dialect and language boundaries, but do not control it. Indeed, *to rely on facts of language to determine boundaries of cultural communication amounts to a form of strong linguistic determinism*. Lexical, phonological, and grammatical facts cannot be ignored, to be sure, and they condition communication across boundaries; there are interesting and important questions to be investigated as to the nature of such conditioning. Such facts have here the same role as human instrumentalities generally; they are means of social action, not its master. People use languages, not the reverse. (Cf. the relation of structures to functions, discussed with regard to structural ethnography in Hymes 1964:43-44; and with regard to inference of cognitive style in Hymes 1966:116-23, 157-58; and with regard to the course of linguistics in Hymes 1967b.)

We come now to the last terminological variable in the definition of cultunit, namely,

(5) *Language*.   From all that has been said, it is clear that "language" cannot be regarded as invariant for the delimitation of culture boundaries in terms of communication. In effect, the term is too gross. From a historical standpoint, one regards language as differentiated into dialects (on some of the problems, see Hockett [1958] and Haugen [1966]); and we have seen cases in which a communicative boundary divides dialects assigned to the same language (western and eastern Ogbia).

From a synchronic standpoint, one must regard a language as a variable system of codes, specialized in function; not all of these codes will be intelligible to all members of a community (e.g., "languages of concealment" in ritual, courtship, and the like, derived perhaps by rules of permutation and deletion from the normal variety; or by substitution of forms not present in the normal variety).

What one wants is a term that can be defined as implying mutual intelligibility, communication, among those who share it in virtue of their sharing of it. Of terms available in the literature either "variety" or "code" might serve. Here I shall adopt "code."

Such a term permits one to treat just those sets of linguistic habits that are specific to one or another communicative function within and across group boundaries; and it is this that is at issue. One can also readily recognize that cultural features may be communicated through codes other than linguistic ones: gesture, objects, music.

The terms "language" and "dialect" may be reserved for the historically delineated sets of features usually intended by such terms as "English," "French,"

"Navaho," "Marathi" and the like. The resources of the English language, say, will be found to be differently organized into functional systems of codes in different sectors of the "English-speaking world." Not all speakers of English will be able to understand each other in English.

It should be clear that the five language-involving terms of the definition of cultunit deal with variables, not with constants that can be taken for granted. The analysis should have indicated that any such set of terms must be regarded in the same way. In order to determine communicative relationships among persons and groups, one must begin with persons and groups, the codes they share, and the purposes to which the codes are put.

I do not know whether or not a single general definition of cultural or communicative unit, suitable for ethnology, can be devised. It does seem clear that more than one kind of unit must be taken into account. So far as language is the means of communication, the most general requirement for the presence of a communicative unit may be expressed as the *sharing of rules for the interpretation of speech*. It must be stressed that such rules include not only rules for the interpretation of codes (in the sense of grammars) but also rules for the interpretation of the use of codes; and that knowledge of the two sorts of rules need not coincide. The concept of *speech area* was introduced earlier to designate a situation in which there was shared knowledge of rules for the interpretation of the use of codes, apart from shared knowledge of any one code. Conversely, those who share knowledge of a code may fail to share knowledge of a given set of rules for its use.

I would tentatively define the basic notion of *speech community* in terms of shared knowledge of rules for the interpretation of speech, including rules for the interpretation of at least one common code. Common rules of use but none of code would imply a *speech area*, as just discussed. Common rules of code, but not of use, might be taken to imply one aspect of *speech field*, that range of settings in which one's knowledge of rules makes communication potentially possible. For a given person or group, one would have to investigate empirically the variety of settings in which the *personal* (or *group*) *repertoire* of codes and rules of use would permit communication. A distinctive hierarchy, or array, or profile of speech fields might result. In this respect one might want also to distinguish *speech network*, as the particular linkages of communication actively participated in by a person or group.[3]

Whether or not these notions prove adequate in their present form, it is clear that some such set of notions is needed. What much ethnological thought has joined together, we must now put asunder, developing concepts adequate to the actual diversity of the phenomena.

ASSUMPTIONS REVISITED

My analysis so far has dealt most directly with the first two of the assumptions found to underly use of language boundaries as criteria in ethnology, those having to do with (1) the division of the world into "one language = one culture" ethnolinguistic units, and (2) the equation of the boundaries of such units with boundaries of mutual intelligibility and communication. The language-involving terms of the cultunit definition have seemed most directly to implicate these two assumptions. With each assumption one finds that the relationship in question is not certain, but problematic.

I must now take up the third and fourth of the assumptions. The silence of the discussion of cultural units on these assumptions suggests that they are taken for granted; here again the relationships in question must be taken as problematic.

Third Assumption

It cannot be taken for granted that a language or code is the medium of communication for particular cultural features. First of all, not all cultural features are acquired or communicated verbally; what is so communicated may differ from one group to another. Some cultural features may require language (e.g., myth); some may not be communicable apart from personal observation, imitation, and practice. For some features verbal means may be optional. Religious training, say, may not involve verbal instruction, as among the Crow in contrast to the Hidatsa (cf. Hymes 1966:126-31). Secondly, the repertoire of a community may comprise several codes, and a given content may be specialized to but one of them. It is likely to be that code, rather than any other, whose distribution and boundaries are relevant; if other codes are relevant, through bilingualism and translation, those relationships must be determined in the given case. In medieval Europe it was the distribution of Latin, not of the domestic languages French, English, and the like, that was most important to the communicative boundaries of religious culture.

We know little systematically about the ways in which specialization of topics among codes may affect communicative independence of groups; a good deal of work is needed before much can be said. It may be necessary to consider that a code can be instrumental to communicative boundaries with regard to cultural features indirectly as well as directly. That is, a code may not be a means for communication with respect to certain features, but may be the communicative instrument basic to a group or relationship within which communication about the features occurs. A code such as Crow might thus demarcate the communication of religious behaviours apart from its use for the purpose. In studying religion, one will need to take into account both what codes are "languages of religion" and what codes unite and bound groups significantly distinct with respect to religion.

Fourth Assumption

The time depth relationship between a code, contents, and a community cannot be taken for granted, but must be empirically determined.

First of all, there can be no assurance that the present association between a code and a community has a time-depth sufficient for the degree of historical independence that is needed. Moerman (1965) has shown for the Lue of Thailand that ethnic affiliation may be impermanent in ways that make language likely to fail as a criterion of past boundaries. A striking example of deceptive present-day association between language and social unit is reported by Salisbury (1962). Among the Siane of New Guinea utterances in some situations must be repeated in a second language; both languages are known by the participants, and the requirement of repetition is not for intelligibility, but for formality. The proportion of primary speakers of each of the two languages in question appears to have shifted in the recent past, so that what is now the dominant language was once not so. The shift amounts to a shift in which language is to count as first language, which as second, in formal settings. Everyone continues to know both (there is in fact a general enthusiasm for acquiring languages). Yet the shift is tantamount to shifting the community from one side to the other of a linguistic boundary that would imply more than a millenium of communicative separation, if linguistic distance could be automatically so taken.

A related situation can be found in North America, according to Jacobs' interpretation (1937) of language distributions in the Pacific Northwest. Here one finds many small groups; connected through trade and local exogamy, the villages are linguistically mixed. Jacobs interprets the present distribution of languages as the result of a recurrent process of shifts in boundaries in a downriver direction at the expense of the original languages of the more favored locations. (That language shift may go against the apparent gradient of social prestige, wealth, and numbers, due to the respective structures of communicative relationships, is attested by Barth [1964] in a careful analysis of a Near Eastern situation.) Jacobs states:

> There must have occurred gradual changes in the percentage of speakers of one or another language in smaller bilingual upriver border villages; in a bilingual border village the percentage of upriver dialect speakers increased, the percentage of lower river dialects speakers diminished. The changing percentages reflect the greater attractiveness of certain locations and the larger numbers moving in such direction.

The actual outcomes depended on the original locations of the groups, and the relative size and number of communities on various rivers (the most populous communities on the coast and Williamette River resisting language shift). The hypothesis of the one recurrent process gives a unified interpretation of many puzzles as to location, and makes sense of the diffusion of certain linguistic traits. Here again equation between present linguistic boundaries and boundaries of social units with time-depth would be quite misleading: the language boundaries have shifted over communities that have themselves remained in place. From this standpoint many Northwest aboriginal communities mapped as having quite distinct languages cannot be regarded as communicatively independent. Many more such cases could be adduced.

While shift in the association between communities and languages as wholes is striking, shift in the association between a community, a retained language, and cultural contents may be important also. One of a community's languages may be found restricted in scope; but the restriction may be the result of encroachment of one or more other languages, such that contents no longer associated with the retained language once were, e.g., the Indian languages of New Mexico, Arizona, Chihuahua, and Sonora (Spicer 1962). Conversely, a language now associated with the communication of certain cultural contents may once have been more restricted in scope. The creolization of pidgins and trade jargons into full-fledged languages is a salient case in point; there is also the emergence of dialects into the status of written, literary, and/or standard languages. It seems likely that the most dramatic of such phenomena are restricted to the recent centuries of European expansion, but only a validated theory able to associate particular processes of linguistic change with particular types of social relationship could assure the ethnologist of this. We have no such theory at present; it seems unlikely that shifts in the roles of codes will be found to be wholly excluded from the world with which the ethnologist deals.

A communicative field may be left intact by a change of language, language boundary, or language use. One instance is the New Guinea trade network in which

Neo-Melanesian seems to have been replacing an earlier pidgin (Harding 1967:6, 186). The Siane, discussed just above, seem clearly to be such a community. The effect of such changes, then, as well as the fact of their occurrence, must be considered with regard to the specific history of each case.

Such time perspective, assessment of communicative history, is strangely absent from recent ethnological discussions. Demarcation of present-day boundaries between languages and dialects seems to be relied upon, backed up, if at all, by genetic classifications at remoter levels. This approach would suffice only if it were true that genetic classification of languages and dialects mirrors communicative history, and if present demarcations of distance and closeness had come about by one, irreversible process of divergence. Perhaps it is just some such image that is implicitly in mind. The downward branching trees of language families may be unconsciously taken as representing the whole of linguistic and communicative history. If so, it must be pointed out that genetic relationship is generally a poor guide.

Two limitations of genetic relationship are particularly worth mention here. First, the evidence for placing languages in genetic families consists of less adaptive features, i.e., those most resistant to reflecting the communicative adaptations of the users of the languages. The greater the time-depth of the relationship the smaller the portion of the present-day features of languages that are pertinent to the genetic connection, and the less likely it is that the genetically interesting features reflect communicative ties. The loanwords in a language, the loanwords from it in other languages, and all features showing diffusional connections within a linguistic area, are more important often to an assessment of the past communicative history of a language in a community. The greater the time-depth of the genetic relationship in question, the greater the importance of diffusional phenomena as indications of communicative relationships.

Second, the present closeness or distance of dialects and languages usually does not reflect a unilinear divergence over time, but a complex ebb and flow. The actual historical relations and subgroupings of related dialects are difficult to establish, and the use of percentages of lexical similarity, or any one line of evidence, is likely to be quite misleading. Dialects may diverge lexically, then converge (cf. Gudschinsky 1955); once converged, they may diverge yet again. Use of all the available lines of evidence is required, if the course of development is to be sorted out.

Particularly interesting consequences of divergence are the emergence of stable new codes, such as the Greek *koiné*, based on a range of Greek dialects; and pidgins (some ultimately becoming creoles) based on extensive admixture of unrelated languages. It is important to note that in at least some cases lexical percentages may imply a depth of independence for a pidgin that is greatly exaggerated.

In short, the present-day alignment of dialects and languages does not necessarily mirror even purely *linguistic* history, let alone the communicative history of the communities in which the dialects and languages are found.

In effect, we must act on Boas's understanding that in an historical context "the problem of the study of language is not one of [genetic] classification but . . . our task is to trace the history of the development of human speech" (Boas 1920:368). From this standpoint, genetic classification and reconstruction are but one portion of a general investigation of the history of languages and their uses.

Much can in fact be done to infer past communicative fields, boundaries, links, through the resources of ethnohistory, areal linguistics, archaeology, and ethnology. There is a fair amount of direct testimony to the past existence of linguistic communication through the presence of diffused features in languages, and of features diffused through languages (such as myths). One might even hope eventually to reconstruct something like a series of maps of communicative fields for an area such as North America. Such work would be the necessary implication of the recognition (e.g., D'Andrade 1966:152a-b; 1962a) of communicative independence as an aspect of validity in comparative ethnology.

The Set of Assumptions

The consequences of the analysis of the four assumptions can be summed up in a restatement such as the following:

(1) The ethnographic world is divided into "sociolinguistic" or communicative units, composed of repertoires of codes and rules of code-use; these units intersect or overlap; their associations with persons, groups, communities, and language varies.

(2) Between such units, mutual intelligibility and communication depend on a complex of factors, of which sameness or similarity is but one.

(3) Whether or not a particular code is the communicative means instrumental to particular cultural features is problematic.

(4) The time depth of an association between a particular code and particular cultural features is problematic.

CONCLUSION

We have seen that the language-involving terms of definitions of cultural units must be regarded as variables, and that the assumptions entailed by use of language as a criterion in ethnology are all problems for investigation, requiring specification in each case. In all probability the hope of a single classification of the cultural world into units for all purposes of comparison must be abandoned, if such a classification requires communicative units indexed by languages. The field worker who is to contribute information to the ethnologist must be advised to look beyond language and dialect boundaries to the factors governing the uses and boundaries of codes both within and between communities. The ethnologist himself must turn to a different perspective for an adequate conception of the relation of languages to cultural units. In so doing, one may contribute not only to the better practice of ethnology, but also to the foundations of anthropological theory. Most usual anthropological statements about language are an inferior sort of fairy tale, spun from unexamined assumptions of the sort I have called "Herderian." We need to build a theory of language that starts from what we can see to be actually the case in the world, man's polymorphous (and to the ethnologist, perhaps perverse) capacity to communicate in codes other than language, to use more languages than one, to make shifting choices as to codes and communication over time.

In short, if ethnology requires assumptions and inferences as to the role of languages in communication, then ethnology must concern itself with the description and history of sociolinguistic systems. Such a concern will join with an ongoing critique of received notions as to the relations between languages, communities, and speech in linguistics itself. A fair amount of literature has recently been devoted to this critique, and to indicating lines along which a more adequate perspective can be constructed (e.g., Ferguson and Gumperz 1960; Ferguson 1966; Gumperz 1961, 1962, 1966; Hymes 1961, 1962, 1966, 1967a; Labov 1966).

From the standpoint of such an enterprise, the causes noted in this paper are not embarrassments, but opportunities. Once the attempt to use languages as demarcations in an *a priori* way is abandoned, the really interesting problem appear. One is faced with basic research into the very nature of the relationships in question. Rather than try to patch up a list of exceptions, one can take the seeming exceptions as part of the empirical range of possibilities, and investigate their nature. What do they tell about the relation of languages to cultural units? about the types and systems of relationship that may occur? What can be said about the distribution of such types and systems? of their history? about the consequences for historical and comparative inference of the presence of each?

Let me repeat at this point that for many cross-cultural studies, the inadequacy of language boundaries as boundary markers of communicative units may be circumvented or compensated for. Nor is it the case that all use of genetic groups as variables must be eschewed. Interesting results may be obtained (as by Driver 1966). The point is that it is one thing to discover what features of culture correlate with genetic linguistic groupings (cf. Jorgensen 1966:160b), and to seek to explain why (since retention alone cannot be taken for granted as the cause); it is quite another to rely on such groupings as evidence of past communicative boundaries. Moreover, the requirement of flexibility with regard to choice of relevant codes and boundaries, depending on the cultural features being investigated, seems quite in keeping with the view of several cross-cultural specialists that the appropriate units of study may differ from one problem to another (D'Andrade 1966:151-52; Ember 1964:296c; Whiting 1964:305a). (In some comparative studies, indeed, one will not seek boundaries to mark the historical independence of units, but seek to define a common baseline or opportunity against which to assess differential response, or covariation, and so select units within boundaries of communication.)

Regarding "Tribes"

My remarks have had to be directed at the general problem of the relation of languages to cultural units. With regard to the specific question of the tribe, the answer will depend upon the ethnologist's decision as to the appropriate definition of "tribe." It is clear now that use of the term "tribe" for peoples hither and yon has no likelihood of finding support in a consistent linguistic correlate. If the approach to the concept of "tribe" suggested by Fried (1966) is adopted, an interesting and perhaps quite specific possibility arises, one which will have the constructive effect of reversing the common ethnological fixation on genetic diversification of languages.

Let me first point out that as a major process of linguistic change, genetic diversification is limited to one portion of human history. It is typical of the process of the gradual peopling of the regions of the world, of periods of migration and local differentiation. It will seldom occur again. The great triumphs of comparative linguistics in method, and the great nineteenth century interest in tracing origins, should not bind us to the fact that the major process of linguistic change is now, and for some time has been, functional reintegration of diverse languages within complex communities. Especially since the spread of European society over the face of the earth, there has begun an interconnected series of processes of linguistic acculturation, pidginization, creolization, language obsolescence and loss, creation of international auxiliary and technical idioms, emergence of *lingua francas* and world languages, etc.

The emergence of tribes as secondary phenomena, as reaction formations, fits easily into such a perspective. From a linguistic standpoint, one's interest in the formation of tribes would not at all be a concern to associate each tribe with a linguistic boundary. One's concern would be with the much more interesting question of the way in which the formation of a tribe is reflected in, and conditioned by, the organization of linguistic resources among the peoples in question. That is the sort of linguistic perspective that is relevant today both to science and to practical affairs. Let us cease to think of languages as if they should reflect some primitively given demarcation of the world, and learn to think about them instead as instruments of human action.

NOTES

[1] Some illustrations of the principle and of awareness of empirical problems may be found in the work of Leibniz (1704; see Slotkin 1965:234), A.L. Schlözer (1735-1809) (see Butterfield 1960:50, 59), and Jefferson (1785; see pp. 96-97 of the 1964 edition).

[2] The commentators on Naroll (1964) and Driver (1966) are cited by name and year, but not listed separately in the references. Those cited are Roland Berndt, Frank D. Bessac, Gertrude E. Dole, Harold E. Driver, Melvin Ember, Frank W. Moore, Gideon and Andrée F. Sjoberg, C.F. Voegelin, and John W.M. Whiting (commenting on Naroll 1964); and R.G. D'Andrade, and Joseph G. Jorgenson (in reference to Driver 1966). Citations from *Current Anthropology* include the column (a, b, c) as a convenience in locating specific passages.

[3] One sort of interrelation between speech field of a community and personal speech networks of community members is noted by Harding (1967) in an interesting study of a New Guinea trade system. In pre-contact communities "there were always a few men, as there are now, who knew the languages of particular alien communities" (203). The trading dominance of the Bilibili islanders (a group of about 200 to 250 traders and pot makers in Astrolabe Bay) was associated with a collective knowledge of the languages of the communities with which they had economic relations, such that "the islanders as a group could serve as informants for most of the languages of the area" (196). In addition to these diversified personal repertoires, there was use of a pidgin form of the Siassi language as a *lingua franca* (203).

REFERENCES

BARTH, FREDRIK. 1964. "Ethnic Processes on the Pathan-Baluchi Boundary." In *Indo-Iranica: Mélanges présentés à Georg Morgenstierne*, pp. 13-20. Wiesbaden: Harrassowitz.
BOAS, FRANZ. 1920. "The Classification of American Languages." *American Anthropologist* 22: 367-76.
BRIGHT, JANE O. and WILLIAM BRIGHT. 1965. "Semantic Structures in Northwestern California and the Sapir-Whorf Hypothesis." *American Anthropologist*, Vol. 67, No. 5, Part 2:249-58.
BRIGHT, WILLIAM (ed.). (1966). *Sociolinguistics*. The Hague: Mouton.
BUTTERFIELD, HERBERT. 1960. *Man on His Past: The Study of the History of Historical Scholarship*. Boston: Beacon Press.
DRIVER, HAROLD E. 1965. "Survey of Numerical Classification in Anthropology." In *The Use of Computers in Anthropology*, ed. Dell Hymes, pp. 302-44. The Hague: Mouton.
———. 1966. "Geographical-Historical versus Psycho-Functional Explanations of Kin Avoidances." *Current Anthropology* 7:131-82.

FERGUSON, CHARLES A. 1966. "National Sociolinguistic Profile Formulas." In *Sociolinguistics*, ed. W. Bright, pp. 309-14. The Hague: Mouton.

FERGUSON, CHARLES A. and JOHN J. GUMPERZ, eds. 1960. *Linguistic Diversity in South Asia: Studies in Regional, Social, and Functional Variation*. Research Center in Anthropology, Folklore, and Linguistics, Publication 13. Bloomington: Indiana University.

FRIED, MORTON H. 1966. "On the Concepts of 'Tribe' and 'Tribal Society'." Transactions of the New York Academy of Sciences, Ser. II, Vol. 28, No. 4:527-40.

FRIEDRICH, PAUL (organizer). 1962. "Multilingualism and Socio-Cultural Organization." *Anthropological Linguistics* 4(1).

GARDE, PAUL. 1961. "Réflexions sur les différences phonétiques entre les langues slaves." *Word* 17:34-62.

GREENBERG, JOSEPH H. 1957. *Essays in Linguistics*. Chicago: University of Chicago Press.

GUMPERZ, JOHN J. 1961. "Speech Variation and the Study of Indian Civilization." *American Anthropologist* 63:976-88.

———. 1962. "Types of Linguistic Communities." *Anthropological Linguistics* 4(1):28-40.

———. 1966. "The Ethnology of Linguistic Change." *Sociolinguistics*, ed. W. Bright, pp. 27-38. The Hague: Mouton.

HARDING, THOMAS G. 1967. *Voyagers of the Vitiaz Strait*. American Ethnological Society, Monograph 44. Seattle: University of Washington Press.

HAUGEN, EINAR. 1966. "Semicommunication: The Language Gap in Scandinavia." *Sociological Inquiry: Journal of the National Sociology Honor Society* 36:280-97. "Explorations in Sociolinguistics." *Sociological Inquiry*, Vol. 36, No. 2.

HOCKETT, CHARLES F. 1958. *A Course in Modern Linguistics*. New York: Macmillan.

HYMES, DELL. 1961. "Functions of Speech: An Evolutionary Approach." In *Anthropology and Education*, ed. Fred Gruber, pp. 55-83. Philadelphia: University of Pennsylvania Press.

———. 1962a. "The Ethnography of Speaking." *Anthropology and Human Behavior*, ed. T. Gladwin and W.C. Sturtevant, pp. 13-53. Washington, D.C.: Anthropological Society of Washington.

———. 1962b. "Comments. Bergsland and Vogt, On the Validity of Glottochronology." *Current Anthropology* 3:136-41.

———. 1964. "Directions in (Ethno)-Linguistic Theory." In *Transcultural Studies of Cognition*, ed. A.K. Romney and R.G. D'Andrade, pp. 6-56. Washington,. D.C.: American Anthropological Association.

———. 1966. "Two Types of Linguistic Relativity." In *Sociolinguistics*, ed. W. Bright, pp. 114-57. The Hague: Mouton.

———. 1967a. "Models of the interaction of Language and Social Setting." *Journal of Social Issues* 23(2):8-28.

———. 1967b. "Why Linguistics Needs the Sociologist." *Social Research* 34:632-47.

———. 1970. "Linguistic Aspects of Comparative Political Research." In *Methodology of Comparative Research*, ed. R.T. Holt and J. Turner, pp. 295-341. New York: The Free Press.

———. 1971. "On Linguistic Theory, Communicative Competence and the Education of Disadvantaged Children." In *Anthropological Perspectives on Education*, ed. M.L. Wax, S.A. Diamond, and F.O. Gearing, pp. 51-66. New York: Basic Books.

JACOBS, MELVILLE. 1937. "Historic Perspective in Indian Languages of Oregon and Washington." *Pacific Northwest Quarterly* 28:55-74.

JEFFERSON, THOMAS. [1785.] *Notes on the State of Virginia*. New York: Harper Torchbooks, 1964.

LABOV, WILLIAM. 1966. *The Social Stratification of English in New York City*. Washington, D.C.: Center for Applied Linguistics.

MILLER, WICK J. 1966. *Speech Communities of the Great Basin and Australia*. Read at the annual meeting, American Anthropological Association, Pittsburgh, 1966.

MOERMAN, MICHAEL. 1965. "Ethnic Identification in a Complex Civilization: Who Are the Lue?" *American Anthropologist* 67:1215-30.

NADEL, S.F. 1942. *A Black Byzantium*. London: Oxford University Press.

———. 1947. *The Nuba*. London: Oxford University Press.

NAROLL, RAOUL. 1964. "On Ethnic Unit Classification." *Current Anthropology* 5:283-312.

OLMSTED, DAVID L. 1954. "Achumawi-Atsugewi Non-reciprocal Intelligibility." *International Journal of American Linguistics* 20:181-84.

SALISBURY, RICHARD F. 1962. "Notes on Bilingualism and Linguistic Change in New Guinea." *Anthropological Linguistics* 4(7):1-13.

SHARP, LAURISTON. 1958. "People Without Politics." *Systems of Political Control and Bureaucracy*, ed. Verne F. Ray, pp. 1-8. Seattle: University of Washington Press.

SLOTKIN, J.S. 1965. *Readings in Early Anthropology.* Chicago: Aldine.

SORENSEN, ARTHUR. 1967. "Multilingualism in the Northwest Amazon." *American Anthropologist* 69:670-84.

SPICER, EDWARD H. 1962. *Cycles of Conquest.* Tucson: University of Arizona Press.

SWADESH, MORRIS. 1959. "The Mesh Principle in Comparative Linguistics." *Anthropological Linguistics* 1(2):7-14.

VOEGELIN, C.F., et al. 1963. "Obtaining an Index of Phonological Differentiation from the Construction of Non-existent Minimax Systems." *International Journal of American Linguistics* 29:4-28.

WOLFF, HANS. 1959. "Intelligibility and Inter-Ethnic Attitudes." *Anthropological Linguistics* 1(3): 34-41.

———. 1967. "Language, Ethnic Identity and Social Change in Southern Nigeria." *Anthropological Linguistics* 9(1):18-25.

WILLIAM LABOV

Field Methods of the Project on Linguistic Change and Variation

0.1. *Earlier sources for current field techniques.* The field methods described here are based on developments in sociolinguistic research which began in the early 1960s. Field methods used in Martha's Vineyard (Labov 1963) were modifications of earlier techniques used in dialectology, and the New York City study (Labov 1966) still showed some focus on lexical items which reflected the dialectological tradition. The New York City study developed techniques for reducing formality in face-to-face interviews and obtaining data on a wide range of styles; it included a number of field experiments such as minimal pair tests, subjective reaction tests, family background tests, self-report tests and tests of linguistic insecurity, as well as the method of rapid and anonymous surveys. These methods were adopted to a greater or lesser extent in a number of sociolinguistic surveys based on individual interviews: of Detroit (Shuy, Wolfram, and Riley 1968); Panama City (Cedergren 1973); Norwich (Trudgill 1972); Salt Lake City (Cook 1969); Phaltan (Berntsen 1973); Philadelphia (Cofer 1972); Bahia Blanca, Argentina (Weinberg 1974); Glasgow (Macaulay and Trevelyan 1973), as well as a number of smaller studies. Descriptions of these methods are available in Labov 1966 (Ch. 1-6); Shuy, Wolfram, and Riley 1968; and Wolfram and Fasold 1974.

A second tradition of field methods stems from the work of Gumperz in Hemnes (1964) which utilized participant-observation techniques to obtain recorded samples of group interaction. Such recordings of group sessions were integrated into the studies of South Harlem (Labov, Cohen, Robins, and Lewis 1968), along with various advances in face-to-face interviewing techniques and field experiments.

Methods for combining participant-observation and individual interviewing have been developed in the various components of the study of the Philadelphia speech community by LCV,[1] particularly in King of Prussia by A. Payne, in the Irish and Italian communities by A. Bower, and in the Puerto Rican community by S. Poplack. The modules used as conversational resources in the interviews are the result of intensive development of early methods by members of the class on The Study of the Speech Community (Linguistics 560) from 1972 to 1976. The current work of Baugh in Pacoima, California, represents the further development of systematic recording through participant-observations, while the current study of Paris by Lennig has carried forward the methods of sampling the community through individual interviews.

[1] The Project on Linguistic Change and Variation was supported by the National Science Foundation. The field methods discussed here were developed under NSF Grants SOC75-00245 and BNS76-80910.

1. Aims and Working Principles

The methods used by LCV are governed by two basic aims which are sometimes seen in opposition. On the one hand, we need a large volume of recorded speech of high enough quality for instrumental analysis of vowels or the precise judgments on the realizations of grammatical particles which are often reduced to rapidly articulated, minimal features of sound. On the other hand, we place a very high value on records of vernacular speech (see below) which show a minimum shift or accommodation of the presence of an outside observer. The tension between these two needs informs the basic dynamics of our developing field methods over the past fifteen years. The following 'methodological axioms' derived from Labov 1972 (pp. 208-9) are actually working principles, based on empirical findings in the sources cited above.

1. *There are no single style speakers.* By "style shifting" we mean to include any consistent change in linguistic forms used by a speaker, qualitative or quantitative, that can be associated with a change in topics, participants, channel, or the broader social context. Some speakers have a much wider range of style shifting than others, and some communities do not show any significant shift on features that are important style indicators in other communities. The most recent sound changes are relatively insensitive to stylistic contexts, but most linguistic changes that are well advanced show a wide range of style shifting.

2. *Styles can be ranged along a single dimension, measured by the amount of attention paid to speech.* This proposal is supported by observations of the factors that lead to style shifting in various interview situations and naturalistic settings, as well as experimental evidence (Mahl 1972, Labov 1972:p. 98). Attention paid to speech appears to be mediated by the process of audio-monitoring, which can be blocked by a wide range of factors. This statement is not equivalent to a naturalistic analysis of style, which might require a very large number of dimensions, but merely states that styles can be so ordered.

3. *The vernacular, in which the minimum attention is paid to speech, provides the most systematic data for linguistic analysis.* The "vernacular" is defined as that mode of speech that is acquired in pre-adolescent years. Its highly regular character is an empirical observation. The vernacular included inherent variation, but the rules governing that variation appear to be more regular than those operating in more formal "super-posed" styles that are acquired later in life. Each speaker has a vernacular form, in at least one language; this may be the prestige dialect (as in the case of "RP"), or a non-standard variety. In some cases, systematic data can be obtained from more formal speech styles, but we do not know this until they have been calibrated against the vernacular.

4. *Any systematic observation of a speaker defines a formal context where more than the minimum attention is paid to speech.* We therefore do not expect to find the vernacular used in the main body of a first face-to-face interview, no matter how casual or friendly the speaker may appear to be. We must assume that there will be distinct changes in a number of linguistic variables when no outside observer is present.

5. *Face-to-face interviews are the only means of obtaining the volume and quality of recorded speech that is needed for quantitative analysis.* In other words,

quantitative analysis demands data obtained through the most obvious kind of systematic observation.

LCV is then faced with the "observer's paradox": Our aim is to observe how people talk when they are not being observed. The problem is well known in other fields under the name of the "experimenter effect," and the problem of minimizing the experimenter effect is one that has received a great deal of attention. We refer to it as a paradox since it can never be solved completely in principle: the remainder of this discussion is devoted to the various means by which we can approximate a solution.

The original sources for the two models for field methods outlined above are both extreme in the ways that they fail as solutions to the observer's paradox. Survey methodology is a highly developed technique for obtaining a representative sample of opinions and attitudes from an enumerated population, but the interactive technique used in such surveys is designed to keep rapport at a moderate level and filter out all information that cannot be coded in the scheme developed. Here the experimenter effect is maximal, and the correspondence of the attitudes expressed to those that operate in every-day life is not easily determined. On the other hand, the opposing approach used by social anthropologists and ethnographers fails as a solution in the opposite way. The participant-observer may gather data on interactive behavior with a minimum of observer effect, but very little linguistic data can be recorded accurately in journals several hours after the event. Many participant-observers feel quite limited in the extent that they can introduce recording apparatus; when they do record group interaction with a minimum of other observational effects, the data is limited in both quality and quantity.

Our basic goal is to modify both methods as far as we can to reduce these limitations, and then combine both approaches to converge on the linguistic system we hope to describe. There will be sources of error in participant-observation and in face-to-face interviews, but they are complementary; by combining both methods, we can estimate the degree and direction of error in our final statement of the rules of the vernacular.

2. Neighborhood Studies

2.1. *Aims and basic design.*   The original sociolinguistic surveys followed the usual pattern of survey methodology by enumerating a population, selecting individuals or households randomly from that population, and then interviewing each of those by a standard instrument. When households are selected as the basic unit, one individual may be randomly selected from that household. Stratified random samples modify this method by selecting only those individuals whose sex, age, class, and ethnicity fill pre-specified cells to obtain representatives of all types. In all of these approaches, the view of the community which is obtained is constructed from the speech produced by those individuals in the interview situation, together with their substantive responses to questions on relations with and attitudes toward others. These data may be supplemented by occasional observations of interaction on the interview site. Such surveys have given us the most accurate and representative view of the social stratification of language, and a partial view of the range of style shifting characteristic of the community. They do not give a view of the linguistic interactions that produce such stratification, which must be reconstructed indirectly, and they do not give as close a view of the vernacular as studies of group interaction do.

The studies of adolescent groups in South Harlem from 1966 to 1968 yielded the most accurate view of the vernacular in group sessions together with extended interviews of individuals. The sociometric diagrams constructed of such groups were extremely valuable in explaining the distribution of linguistic forms (Labov 1972, Ch. 7). This approach was not extended to the adult community, however.

Six neighborhood studies conducted by LCV from 1972 to 1976 are designed to obtain a large amount of linguistic and social data on the major social networks of the neighborhoods. They include long-range participant-observation which permits unlimited access to the linguistic competence of the central figures of those networks, along with recordings of group interaction in which the vernacular is displayed with minimum interference from the effects of observation.

At the same time, the neighborhood studies utilize systematic sociolinguistic interviews to obtain comparable data on all members of the social network.

2.2. *Selection of a neighborhood.* The neighborhoods selected for study form a judgment sample of the city in the largest sense: the priorities of selection are ordered in accordance with major residential, class, and ethnic groups most characteristic of the city. There are not enough neighborhoods involved to form a sample representative of the city as a whole, however, and without supplementary data these neighborhood studies cannot be considered to yield a representative view of the Philadelphia speech community. Their primary function is to achieve depth, rather than breadth.

Information on census tracts and previous studies of ethnic distributions in Philadelphia are consulted to identify blocks that are located centrally in the main ethnic and class groups. Data from our own random and anonymous surveys are also utilized for this purpose. Within each of these areas, a single block is selected as an initial research site. These characteristics motivate our selection of a block.

a. Residentially stable with close to full occupation of dwelling units, and many adult residents who have lived in the area since childhood.

b. Relatively soft interfaces between public and private space, with a resultant high level of interaction of residents.

c. A moderate number of shopping and recreation sites in the immediate vicinity, with a consequent high level of local interaction.

2.3. *Entry into the neighborhood.* The first entry into neighborhood social networks utilizes two basic strategies. One is contact with individuals and small groups who make themselves available for social interaction on the block. Studies of the use of public and private space, along with particular sketches and surveys of the block in question, provide an overall view of the times and places at which people make themselves so available. The second approach is through persons who are centrally located in social institutions with an overview of the neighborhood: local stores, groceries, barber shops, post offices, fraternal organizations, churches and schools. In middle-class neighborhoods with widely detached houses, the second strategy has proven most effective, particularly with the use of higher status institutions such as churches and schools. In working class neighborhoods, first contacts have been most frequently made through informal channels.

The initial presentation of LCV field workers is consistent in general principles, though it may vary in detail with the personality, age, and sex of the field worker. We present an accurate view of our aims and interests in the broadest sense, including the study of language features characteristic of the neighborhood without singling language out for specific attention. Our overall aim is getting to know the neighborhood: how people get along; how it has changed or maintained itself; whether living on the block brings people together or pulls them further apart, and how this neighborhood may be different from others. In talking about the motivation and results of our study, we emphasize the problems that are the joint concern of our work and the people in the neighborhood: the changes that are taking place in American cities, how living in the cities affects people and their ways of life. As our contacts with people grow, it appears that we have a particular interest in language and local dialect, and our continued interest in recording is motivated by this concern. But our interest in language is placed within a larger framework of interest in narrative accounts of daily life, in confrontations and accommodations, in relations of ethnic groups and educational problems. Since the papers and publications of members of LCV reflect this wider range of interest, we have no difficulty in justifying a long-term involvement with the social life of the neighborhood along with formal inquiry and field experiments specifically concerned with language.

2.4. *The sociolinguistic interview.* The first recorded conversation with a member of the speech community usually follows a well developed strategy which may be entitled "the sociolinguistic interview." In conception and design, current methods are descended from the interviews developed in sociolinguistic surveys (Labov 1966:Ch. 5, Appendix A; Shuy, Wolfram, and Riley 1968; Labov, Cohen, and Robins 1965). However, the developments of the past ten years have carried this technique considerably beyond that starting point, eliminating many of the elements that still showed the inheritance from traditional dialectology. Our present methods are informed considerably by studies of conversation outside of the interview.

The sociolinguistic interview is governed by a number of goals, some complementary but others contradictory:

1. to record with reasonable fidelity from one to two hours of speech from each speaker.
2. to obtain the full range of demographic data necessary for the analysis of sociolinguistic patterns (age; residential, school, occupation, and language history; family location and relations; income, rent or house values; group memberships and associations).
3. to obtain comparable responses to questions that define contrasting attitudes and experiences among various sub-cultures (experience of the danger of death; fate; premonitions; fighting and rules for a fair fight; attitudes towards other racial and ethnic groups; educational aspirations).
4. to elicit narratives of personal experience, where community norms and styles of personal interaction are most plainly revealed, and where style is regularly shifted towards the vernacular.
5. to stimulate group interaction among the people present, and so record conversation not addressed to the interviewer.
6. to isolate from a range of topics those of greatest interest to the speaker, and allow him or her to lead in defining the topic of conversation.

7. to trace the patterns of communication among members of the neighborhood, and establish the position of the speaker in the communication network.

8. to obtain a record of overt attitudes towards language, linguistic features and linguistic stereotypes.

9. to obtain specific information on linguistic structures through formal elicitation: reading texts and word lists.

10. to carry out field experiments on subjective reactions towards perceptions of linguistic forms (minimal pair and commutation tests; self-report tests; subjective reaction tests; family background tests).

The technique of the sociolinguistic interview must be responsive to this variety of goals. Goals 2–3 and 7–10 are best carried out within a reasonably formal framework, where interviewers are guided by protocols that give comparable results. If the language style involves shifts towards more careful speech, that may be a necessary price to be paid for comparability. On the other hand, the predominant concern of the interviewer is in shifting the style towards the vernacular; goals 4–6 implement this shift. If the drive towards personal narrative, interest and tangential shifting becomes over-dominant, we wind up with large bodies of speech, close to vernacular style, of great intrinsic interest, but very difficult to use in obtaining measures of language structure and use across the community.

It is important to note that the steps needed to record a high quality signal (goal 1) may increase the observer effect. The use of a lavaliere dynamic microphone such as the Sennheiser MD-214 reduces the obtrusiveness of a table microphone, and insures optimal signal-to-noise ratio. But careful pre-testing of recording, and monitoring of a VU-meter, are essential to avoid distortion and insure consistent results, and any steps taken to reduce this monitoring have proven counterproductive. Further details on recording techniques are given in section 2.5.

The technical development of the sociolinguistic interview is aimed at maximizing overall progress in achieving goals 1–10. This development involves two technical devices: (a) the module and (b) the conversational network.

2.4.1. *The module.* The conversational module is a group of questions focusing on a particular topic: i.e., children's games, premonitions, the danger of death, aspirations, etc. The generalized set of such modules, Q-GEN-II, represents a conversational resource on which the interviewer draws in constructing an interview schedule.

Many questions within a particular module have been shaped over a number of years by three processes:

a. Responses to generalized foci of interest. Attention to goal 6 has led to the recognition that several general foci of interest apply across many speech communities: death and the danger of death; sex; and moral indignation. The ways in which these concerns appear in an interview format may be particular to each community, particularly in the case of sex. But other questions can be shaped generally for many communities: e.g., "Did you ever have a dream that really scared you?" "Were you ever in a situation where you were in serious danger of getting killed?"

b. Colloquial format. Many inexperienced interviewers, formulating questions without preparation, will exhibit a bookish lexicon and grammar, or show the influence of survey methodology. The questions formulated in our modules provide a guide to colloquial style, which may then be further modified to fit the particular style of the interviewer and the current lexicon of the speech community.

c.   Shortening. Questions formulated without preparation tend to be quite long, with many re-starts. One governing principle is that module questions should take less than five seconds to deliver and in many cases, less than one second.

d.   Feedback. Questions may first be formulated from an outsider's point of view, as in "Do you play the numbers around here?" But information from many speakers is accumulated to transform the question into one that presupposes a generalized state of affairs, and looks to the particular issues of interest.

All three of these formatting processes have operated effectively to produce the central question from our Module 9, on Family:

Did you ever get blamed for something you didn't do?

The normal practice is for an interviewer to become intimately accquainted with a module format, and to adapt questions to his own colloquial style. However, some questions are marked with a double asterisk (**) to indicate that they should be asked in exactly the words indicated, first to achieve comparability, and second because experience has shown that the wording is close to optimal.

Modules show a certain degree of hierarchical structure. A section usually begins with a general question, and then proceeds to more detailed issues, which may be penetrated to the extent the interviewer's and speaker's interests allow. Others contain check lists, as in Module 2, Children's Games, which are to be run through rapidly to test the subject's recognition of certain items.

2.4.2. *The network.*   The modules are combined into a conversational network by the interviewer. Modules are selected by the interviewer from the general resource file Q-GEN-II to construct a conversational network, in which modules are connected at transitional points through close associations. Most modules begin and end with transitional questions which permit links to many other networks. This Module 3, Fights, begins with the question:

0.   What did (do) fights start about around here?

with choice of past or present form dictated by the age of the speaker. This may be linked with Module 2, Games, where arguments start over tough tackles, or with Module 11, Peer Groups, in the discussion of friends getting mad at each other. Module 3 ends with

5.   Do girls fight around here?
.1.   Did you ever get into a fight with a girl?

and can lead into Module 4.1, Dating patterns, going steady, etc., which can begin with the question "What are the girls *really* like around here?" Such transitions can be initiated by the interviewer or may occur naturally in the course of the conversation. Generalized networks for particular communities are sometimes created, showing various points of entry into the network depending on the age, sex, and social class of the subjects.

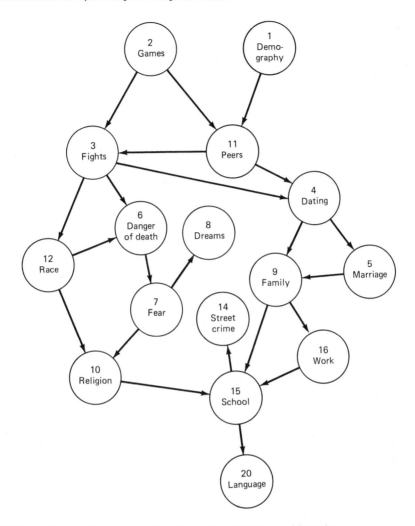

FIGURE 1.   Characteristic network of modules for adolescent or young adult speaker.

Figure 1 shows a typical network of topics used with working class adults in Philadelphia. The interview is entered via Module 1, Demography, and then proceeds either to Module 16, Work, or to Module 2, Boys' Games. From that point, one can proceed to Module 11, Peer Group, or to Module 15 and then to the sub-network formed by Fights (3), Crime in the Streets (14), Danger of Death (6), Fear (7), Dreams (8), and Religion (10). Another sub-network is formed by Family (9), Dating (4), and Marriage (5).

The Language module (20) is indicated separately, since this is introduced in a variety of ways as a distinct area of interest, sometimes in a continued interview (see below).

2.4.3. *The use of modules and networks.*   The modules, assembled into networks, form a set of conversational resources to assist in accomplishing the

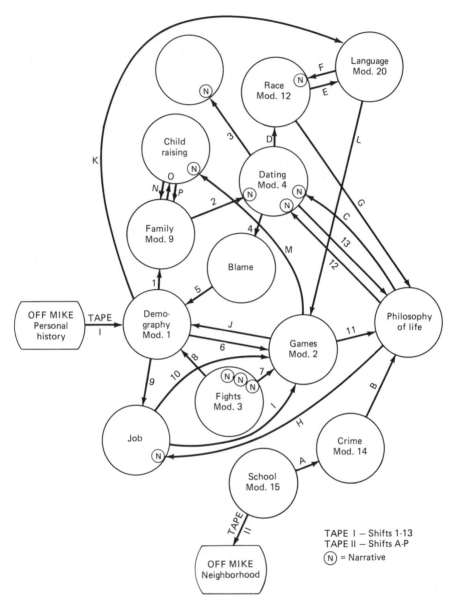

FIGURE 2. Topic shifting in a sociolinguistic interview with Diane S., 21, Kensington.
Interviewer: Anne Bower.

aforementioned goals 1–10. The network is a guide for the interviewer as he or she constructs a simulated conversation which follows principles quite similar to the unfocused conversations of everyday life. The interviewer does initiate topics, often with questions; this is an expected role. But there is no rigid insistence upon a pre-set order of topics, and ideally the interviewer plays a part in the conversation which approaches that of any other participant: volunteering experience, responding to new issues, and following the subject's main interests and ideas wherever they go (see 2.4.4 below). Interviewers vary in the degree to which they utilize the structure of the network, but the most successful interviews follow a path which is both natural to the speaker and comparable to other paths. Figure 2 shows the networks of interview topics followed in an interview between A. Bower of LCV and Diane S., 21, of Kensington. An hour and a half of conversation began with child raising, then shifted to demographic data, to Diane's job (Mod. 16) and then to family (Mod. 9). The discussion of dating (Mod. 4) then turned back to family in the form of daughter-mother relationships, which allowed the interviewer to include the central question on blame ("Did you ever get blamed for something you didn't do?"), particularly valuable for stimulating narratives centered on moral indignation. The interviewer then returned to demographic questions and obtained a large amount of data on the family as a whole before shifting rather abruptly to girls' games (Mod. 2.3), which led to narratives of fights and the rules for fair fights (Mod. 3) and back to family relationships as the question of punishment came up.

The interviewer sensed that Diane had a strong interest in children's games, and returned many times to this theme ". . . back to the games you played as a kid"; each time, this theme led in a new direction by a different set of associations. The second discussion of games led to a discussion of friends, their teen-age games, and back to dating, which involved a side discussion of Diane's philosophy of life, and then a natural extension to marriage (Mod. 5), ethnic differences (Mod. 12), and back to jobs, school (Mod. 15), crime in the neighborhood (Mod. 14). Diane's job again, and her philosophy of life again. The interviewer returned a third time to the theme of Diane's childhood:

"Getting back to when you were a kid, was there anyone you didn't like?"

This led to a general discussion of the block, and a discussion of the meaning of "step" vs. "stoop", and then into language (Mod. 20). A fourth return to childhood games, and "Mischief Night" in particular, led to a much wider variety of topics, ending with more family information and a discussion of family relationships on the block.

The associational network of this interview was similar to that of the spontaneous conversations we monitored for topic structure. At the same time, it was guided by the interviewer to gradually build up a complete view of Diane's family relationships and the residential, educational, and job history of the other people in her social network, and a great deal of information on social relations in the neighborhood (goal 2). The interviewer is particularly alert to Diane's display of interest (goal 6), and recognized that pre-adolescent and adolescent activities formed an "ultra-rich" topic which could be used again and again without exhausting interest. Figure 2 shows by the letter *N* the location of narratives of personal experience (goal 4). All in all, nine of the ten aims of the interview process were well developed in this interview.

2.4.4. *The principle of tangential shifting.*[2] Throughout the sociolinguistic interview, there is careful attention to any contribution by the speaker which represents a tangent or shift of topic away from the topic which the interviewer

---

[2] This terminology and the principle are the work of Ivan Sag and Group 3 of the Linguistics 560 class, "Study of the Speech Community," from 1972 to 1973.

initiated. The sociolinguistic interview is considered a failure if the speaker does no more than answer questions. It is the additional material that the speaker provides, beyond the initial question, which provides the main substance of the interview. Figure 3 explains the notational system used in transcribing the interview illustrated in Figure 4. The square brackets enclose topics initiated by the interviewer, and the circles the responses of the speaker on a given topic. Arrows that lead to new topics without intervention of square brackets show initiation of new topics by the speaker. In some cases, a dashed circle follows a formal question; this indicates a short interchange of questions between interviewer and subject, which led the speaker herself to initiate a new topic. Dashed lines between topics indicate indirect guidance of the interviewer, encouraging the speaker to shift tangentially to a new topic.

If we examine all of the topical transitions in Figure 4, we obtain the following proportions:

Topics initiated by a question of the interviewer	38
Topics initiated by the speaker	42
Tangential shifts encouraged by the interviewer	9
Question-and-answer series terminated by a new topic introduced by speaker	9

We can see in this interview a balance between the impetus provided by the interviewer and that provided by the subject. Figure 4 also shows that the latter part of the interview clearly marked a shift towards speaker-initiation, as we would expect.

FIGURE 3.   Notational key for transcription of topic shifting in the interview with Diane S., 21, Kensington.

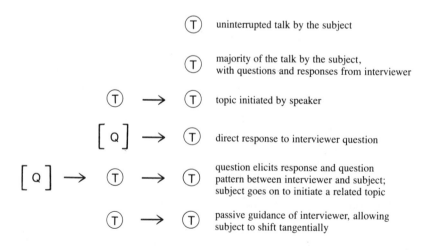

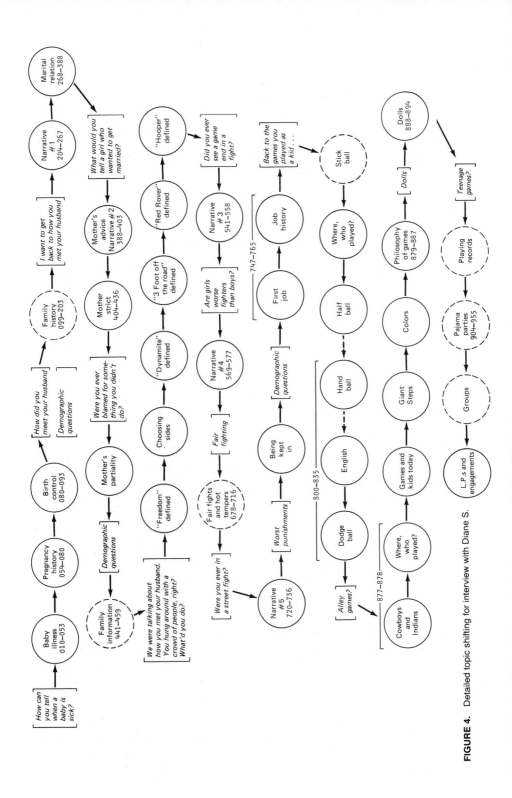

FIGURE 4. Detailed topic shifting for interview with Diane S.

39

2.4.5. *Power relationships in the interview setting.*   One of the crucial elements that determine the course of a sociolinguistic interview and further contacts is the relative degree of authority of the interviewer and speaker. The "observer's paradox" is not to be seen as absolute, but closely linked to the perceived relationship of an outside observer in a dominating class (Encrevé 1976). The interviewer is engaged in an occupation that clearly points to membership in a middle-class institution of some kind—research or journalism. Any identification of the interviewer as a teacher would stress the fact that he is a person that information flows from, not to.[3] The basic counter-strategy of the sociolinguistic interview is to emphasize the position of the interviewer as a learner, in a position of lower authority than the person he is talking to.

This favorable interactive position can only be achieved by a thoroughgoing rejection of the authority that stems from association with the dominating social class. Sociolinguistic interviewers must continually monitor their behavior for any signs of this authority. They must review their lexical and grammatical choices to remove any evidence of bookishness or influence of literary language, and ruthlessly plane away all remains of conspicuous ostentation to achieve a plain, unvarnished style. On the positive side, the sociolinguistic interviewer will develop his own use of colloquial idiom, even at the expense of generalized intelligibility. The extent and style of morphological condensation will show similar adjustments, in the direction of the local dialect. It is not uncommon for interviewers to make partial phonetic shifts towards a local dialect; as long as this is not so extreme as to be seen as an imitation of that dialect, it will be accepted as a symbolic entry into the local value system.

On the interactive level, the interviewer will work to develop a position of lower authority and lesser consequence in the conversation. One part of this behavior is a consequence of the principles already developed. In monitoring the rise and fall of interest shown by the speaker, he naturally attends closely to everything being said, and gives the other more than the time needed to finish one idea and launch into a new one. His interest must not be a mechanical one, and he must not be distracted from the content of what is being said by too much attention to the speaker's phonology or syntax. The interviewer must have a keen appreciation of the strengths and expertise of the speaker: a genuine and profound interest in what the speaker knows. If he pays attention, he is bound to learn and absorb knowledge that will be fed back into future interviews, and raise his discussions with others to a higher level of interest and expertise.

Experienced interviewers work towards steadily removing themselves from a position of consequence in the conversation being conducted. When a third or fourth person appears, their attention will then not be drawn to the interviewer and what he is doing, but rather to the subject of the conversation, and it is quite possible for a face-to-face conversation between the interviewer and speaker to gradually shift to a general conversation where the interviewer plays a very small part.

In one respect, the interviewer should retain his authority: in his own area of expertise in making recordings. He should feel free to suggest where the others

---

[3] This impression is confirmed by the concrete experience of two graduate students who spent a summer interviewing in two areas of Philadelphia to obtain data on the use of tense markers in narrative. They presented themselves as school teachers who wanted to know about the community. Though they met with the usual warm reception in working-class areas, they obtained very few personal narratives and very little relevant data as a consequence.

might sit so that he can get the best sound; if outdoors, to move out of the wind or away from the street; if indoors, to turn off the sound on the television set, turn off electric fans, or move away from a noisy motor. Once subjects have agreed to make a recording, they have the same investment in obtaining good results as the interviewer, and they will be even more disappointed if the playback is distorted by reverberation or outside noise.

2.4.6. *Continued interviews.* Given the nature of our neighborhood studies as continuous contact with the speech community, there is no imperative to complete an interview schedule in a single session. In many cases, the goals 1–10 are carried out in several sessions. In fact, the recording of group interaction under goal 5 is best carried out by participant-observation in the months following the initial interview (see the discussion of group sessions in section 4, below). But the goals of the individual interview are quite distinct from those of group sessions, and it is therefore necessary and desirable to continue the format of the initial interview in second or third meetings with subjects as individuals or pairs. The familiarization process which is evident throughout the individual interview (Labov 1972:97-98) continues to reduce the level of formal constraints in these continued sessions, but the fundamental dynamics are the same as those sketched above.

In current neighborhood studies of Philadelphia, a second complete series of individual interviews was carried out centered around a group of communication modules. These modules outline the location of the speaker's social networks— both family and friends—in relation to the block. They investigate the kinds of help that neighborhood people give each other that bring them into social relations—re-directing mail, baby-sitting, relaying maternity clothes, emergencies, and sickness. A second area deals with socializing—sports, afternoon and evening gatherings. A third module deals with the telephone, of special interest to us in obtaining data that relates the neighborhood studies to telephone interviews (see section 3, below). A fourth module concerns privacy and the lack of it: gossip, friendship, and the breaking off of social relations.

The ultimate extension of such continued interviews is a series of confidential conversations that the field worker recorded with the central informant in each neighborhood: She obtained a sketch of the social position and history of each resident on the block, from the point of view of her informant. After several years of intimacy and familiarization, this catalogue laid bare many of the determinants of social behavior that would have been hidden from view in initial interviews. Because such data is charged with strong social significance, the recordings are separated from the normal archiving procedures and are not available even to members of the research staff without special precautions (see section 7, below).

Continued interviews allow us to resolve part of the contradiction inherent in the interview format: The need to follow the principles of unfocused conversation and tangential shifting conflicts with the need to acquire comparable data. As we review first interviews, we find that questions needed for comparability (such as attitudes towards fate or educational aspirations) were sometimes passed by in the course of following the speaker's natural interests, and for one reason or another, the interviewer never returned through the conversational network to that area. These ommissions are then systematically repaired in the second interview.

The construction of effective subjective reaction, self-report, and family background tests often requires long familiarity with the speech community, and it regularly happens that these are not completed until many first interviews have been carried out. Such tests will regularly find a place in continued interviews.

2.4.7. *The re-construction of modules through feedback.*   Throughout our research in the speech community, new information on speakers' activities, interests, and the central concerns of the neighborhood flows back through answers to questions and through new topics initiated by the speakers. In constructing new questions, and improving old ones, we regularly feed back this new information into the module construction. The quality of the conversations that follow shows a steady shift towards more involvement of the speaker, longer discussions, and more narrative.

A first approach to a new neighborhood, sub-culture, or geographic area inevitably involves the interviewer in the position of the outsider. The position as an outsider reinforces the initial appeal for help, and most people respond favorably to that appeal. But it will appear that it is very difficult to maintain a conversation of any length or involvement with someone who is a rank beginner: there is simply too much to explain, and no handle on where to start. It is only when the new person shows some understanding of the critical issues, and asks questions that point at real problems of concern to local people, that the conversation takes on life. An outsider cannot easily reach the areas of disputed knowledge that form the focus of extended discussion. Therefore the interviewer is continually reconstructing modules in order to advance more rapidly into the areas of interest.

Module 11.1 shows the beginnings of such development in the discussion of girls' social activities. Question 1 concerns pajama parties, and begins with a pair of very general inquiries:

    1.   Do you ever have pajama parties?
    .1. What do you do?

These have too little focus to produce very much response from most adolescent girls. But the following questions feed back into the interview situation the results of a few productive early sessions:

    .1. Do you play the ouija board?
    .2. Have you ever had a seance?
    .3. Do levitation?

In a variety of speech communities throughout the United States, these questions have opened up an area of excited discussion. But the process of feedback is not complete here, and there are several routes to follow. An experienced interviewer will avoid the issue as to whether levitation or ouija boards "really work," and go on to inquire into cases where the subjects were "really scared." Candles often go out at crucial moments; boards say things that seem to go beyond coincidence, and as soon as disbelief is suspended, stories multiply.

2.5. *Field experiments.*   The study of sociolinguistic stratification in New York City (Labov 1966) introduced a series of field experiments into the interview format which were further developed in the South Harlem study and elsewhere. They may be characterized briefly where descriptions are available in the literature.

2.5.1. *Minimal pair tests.* The simplest form of controlled inquiry into speech perception is a list of pairs: The speaker is asked to repeat each one, and then say whether they are the same or different (Labov 1966:596; Labov, Cohen, and Robins 1965). Ways in which such tests fail to reflect the vernacular or productive system are outlined in Labov, Yaeger, and Steiner (1972:230-35), and in particular, cases where the speaker pronounces the two words differently but says they are the same.

2.5.2. *Commutation tests.* References to commutation tests may be found in Harris 1951, but we do not know of any systematic report on commutation tests before Labov, Yaeger, and Steiner (1972:236-57). A pair of words distinguished by one phonemic opposition appears in a randomized list of five instances of each. In one form of the test, one native speaker reads the list, and another identifies the words. In another, a listener may be asked to identify his own pronunciations recorded from a previous reading. Commutation tests were introduced when it was found that in many dialects there were marginal oppositions that were consistently maintained in speech (though with a small margin of security) but that could not be labelled in minimal pair or commutation tests by native speakers.

In Philadelphia, we have been systematically investigating the near-merger of /er/ and /ər/ as in *merry* vs. *Murray*, and the full merger of /ohr/ and /uhr/ as in *tore* vs. *tour*, using minimal pair and commutation tests.

2.5.3. *Embedded contrast tests.* The development of a more naturalistic contrast test was motivated by the failure of native speakers to label contrasts in commutation tests that they themselves made in speech. It is possible that a speaker could fail to label a contrast in a formal test but could utilize the phonetic contrast unconsciously to distinguish words in the course of ordinary conversation. To test this possibility, we devised embedded contrast tests which focus on a moral problem without any evidence of attention to the problem of phonological contrast. Earlier reading tests (Labov 1966:598) have embedded phonological contrast in close connection without a focus of attention ("...ask a subway guard. My God! I thought...that's one way to get lost in New York City"). But no semantic interpretation depended on the contrast.

Embedded contrast tests use a narrative that develops a series of well-balanced semantic alternatives that can be resolved in one way or another through a single lexical choice. That choice is then maintained through a following series of sentences that are completely consistent with either choice. When the experimenter obtains the subject's judgment on the moral issues involved, the semantic interpretation that he made is well fixed and easy to determine.

The most highly developed example of an embedded contrast experiment is "The Coach." After it appeared that Philadelphians cannot pass a commutation test with *merry* vs. *Murray*, but still maintain a consistent difference in speech, we decided to examine the possibility that listeners could use the distinction in unreflecting semantic interpretation of connected text. It was necessary to avoid any focus on language, so that contrasts such as *Murray* vs. *merry* were to be avoided. The contrast was tested through the unobtrusive pair, 'Merion' (a Philadelphia suburb) and 'Murray in'.

The necessary context was established through a fairly long narrative about a coach of a Little League team under pressure to play girls on his team. The name

Murray was established for a boy who tried very hard but couldn't catch anything. The name Merion was established as a nickname for a girl whose rich and overbearing mother came from Lower Merion. The coach gave both Murray and Merion the title of First Utility Outfielder. At a crucial moment in the series, the center fielder was injured, and the coach found himself in a dilemma: which first utility outfielder to play? He considered the alternatives and decided,

> "No help for it. I've got to play [mərɪən] there!"

In various versions of the text, the word in phonetics is the natural pronunciation of a Philadelphia speaker who had intended to say 'Merion'; in a second version, the words 'Murray in' are intended. The resultant difference [ə] in the first vowel is about 100 Hz. F2. Two other versions use exaggerated differences of 250 Hz. F2.

After the final question, "Did he do the right thing?" the subject's opinion on the moral issues demonstrates whether he interpreted the phonetic form as 'Murray in' or 'Merion'. The semantics are balanced enough to give about equal numbers of each response for those who do not hear the difference. The experimenter then replays the section where the coach reasons through the problem and in this version the opposing phoneme is used in the key sentence. The subject then has a second opportunity to demonstrate whether or not he can utilize the phonetic difference to distinguish words.

2.5.4. *Self-report tests.*   A self-report test presents subjects with a recorded set of phonetic variants, and asks them to select the one that they themselves use most often (Labov 1966:456-74, Trudgill 1972). It is found that subjects regularly shift in the direction of the prestige norm, though a reverse shift was found by Trudgill among men in Norwich (1972). In Philadelphia, we have utilized self-report tests in continued interviews for the major sound changes in progress.

2.5.5. *Subjective reaction tests.*   The original subjective reaction or subjective evaluation tests (Labov 1966:405-54) were a linguistic adaptation of Lambert's "matched guise" tests (Lambert et al. 1960). A subject makes judgments of the personalities or social attributes of a recorded series of speakers. Among these speakers, the same person recurs using different linguistic forms. Whereas Lambert's methods use linguistically unanalyzed forms of the dialects or languages that are judged impressionistically by experts to be characteristic, the linguistic approach concentrates the variables of interest in individual sentences, and contrasts reactions to these with reactions to neutral sentences or with different values of the same variable, as used by the same speaker.

Subjective evaluation tests were utilized in the South Harlem study in a way that elicited covert as well as overt value systems (Labov et al. 1968:II, 217-88; Labov 1972:250) and the general principles behind the linguistic adaptation are given in Labov 1972:247-51. In our Philadelphia study, a subjective evaluation test has been developed by S. Herman, with a balanced design using four speakers and five linguistic variables.

2.5.6. *Family background tests.*   Many linguistic investigators have examined the ability of subjects to identify speakers' class or ethnic background on the basis of their speech, e.g., Shuy, Baratz, and Wolfram 1969. Such tests are not controlled for either linguistic features or voice qualifier, but they do reveal something of the subjects' sensitivity to markers of ethnic identity, and stimulate research to determine what those features are. The South Harlem study used marginal speakers to determine how judges could be systematically wrong, though some degree of special sensitivity on the part of black subjects emerged (Labov et al. 1968:II, 266-83). Underwood (1975) used a series of ten adjective pairs to register reactions by Arkansas subjects to ten different dialects, unanalyzed, but added a request for racial identification; this showed that Arkansawyers regularly transferred their negative reaction to white South Carolineans who they judged to be black.

In Philadelphia, we have begun work with a family background test that is specialized to narrative style, in order to see if there are subjective correlates to the larger discourse features that seem to be characteristic of the Italian, Irish, or Jewish subgroups.

2.5.7. *Linguistic insecurity tests.* The New York City study used eighteen alternative pronunciations to measure linguistic insecurity (Labov 1966:474-81). Subjects are asked to circle one of two numbers corresponding to the pronunciation that they think is correct and afterwards, to do the same to indicate their own pronunciation. The items used were lexical alternants that had become stereotypes of correctness or pretension in New York City such as [ant] vs. [ænt] for *aunt*, or [ve^{i}z] vs. [va:z] for *vase*. Here the measure of insecurity was the number of items where the two judgments were different. Underwood (1975) used a similar test for analyzing insecurity among Arkansas subjects, using phonological alternations such as [dɔg] vs. [dɔ°g] for *dog* as a token of the long open *o* class. These were then compared to the phonetic realizations of this phoneme in spontaneous speech.

In Philadelphia, we have adapted the New York City model in our continued interviews, and added a series of grammatical features.

2.5.8. *Frequency tests.* Our research on the social significance of linguistic variation has been primarily confined to the examination of the social distribution of variants in production. The question of subjective correlates of these stable quantitative patterns remains an open question. The subjective reaction tests for (r) in New York City showed a strong differential reaction to variable (r) as against categorical [r] pronunciation (Labov 1966:430-36), but the fine-grained pattern of stylistic and social differentiation within the variable class was not tested for subjective reactions. In Philadelphia, we have begun to develop field tests for examining subjective reactions to differing distributions of the variable. There is indirect evidence that quantitative perceptions are transformed into qualitative subjects, often categorical. In Philadelphia, a test developed by S. Herman examines differential responses to the realization of (ing). Subjects are asked to judge a speaker's success in improving his speech, and hear a story read in which every sentence has one progressive suffix. There are three forms of the stimulus tapes: in A the first five are [ɪŋ], the second five [ɪn]; in B, the order of the blocks is reversed; and in C, the two forms alternate. If speakers are continuously sensitive to frequencies, then reactions to A, B, and C may be quite similar, but if monitoring of frequencies is terminated by categorical judgments, A and B should produce very different types of reactions.

3. The Telephone Survey

3.1. *The sampling problem.* The sociolinguistic study of New York City
was a survey of individuals on the Lower East Side, enumerated and selected in the
course of a prior survey carried out by sociologists. Studies of Detroit, Norwich,
Panama City, and Montreal were also surveys of individuals, randomly selected
from a population with various adjustments, to obtain social stratification and deal
with refusals or absences. The strength of these surveys is their representative
character: By following the principles of survey methodology, we can be sure that
our results hold true within some degree of error for some well-defined population.
The South Harlem study also included a random survey of adults. But the primary
data were obtained from the studies of adolescent groups in the 112th to 118th Street
area. Given the nature of adolescent organization, we can state that within a certain
area, we studied all the named groups, and various efforts were made to estimate the
relation of these groups to the total population, including a complete enumeration of
one apartment building (Labov et al. 1968:31-40).
      The weakness of these studies lies in their approximation of the language
obtained to the vernacular, and in the problem of explanation. After an individual is
placed in a certain position in the pattern of stylistic and social stratification, we
must resort to speculation and indirect evidence to find the factors responsible for
his achieving that position. In the course of the interview, he may refer to
organizations he is a member of, to family or friends he sees in daily life, to
reference groups that might influence his language. But we rarely have recordings of
his interaction with those groups, and our speculations on how they might affect his
language must remain speculations.

3.2. *The Philadelphia sample.* In the Philadelphia study, we have concentrated our major efforts on six neighborhood studies. These include two working-
class neighborhoods that are predominantly Italian and Irish; a lower-class Puerto
Rican neighborhood; a lower-middle-class neighborhood that is predominantly
Catholic with a fair variety of ethnic representation. In addition, we have access to
data from a number of other neighborhood studies that include working-class and
middle-class neighborhoods, black and white, carried out by students and others
associated with our research project. These neighborhood studies give us a view of
characteristic Philadelphia patterns in a wide range of geographic areas, with a fairly
wide spread of social class membership within and across neighborhoods. But the
neighborhoods were not chosen as part of a systematic enumeration and random
selection, and we cannot say for certain which part or how much of Philadelphia
they represent. By emphasizing deeper studies of groups and social networks, we
gain in the possibilities of explaining linguistic behavior, but lose the representative
character of the earlier studies.
      To make up for this limitation, we planned to supplement these scattered deep
studies with a shallow but broad study, which would have sources of error
complementary with those of the neighborhood studies. To obtain the full benefit of
a convergence of two methods, the second survey should exploit the dimensions of
breadth and representativeness in a single style, without attempting to obtain
samples of the vernacular or social interaction, or the benefits of the long and
penetrating interviews carried out in the neighborhoods.

3.3. *Design of the Telephone Survey.* To meet these requirements, the Telephone Survey was designed and carried out by D. Hindle. Subjects were selected through a random choice of listed telephone numbers. They were asked to participate in a short interview dealing with communication in Philadelphia, with emphasis on telephone communication, and special words and sounds of the Philadelphia dialect that might be the sources of misunderstanding. The interviews last no more than 15 minutes. They include enough spontaneous conversation to allow us to chart the speaker's vowel system instrumentally. Word lists and minimal pairs were included. In addition, the Telephone Survey included questions on the interpretation and acceptability of syntactic features of the Philadelphia dialect: positive *anymore*, the *be* auxiliary with *done* and *finished*.

After the subjects indicated that they would participate in the interview, they were asked for permission to record. If permission was denied (2%), a short form was conducted without recording. The signal was recorded from a point prior to the telephone loudspeaker, on a Sony TC-120 cassette recorder.

The question naturally arose as to whether telephone signals are good enough to permit instrumental measurements of vowels. The telephone band is sharply limited to a range of 80-3000 Hz. But a test of the same signal recorded directly with a Nagra-IV and a Sennheiser dynamic microphone, and recorded after telephone transmission, indicated that for all but the high vowels, the errors in telephone measurement were within an acceptable range.

From a total selection of 238 listed numbers, 196 subjects were contacted by telephone. There were 87 refusals, and 109 interviews were completed. Of these, 60 were analyzed instrumentally for comparison with the white neighborhood samples, and 3 who appeared to be members of the black community were studied separately.

3.4. *Evaluation of the Telephone Survey.* The telephone survey is therefore a representative sample, within limits, of Philadelphians who list their telephones. The sample covers a wide range of the city geographically, and a wider range of socio-economic classes than the neighborhood studies. There are two major problems in determining the representativeness of the sample. The population that cannot afford telephones is not represented at all, and we must consider that the telephone survey is sharply truncated at the lower end. We are informed by the Bell Telephone Survey Company that only two-thirds of the subscribers in Philadelphia list their telephones, and one-third pay to have their telephones unlisted.

One way to compensate for unlisted telephones is to undertake a survey with a random selection of numbers, without drawing on telephone listings. A second way is to compare the linguistic behavior of people in our neighborhood studies who list their telephones with those who do not. Our current method is the second. Indications to this point confirm the report of the New York City Telephone Company (New York Times, September 14, 1977:35); there is no correlation between listing of telephones and socio-economic class. We find that about the same proportion of our subjects in each neighborhood pay to have their telephones unlisted as those reported for the city as a whole. Further comparison of the two populations will make the effect of this limitation to listed telephones more precise.

The Telephone Survey is thus designed to supplement the strengths of the neighborhood study with the advantages of random selection, and compensate for the limitations of the neighborhood studies in this respect. At the same time, the limitations of the telephone interviews, in their formal character, limited length and low sound quality are compensated for by the very high quality of the neighborhood data in this respect.

4. Group Sessions

Some progress can be made in shifting towards the vernacular in individual interviews. But the best records of vernacular speech have been obtained in group sessions, where the effects of observation are minimized through the controlling interaction of peers. Gumperz's work in Hemnes (1964) was the first to record such group interaction systematically. The South Harlem study used group sessions among adolescents as the primary means of obtaining records of the Black English Vernacular. The techniques for setting up and conducting such sessions are given in detail in Labov et al. (1968:I, 57-64), with examples of the types of interaction transcribed. In these sessions, each speaker was recorded on a separate track through a lavalier microphone, with as many as ten persons present; a variety of tape recorders was used and the transcriptions coordinated. Speech was recorded during card games, eating and drinking, and spontaneous conversation that included narratives, ritual insults, and confrontations.

To date, the South Harlem groups are the only ones that have been studied quantitatively, but other work is in progress. J. Baugh is currently analyzing data from the black community of Pacoima, California, where he used group sessions as well as individual interviews. The comparison of these materials with Baugh's variable rule re-analysis of the South Harlem data (1980)[4] will greatly extend our knowledge of the vernacular, since the Pacoima subjects are young adults. M. Goodwin has recorded groups of black youth in Philadelphia, using a single tape recorder, as part of her long-term participant-observation. Both Goodwin's and Baugh's materials are limited in the quality of recording, but show great success in minimizing the effects of observation.

In our Philadelphia study, A. Payne conducted an extended series of group sessions among the youth of King of Prussia and surrounding communities. Here a quadriphonic fourtrack tape recorder was used (Sony TC 388-4) with four lavalier dynamic microphones (Sennheiser MD-214). Transcriptions from six of these sessions were made by G. Jefferson. Since it is possible on this equipment to isolate one or more tracks, or hear them all together, the tracking and coordination of spontaneous conversation are much more feasible, and the total amount of accurate transcription, in Jefferson's estimation, is much higher than with recordings of groups from a single microphone.

In the course of participant-observation in South Philadelphia, A. Bower has recorded a number of groups at the homes of her informants. These recordings form a reliable record of the vernacular in this area. No such records of adult group interaction are available from the earlier sociolinguistic studies such as New York City, Detroit, Panama City, or Norwich. In Philadelphia, we will be able to calibrate the nature of style shifting within the interview with speech used in such group gatherings, and so derive quantitative measures of distance from the vernacular.

[4] See John Baugh, "A Reexamination of the Black English Copula," in Section Four of this volume.

In Montreal, the research group headed by G. Sankoff collected recordings of people in a variety of social contexts. Anthropology students were recruited who could persuade someone to allow them to accompany them throughout the course of a day, carrying a cassette tape recorder. This model was developed further by A. Payne in our Philadelphia study. She accompanied Carol Myers, one of her main informants, throughout her working day and at home, using a Nagra-IV tape recorder and a Sennheiser 404 condenser microphone. Recordings made in the travel agency where the informant worked have remarkable clarity and variety of social interaction which have made them a valuable base for analysis of conversation, and for deeper analysis of phonetic variation. A second series of tape recordings was made at a bridge game, with each player using a separate lavalier microphone.

D. Hindle is currently engaged in a detailed analysis of the Alice B. materials, using instrumental measurements of vowel position to relate linguistic performance to social interaction. Through this study, we hope to obtain further insight into the mechanism of linguistic change by determining the circumstances under which the most advanced tokens of a sound change in progress are realized.

In the light of the many advantages of group sessions, it is easy to disregard some of their limitations. First of all, there is no known way of sampling the groups of a society, and no way of determining what proportion of the total number of intersecting collections of people have been recorded. If we could enumerate all the groups in a neighborhood, it would still not be possible to record more than a few in group sessions, and the opportunity to study those would be the result of many accidental factors. It is possible to obtain very good sound quality in group sessions, though the equipment most often used does not give this result. But even with the best equipment, we find that some individuals do not talk very much in a group. In our South Harlem studies, the most extreme example was Jesse H., who never spoke a single word in two group sessions. Yet Jesse was well known to be a person of consequence, who others turned to for advice, and in individual interviews he talked freely and at great length.

5. Rapid and Anonymous Surveys

The various methods set out in the preceding sections converge upon the general object of characterizing the speech community in ways that are relatively independent of the social position of the observer. The method of rapid and anonymous surveys (hereafter R&A) provides another source of data that is even more distinct in its perspective and in the strengths and weaknesses of the data provided.

The initial example of R&A studies in the sociolinguistic literature was carried out in New York City department stores, and is described in detail in Labov 1972, Ch. 2. Employees of three large department stores were asked for directions for an item that was in fact located on the fourth floor. The phonetic realization of (r) in *fourth floor* was thus recorded twice in handwritten notes.

The department store survey provided sources of error that were complementary with the survey of the Lower East Side. The East Side interviews recorded a great deal of data of high quality, supported by full demographic information; yet they were limited in geographic range within the city, and had only partial success in overcoming the effects of observation. The department store data was quite limited in volume and quality, and there was very little information on the background of the speakers; but it included a much larger geographic base, and the effects of observation were minimal. Furthermore, a great deal of data could be accumulated in a very short time.

Several similar studies were carried out by students of sociolinguistic stratification in other areas (Allen 1968), and the method has proved quite effective in giving a rapid profile of a single variable in a new area. R&A studies may be seen as specimens of the more general class of "unobtrusive observations" (Webb et al. 1966).

In our current studies of Philadelphia, we have used R&A methodology to trace the path of a particular sound change in progress which is most easily traced by impressionistic means. The cluster (str) represents the variation between a hissing and a hushing sibilant before /tr/, though it also extends to /st/ clusters without a following /r/ and across word boundaries. We obtained data on (str) in a wide variety of Philadelphia neighborhoods by asking for directions in the neighborhood of a given street which had a name of a form *X Street*. However, we asked

"Can you tell me how to get to *X* Avenue?"

In the great majority of cases, the informants would respond "*X* Street?" with considerable emphasis on *street*. This technique for obtaining extra emphasis on the variable without formal elicitation was also used effectively in an R&A inquiry in Paris, with B. Simblist, where we inquired for "la rue Taba" in the vicinity of rue Tabac, in order to obtain data on the palatalization of final /k/.

The sampling techniques of R&A methods can be quite precise, and represent a well-defined population: i.e., all those people found in a public place during a certain time. Salespeople in department stores are a fixed quantity, and easy to represent. But R&A studies carried out in residential areas are samplings of the population found on the street, and the relation of this population to the total residential population is not known.

6. Rating the Methods of Acquiring Sociolinguistic Data

Seven methods of gathering data are used: sociolinguistic surveys of individuals; interviews in the neighborhood studies as first interviews; and as continued interviews; group sessions; participant-observation; telephone interviews; and rapid and anonymous surveys. Each of these are rated on seven different criteria: the possibility of obtaining a representative sample; the demographic data obtained; the comparability of the data obtained; success in minimizing the effects of observation; the quality of the sound recorded; the volume of data obtained; and the feasibility of including field experiments.

The ratings are in accordance with the discussions in the preceding pages. It can readily be seen that no one method is excellent in all respects, and some are very sharply limited. But the joint use of several such methods allows us to converge upon our ultimate object: to obtain reliable and valid records of the language used in the speech community.

7. Policy towards the Protection of Data and Subjects' Rights

This report on methods would not be complete if it did not deal with several questions of social policy that must confront anyone who collects recorded data from the speech community. One is the issue of candid recording; a second is the protection of the anonymity of the subjects and preservation of the confidentiality of the data gathered. This inevitably involves the problem of access to the records by other researchers.

7.1. *Candid recording.* In general, we have set a simple and clear policy to forbid candid recording: At all times, the speaker who is recorded must know that he is being recorded. This principle follows equally from practical and ethical considerations. It is our opinion that researchers who engage in candid recording will eventually cause repressive legislation. The policy we have maintained for some time is consistent with the procedures advocated by the Committee on Human Subjects at the University of Pennsylvania.

From a practical viewpoint, such candid recordings have little value for linguistic research, since the quality of the data gathered is so poor that the interpretation of the words uttered is often arbitrary. To obtain good sound recording, it is necessary to pay close attention to signal level and monitor equipment at many points in the process. Even when recording is done on an informed and principled basis, many field workers fail to achieve high quality recordings through their reluctance to pay attention to their equipment. A hidden tape recorder and a hidden microphone produce data that is as doubtful as the method itself.

Some researchers have taken advantage of the presence of built-in microphones to deceive subjects in what seems to them an innocuous way. They use a lavalier microphone during the interview proper, and then disconnect that microphone, leaving the built-in microphone operating. We have never employed this device in LCV. Recordings of this type have little value for us; but even if the recordings from the built-in microphone had satisfactory quality from a distance of a meter or two, it seems to us that the effects of such mild deceit will be damaging in the long run. The subject is usually told afterwards that he was recorded, and asked for permission to use the material. It should be borne in mind that when he grants permission, it is a matter of record that such indirect means were used. Long-term contacts with a neighborhood can only suffer from such techniques.

There remain many situations where it may happen that speakers are recorded without their knowledge. In the course of a recorded interview, new parties may arrive on the scene without being invited. It is not necessarily the responsibility of the interviewer to interrupt whoever is speaking in order to enter into new negotiations. It is our practice to make such a re-introduction whenever a natural pause or break in the conversation makes it practical, if others do not do so first.

Finally there is an issue concerning recording in public places. No one will object to recording a band in a parade, or a street corner orator. Our South Harlem records include a recording of a confrontation between John Lewis and a pitchman who objected to Lewis's recording him. Lewis stoutly maintained that if the man was honest he would have had no objection to being recorded, and refused to back down. The general principle is to avoid any act that would be embarrassing to explain if it became a public issue, and here Lewis felt no embarrassment.

There is no consensus on the rules for recording in public places. Some members of LCV believe that if a party is talking loud enough in a restaurant for any stranger to hear, it is quite legitimate to record them; others disagree. Though it is not likely that such data will be important for quantitative analysis of linguistic change and variation, there are times when it may be valuable quantitative evidence on the use of syntactic or discourse structures. It is possible that such data can be recorded more efficiently in Gregg shorthand, and some members of the staff are currently making efforts to develop the use of this phonetic method.

7.2. *Protection of anonymity.* All subjects recorded by LCV are assured that no one will listen to the tape recordings except members of the research group. Though this is not an important consideration for every subject we deal with, it is a standard policy maintained over more than a decade. When excerpts or charts are published, it is always with pseudonyms and pseudostreets, and considerable care is taken to be sure that no quotation permits the identification of the person.

7.3. *Access to tape recordings.* At present, the archives of LCV amount to approximately 4,000 hours of tape recordings, covering a number of research projects over a span of 15 years. Access to these materials is limited to members of the research group, in accordance with our statements to subjects. The strict commitment to this policy makes it impossible for LCV to adopt the practice of the University of Montreal group, who made their tape recordings available to any scholar interested in Canadian French. In any case, we do not believe that it is possible for someone to do an effective analysis of recorded speech without any familiarity with the speech community it comes from. When a new person joins our research group, and makes a significant contribution to the materials by contributing from his or her own field work, then access to the general body of tape recordings is given on the same basis as to other members of the staff.

With these limitations to a generalized access, it should be stated that any tape recordings that form the basis of our conclusions are available to corroborate those conclusions, in the same way that any library sources are. Visitors from other research groups, conducting parallel studies, are frequently given the opportunity to listen to a wide variety of materials from our tape recordings, with the general understanding that we are engaged in the joint study of linguistic change and variation. Reliability tests or new instrumental analyses can be made from any of these tape recordings by scholars who have reason to believe that it would be important to do so, as long as they subscribe to the same general policies outlined in this section. Towards this end, we will continue to publish our analyses of data with each individual citation identified by tape number, sex, and the speech community that is represented.

REFERENCES

ALLEN, P. 1968. "/r/ variable in the speech of New Yorkers in department stores." Unpublished research paper SUNY, Stony Brook.
BAUGH, JOHN. 1980. "A reexamination of the Black English copula." *Locating Language in Time and Space*, ed. W. Labov, New York: Academic Press. [Included in this volume.]

BERNTSEN, MAXINE. 1973. "The speech of Phaltan: A study in linguistic variation." Unpublished University of Pennsylvania dissertation.

CEDERGREN, HENNRIETTA J. 1973. "The interplay of social and linguistic factors in Panama." Unpublished Cornell University Ph.D. dissertation.

COFER, THOMAS M. 1972. "Linguistic variability in a Philadelphia speech community." Unpublished University of Pennsylvania dissertation.

COOK, STANLEY. 1969. "Language change and the emergence of an urban dialect in Utah." Unpublished University of Utah dissertation.

ENCREVÉ, PIERRE. 1976. "Labov, linguistique, sociolinguistique." Introduction to William Labov, *Sociolinguistique*. Paris: Les Éditions de Minuit.

GUMPERZ, JOHN. 1964. "Linguistic and social interaction in two communities." In J. Gumperz & D. Hymes (eds.), *The Ethnography of Communication* [*American Anthropologist* 66 No. 6, Part 2:137-53].

HARRIS, ZELLIG. 1951. *Structural Linguistics*. Chicago: University of Chicago Press.

LABOV, WILLIAM. 1963. "The social motivation of a sound change." *Word* 19:273-309. Also Chapter 1 of W. Labov, *Sociolinguistic Patterns*. Philadelphia: University of Pennsylvania Press, 1972.

———. 1966. *The Social Stratification of English in New York City*. Washington, D.C.: Center for Applied Linguistics.

———. 1971a. "Methodology." In W. Dingwall (ed.), *A Survey of Linguistic Science*. College Park, Md.: Linguistics Program, University of Maryland, pp. 412-97.

———. 1971b. "Some principles of linguistic methodology." *Language in Society* 1:97-120.

———. 1972. *Sociolinguistic Patterns*. Philadelphia: University of Pennsylvania Press.

LABOV, WILLIAM, PAUL COHEN, and CLARENCE ROBINS. 1965. *A Preliminary Study of the Structure of English Used by Negro and Puerto Rican Speakers in New York City*. Final report, Cooperative Research Project No. 3091, Washington, D.C.: Office of Education.

LABOV, WILLIAM, PAUL COHEN, CLARENCE ROBINS, and JOHN LEWIS. 1968. *A Study of the Non-Standard English of Negro and Puerto Rican Speakers in New York City*. Philadelphia: U.S. Regional Survey.

LABOV, WILLIAM, MALCAH YAEGER, and RICHARD STEINER. 1972. *A Quantitative Study of Sound Change in Progress*. Report on National Science Foundation Contract GS-3287. Philadelphia: U.S. Regional Survey.

LAMBERT, W., ET AL. 1960. "Evaluation reactions to spoken languages." *Journal of Abnormal and Social Psychology* 60:44-51.

MACAULAY, RONALD K.S., and GAVIN D. TREVELYAN. 1973. *Language, Education and Employment in Glasgow*. 2 volumes. Report to the Social Science Research Council.

MAHL, GEORGE. 1972. "People talking when they can't hear their voices." In A. Siegman and B. Pope (eds.), *Studies in Dyadic Communication*. New York: Pergamon Press.

SHUY, ROGER W., JOAN C. BARATZ, and WALTER A. WOLFRAM. 1969. *Sociolinguistic Factors in Speech Identification*. Report on NIMH Project MH 15048-01. Washington,. D.C.: Center for Applied Linguistics.

SHUY, ROGER W., WALTER A. WOLFRAM, and WILLIAM K. RILEY. 1968. *Field Techniques in an Urban Language Study*. Washington, D.C.: Center for Applied Linguistics.

TRUDGILL, PETER J. 1972. "Sex, covert prestige, and linguistic change in the urban British English." *Language in Society* 1:179-95.

UNDERWOOD, GARY N. 1975. "Subjective reactions of Ozarkers to their own English and the English of other Americans." *Journal of the Linguistic Association of the Southwest* 1:63-77.

PETER TRUDGILL

Sex and Covert Prestige: Linguistic Change in the Urban Dialect of Norwich

In this chapter we present some data which illustrate the phenomenon of sex differentiation in language, drawing upon evidence from one variety of British English. We then examine an explanation for this differentiation, and consider what role it plays in the propagation of linguistic change.

The results from which the following figures are taken are based on an urban dialect survey of the city of Norwich carried out in the summer of 1968 with a random sample, 60 in number, of the population of the city, and reported in detail in Trudgill (1974). This sociolinguistic research was concerned mainly with correlating phonetic and phonological variables with social class, age, and stylistic context. Some work was also done, however, in studying the relationships that obtain between linguistic phenomena and sex.

In order to relate the phonological material to the social class of informants and the other parameters, a number of phonetic and phonological variables were developed, and index scores were calculated for individuals and groups in the manner of Labov (1966a). The first of these variables that I wish to discuss is the variable (ng). This is the pronunciation of the suffix *-ing* in *walking, laughing,* etc., and is a well-known variable in many types of English. In the case of Norwich English there are two possible pronunciations of this variable: [ɪŋ], which also occurs in the prestige accent, *RP,* and [ən~n̩]. The former is labelled (ng)-1 and the latter (ng)-2.

Index scores were developed for this variable by initially awarding 1 for each instance of (ng)-1 and 2 for each instance of (ng)-2. These scores were then summed and divided by the total number of instances, to give the mean score. Indices were finally calculated by subtracting 1 from the mean score and multiplying the result by 100. In this case, this gives an index score of 000 for consistent use of *RP* (ng)-1, and 100 for consistent use of (ng)-2, and the scores are equivalent to the simple percentage of non-*RP* forms used. (For variables with more than two variants this simple relationship, of course. does not apply.) Indices were calculated in the first instance for individual informants in each contextual style and subsequently for each group of informants. The four contextual styles:

word list style: *WLS*
reading passage style: *RPS*
formal speech: *FS*
casual speech: *CS*

are equivalent to the styles discussed by Labov (1966a) and were elicited in a similar manner. Indices for other variables were calculated in the same way.

Table 10-1 shows the average (ng) index scores for informants in the five social class groups obtained in the survey, in the four contextual styles. The social class divisions are based on an index that was developed using income, education, dwelling type, location of dwelling, occupation, and occupation of father as parameters. The five classes have been labelled:

MMC: middle middle class
LMC: lower middle class
UWS: upper working class
MWC: middle working class
LWC: lower working class

TABLE 10-1   (ng) Index scores by class and style

Class	Style				N
	WLS	*RPS*	*FS*	*CS*	
MMC	000	000	003	028	6
LMC	000	010	015	042	8
UWC	005	015	074	087	16
MWC	023	044	088	095	22
LWC	029	066	098	100	8

The table shows very clearly that (ng) is a linguistic variable in Norwich English. Scores range from a high of 100 percent non-*RP* forms by the LWC in *CS* to a low of 0 percent by the MMC in *RPS* and by the MMC and LMC in *WLS*. The pattern of differentiation is also structured in a very clear manner. For each of the social classes, scores rise consistently from *WLS* to *CS*; and for each style scores rise consistently from MMC to LWC.

In his study of this same variable in American English, Fischer (1958) found that males used a higher percentage of non-standard [n] forms than females. Since we have shown that (ng) is a variable in Norwich English, we would expect, if sex differentiation of the type we have been discussing also occurs here, that the same sort of pattern would emerge. Table 10-2 shows that this is in fact very largely the case. In 17 cases out of 20, *male* scores are greater than or equal to corresponding *female* scores. We can therefore state that a high (ng) index is typical not only of WC speakers in Norwich but also of *male* speakers. This pattern, moreover, is repeated for the vast majority of the other nineteen variables studied in Norwich.

TABLE 10-2   (ng) Index scores by class, style and sex

Class	Sex	WLS	RPS	FS	CS
		\多Style			
MMC	M	000	000	004	031
	F	000	000	000	000
LMC	M	000	020	027	017
	F	000	000	003	067
UWC	M	000	018	081	095
	F	011	013	068	077
MWC	M	024	043	091	097
	F	020	046	081	088
LWC	M	060	100	100	100
	F	017	054	097	100

In the previous chapter we examined a number of different explanations for this phenomenon. In this chapter we seek an explanation in terms of the fact that WC speech, like other aspects of WC culture, appears, at least in some western societies, to have connotations of masculinity (see Labov, 1966a:495), probably because it is associated with the roughness and toughness supposedly characteristic of WC life which are, stereotypically and to a certain extent, often considered to be desirable masculine attributes. They are not, on the other hand, widely considered to be desirable feminine characteristics. On the contrary, features such as "refinement" and "sophistication" are much preferred in some western societies.

As it stands, this argument is largely speculative. What it requires is some concrete evidence. This need for evidence was discussed by Labov (1966b:108) who wrote that in New York

> the socio-economic structure confers prestige on the middle-class pattern associated with the more formal styles. [But] one can't avoid the implication that in New York City we must have an equal and opposing prestige for informal, working-class speech—a covert prestige enforcing this speech pattern. We must assume that people in New York City want to talk as they do, yet this fact is not at all obvious in any overt response that you can draw from interview subjects.

It is suspected, in other words, that there are hidden values associated with non-standard speech, and that, as far as our present argument is concerned, they are particularly important in explaining the sex differentiation of linguistic variables. Labov, however, has not been able to uncover them or prove that they exist. We can guess that these values are there, but they are values which are not usually overtly expressed. They are not values which speakers readily admit to having, and for that reason they are difficult to study. Happily, the urban dialect survey carried out in Norwich provided some evidence which argues very strongly in favour of our hypothesis, and which managed, as it were, to remove the outer layer of overtly expressed values and penetrate to the hidden values beneath. That is, we now have some objective data which actually demonstrates that for male speakers WC non-standard speech is in a very real sense highly valued and prestigious.

Labov has produced evidence to show that almost all speakers in New York City share a common set of linguistic norms, whatever their actual linguistic performance, and that they hear and report themselves as using these prestigious linguistic forms, rather than the forms they actually do use. This "dishonesty" in reporting what they say is of course not deliberate, but it does suggest that informants, at least so far as their conscious awareness is concerned, are dissatisfied with the way they speak, and would prefer to be able to use more standard forms. This was in fact confirmed by comments New York City informants actually made about their own speech.

Overt comments made by the Norwich informants on their own speech were also of this type. Comments such as "I talk horrible" were typical. It also began to appear, however, that, as suggested above, there were other, deeper motivations for their actual linguistic behaviour than these overtly expressed notions of their own "bad speech." For example, many informants who initially stated that they did not speak properly, and would like to do so, admitted, if pressed, that they perhaps would not *really* like to, and that they would almost certainly be considered foolish, arrogant or disloyal by their friends and family if they did. This is our first piece of evidence.

Far more important, however, is the evidence that was obtained by means of the Self-Evaluation Test, in which half of the Norwich informants took part. This is particularly the case when the results of this test are compared to those obtained by a similar test conducted by Labov in New York. In the Norwich Self-Evaluation Test, 12 lexical items were read aloud, to informants, with two or more different pronunciations. For example:

tune   1. [tjʉ:n]   2. [tʉ:n]

Informants were then asked to indicate, by marking a number on a chart, which of these pronunciations most closely resembled the way in which they normally said this word.

The corresponding Self-Evaluation Test in New York for the variable (r)— presence or absence of post-vocalic /r/ (a prestige feature)—produced the following results. Informants who in *FS* used over 30 percent /r/ were, very generously, considered to be (post-vocalic) /r/-users. Seventy percent of those who, in this sense, were /r/-users reported that they normally used /r/. But 62 percent of those who were *not* /r/-users *also* reported that they normally used /r/. As Labov says (1966a:455): "In the conscious report of their own usage...New York respondents are very inaccurate." The accuracy, moreover, is overwhelmingly in the direction of reporting themselves as using a form which is *more* statusful than the one they actually use. Labov (1966a:455) claims that "no conscious deceit plays a part in this process" and that "most of the respondents seemed to perceive their own speech in terms of the norms at which they were aiming rather than the sound actually produced."

The full results of this test are shown in table 10-3. It shows that 62 percent of non-/r/-users "over-reported" themselves as using /r/, and 21 percent of /r/-users "under-reported," although in view of Labov's 30 percent dividing line, the latter were very probably simply being accurate.

TABLE 10-3   Self-evaluating of (r)—New York

	Percentage reported		
Used	/r/	ø	
/r/	79	21	= 100
ø	62	38	= 100

In the Norwich test, the criteria used were much more rigorous. In comparing the results obtained in the Self-Evaluation Test to forms actually used in Norwich, *casual speech* was used rather than *formal speech*, since *CS* more closely approximates everyday speech—to how informants normally pronounce words, which is what they were asked to report on. Moreover, informants were allowed *no* latitude in their self-evaluation. It was considered that the form informants used in everyday speech was the variant indicated by the appropriate *CS* index for that individual informant. For example, an (ng) index of between 050 and 100 was taken as indicating an (ng)-2 user rather than (ng)-1 user. In other words, the dividing line is 50 percent rather than Labov's more lenient 30 percent. If, therefore, the characteristics of the Norwich sample were identical to those of the New York sample, we would expect a significantly *higher* degree of *over-reporting* from the Norwich informants.

TABLE 10-4   Self-evaluation of (yu)

	(yu) Percentage reported		
Used	1	2	
1	60	40	= 100
2	16	84	= 100

The results, in fact, show the exact reverse of this, as can be seen from table 10-4.

This table gives the results of the Self-Evaluation Test for the variable (yu), which is the pronunciation of the vowel in items such as *tune, music, queue, huge*. In Norwich English items such as these have two possible pronunciations: (yu)-1 has [j] as in *RP*-like [kju:~kjʉ:]; (yu)-2 omits [j] as in [kʉ:~kɜʉ], *queue*.

Table 10-4 provides a very striking contrast to the New York results shown in table 10-3 in that only 16 percent of (yu)-2 users, as compared to the equivalent figure of 62 percent in New York, over-reported themselves as using the more statusful *RP*-like variant (yu)-1 when they did not in fact do so. Even more significant, however, is the fact that as many as 40 percent of (yu)-1 users actually *under*-reported—and the under-reporting is in this case quite genuine.

A further breakdown of the scores given in table 10-4 is also very revealing. Of the 16 percent (yu)-2 users who over-reported, *all* were women. Of the (yu)-1 users who under-reported, half were men and half women. Here we see, for the first time, the emergence of the hidden values that underlie the sex differentiation described earlier in this chapter. If we take the sample as a whole, we have the percentages of speakers under- and over-reporting shown in table 10-5. Male informants, it will be noted, are strikingly more accurate in their self-assessment than are female informants.

TABLE 10-5   Percentage of informants over- and under-reporting (yu)

	Total	Male	Female
Over-r	13	0	29
Under-r	7	6	7
Accurate	80	94	64

The hidden values, however, emerge much more clearly from a study of the other variables tested in this way, (er), (ō) and (ā), illustrated in tables 10-6, 10-7, and 10-8, respectively. The variable (er) is the vowel in *ear, here, idea*, which in Norwich English ranges from [ɪə] to [ɛ:]; (ō) is the vowel in *road, nose, moan* (but not in *rowed, knows, mown,* which are distinct) and ranges from [ɵu] through [u:] to [ʊ]; and (ā) is the vowel in the lexical set of *gate, face, name*, which ranges from [eɪ] to [æɪ].

For each of these variables, it will be seen, there are more male speakers who claim to use a *less* prestigious variant than they actually do than there are who over-report, and for one of the variables (ō), the difference is very striking: 54 percent to 12 percent. In two of the cases, moreover, there are more male speakers who under-report than there are who are accurate.

TABLE 10-6   Percentage of informants over- and under-reporting (er)

	Total	Male	Female
Over-r	43	22	68
Under-r	33	50	14
Accurate	23	28	18

TABLE 10-7   Percentage of informants over- and under-reporting (ō)

	Total	Male	Female
Over-r	18	12	25
Under-r	36	54	18
Accurate	45	34	57

TABLE 10-8   Percentage of informants over- and under-reporting (ā)

	Total	Male	Female
Over-r	32	22	43
Under-r	15	28	0
Accurate	53	50	57

Although there are some notable differences between the four variables illustrated here,[1] it is clear that Norwich informants are much more prone to under-report than New York informants, and that—this is central to our argument—*male*

---

[1] These differences may be due to a skewing effect resulting from the necessity of using only a small number of individual lexical items to stand for each variable in the tests. (Informants' reports of their pronunciation of *tune*, for example, do not *necessarily* mean that they would pronounce or report *Tuesday* or *tube* in the same way.)

informants in Norwich are much more likely to *under*-report, *female* informants to *over*-report.

This, then, is the objective evidence which demonstrates that male speakers, at least in Norwich, are at a subconscious or perhaps simply private level very favourably disposed towards non-standard speech forms. This is so much the case that as many as 54 percent of them, in one case, claim to use these forms or hear themselves as using them *even when they do not do so*. If it is true that informants "perceive their own speech in terms of the norms at which they are aiming rather than the sound actually produced" then the norm at which a large number of Norwich males are aiming is *non-standard WC speech*. This favourable attutude is never overtly expressed, but the responses to these tests show that statements about "bad speech" are for public consumption only. Privately and subconsciously, a large number of male speakers are more concerned with acquiring prestige of the covert sort and with signalling group solidarity than with obtaining social status, as this is more usually defined. (This does not, of course, mean, as Spender (1980) would have it, that the male linguistic "variety" is "the norm." Nor does it mean that "females have no identity and cannot develop solidarity." It would be nonsensical to maintain anything like this, and no sociolinguist has ever maintained anything of the kind. Spender's account of sociolinguistic research is at this point simply a caricature.) By means of these figures, therefore, we have been able to demonstrate both that it is possible to obtain evidence of the "covert prestige" associated with non-standard varieties, and that, for Norwich men, working-class speech is statusful and prestigious. The clear contrast with scores obtained by female informants, with as many as 68 percent of the women over-reporting, in one case, underlines this point and indicates that women are much more favourably disposed towards MC standard forms. This in turn explains why the sex-differentiation pattern of table 10-2 takes the form it does.

Why it should have been possible to obtain this sort of evidence of covert prestige from Norwich speakers but not from New York speakers it is difficult to say. This may be due to the fact that WC speakers in Britain have not accepted MC values so readily or completely as WC speakers in America. If this is the case, it could be explained by "the conspicuous lack of corporate or militant class consciousness [in America], which is one of the most important contrasts between American and European systems of stratification" (Mayer, 1955:67) and by the related lack of "embourgoisement" of the British WC (cf. Goldthorpe and Lockwood, 1963).

On the other hand, tables 10-9 and 10-10 show that this cannot be the whole story. These tables illustrate the amount of over- and under-reporting of (er) and (ō) respectively by male speakers as a whole, and then by MC as opposed to WC male speakers. It can be seen that there is no significant difference in the behaviour of the two classes. The MC, it is true, shows a slightly greater tendency to over-report than the WC, but this is very small. The significant parameter controlling presence or absence of this "covert prestige" is therefore sex rather than social class. Recognition of these hidden values is something that is common to a majority of Norwich males of whatever social class (and something that they do not share with WC female informants). Many MC males appear to share with WC males the characteristic that they have not so completely absorbed the dominant mainstream societal values as have their American counterparts.

TABLE 10-9   Percentage male informants over- and under-reporting (er)

	Total	MC	WC
Over-r	22	25	21
Under-r	50	50	50
Accurate	28	25	29

TABLE 10-10   Percentage male informants over- and under-reporting (ō)

	Total	MC	WC
Over-r	12	15	11
Under-r	54	54	54
Accurate	34	30	35

Having established that covert prestige does in fact exist, and can be shown to exist, we are now in a position to move on to a discussion of one of the problems that arises from the Norwich data. It was shown in table 10-2 that for the variable (ng) men had higher index scores than women. We also stated that the same pattern occurred for the vast majority of other Norwich variables, and we have since been able to offer at least a partial explanation of why this pattern occurs. There is one Norwich variable, however, which does not conform to this pattern of sex differentiation. This is the variable (o), the pronunciation of the vowel in the lexical set of *top, dog, box*. There are two main variants in Norwich English: (o)-1, a rounded *RP*-like vowel [ɒ]; and (o)-2, an unrounded vowel [ɑ~a]. Table 10-11 gives index scores for this variable by social class, contextual style, and sex, and shows a pattern of differentiation markedly different from that shown for (ng) in table 10-2.

TABLE 10-11   (o) Indices by class, style, and sex

Class		Style			
	Sex	WLS	RPS	FS	CS
MMC	M	000	000	001	003
	F	000	000	000	000
LMC	M	004	014	011	055
	F	000	002	001	008
UWC	M	011	019	044	060
	F	023	027	068	077
MWC	M	029	026	064	078
	F	025	045	071	066
LWC	M	014	050	080	069
	F	037	062	083	090

As far as the two MC groups are concerned, in all eight cases men again have scores that are higher than or equal to those of women. The striking fact to emerge from this table, however, is that for the three WC groups the normal pattern of sex differentiation is almost completely *reversed*. In ten cases out of twelve, women have higher scores than men. If it is true that for Norwich men WC non-standard speech forms have high covert prestige, then this would appear to be a counter-example which we have to explain. (This is the only Norwich variable for which a reversal of the pattern of sex differentiation was found.)

In order to be able to handle this problem we must first turn our attention to the examination of another variable, the variable (e). This is the pronunciation of the vowel in *tell, bell, hell,* for which there are three main variants: (e)-1 = [ɛ]; (e)-2 = [ɜ]; (e)-3 = [ʌ]. Table 10-12 shows index scores for this variable by class and style.

TABLE 10-12   (e) Indices by class and style

Class	Style			
	WLS	*RPS*	*FS*	*CS*
MMC	003	000	001	002
LMC	007	012	023	042
UWC	027	039	089	127
MWC	030	044	091	087
LWC	009	026	077	077

The figures given in this table illustrate quite clearly that the pattern of class differentiation for (e) differs rather strikingly from the normal pattern of differentiation illustrated for (ng) in table 10-1. The difference lies in the fact that the bottom group, the LWC, consistently has scores that are *lower* (more nearly standard) than those of both the UWC and MWC. A regular pattern of differentiation could only be obtained by placing the LWC scores between those for the LMC and UWC. It should also be noted that the MWC has a *lower* score than the UWC in *CS*. In *CS*, in fact, the class differentiation pattern for the WC is completely the reverse of the normal pattern.

The answer to the problem of why this should be the case lies in some research that was carried out into linguistic change in Norwich English. It was noted several times in the course of this research that the LWC, as a relatively underprivileged group, appeared to be isolated from certain innovating tendencies. Since we have found in the case of (e) that the LWC is differentiated from the UWC and the MWC in an unusual way, we can guess that high scores for this variable (that is, a large amount of non-standard centralization) represent an *innovation* in Norwich English: The variable (e) is involved in linguistic change, in that centralization of this vowel is increasing. We can further hypothesize that in the vanguard of this linguistic change, which would appear to be leading Norwich English in a direction away from the RP standard, are the *upper* members of the WC. The LWC and LMC are also participating in this change, but at a lower level, and the MMC are not participating at all, or very little.

This hypothesis is in fact confirmed by the pattern of age differentiation illustrated in table 10-13. This illustrates that younger people in Norwich, those aged under 30 and in particular those aged under 20, have much higher (e) scores than the rest of the population. This is particularly true of the crucial *CS* scores. Only the youngest two age groups achieve scores of 100 or over. This large amount of age differentiation confirms that a linguistic change is in fact taking place in Norwich.

TABLE 10-13　　(e) Indices by age and style

Age	Style			
	WLS	*RPS*	*FS*	*CS*
10−19	059	070	139	173
20−29	021	034	071	100
30−39	025	031	059	067
40−49	015	026	055	088
50−59	006	013	035	046
60−69	005	018	055	058
70 +	005	031	050	081

It is therefore possible to suggest that linguistic changes in a direction away from the standard norm are led in the community by members of the UWC and MWC. In particular, because of the covert prestige non-standard forms have for them, we would expect changes of this type to be spear-headed by MWC and UWC *men*. (Correspondingly, standard forms will tend to be introduced by MC women.) This point is confirmed in the case of (e), since the highest (e) index score of all was obtained in *CS* by *male* MWC 10 to 19-year-olds, who had a mean index of 200, i.e. they all consistently used (e)-3 in *CS*.

It is interesting to relate this change in a non-standard direction to the concept of covert prestige. We have already seen that for Norwich men this kind of prestige is associated with non-standard forms. But it also appears to be the case that very high covert prestige is associated with WC speech forms by the young of *both sexes*. Tables 10-14 and 10-15 illustrate this point. They compare the figures obtained in the Self-Evaluation Test for (er) and (ō) respectively by male WC speakers as a whole with those obtained by male WC speakers aged under 30. In the case of female speakers, because of the size of the sample at this point, it was not possible to remove class bias from the data, and the figures for female speakers also shown in tables 10-14 and 10-15 simply compare scores obtained by female speakers as a whole with those of the female under-30 group.

TABLE 10-14　　Percentage of informants over- and under-reporting (er) by age

Percentage	Male		Female	
	Total WC	*WC 10−29*	*Total female*	*10−29*
Over-r	21	8	68	40
Under-r	50	58	14	20
Accurate	29	33	18	40

TABLE 10-15   Percentage of informants over- and under-reporting (ō) by age

	Male		Female	
Percentage	*Total WC*	*WC 10–29*	*Total female*	*10–29*
Over-r	8	8	25	0
Under-r	50	58	18	50
Accurate	42	33	57	50

In the case of (er) it is clear that younger informants are rather more accurate in their self-evaluation than are older informants. With the female informants this is particularly striking: 40 percent accuracy as compared to only 18 percent accuracy from the female sample as a whole. In the case of (ō), the differences are rather more striking. The younger informants are slightly less accurate than the sample as a whole, but this is due to a greater tendency—and in the case of the female informants a *much* greater tendency—to under-report. It is therefore not only male speakers who attach covert prestige to WC speech forms, but also the younger female informants. (This point has been consistently overlooked by other writers on this topic—see especially Spender, 1980:38). Whether this is a feature which is repeated in every generation of female speakers, or whether it reflects a genuine and recent change in ideology, it is not possible at this stage to say. What is clear, however, is that the linguistic change associated with (e) is being caused, at least in part, by the covert prestige which the WC form [ʌ] has for certain Norwich speakers. Group-identification of a kind considered desirable by these speakers is signalled by the usage of the non-standard form, and this leads to its increase and exaggeration. Covert prestige, therefore, leads not only to the differentiation of the linguistic behaviour of the sexes, but also to the exaggeration of certain non-standard features, particularly by UWC and MWC men and by the young, which in turn leads to linguistic change.

If we now return once again to the unusual pattern associated with (o) illustrated in table 10-1, we might again hypothesize that the deviant configuration of scores obtained for this variable is due, as in the case of (e), to a linguistic change in progress. However, this does not at first sight appear possible, since, if the RP form [ɒ] were being introduced into Norwich English, we would clearly expect this process to be spear-headed by MC women. The answer would appear to lie in the fact that [ɒ] is not *only* an *RP* form. It is *also* the form that occurs in the speech of the Home Counties and, perhaps more importantly, in Suffolk. Field records made in the 1930s by Lowman,[2] some of which are published in Kurath and McDavid (1961), give the pronunciation of the vowel in items such as *bog* as [ɒ] in Suffolk and this pronunciation is also recorded for the Suffolk localities in Orton and Tilling (1969).

It would therefore seem to be the case that the unusual pattern of sex differentiation of (o) is due to the following processes. The form [ɒ] in items such as *top, dog* is being introduced as a linguistic innovation into Norwich English. This is demonstrated by the scores shown for different age groups in table 10-16. The introduction of this innovation, moreover, is taking place in two ways. First, [ɒ] is being introduced into Norwich English from *RP* by MC women, who are not only

---

[2] I am very grateful to R.I. McDavid who went to a great deal of trouble to enable me to consult these records.

oriented towards *RP*, as the Self-Evaluation Tests show, but also have access to *RP* forms, in a way that WC women do not, because of their social class position. Secondly, this form is being introduced, as a result of geographical diffusion processes, from the non-standard WC speech forms of the Home Counties and particularly Suffolk by WC men, who not only are favourably disposed towards non-standard forms just as MC men are, but also, because of their social class position, have access to these forms as a result of occupational and other forms of social contact with speakers of [ɒ]-type accents. The variable (o) therefore represents a relatively rare example of two different types of linguistic change (change "from below" and "from above" in the terms of Labov, 1966a:328) both leading in the same direction, with the result that it is now only WC women who, to any great extent, preserve the unrounded vowel.

TABLE 10-16　(o) Indices by age and style

Age	Style			
	WLS	*RPS*	*FS*	*CS*
10–29	017	017	045	055
30–49	020	030	039	063
50–69	021	037	058	067
70 +	043	043	091	093

We have therefore been able to argue that "covert prestige" can be associated with certain linguistic forms, and that it is possible in some cases to provide evidence to show that this is in fact the case. This covert prestige reflects the value system of our society and of the different sub-cultures within this society, and takes the following form: for male speakers, and for female speakers under 30, non-standard WC speech forms are highly valued, although these values are not usually overtly expressed. These covert values lead to sex-differentiation of linguistic variables of a particular type that appears to be common to at least many varieties of language in urban societies. Covert prestige also appears to lead to linguistic changes "from below," with the result, for example, that in Norwich English non-standard variants of (e) are currently on the increase. A study of the actual form the sex differentiation of a particular linguistic variable takes, moreover, can also usefully be employed in an examination of whether or not the variable is involved in linguistic change. Levine and Crockett (1966) have demonstrated that in one American locality "the community's march toward the national norm" is spear-headed in particular by middle-aged MC women (and by the young). In Norwich, at least, there appears to be a considerable number of young WC men marching resolutely in the other direction.

REFERENCES

FISCHER, J.L. 1958. "Social Influences on the Choice of a Linguistics Variant." *Word*, 14:47-56.
GOLDTHORPE, J., and LOCKWOOD, D. 1963. "Affluence and British Class Structure." *Sociological Review*, Chap. 11:133-63.
KURATH, H., and McDAVID, R.I. 1961. *The Pronunciation of English in the Atlantic States*. Ann Arbor: University of Michigan Press.

LABOV, W. 1966a. *The Social Stratification of English in New York City.* Washington, D.C.: Center for Applied Linguistics.

LABOV, W. 1966b. "Hypercorrection by the Lower Middle Class as a Factor in Linguistic Change." In W. Bright (ed.), *Sociolinguistics.* The Hague: Mouton.

LEVINE, L., AND CROCKETT, H.J. 1966. "Speech Variation in a Piedmont Community: Post-vocalic *r.*" In S. Lieberson (ed.), *Explorations in Sociolinguistics.* The Hague: Mouton.

MAYER, K.B. 1955. *Class in Society.* New York: Random House.

ORTON, H., AND TILLING, P.M. 1969. *Survey of English Dialects*, Vol. 3: The East Midland Counties and East Anglia. Leeds: E.J. Arnold.

SPENDER, D. 1980. *Man-made Language.* London: Routledge and Kegan Paul.

TRUDGILL, P. 1974. *The Social Differentiation of English in Norwich.* London: Cambridge University Press.

~~~~~~

LANGUAGE IN SOCIAL INTERACTION

Section Two is concerned with the analysis of discourse in face-to-face interaction between individuals. The term "discourse" has been used in recent years to signify both a component of language beyond the sentence and the functional role of language in social interaction. Considerable attention has been focused on the speech act, the minimal or basic unit or move in verbal interaction. Examples of speech acts are directives, requests, declarations, and greetings. Speech acts are in turn located in larger units of discourse, such as conversations, arguments, interviews, and narrations. Since it is evident, to use the formulation of the philosopher J.L. Austin, that speakers "do things with words," discourse is an important component of language structure and language use. And yet it is only comparatively recently that it has been given serious attention. The papers in this section reflect the interesting intersections of disciplines, including anthropology, linguistics, philosophy, and sociology, that have been involved in discourse analysis, as well as the diversity of theoretical and methodological perspectives.

In the study of discourse, attention to verbal units and their structure on the one hand and the social interactional properties of face-to-face behavior on the other must go together. For the analysis of the actual linguistic forms that individuals use in speaking to one another cannot be separated from such social processes as showing respect and deference, taking turns at talk, and correctly beginning and ending interactions. Analysts of discourse and verbal interaction have focused on such issues as the determination of units of talk, the development of systems of transcription, and the discovery of general principles of language use. The authors in this section deal with conversation as well as other forms of discourse and with verbal and nonverbal communication. These perspectives are reflected in several locations within the United States along with other societies and cultures.

HARVEY SACKS and EMANUEL SCHEGLOFF are acknowledged masters of conversational analysis. They and their students have developed methods, vocabulary, and a transcription system for their analysis. They have paid particular attention to the organization of turn-taking in conversation. One crucial aspect of turn-taking is how to terminate it, that is, how to conclude a conversation, which is the topic of their paper. ERVING GOFFMAN's writings have always been at the forefront of the study of social interaction, constantly pointing out the complicated and subtle structure of seemingly simple and mundane communication. His paper in this volume demonstrates the interplay of social interactional and linguistic factors and rules in a very common form of verbal behavior which has previously received very little attention. Notice that interaction with the self is a significant type of communication. JOHN GUMPERZ, in a framework which combines social interactional and ethnographic approaches to language use, reveals the unstated social and cultural assumptions and understandings that are involved in conversational interaction. He points out that speakers and listeners are constantly involved in processes of inference and contextualization, relating what is said to socio-cultural and interactional meanings. The final two papers in this section focus on particular cases of language use in American society. MARILYN MERRITT, very much in the tradition of Goffman, Sacks, and Schegloff, teases out the linguistic and social interactional meanings and functions of the very American "OK," with a careful study of its use in small convenience stores. The significance of CAROL BROOKS GARDNER's paper is her attention to interactional aspects of communicative events between men and women. Her investigation of public, impersonal street remarks is most revealing of urban male–female relations in the United States. It is interesting to compare Gardner's social interactional approach to men's and women's verbal relations with the different perspectives of PETER TRUDGILL (Section One), who studies phonological and grammatical variation in England, and SUSAN GAL, who analyzes language choice and change in a bilingual Alpine community (Section Four).

SELECTED BIBLIOGRAPHY

GOFFMAN, E. 1974. *Frame Analysis*. New York: Harper and Row.
———. 1981. *Forms of Talk*. Philadelphia: University of Pennsylvania Press.
GUMPERZ, J.J. 1981. *Discourse Strategies*. New York: Cambridge University Press.
PSATHAS, G. (ed.). 1979. *Everyday Language: Studies in Ethnomethodology*. New York: Irvington Publishers.
SCHENKEIN, J. (ed.). 1978. *Studies in the Organization of Conversational Interaction*. New York: Academic Press.
SEARLE, J. 1969. *Speech Acts*. New York: Cambridge University Press.
SUDNOW, D. (ed.). 1972. *Studies in Social Interaction*. New York: Free Press.

EMANUEL A. SCHEGLOFF and HARVEY SACKS

Opening Up Closings

Our aim in this paper is to report in a preliminary fashion on analyses we have been developing of closings of conversation. Although it may be apparent to intuition that the unit 'a single conversation' does not simply end, but is brought to a close, our initial task is to develop a technical basis for a closing problem. This we try to derive from a consideration of some features of the most basic sequential organization of conversation we know of—the organization of speaker turns. A partial solution of this problem is developed, employing resources drawn from the same order of organization. The incompleteness of that solution is shown, and leads to an elaboration of the problem, which requires reference to quite different orders of sequential organization in conversation—in particular, the organization of topic talk, and the overall structural organization of the unit 'a single conversation'. The reformulated problem is used to locate a much broader range of data as relevant to the problem of closings, and some of that data is discussed in detail. Finally, an attempt is made to specify the domain for which the closing problems, as we have posed them, seem apposite.

This project is part of a program of work undertaken several years ago to explore the possibility of achieving a naturalistic observational discipline that could deal with the details of social action(s) rigorously, empirically, and formally.[1] For a variety of reasons that need not be spelled out here, our attention has focused on conversational materials; suffice it to say that this is not because of a special interest in language, or any theoretical primacy we accord conversation. Nonetheless, the character of our materials as conversational has attracted our attention to the study of conversation as an activity in its own right, and thereby to the ways in which any actions accomplished in conversation require reference to the properties and organization of conversation for their understanding and analysis, both by participants and by professional investigators. This last phrase requires emphasis and explication.[2]

We have proceeded under the assumption (an assumption borne out by our research) that insofar as the materials we worked with exhibited orderliness, they

This is an expanded version of a paper originally delivered at the annual meeting of the American Sociological Association, San Francisco, September 1969. It appeared in *Semiotica*, Vol. 8, 1973, pp. 289-327. Bibliographic update July 1982, reprinted with permission of Emanuel A. Schegloff.

[1] Products of that effort already published or in press include: Sacks (1972a; 1972b), Schegloff (1968; 1972), Jefferson (1972), Schenkein (1972), Moerman (1967; 1970). Since original publication, many additional "products of that effort" have appeared, by these and other authors: cf. selected papers and bibliographies in such collections as Sudnow (1972), Schenkein (1978), Psathas (1979), *Sociological Inquiry* (1980), and Atkinson and Heritage (forthcoming), as well as Goodwin (1981).

[2] Here our debts to the work of Harold Garfinkel surface. Elsewhere, though they cannot be pinpointed, they are pervasive.

did so not only for us, indeed not in the first place for us, but for the coparticipants who had produced them. If the materials (records of natural conversations) were orderly, they were so because they had been methodically produced by members of the society for one another, and it was a feature of the conversations that we treated as data that they were produced so as to allow the display by the coparticipants to each other of their orderliness, and to allow the participants to display to each other their analysis, appreciation, and use of that orderliness. Accordingly, our analysis has sought to explicate the ways in which the materials are produced by members in orderly ways that exhibit their orderliness, have their orderliness appreciated and used, and have that appreciation displayed and treated as the basis for subsequent action. In the ensuing discussion, therefore, it should be clearly understood that the 'closing problem' we are discussing is proposed as a problem for conversationalists; we are not interested in it as a problem for analysts except insofar as, and in the ways, it is a problem for participants. (By 'problem' we do not intend puzzle, in the sense that participants need to ponder the matter of how to close a conversation. We mean that closings are to be seen as achievements, as solutions to certain problems of conversational organization. While, for many people, closing a conversation may be a practical problem in the sense that they find it difficult to get out of a conversation they are in, that problem is different from the problem of closing that we are concerned with. The problem we are concerned with sets up the possibilities of a practical problem but does not require that such practical problems occur. Our discussion should then be able to furnish bases for the existence of practical problems of closing conversations.)

The materials with which we have worked are audiotapes and transcripts of naturally occurring interactions (i.e., ones not produced by research intervention such as experiment or interview) with differing numbers of participants and different combinations of participant attributes.[3] There is a danger attending this way of characterizing our materials, namely, that we be heard as proposing the assured relevance of numbers, attributes of participants, etc., to the way the data are produced, interpreted, or analyzed by investigators or by the participants themselves. Such a view carries considerable plausibility, but for precisely that reason it should be treated with extreme caution, and be introduced only where warrant can be offered for the relevance of such characterizations of the data from the data

---

[3] Considerations of space preclude the extensive citation of data in the text. Nonetheless, we intend our analysis to be thoroughly empirical; throughout it characterizes and analyzes conversational materials we have collected over the last several years, and we invite its assessment on natural conversational materials readers may collect.

A further reason for limitations on data citation may be mentioned, which reflects on the nature of the problem with which we are dealing. Investigations of greetings (Sacks, 1967) or summons-answer sequences (Schegloff, 1968) appear to satisfy data citation requirements with a few cases, such as "hello", "hello". It would be redundant to cite multiple instances of such exchanges, or minor variants of them (though some variants would require separate treatment). Failure to do such multiple citation would not represent a paucity of empirical evidence. But, while conversational openings regularly employ a common starting point—with greetings, etc.—and then diverge over a range of particular conversations, conversational closings converge from a diverse range of conversations-in-their-course to a regular common closure with "bye bye" or its variants. Multiple citations of "bye bye" would be as redundant as multiple citations of "hello". However, as will be seen below, we find analysis of terminal "bye bye" exchanges inadequate as an analysis of closings, in a way that greeting exchanges or summons-answer sequences are not inadequate for openings. Consequently, we find we have to deal with the divergent sources out of which conversationalists, in their respective conversations, collaborate in arriving at farewell exchanges. While a single "hello" citation can stand proxy for a host of actual occurrences

themselves.[4] We offer some such warranted characterization of our material at the end of this paper. The considerations just adduced, however, restrain us from further characterizing it here.

In addressing the problem of closings, we are dealing with one part of what might be termed the overall structural organization of single conversations. While one can certainly address other closing or completion loci, e.g., utterance completion, topic closure, etc., the unit whose closing is of concern here is 'a single conversation'. While therefore in one sense we are dealing with closing, in another we are dealing with one aspect of the structure of the unit 'a single conversation', other aspects of which include 'openings', and topical structure. As we shall see, dealing with the one aspect of the overall structural organization of conversation will require reference to other orders of conversation's organization. And because an adequate account of the order of organization, 'overall structural organization', would require space far beyond that available to us, and knowledge beyond that in hand (as well as reference to other orders of organization, such as the organization of the unit 'a topic', about which not enough is now known), our account will remain in many respects indicative rather than complete. It is in that sense a preliminary account of how to deal with 'closings', and an even more rudimentary account of overall structure in general.

Not all conversational activity is bounded and collected into cases of the unit 'a single conversation'. That unit, and the structure that characterizes and constitutes it, is therefore not necessarily relevant wherever conversational activity occurs. On the other hand, other orders of organization, most notably those organizing utterances and the speaker turns in which they occur, are coterminous with, and indeed may be taken as defining, conversational activity (though not all talk; not, for example, formal lecturing). On that account, they may be regarded as fundamental (for more compelling reasons for so regarding them, see Sacks, 1967). We will return to the theme of conversational activity that does not seem to constitute instances of the unit 'a single conversation' at the end of this paper. In view of the preceding argument, however, it seems useful to begin by formulating the problem of closing technically in terms of the more fundamental order of organization, that of turns.

I

Elsewhere (Sacks, 1967; Sacks et al., 1974), two basic features of conversation are proposed to be: (1) at least, and no more than, one party speaks at a time in a single

---

because of its standardized usage, the same is not true for the range of goings-on from which conversationalists may undertake to move toward closing. It is here that space limitations preclude reproduction of the range of materials we hope to be giving an account of. (Joan Sacks brought some of these points to our attention.)

[4] For example, that all the conversations are in 'American English' is no warrant for so characterizing them. For there are many other characterizations which are equally 'true', e.g., that they are 'adult', 'spoken' (not yelled or whispered), etc. That the materials are all 'American English' does not entail that they are RELEVANTLY 'American English', or relevantly in any larger or smaller domain that might be invoked to characterize them. All such characterizations must be warranted, and except for the account we offer in the final section of the paper, we cannot warrant them now. Ethnic, national, or language identifications differ from many others only in their *prima facie* plausibility, especially to those in the tradition of anthropological linguistics. The basis for this position may be found in Sacks (1972a); a discussion of unwarranted ethnic characterizations of materials and findings may be found in Moerman (1967).

conversation; and (2) speaker change recurs. The achievement of these features singly, and especially the achievement of their cooccurrence, is accomplished by coconversationalists through the use of a 'machinery' for ordering speaker turns sequentially in conversation. The turn-taking machinery includes as one component a set of procedures for organizing the selection of 'next speakers', and, as another, a set of procedures for locating the occasions on which transition to a next speaker may or should occur. The turn-taking machinery operates utterance by utterance. That is to say: in contrast to conceivable alternative organizations (e.g., in which the occasions of speaker transition and the mode or outcome of next speaker selections would be predetermined for the whole conversation, from its outset, by mappings into other attributes of the parties; see Albert, 1965), it is within any current utterance that possible next speaker selection is accomplished, and upon possible completion of any current utterance that such selection takes effect and transition to a next speaker becomes relevant. We shall speak of this as the 'transition relevance' of possible utterance completion. It is in part the consequence of an orientation to the feature, 'speaker change RECURS', which provides for the RECURRENT relevance of transition to a next speaker at any possible utterance completion point (except where special techniques have been employed to modify that relevance).

These basic features of conversation, the problem of achieving their cooccurrence, and the turn-taking machinery addressed to the solution of that problem are intended, in this account, not as analysts' constructs, but as descriptions of the orientations of conversationalists in producing proper conversation. Conversationalists construct conversations in their course, and in doing so they are oriented to achieving the cooccurrence of the features cited above, and employ the turn-taking machinery to do so. We cannot here present a detailed demonstration of this claim (cf. Sacks et al., 1974), but an indication of one direction in which such a demonstration might be pursued may be offered. If the features are normative, i.e., are oriented to by conversationalists, then the machinery for achieving their cooccurrence should include procedures for dealing with violations, and indeed should locate failure to achieve the features, singly and jointly, as 'violations', as in need of repair. A minimal requirement for this would be that the machinery locates as 'events' cases of the nonachievement of the features. That it does so may be suggested by such matters as the occurrence of conversationalists' observations about 'someone's silence' when no one in a setting is talking. The noticeability of silence reflects an orientation by conversationalists to the 'at least . . . one at a time' feature; the feature must be oriented to by conversationalists, and not merely be an analytic construct, if conversationalists do accomplish and report the noticing. The attributability of the silence reflects an orientation to the next-speaker-selection component of the turn-taking machinery that can have generated a 'some speaker's turn' at a given point in the course of the conversation, so that a silence at that point may be attributable to that 'speaker'. [Note: A key to the symbols used in the transcriptions appears at the end of this paper.]

> E: He hadtuh come out tuh San Francisco. So he called hhh from their place, out here to the professors, en set up, the, time, and hh asked them to hh- if they'd make a reservation for him which they did cuz they paid for iz room en etcetera en he asked them tuh:: make a reservation for iz parents. En there was a deep silence she said at the other end 'e sez "Oh well they'll pay for their own uh"—hhh—"room an' accommodations."

(What is reported seems to involve that the silence that was noted was dealt with by appending a clarification to the request, the silence being heard by the speaker as not his, and then being transformed into his own pause by his producing such a continuation as they might then reply to appropriately. That the silence is heard as the other's, but treated as one's own for talk purposes is a delicately interesting matter.)

Similarly, there are available and employed devices for locating cases of 'more than one at a time' as events, and for resolving them, or warrantedly treating them as violations. Again, that such devices are available to, and employed by, conversationalists requires treatment of the feature 'no more than one at a time' as normative, as oriented to by conversationalists, rather than as theorists' devices for imposing order on the materials.

It may be noted that whereas these basic features with which we began (especially the feature of speaker change recurrence), and the utterance by utterance operation of the turn-taking machinery as a fundamental generating feature of conversation, deal with a conversation's ongoing orderliness, they make no provision for the closing of conversation. A machinery that includes the transition relevance of possible utterance completion recurrently for any utterance in the conversation generates an indefinitely extendable string of turns to talk. Then, an initial problem concerning closings may be formulated: HOW TO ORGANIZE THE SIMULTANEOUS ARRIVAL OF THE CO-CONVERSATIONALISTS AT A POINT WHERE ONE SPEAKER'S COMPLETION WILL NOT OCCASION ANOTHER SPEAKER'S TALK, AND THAT WILL NOT BE HEARD AS SOME SPEAKER'S SILENCE. The last qualification is necessary to differentiate closings from other places in conversation where one speaker's completion is not followed by a possible next speaker's talk, but where, given the continuing relevance of the basic features and the turn-taking machinery, what is heard is not termination but attributable silence, a pause in the last speaker's utterance, etc. It should suggest why simply to stop talking is not a solution to the closing problem: any first prospective speaker to do so would be hearable as 'being silent' in terms of the turn-taking machinery, rather than as having suspended its relevance. Attempts to 'close' in this way would be interpretable as an 'event-in-the-conversation', rather than as outside, or marking, its boundaries, and would be analyzed for actions being accomplished in the conversation, e.g., anger, brusqueness, pique, etc. Again, the problem is HOW TO COORDINATE THE SUSPENSION OF THE TRANSITION RELEVANCE OF POSSIBLE UTTERANCE COMPLETION, NOT HOW TO DEAL WITH ITS NONOPERATION WHILE STILL RELEVANT.

II

How is the transition relevance of possible utterance completion lifted? A proximate solution involves the use of a 'terminal exchange' composed of conventional parts, e.g., an exchange of 'good-byes'. In describing how a terminal exchange can serve to lift the transition relevance of possible utterance completions, we note first that the terminal exchange is a case of a class of utterance sequences which we have been studying for some years, namely, the utterance pair, or, as we shall refer to it henceforth, the adjacency pair.[5]

---

[5] Erving Goffman has given attention to a range of members of this class from a somewhat different perspective, in his chapters on "Supportive Interchanges" and "Remedial Interchanges" in *Relations in Public* (1971). More recently (1975) he has addressed himself still more directly to this area.

While this class of sequences is widely operative in conversation, our concern here is with the work they do in terminations, and our discussion will be limited to those aspects of adjacency pairs that fit them for this work. Briefly, then, adjacency pairs consist of sequences which properly have the following features: (1) two utterance length, (2) adjacent positioning of component utterances, (3) different speakers producing each utterance.

The component utterances of such sequences have an achieved relatedness beyond that which may otherwise obtain between adjacent utterances. That relatedness is partially the product of the operation of a typology in the speakers' production of the sequences. The typology operates in two ways: it partitions utterance types into 'first pair parts' (i.e., first parts of pairs) and second pair parts; and it affiliates a first pair part and a second pair part to form a 'pair type'. 'Question-answer,' 'greeting-greeting,' 'offer-acceptance/refusal' are instances of pair types. A given sequence will thus be composed of an utterance that is a first pair part produced by one speaker directly followed by the production by a different speaker of an utterance which is (a) a second pair part, and (b) is from the same pair type as the first utterance in the sequence is a member of. Adjacency pair sequences, then, exhibit the further features (4) relative ordering of parts (i.e., first pair parts precede second pair parts) and (5) discriminative relations (i.e., the pair type of which a first pair part is a member is relevant to the selection among second pair parts).

The achievement of such orderliness in adjacency pair sequences requires the recognizability of first pair part status for some utterances. That problem is handled in various ways; constructionally, as when the syntax of an utterance can be used to recognize that a question is being produced, or through the use of conventional components, as when "hello" or "hi" is used to indicate partially that a greeting is being produced, to cite but two procedures.

A basic rule of adjacency pair operation is: given the recognizable production of a first pair part, on its first possible completion its speaker should stop and a next speaker should start and produce a second pair part from the pair type of which the first is recognizably a member.

Two sorts of uses of adjacency pairs may be noticed. We are interested in only one of them here, and mention the other for flavor. First, for flavor: wherever one party to a conversation is specifically concerned with the close order sequential implicativeness of an utterance he has a chance to produce, the use of a first pair part is a way he has of methodically providing for such implicativeness.[6] So, if he is concerned to have another talk directly about some matter he is about to talk about, he may form his own utterance as a question, a next speaker being thereby induced to employ the chance to talk to produce what is appreciable as an answer. Such uses of adjacency pairs occur freely in conversation. Secondly, wherever, for the operation of some TYPE OF ORGANIZATION, close ordering of utterances is useful or required, we find that adjacency pairs are employed to achieve such close ordering. So, in the case of that type of organization which we are calling 'overall structural organization', it may be noted that at least initial sequences (e.g., greeting exchanges), and ending sequences (i.e., terminal exchanges) employ adjacency pair

---

[6] By 'sequential implicativeness' is meant that an utterance projects for the sequentially following turn(s) the relevance of a determinate range of occurrences (be they utterance types, activities, speaker selections, etc.). It thus has sequentially organized implications.

formats. It is the recurrent, institutionalized use of adjacency pairs for such types of organization problems that suggests that these problems have, in part, a common character, and that adjacency pair organization is specially fitted to the solution of problems of that character. (Lifting the transition relevance of possible utterance completion being that sort of problem, adjacency pair organization would be specially adapted to its solution, in the form of the terminal exchange.)

The type of problem adjacency pairs are specially fitted for, and the way they are specially suited for its solution, may very briefly be characterized as follows. Given the utterance by utterance organization of turn-taking, unless close ordering is attempted there can be no methodic assurance that a more or less eventually aimed-for successive utterance or utterance type will ever be produced. If a next speaker does not do it, that speaker may provide for a further next that should not do it (or should do something that is not it); and, if what follows that next is 'free' and does not do the originally aimed-for utterance, it (i.e., the utterance placed there) may provide for a yet further next that does not do it, etc. Close ordering is, then, the basic generalized means for assuring that some desired event will ever happen. If it cannot be made to happen next, its happening is not merely delayed, but may never come about. The adjacency pair technique in providing a determinate 'when' for it to happen, i.e., 'next', has then means for handling the close order problem, where that problem has its import, through its control of the assurance that some relevant event will be made to occur.

But, it may be wondered, why are two utterances required for either opening or closing? It is plain, perhaps, why adjacency pairs are relevant to getting answers to ever happen for questions; for one thing, the parts of question-answer pairs are rather different sorts of objects. It might appear, however, that the problem of closing could be handled with just one utterance. That is, if two utterances are needed, then a pair format is understandable; but why are two utterances needed?

What two utterances produced by different speakers can do that one utterance cannot do is: by an adjacently positioned second, a speaker can show that he understood what a prior aimed at, and that he is willing to go along with that. Also, by virtue of the occurrence of an adjacently produced second, the doer of a first can see that what he intended was indeed understood, and that it was or was not accepted. Also, of course, a second can assert his failure to understand, or disagreement, and inspection of a second by a first can allow the first speaker to see that while the second thought he understood, indeed he misunderstood. It is then through the use of adjacent positioning that appreciations, failures, corrections, etcetera can be themselves understandably attempted. Wherever, then, there is reason to bring attention to the appreciation of some implicativeness, 'next utterance' is the proper place to do that, and a two-utterance sequence can be employed as a means for doing and checking some intendedly sequentially implicative occurrence in a way that a one-utterance sequence can not.

(The foregoing is not at all exclusive, though it is sufficient. For example, in the case of initial sequences, their paired status also permits the use of their assertion to be inspected, in the case of telephone calls in particular, for who is talking or whether who is talking is recognizable from just that presentation; cf. Schegloff, 1979.)

We are then proposing: If WHERE transition relevance is to be lifted is a systematic problem, an adjacency pair solution can work because: by providing that transition relevance is to be lifted after the second pair part's occurrence, the occurrence of the second pair part can then reveal an appreciation of, and agreement to, the intention of closing NOW which a first part of a terminal exchange reveals its speaker to propose. Now, given the institutionalization of that solution, a range of ways of assuring that it be employed have been developed, which make drastic difference between one party saying "good-bye" and not leaving a slot for the other to reply, and one party saying "good-bye" and leaving a slot for the other to reply. The former becomes a distinct sort of activity, expressing anger, brusqueness, and the like, and available to such a use by contrast with the latter. It is this consequentiality of alternatives that is the hallmark of an institutionalized solution. The terminal exchange is no longer a matter of personal choices; but one cannot explain the use of a two-utterance sequence by referring to the way that single utterance closings are violative, for the question of why they are made to be violative is then left unexamined.

In referring to the components of terminal exchanges, we have so far employed "good-bye" as an exclusive instance. But, it plainly is not exclusively used. Such other components as "ok", "see you", "thank you", "you're welcome", and the like are also used. Since the latter items are used in other ways as well, the mere fact of their use does not mark them as unequivocal parts of terminal exchanges. This fact, that possible terminal exchanges do not necessarily, by their components alone, indicate their terminal exchange status, is one source for our proposal that the use of terminal exchanges is but a proximate solution to the initially posed problem of this paper. We turn now to a second problem, whose examination will supply some required additions.

III

In the last section we focused on one type of placing consideration relevant to closing conversation: the close order organization of terminal exchanges. By the use of an adjacency pair format, a place could be marked in a string of utterances in such a way that on its completion the transition relevance of utterance completion might be lifted. The second part of a terminal exchange was proposed to be such a place. The second part of a terminal exchange had its positioned occurrence provided for by the occurrence of a first part of such an exchange. No discussion was offered about the placement of the first part of terminal exchanges. Here we begin to take up that issue, and to develop what sorts of problems are involved in its usage.

While it should be experientially obvious that first parts of terminal exchanges are not freely occurrent, we shall here try to develop a consideration of the sorts of placing problems their use does involve. First, two preliminary comments are in order. (1) Past and current work has indicated that placement considerations are general for utterances. That is: a pervasively relevant issue (for participants) about utterances in conversation is 'why that now', a question whose analysis may (2) also be relevant to finding what 'that' is. That is to say, some utterances may derive their character as actions entirely from placement considerations. For example, there do not seem to be criteria other than placement (i.e., sequential) ones that will sufficiently discriminate the status of an utterance as a statement, assertion, declarative, proposition, etc., from its status as an answer. Finding an utterance to be an answer, to be accomplishing answering, cannot be achieved by reference to phonological, syntactic, semantic, or logical features of the utterance itself, but only by consulting its sequential placement, e.g., its placement after a question. If terminal exchanges are not necessarily marked as such by their components (as was suggested above), we are well advised to consider the contribution of their placement to their achievement of that status.

Addressing considerations of placement raises the issue: what order of organization of conversation is the relevant one, by reference to which placement is to be considered. We dealt earlier with one kind of placement issue, i.e., the placement of SECOND parts of terminal exchanges, and there the order of organization by reference to which placement was done and analyzed was the adjacency pair, which is one kind of 'local', i.e., utterance, organization. It does NOT appear that FIRST parts of terminal exchanges, which is what we are now concerned with, are placed by reference to that order of organization. While they, of course, occur after some utterance, they are not placed by reference to a location that might be formulated as ' 'next' after some 'last' utterance or class of utterances'. Rather, their placement seems to be organized by reference to a properly initiated closing SECTION, and it is by virtue of the lack of a properly initiated closing section that the unilateral dropping in of the first part of a terminal exchange is only part of the solution to the closing problem. We shall need, therefore, to concern ourselves with the proper initiation of closing sections. To do so adequately, and to understand the basis for this order of organization as the relevant one for closing, we will explore some aspects of overall conversational organization as the background for a subsequent consideration of the placement issue. In view of the background character of our purpose, the discussion is necessarily minimal and somewhat schematic.

The aspect of overall conversational organization directly relevant to the present problem concerns the organization of topic talk. (The last phrase is ambiguous, being understandable both as the organization of the unit 'a topic', and as the organization of a set of such units within the larger unit 'a single conversation'. While the former of these is also relevant to closings, it is the latter that we intend in the present context.) If we may refer to what gets talked about in a conversation as 'mentionables', then we can note that there are considerations relevant for conversationalists in ordering and distributing their talk about mentionables in a single conversation. There is, for example, a position in a single conversation for 'first topic'. We intend to mark by this term not the simple serial fact that some topic gets talked about temporally prior to others, for some temporally prior topics such as, for example, ones prefaced by "First, I just want to say . . .", or topics that are minor developments by the receiver of the conversational opening of "how are you" inquiries, are not heard or treated as 'first topics'. Rather, we want to note that to make of a topic a 'first topic' is to accord it a certain special status in the conversation. Thus, for example, to make a topic 'first topic' may provide for its analyzability (by coparticipants) as 'the reason for' the conversation, that being, furthermore, a preservable and reportable feature of the conversation.[7] In addition, making a topic 'first topic' may accord it a special importance on the part of its initiator (a feature which may, but need not, combine with its being a 'reason for the conversation').

---

[7] By "preservable and reportable" we mean that in a subsequent conversation, this feature, having been analyzed out of the earlier conversation and preserved, may be reported as "he called to tell me that . . .". We think that such references to prior conversation are orderly, and can be made available for criterial use, but the argument cannot be developed here.

These features of 'first topics' may pose a problem for conversationalists who may not wish to have special importance accorded some 'mentionable', and who may not want it preserved as 'the reason for the conversation'. It is by reference to such problems affiliated with the use of first topic position that we may appreciate such exchanges at the beginnings of conversations in which news IS later reported, as:

A: What's up.
B: Not much. What's up with you?
A: Nothing.

Conversationalists, then, can have mentionables they do not want to put in first topic position, and there are ways of talking past first topic position without putting them in.

A further feature of the organization of topic talk seems to involve 'fitting' as a preferred procedure. That is, it appears that a preferred way of getting mentionables mentioned is to employ the resources of the local organization of utterances in the course of the conversation. That involves holding off the mention of a mentionable until it can 'occur naturally', that is, until it can be fitted to another conversationalist's prior utterance, allowing his utterance to serve as a sufficient source for the mentioning of the mentionable (thereby achieving a solution to the placement question, the 'why that now', whose pervasive relevance was noted earlier, for the introduction of the topic).

> (At 56 minutes into the conversation)
>   (15.0)

Ken: Well, we were on a discussion uh before Easter that we never finished on
    → uh on why these guys are racing on the street?
(1)   (3.0)
Ken: You know. D'you remember that?
Roger: Oh, I was in a bad accident last night. My legs are all cut up. I was uh-
    → speakina racing on the streets, picking up the subject. We were doin
        th'Mulholland stretch again and one guy made a gross error an' we
        landed in-in the wrong si(hh)de of the mountain hehh I was wearin a belt
        but my knees an' everything got all banged up.

(At one hour, 13 minutes into conversation)

((Ken is talking about people liking to do things, but having to work hard at making it happen))

Ken: Al likes to uh t- to ride sailboats or-or something / / (   )
Roger: Not any more hah hehhh ah hah heh
Ken: Why? What happened?
Roger: She's gone hehh
(2) Al: She is sold. She's gonna be sold.
Ken: Oh. Well, he used to.
Al: Mm hm,
Ken: [[Or-he-he still does in-in the back of his mind probly.
Roger: → Now he / / likes to drive / / fast Austin Healey's now.*
Ken: Or-
Ken: Or he-he/ /he

* Roger has sold Al the Austin Healey.

Al:	$\longrightarrow$ NOT ANY MORE.
Roger:	What happened?
Al:	$\longrightarrow$ IT BLEW UP.
Roger:	*Did*ju really?!
	(1.0)
Roger:	Whadju *do* to it?
Al:	The uh engine blew — I don't know, the valves an' everything went — phooh!
	(1.0)
Roger:	Are you kidding?
Al:	There's three hundred an' fifty dollars worth of work to be done on the engine now.

What we have, then, is that some mentionables ought not or need not be placed in first topic position, and may or are to be held off in the ensuing conversation until they can be fitted to some last utterance. There is, however, no guarantee that the course of the conversation will provide the occasion for any particular mentionable to 'come up naturally'.[8] Thus, the elements of topical organization so far discussed leave open the possibility that for some mentionable which a conversationalist brings to the conversation, no place for its occurrence will have been found at any point in the developing course of that conversation. This can be serious because some mentionables, if not mentioned in some 'this conversation', will lose their status as mentionables, or as the kind of mentionable they are, e.g., they may lose their status as 'news.'

B:	I saw you with your uh filling out a thing for the U. of ——— bookstore. Does that mean you're going there?
A:	Oh yes. Sorry. I didn't know I hadn't told you.
B:	Well, oh you never tell me anything. When well/ /
A:	Well I tell you if I talk to you when something has just happened.
B:	I su-pose
A:	But I don't always remember how long it's been since I've seen people.

This being the case, it would appear that an important virtue for a closing structure designed for this kind of topical structure would involve the provision for placement of hitherto unmentioned mentionables. The terminal exchange by itself makes no such provision. By exploiting the close organization resource of adjacency pairs, it provides for an immediate (i.e., next turn) closing of the conversation. That this close-ordering technique for terminating not exclude the possibility of inserting unmentioned mentionables can be achieved by placement restrictions on the first part of terminal exchanges, for example, by requiring 'advance notices' or some form of foreshadowing.

These considerations about topical structure lead us back to one element of the placement considerations for closings mentioned before, to wit, the notion of a properly initiated closing section. One central feature of proper initiations of closing

---

[8] This is so even when the occasion for the conversation was arranged in the interests of that topic. For example, there was a report several years ago in the student newspaper of the School of Engineering at Columbia University about a meeting arranged with the Dean to air student complaints. No complaints were aired. In answer to a reporter's question about why this happened, a student who had been at the meeting replied, "The conversation never got around to that."

sections is their relationship to hitherto unmentioned mentionables, and some methods for initiating closings seem designed precisely for such problems as we have been discussing.

IV

The first proper way of initiating a closing section that we will discuss is one kind of (what we will call) 'pre-closing'. The kind of pre-closing we have in mind takes one of the following forms, "We-ell...", "O.K...", "So-oo", etc. (with downward intonation contours), these forms constituting the entire utterance. These pre-closings should properly be called 'POSSIBLE pre-closing', because providing the relevance of the initiation of a closing section is only one of the uses they have. One feature of their operation is that they occupy the floor for a speaker's turn without using it to produce either a topically coherent utterance or the initiation of a new topic. With them a speaker takes a turn whose business seems to be to 'pass,' i.e., to indicate that he has not now anything more or new to say, and also to give a 'free' turn to a next, who, because such an utterance can be treated as having broken with any prior topic, can without violating topical coherence take the occasion to introduce a new topic, e.g., some heretofore unmentioned mentionable. AFTER such a possible pre-closing is specifically a place for new topic beginnings.

When this opportunity, provided by possible pre-closings of the sort we are discussing, is exploited, that is, when another thereupon mentions a hitherto unmentioned mentionable, then the local organization otherwise operative in conversation, including the fitting of topical talk, allows the same possibilities which obtain in any topical talk. The opening that a possible pre-closing makes for an unmentioned mentionable may thus result in much more ensuing talk than the initial mentionable that is inserted; for that may provide the occasion for the 'natural occurrence' of someone else's mentionables in a fitted manner. It is thus not negative evidence for the status of utterances such as "We-ell", etc. as possible pre-closings that extensive conversational developments may follow them. (In one two-party conversation of which we have a transcript running to eighty-five pages, the first possible pre-closing occurs on page twenty.) The extendability of conversation to great lengths past a possible pre-closing is not a sign of the latter's defects with respect to initiating closings, but of its virtues in providing opportunities for further topic talk that is fitted to the topical structure of conversation.

We have considered the case in which the possible pre-closing's provision for further topic talk is exploited. The other possibility is that coconversationalists decline an opportunity to insert unmentioned mentionables. In that circumstance, the pre-closing may be answered with an acknowledgement, a return 'pass' yielding a sequence such as:

A: O.K.
B: O.K.

thereby setting up the relevance of further collaborating on a closing section. When the possible pre-closing is responded to in this manner, it may constitute the first part of the closing section.

We have referred to utterances of the form "O.K.", "We-ell", etc. as possible pre-closings, intending by that term to point to the use of such utterances not only possibly to initiate a closing section, but also, by inviting the insertion of unmentioned mentionables, to provide for the reopening of topic talk. On their occurrence, they are only POSSIBLE pre-closings because of this specific alternative they provide for.[9] But there is another sense in which they are only POSSIBLE pre-closings. Clearly, utterances such as "*O.K.*", "We-ell", etc. (where those forms are the whole of the utterance), occur in conversation in capacities other than that of 'pre-closing'. It is only on some occasions of use that these utterances are treated as pre-closings, as we have been using that term. To recommend that the terminal exchange solution initially sketched must be supplemented by an analysis of the placement of terminal exchanges; that the placement be seen in terms of properly initiated closing sections; that closing sections can be properly initiated by possible pre-closings; and that utterances of the form "We-ell" can be pre-closings is not of great help unless it can either be shown (1) that utterances of the form "we-ell" are invariably pre-closings, which is patently not the case, or (2) some indication can be given of the analysis that can yield utterances of the form "we-ell" to be possible pre-closings. One consideration relevant to such a finding (by participants in the conversation; it is their procedures we seek to describe) is the placement of utterances of the form "we-ell" in the conversation.

One way of discriminating the occasions on which such utterances are found to constitute possible pre-closings turns on their placement with respect to topical organization (not in the sense of the organization of mentionables over the course of the conversation which we have hitherto intended, but in the sense of 'the organization of talk on a single topic'). In brief, utterances of the form "we-ell", "*O.K.*", etc., operate as possible pre-closings when placed at the analyzable (once again, to PARTICIPANTS) end of a topic.

To do justice to a discussion of this placement would require an analysis of the organization of 'talk about a topic' which cannot be developed here (work on such analysis is in progress). But we can at least note the following. Not all topics have an analyzable end. One procedure whereby talk moves off a topic might be called 'topic shading', in that it involves no specific attention to ending a topic at all, but rather the fitting of differently focused but related talk to some last utterance in a topic's development. But coconversationalists may specifically attend to accomplishing a topic boundary, and there are various mechanisms for doing so; these may yield what we have referred to above as 'analyzable ends,' their analyzability to participants being displayed in the effective collaboration required to achieve them.

For example, there is a technique for 'closing down a topic' that seems to be a formal technique for a class of topic types, in the sense that for topics that are of the types that are members of the class, the technique operates without regard to what the particular topic is. It does not, then, operate by the determinate, substantively fitted development of the on-going topic talk as a way of bringing that topic talk to an end, but is usable independent of whatever other technique would be topic specific. We have in mind such exchanges as:

A: Okay?
B: Alright.

Such an exchange can serve, if completed, to accomplish a collaboration on the shutting down of a topic, and may thus mark the next slot in the conversational

---

[9] We return to the idea of "specific alternatives' in section VI, where it is more fully discussed.

sequence as one in which, if an utterance of the form "We-ell", "O.K.", etc. should occur, it may be heard as a possible pre-closing.[10]

Another 'topic-bounding' technique (which we can here merely gloss) involves one party's offering of a proverbial or aphoristic formulation of conventional wisdom which can be heard as the 'moral' or 'lesson' of the topic being thereby possibly closed. Such formulations are 'agreeable with'. When such a formulation is offered by one party and agreed to by another, a topic may be seen (by them) to have been brought to a close. Again, an immediately following "We-ell" or "O.K." may be analyzed by its placement as doing the alternative tasks a possible pre-closing can do.

Dorrinne: Uh-you know, it's just like bringin the- blood up.

Theresa: Yeah well, THINGS UH ALWAYS WORK OUT FOR THE / / BEST

Dorrinne: Oh certainly. Alright / / Tess.

(1) Theresa: Uh huh,

Theresa: Okay,

Dorrinne: G'bye.

Theresa: Goodnight,

(2) Johnson: . . .and uh, uh we're gonna see if we can't uh tie in our plans a little better.

Baldwin: Okay / / fine.

Johnson: ALRIGHT?

Baldwin: RIGHT.

Johnson: Okay boy.

Baldwin: Okay.

Johnson: Bye / /bye.

Baldwin: G'night.

There is a type of overall conversational organization in which bounding a topic (rather than 'topic shading') is especially relevant, and in which a sequence made up of a topic closing exchange followed by a possible pre-closing is specially prominent, which we shall call 'monotopical conversation'. With the term 'monotopical' we intend not an *ex post facto* finding that a single topic was talked

---

[10] Although, as argued in the text, this kind of 'shutting down a topic' operates independent of the particular topic talk in progress, it cannot be used at any place in that topic talk without, once again, being seen to accomplish other activities as well, such as 'avoiding the issue', embarrassment, brusqueness, etc. Which is to say that there may be a placement issue for topic closing, as there is for conversational closing. That issue properly belongs in the analysis of topical organization, however, and cannot be developed here.

While 'shutting down a topic' operates in a manner independent of the particular topic in progress, it is not the 'normal', i.e., unmarked, way for talk to move off any topic whatsoever. We mentioned earlier that talk may be moved off a topic without special attention to ending it. To undertake the shutting down of a topic by the sort of exchange discussed in the text may mark that topic as a possibly last one, that marking conferring upon the following conversational slot its distinctive relevance for possible pre-closings. Such a view is supported by noting that the class of types of topics for which the technique operates formally includes 'making arrangements' as a topic type, and that topic type we independently find to be 'closing-relevant' (see section VII). Other types that are members of the class appear to be 'request-satisfaction topics', and 'complaint-remedy topics'. For topics of these types, "O.K.:O.K." can operate as a shutting down technique formally. Both may have some special relationship to 'expectably monotopical' conversation, discussed below.

about, especially in view of the complexity with which topic talk is done, wherein each successive utterance can revise what the topic has been 'all along'. We have in mind, rather, conversations produced from their beginnings with an orientation to their expectable monotopicality.[11] That such conversations do occur can be seen in the techniques conversationalists employ to adapt to that structure or circumvent it while retaining its relevance. Thus, conversations whose initiator begins with the announcement "Two things: . . ." (as a student might say as he seats himself during an instructor's office hours) may serve to counter an otherwise expectable construction of the conversation around one topic, i.e. 'the reason' for his appearance (a construction possibly involving on the part of the other a finding as to where he is in the structure of the conversation by finding where he is in the developing structure of the first topic). Other devices may make room for some talk about matters other than a single topic while preserving an orientation to monotopicality, for example, "Before I come to what I called about. . .". If by 'monotopical' we mean, procedurally, the use of a first topic end as the occasion for initiating a closing section, then the use of some preface like this last may serve to exempt that which it prefaces from being counted as initial topic.

For conversations produced by reference to expectable monotopicality, the close of the topic (or the first nonexempted topic) properly serves as the occasion for the initiation of the closing section. In such circumstances, topics will regularly be bounded, rather than being shaded into other topics. Topic bounding may be accomplished by any of the range of techniques available, including the aphoristic technique and the 'shutting down' technique glossed earlier, and an analyzable possible pre-closing by the initiator, when placed where a topic closing technique might be placed, may itself show the satisfactory (to the party so acting) resolution of the topic, a resolution (and closing) which may thus not have to be separately accomplished. Conversely, where a closing initiation attempt by a called-upon party fails to achieve collaboration from an initiator of a conversation, this may indicate dissatisfaction by the initiator with the putative resolution of the topic.

The discussion in this section, it should be noted, has dealt with only one kind of possible pre-closing, and the suggestions we have offered concerning the placement that allows the analysis of an utterance as a possible pre-closing has reference only to that form. We will deal with others shortly. In regard to the form we have been concerned with, we should note that the techniques of topic bounding we have discussed are not specified for the place of a topic in the serial organization of topics. They are not techniques for first topic, fifth topic, intendedly last topic,[12] etc., but for any topic (in terms of serial organization). That makes all the more fitting the character of possible pre-closings as specifically inviting the reopening of topic talk. For, given that the use of an "*O.*K." or a "we-ell" after the close of a

[11] This is not the place to elaborate on the bases for expectations of monotopicality. It appears to be related to the articulation of the unit 'a single conversation' to features 'external' to that unit, such as compositional features of the interaction, analysis of relative interactional states of the participants (e.g., involvement in other courses of action of competing priority), and the placement of the conversation in the course of a history of interaction of the parties, and in the interactional occasion on which it occurs. The last of these we return to briefly at the end of this paper.

[12] The relationship between 'shutting down' techniques and a class of topic types is no exception. For while 'shutting down' may be specially usable with the topic type 'making arrangements', and that topic type may be closing-relevant, it is not by virtue of the latter feature of 'making arrangements' that 'shutting down' is specially usable to end it.

topic can be analyzed (by coparticipants) as a possible pre-closing without regard to which serial topic in a conversation has been closed, the absence of the reopening alternative might have the consequence of systematically excluding from possible use in the present conversation the whole range of unmentioned mentionables which the participants might have to contribute. In their use of the etiquette of invitation, that is, the offering of the floor to another, possible pre-closings operate to allow a distribution of the opportunities and responsibilities for initiating topic talk and using unmentioned mentionables among various participants in the conversation. It is when the participants to a conversation lay no further claim to these opportunities and responsibilities that the potential of the possible pre-closing for initiating a closing section may be realized.

V

What the preceding discussion suggests is that a closing section is initiated, i.e., turns out to have begun, when none of the parties to a conversation care or choose to continue it. Now that is a WARRANT for closing the conversation, and we may now be in a position to appreciate that the issue of placement, for the initiation of closing sections as for terminal exchanges, is the issue of warranting the placement of such items as will initiate the closing at some 'here and now' in the conversation.[13] The kind of possible pre-closing we have been discussing—"$O.K.$", "we-ell", etc.—is a way of establishing one kind of warrant for undertaking to close a conversation. Its effectiveness can be seen in the feature noted above, that if the floor offering is declined, if the "$O.K.$" is answered by another, then together these two utterances can constitute not a possible, but an actual first exchange of the closing section. The pre-closing ceases to be 'pre-' if accepted, for the acceptance establishes the warrant for undertaking a closing of the conversation at some 'here'.

Having seen that this kind of pre-closing establishes a particular warrant for undertaking the closing of a conversation, we may now examine other kinds of pre-closings and the kinds of warrants they may invoke for initiating the beginning of a closing section. To provide a contrast with the ensuing discussion, let us make one further observation on the kind of pre-closing we have just been discussing. The floor-offering-exchange device is one that can be initiated by any party to a conversation. In contrast to this, there are some possible pre-closing devices whose use is restricted to particular parties. The terms in which such parties may be formulated varies with conversational context.[14] For now, we can offer some observations about telephone contacts, where the formulation of the parties can be specified in terms of the specific conversation, i.e., caller—called.[15] What we find is that there are, so to speak, 'caller's techniques' and 'called's techniques' for inviting the initiation of closing sections. Before detailing these, we may make the general point (in pursuit of the claim at the beginning of this paper about the relationship of closings to overall structural organization) that it is of interest that closing sections of such conversations may be produced in ways which specifically employ, as relevant, features of their beginnings (namely, who initiated them), thus

---

[13] The earlier noted attributions of brusqueness, anger, pique, etc., can now be appreciated as alternative possible warrants for closing attempts, when a closing initiation has not availed itself of the sequentially organized possibilities for warrants.

[14] For explication of the problem this sentence alludes to, see Sacks, 1972, and Schegloff, 1972.

[15] For justification, see Schegloff, 1970, chap. 2.

giving support to the proposal that the unit 'a single conversation' is one to which participants orient THROUGHOUT its course.

While there are specific components whose use may be restricted to callers or called parties in inviting the initiation of conversational closings, we may note one feature that many of them have in common, namely, that they employ as their warrant for initiating the closing at some 'here' the interests of the other party. It is in the specification of those interests that the techniques become assigned to one or another party. Thus, the following invitation to a closing is caller-specific and makes reference to the interests of the other.

> A discussion about a possible luncheon has been proceeding:
>
> A: Uhm livers 'n an' gizzards 'n stuff like that makes it real yummy. Makes it too rich for *me* but: makes it yummy.
> A: *Well* I'll letchu go. I don't wanna tie up your phone.

And, on the other hand, there are such called-specific techniques, also making reference to the other's interests, as

> A: This is costing you a lot of money.

There are, of course, devices usable by either party which do not make reference to the other's interests, most familiarly, "I gotta go".

One feature common to the possible pre-closings so far discussed is that they make no reference to the particulars of the conversation in which they occur. While some of them retain and employ some elements of the conversation's beginning, such as who called, no conversationally developed materials are referred to in warranting the closing of the conversation. There are, in addition, devices which DO make use of conversationally developed materials. Near the beginning of the conversation we will cite, the called (the receiver of the call) says:

> B: Are you watching Dakta:ri?
> A: N:no.
> B: Oh my gosh Officer Henry is ul-locked in the cage wi-(0.4) wi' the lion, hheh

And several minutes later, the caller initiates the closing with

> A: Okay, I letcha go back tuh watch yer Daktari.

Such devices again reinforce our understanding of the orientation of conversationalists to 'a single conversation' as a unit, and to 'THIS single conversation' as an instance, in which ITS development to some point may be employed as a resource in accomplishing its further development as a specific, particularized occurrence. Such materials can be picked up any place in a conversation and seemingly be preserved for use in the conversation's closing. One place they systematically can occur is in the beginnings of conversations (not only in the beginnings of telephone conversations but in face-to-face interactions as well). The "routine" questions employed at the beginnings of conversations, e.g., "what are you doing?", "where are you going?", "how are you feeling?", etc., can elicit those kinds of materials that will have a use at the ending of the conversation in warranting its closing, e.g.,

"Well, I'll let you get back to your books", "why don't you lie down and take a nap?", etc.[16] By contrast with our earlier discussion of such possible pre-closings as "O.K." or "We-ell", which may be said to accomplish or embody a warrant for closing, these may be said to announce it. That they do so may be related to the possible places in which they may be used.

Insofar as the possible pre-closings which announce a warrant for closing draw upon materials particular to the conversations in which they occur, it is not feasible to specify exhaustively their privileges of occurrence. One technique which announces its warrant, but does not make reference to materials derived from the conversation, and which is generally usable (i.e., not restricted to particular users) can be briefly discussed, namely "I gotta go" (and its variants and expansions, such as "The baby is crying, I gotta go", "I gotta go, my dinner is burning", etc.).

We noted before that the possible pre-closings which accomplish a warrant without announcing it are placed after the close, or the closing down, of a topic (indeed, such placement may be required for their recognition as possible pre-closings). The overt announcement we are now considering can be used to interrupt a topic. While exchanges such as "O.K.; O.K." respect in their placement certain local orders of organization, such as the organization of talk on a topic or adjacency pairs (the first "O.K." not being placed after the first part of an adjacency pair, or not being recognizable as a possible pre-closing if it is), the overt announcement, "I gotta go" need not respect such boundaries, and can even interrupt not-yet-possibly-completed utterances. That is not to say that "I gotta go" may not be placed with a respect for such local organization. It can be placed after a topic close, and we can speculate on reasons for its being used at such a place in preference to the "O.K." which could also be used there. While "'I gotta go" cannot prohibit further talk, while others may insert an unmentioned mentionable after it, it does not specifically invite such a sequel, as "O.K." does. For the initiation of a closing section in a way that discourages the specific alternative of reopening topic talk, this pre-closing may be more effective.

One implication of the preceding discussion which we can but hint at now is that from the inventory of possible pre-closing devices, one criterion of selection may be the placement that the item is to be given. That is, the availability of alternative mechanisms for accomplishing the invitation or initiation of a closing section affords us (as analysts) an interesting problem: how can some actually employed mechanism or component be selected? Investigation of this problem can be expected to show that such a selected item operates not only to initiate or invite the initiation of the closing of a conversation (which any of the other available components might do also, and which therefore will not account for the use of the particular component employed), but accomplishes other interactionally relevant activities as well. What we have suggested above is that one such consideration in the selection among components to invite or initiate the closing section is the placement it will be given in terms of the local (utterance-to-utterance) and topical organization.

---

[16] Such a use of materials gathered earlier in the conversation need not be restricted to materials about the other's circumstances or interests. An initiator of a conversation may insert at its beginning materials for his own use at its closing e.g., "I'm just leaving to see the doctor, but I wanted to ask you...". This technique may also allow the caller to provide for a conversation's monotopicality when, for the conversationalists involved, it would not otherwise be expectable.

Another implication should be noted. It is the import of some of the preceding discussion that there are slots in conversation 'ripe' for the initiation of closing, such that utterances inserted there may be inspected for their closing relevance. To cite an example used earlier, "why don't you lie down and take a nap" properly placed will be heard as an initiation of a closing section, not as a question to be answered with a "Because..." (although, of course, a coparticipant can seek to decline the closing offering by treating it as a question). To cite actual data:

B has called to invite C, but has been told C is going out to dinner:

B:	Yeah. Well get on your clothes and get out and collect some of that free food and we'll make it some other time Judy then.
C:	Okay then Jack
B:	Bye bye
C:	Bye bye

While B's initial utterance in this excerpt might be grammatically characterized as an imperative or a command, and C's "Okay" as a submission or accession to it, in no sense but a technical syntactic one would those be anything but whimsical characterizations. While B's utterance has certain imperative aspects in its language form, those are not ones that count; his utterance is a closing initiation; and C's utterance agrees not to a command to get dressed (nor would she be inconsistent if she failed to get dressed after the conversation), but to an invitation to close the conversation. The point is that no analysis—grammatical, semantic, pragmatic, etc.—of these utterances taken singly and out of sequence, will yield their import in use, will show what coparticipants might make of them and do about them. That B's utterance here accomplishes a form of closing initiation, and C's accepts the closing form and not what seems to be proposed in it, turns on the placement of these utterances in the conversation. Investigations which fail to attend to such considerations are bound to be misled.

VI

We have been considering the problem of the placement of the initiation of closing sections, and have found that this problem and the selection of a technique to accomplish initiation of the closing are related to the issue of warranting the initiation of a conversation's closing. That issue, it may be recalled, concerned how to warrant undertaking, at some 'here and now' in a conversation, a procedure that would achieve a solution to the problem of coordinating a stop to the relevance of the transition rule and that would at the same time respect the interests of the parties in getting their mentionables into the conversation. One such warrant could be found when the specific alternative to closing—reopening topic talk—had no interest displayed in it by any of the participants. It should be noted that the use of a possible pre-closing of the form "*O.*K.", or "we-ell" can set up 'proceeding to close' as the central possibility, and the use of unmentioned mentionables by coparticipants as specific alternatives. That is to say, the alternatives made relevant by an utterance of that form are not symmetrical. Closing is the central possibility, further talk is alternative to it; the reverse is not the case (an asymmetry hopefully captured by the term 'possible pre-closing'; 'possible topic reopener' would not do). Unless the alternative is invoked, the central possibility is to be realized.

There is another form of the warranting problem, with concomitant contrasts in placement and utterance type, which reverses this asymmetry. We will refer to it as 'pre-topic closing offerings'. We have in mind data such as the following:

(1) A: Allo
     B: Did I wake you?
     A: Who's it.
     B: Nancy
     A: Oh hi
     B: →Hi, did I wake you
     A: Uh no no, not at all hh/ /h
     B: (   ) hh after a while it started ringin I kept thinkin maybe I should hang up (but I) you know hh
     A: No no no, it's O.K. / / I was just uh rushing a little that's all hh
     B: Oh good.
     A: hh Umm don't bring any sausage because . . . etc.

(2) A: Hello?
     B: Good morning.
     A: Oh hi / / how are you hhh
     B: Lisa
     B: →Fine. Did I wake you up?
     A: No no no, I was reading . . etc.

(3) A: Buh nobody fought with huh like *I* fought with huh.
                    (1.4)
     A: Uhb-uh fer example, uh d-oh about two weeks before she uh died I hh I don't know what possessed me. I really don't. I found myself in my car, driving ovuh tuh see her *alone*.
                    (1.3)
     A: An' I uh::: it *koo- took* me about oh I don't known how long t'find a parking space in that area there,
                    (0.4)
     B: yeah
     A: →About a *half* hour. Are yih busy?
     B: Uh *no*. My liddle gran'daughter is here.
     A: Oh. Oh so it's hard f'you to / / uh,
     B: That's *al*right
     A: -to uh::, to listen. Then uh, look, enjoy yer gran'daughter, hh
     B: I'll be taking her home soon,
     A: An' I'll try to uh:::uh to see you / / on-
     B: Yeah, it could be-would / / be (nice).
     A: -on Thursday.   (etc. to closing)

(4) B: Hello
     A: Vera?
     B: Ye:s
     A: Well you know, I had a little difficulty getting you. ((short discussion of the difficulty))
     A: →Am I taking you away from yer dinner?
     B: No::, no, I haven't even started tuh get it yet.
     A: Oh, you (h)have / / n't.
     B: hhheh heh

```
        A:      Well I- I never am certain, I didn't know whether I'd be too early or too
                late / / or ri-      etc.
  (5)  A:      . . . (Karen Sweet)
        B:      Well, howarya(h)
        A:      Fine, how are you.
        B:      Well just fine.
        A:    →Were you eating,
                      (1.0)
        B:      Some grapes, ehh / / heh heh
        A:      heh, I was just lookin at mine.
```

Such questions as "Did I wake you", "Are you busy", "Am I taking you away from
your dinner", and others (e.g., "Is this long distance?", "Are you in the middle of
something?", etc.) are placed not at the analyzable close of some unit, such as a
topic, but at, or near, the beginning of one. One consequence of this is that, instead
of some activity such as topic talk being a specific alternative to the closing they
otherwise prefigure, the central possibility is an undertaking, or continuation, of the
unit at the beginning of which they are placed (be it a 'topic', a 'conversation', or a
'silence' as when about to 'hold' in a telephone conversation), and closing is the
specific alternative to that. When such pre-topic closing offerings are declined, then
the offering or some component of the declining utterance may be topically
elaborated in its own right, or the offering becomes a pre-sequence for the offerer's
topic talk. If the pre-topic closing offering is accepted, there follows a closing
section, one component of which routinely is making arrangements for resumption
of the conversation (as in the data from (3) above).[17]

Of special interest here are what might be called 'pre-first-topic closing-
offerings', of which all but one of the data citations above are instances (the
exception being the data from (3)). These are not simply special cases of pre-topic
closing offerings, specifying the 'topic' as 'first topic'. Rather, by virtue of the
special status of 'first topic' discussed earlier, inquiries such as "Are you busy?",
"Are you eating?", etc., placed before first topic are more importantly seen as
placed before 'the conversation'. The bases for the insertion of such inquiries before
'first topic' cannot be discussed at length here, but two may be briefly indicated.
First, such inquiries may be heard (by participants) to be warranted (i.e., to have the
'why that now' explained) by features of the contact to that point (e.g., by the
'number of rings before answering', as in the data from (1) above) or by assumedly
mutually oriented-to features of the interaction such as its time and place (on the
mutual orientation to the time and place of a conversation by participants, see
Schegloff, 1972,[18] e.g., the orientation to the social time of day displayed by "Am I

---

[17] These features of pre-topic closing offerings seem to be related in their capacity not only to
prefigure the undertaking of some conversational unit in the absence of a reason to the contrary, but also
to project a certain contour or length for the unit, such that, if the offer to close is not accepted on the
occasion of the offering, no opportunity to close will soon present itself which respects the organization
of that unit (for example, it may require an interruption).

[18] These alternatives may shade into each other. "Did I wake you?" may be heard as displaying its
speaker's orientation to the time of the conversation if asked at a time the speaker might know the other to
have possibly been sleeping; i.e., it can be heard as referring to time if it is the right time for such a ·
question. If not, it can be heard as picking up on a feature of the interaction to that point, e.g., number of
rings before answering, voice quality leading to talk about 'colds', etc.

taking you away from your dinner?", in the data above. Secondly, such inquiries may be heard as attentive to the 'priorities assessment' that may be relevant in initiating a conversation. Where the initiator of a conversation is unable to assess the comparative priorities of possibly ongoing activities of the other and the prospective conversation (for a fuller discussion of this issue concerning openings, see Schegloff, 1970, chap. 2), as when first coming upon the scene (e.g., knocking at the door) or calling on the telephone, an inquiry concerning possibly ongoing priority activities may be introduced, as a way of finding whether an initiated conversation shall be prosecuted. Since the subject of the inquiry is thus selected as one which might have priority over the proposed conversation, an affirmative answer may have the consequence of accepting what turns out to be a closing offering.

Pre-first-topic closing offerings have been introduced here to suggest that, just as possible pre-closings do not foreclose the possibility of further topic talk in the conversation (i.e., raising the possibility of closing does not ensure it), so does the opening of a conversation not preclude the possibility of immediately closing it. When the latter possibility is actualized, although by reference to the basic features discussed at the beginning of this paper, 'conversation' may technically be said to have taken place, the participants may find that 'no conversation occurred'. The possibilities for both conversational continuation and for conversational closing are thus present, if appropriate techniques are used, from the very beginning of a conversation to its end.

VII

After initial formulation of the closing problem for conversation in terms of the suspension of the transition property of utterance completions, a technique was described which is used to come to terms with that problem—the terminal exchange. It was found that that exchange by itself was insufficient and that an adequate description of closing would have to provide for the proper placement of terminal exchanges which do not have unrestricted privileges of occurrence. The needed supplement was found to consist in properly initiated closing sections, and we described a variety of techniques for properly initiating closing sections, their placement, and the warrant they establish for closing a conversation.

Once properly initiated, a closing section may contain nothing but a terminal exchange and accomplish a proper closing thereby. Thus, a proper closing can be accomplished by:

A: *O*.K.
B: O.K.
A: Bye Bye
B: Bye

Closing sections may, however, include much more. There is a collection of possible component parts for closing sections which we cannot describe in the space available here. Among others, closings may include 'making arrangements', with varieties such as giving directions, arranging later meetings, invitations, and the like; reinvocation of certain sorts of materials talked of earlier in the conversation, in particular, reinvocations of earlier-made arrangements (e.g., "See you Wednesday") and reinvocations of the reason for initiating the conversation (e.g., "Well, I just wanted to find out how Bob was"), not to repeat here the earlier discussion of materials from earlier parts of the conversation to do possible pre-closings; and components that seem to give a 'signature' of sorts to the type of conversation, using the closing section as a place where recognition of the type of conversation can be displayed (e.g., "Thank you"). Collections of these and other components can be combined to yield extended closing sections, of which the following is but a modest example:

B:	Well that's why I *said* "I'm not gonna say anything, I'm not making *any com*ments / / about anybody"
C:	Hmh
C:	Ehyeah
B:	Yeah
C:	Yeah
B:	*Al*righty. Well *I'll* give you a call before we decide to come down. O.K.?
C:	O.K.
B:	*Al*righty
C:	O.K.
B:	We'll see you then
C:	O.K.
B:	*Bye* bye
C:	Bye

However extensive the collection of components that are introduced, the two crucial components (FOR THE ACHIEVEMENT OF PROPER CLOSING; other components may be important for other reasons, but not for closing *per se*) are the terminal exchange which achieves the collaborative termination of the transition rule, and the proper initiation of the closing section which warrants the undertaking of the routine whose termination in the terminal exchange properly closes the conversation. It should be noted again, however, that at any point in the development of the collection of components which may occur between a proper initiation of a closing up to and including the terminal exchange, and even the moments immediately following it, there are procedures for reopening the conversation to topic talk (cf. Button, forthcoming). A necessary brief description of some procedures for doing so may indicate why we have referred to this conversational part as a closing SECTION, thereby ascribing to it the status of an oriented-to conversational unit.

One way topic talk may be reopened at any point has already been discussed in another context. We noted earlier that some possible pre-closings specifically invite the insertion of unmentioned mentionables and if that invitation is accepted by a coparticipant, then considerable topic talk may ensue, since other participants may find in the talk about the newly introduced mentionable occasions for the natural fitting of a topic of their own. The same procedure of fitting, of topics 'naturally' coming up, can arise from any of the proper components of closing sections. If one component of a closing section can be reinvocation of earlier talked-about materials, then on any occasion of such an invocation, occasions for fitting new topics to that reinvocation may arise. The same is true for other components of closings, each of which may 'lead to' some fitted other topic 'coming up naturally'. Since most closing components have their roots in the body of the conversation, it appears that 'new' topics can enter into a closing section only by their fit to, or their coming up 'naturally' from 'old' materials. This character of closing sections as 'not a place for new things to come up' is consistent with techniques for initiating them such as possible pre-closings, whose warrant (when their closing options are accepted) is that none of parties has further mentionables to introduce.

The suggestion above that there are procedures at any point in a closing section for reopening topic talk was not, however, intended primarily to refer to this process whereby new materials are introduced by 'hooking' them onto old materials properly appearing as reinvocations. There are also ways in which new materials may be introduced, so to speak, in their own right, and these reflect the sectional character of closings. When such new materials are inserted into a closing, they are specially 'marked'; we can here discuss only two forms of such marking.

One form of marking, used elsewhere in conversation and not only in closings, we can refer to as 'misplacement marking'. Classes of utterances or activities which have a proper place in a conversation but are to be done in some particular conversation in other than their proper place, or an utterance (type) which has no particular proper place but is nonetheless 'out of place' where it is to be done, may have their occurrence misplacement marked. As an example of the former: 'introductions' are properly done at or near the beginnings of conversations. On occasion, however, they may not occur until well into the conversation, as may happen in conversations between adjacently seated passengers in an airplane or train. Such introductions may be prefaced with a misplacement marker, e.g., "By the way, my name is...". As an example of the latter sort of occasion alluded to above, we may note that interruptions of an organizational unit for utterances, such as an adjacency pair, may be similarly misplacement marked. Thus, an utterance inserted after a question has been asked but before it has been answered, may begin with "By the way...".

Misplacement markers, thus, display an orientation by their user to the proper sequential-organizational character of a particular place in a conversation, and a recognition that an utterance that is thereby prefaced may not fit, and that the recipient should not attempt to use this placement in understanding their occurrence. The display of such orientation and recognition apparently entitles the user to place an item outside its proper place. In the case of closings, we find that utterances introducing new materials may be misplacement marked when those utterances do not occur between the parts of an adjacency pair and do not accomplish an activity which has a proper place elsewhere in the conversation. That such utterances, but not ones which use proper closing components, are misplacement marked suggests an orientation by conversationalists to the status of 'closings' as an organizational unit—what we have referred to as a 'section'—with a proper character with which the misplacement marked utterance is not consistent.

Caller: You don'know w- uh what that would be, how much it costs.
Crandall: I would think probably, about twunty five dollars.
Caller: Oh boy hehh hhh!
Caller: Okay, thank you.
Crandall: Okay dear.
Caller: →OH BY THE WAY. I'd just like tuh say thet uh, I *DO* like the new
            programming, I've been listening, it's uh / /
                    (   )
Crandall: *Good girl!*

Crandall: Hey listen do me a favor wouldja write Mister Fairchild 'n tell im that, I
             think that'll s-shi-break up his whole day for im.
Caller: ehhh heh heh hhh!
Crandall: Okay?
Caller: ⌜Okay,
Crandall: ⌞Thank you.
Caller: bye bye,
Crandall: Mm buh(h) bye.

A second form of marking which displays an orientation to a closing section
as 'not a place for new materials' we may refer to as 'contrast marking'. It is best
discussed in connection with data:

> A, who is visiting the city, and B, who lives there, have been engaged in an extensive
> making of arrangements to see each other.
>
> A: I mean b'cause I-eh you're going to this meeting at twelve thirty, en I don't
>   want to uh inconvenience *you*,
> B: Well, even if you get here et abayout eh ten thirty, or eleven uh' clock, we
>   still have en hour en a hahf,
> A: *O*.K., *A*lright,
> B: Fine, We c'd have a bite, en / / (talk),
> A: Yeh, Weh- *No!* No, *don't* prepare any / / thing.
> B: And uh- I'm not gunnah pre*pare*, we'll juz whatever it'll / / be, we'll
>   (   ).
> A: *No!* No, I don't mean that. I min- because uh, *she* en I'll prob'ly uh be
>   spending the day togethuh, so uh::: we'll go out tuh lunch, or something like
>   that. hh So I mean if you:: have a cuppa cawfee or something, I mean / / that
>   uh that'll be fine. But / / uh-
> B: Yeah
> B: Fine.
> A: *Othuh* th'n that don't / / uh
> B: Fine.
> A: Don't bothuh with anything else. I-huh:::
>   (1.2)
> A: →I-uh::: I *did* wanna tell you, en I didn" wanna tell you uh:: last night. Uh
>   because you had entert-uh, company. I-I-I had something- *terrible* t'tell you.
>   So / / uh
> B: How terrible *is* it.
> A: Uh, tuh- as worse it could *be*.
>   (0.8)
> B: W-y' mean Ada?
> A: Uh yah
> B: Whad' she do, die?
> A: Mmhmmm.

The data of particular interest here are in A's seventh utterance in the segment, "I *did*
wanna tell you." While there are various interesting issues raised by this data, we
want briefly only to indicate one of them. The stress (as well as the verb form
employed which allows the stress) accomplishes one half a contrast whose other half
is not explicit (the rest of the utterance does not supply it), and whose paraphrase
might be, "There *is* something else I wanted to tell you". A stress on the second part
of a contrast pair whose first part is not explicit can nonetheless serve to display the

relevance of the first part. Thus, to cite another example, a particularly clear display of what is 'going through someone's mind' though it is not spoken or gesturally, etc., conveyed, is provided by a person waiting to take an elevator down, who is told upon its arrival that the elevator is going up, pauses a moment, and then says, "I guess I *will* wait". The contrast accent displays his prior, now abandoned, decision to 'go along for the ride'. In the case of "I *did* wanna tell you", the presumptive character of closing sections as 'not the place for new materials' can be seen to be here prospectively overruled by new materials, which however are specially marked.

The insertion of misplacement marked new materials into closing sections, it may be added, marks the new materials themselves in a distinctive way. While in the case of the data just discussed, this appears to be 'deferred bad news', regularly the placing of new materials in closing sections is a way of achieving for them the status of 'afterthoughts'.

Having offered some suggestions about the status of closings as sectional units, we think it is in point to suggest several virtues of a sectional solution to the problems we have formulated as the problems of closing.

One aspect of the problem of closing, formulated by reference to the organization of speaker turns, it may be recalled, was that that organization generates an indefinitely extendable, but internally undifferentiated, string of turns. We noted earlier the importance of having a marked place for a problem whose focus was coordination in terminating the transition rules, and described the contribution that a terminal exchange, employing adjacency pair organization, made to the solution of that problem. That contribution was limited, however, by the placement problem for terminal exchanges, i.e., the impropriety of a closing produced by an 'unprepared' terminal exchange. That placement problem is solved by the use of properly initiated closing sections. It is the closing section which, through its terminal exchange, marks a place at which collaboration on termination of the transition rule can be located. An important part of the solution to the closing problem thus involves locating the solution to the initial problem we formulated not so much in the conversation as a whole, but in a closing section; one can close a conversation by closing a section which has as its business closing a conversation. When an initiated closing is aborted by reopening topic talk, a next effort to close does not proceed by simple insertion of a terminal exchange, but by the initiation of another closing section, again providing a unit within which the terminal exchange can be located.

A second virtue of a sectional solution can be mentioned again here briefly. Given the feature of closing sections as 'porous', i.e., the availability at any point of procedures for reopening topic talk, sectional solution has the virtue of possibly providing multiple opportunities for the introduction of unmentioned mentionables, a virtue whose importance vis-à-vis this conversational system's topical organization should be evident from the earlier discussion.

One final virtue of a sectional solution to the closing problem may be suggested, concerning the articulation of conversations (i.e., the unit 'a single conversation') with the interaction episodes, occasions, or streams of behavior in which they occur. One order of relevance termination can have, and one basis for the importance of the clarity of terminal exchanges, is that other actions by the participants may be geared to, or properly occasioned by, the occurrence of conversational termination. In telephone conversations, hanging up and breaking the communication medium properly awaits termination, and properly follows its occurrence. In face-to-face interaction, a whole range of physical doings and positionings, ruled out by the proprieties of maintaining a show of attention and interest,[19] become available and/or required upon termination, for example, those related to leave-taking. Insofar as the actions that may be occasioned by termination of the conversation require preparation, there is use for a place IN the conversation to prepare for actions that should follow its termination in close order.[20] Closing sections, in foreshadowing the imminent occurrence of termination, allow such a possibility. Indeed, topics may be improvised for insertion into a closing sequence to extend the time available for such preparations, as when visitors gather their belongings before departure (thus yielding a derivative problem when such improvised topics assume a 'life of their own' and cannot easily be brought to a close when the preparations they were to accommodate have been completed). The sectional organization of closings thus provides a resource for managing the articulation between the conversation and the interaction occasion in which it occurs.

The source of many of these virtues resides in the potential for reopening topic talk at any point in the course of a closing section. This invites our understanding that to capture the phenomenon of closings, one cannot treat it as the natural history of some particular conversation; one cannot treat it as a routine to be run through, inevitable in its course once initiated. Rather, it must be viewed, as must conversation as a whole, as a set of prospective possibilities opening up at various points in the conversation's course; there are possibilities throughout a closing,

---

[19] Cf. Goffman, 1961; 1963; 1967.

[20] One reader of this paper in manuscript understood it to claim that closing can be accomplished by 'verbal means' alone, and that 'non-verbal accompaniments' are not involved. Thus, for example, 'taking leave' or breaking copresence is not explicitly mentioned, yet closing would not appear to have been effected if the parties remain in copresence after having gone through such sequences as we describe. Nothing in this paper, however, denies the possible relevance of 'non-verbal behavior' to conversational closing, e.g., the possibility of doing the work of possible pre-closings in face-to-face interaction by posture shifts, extended eye scans, increasing inter-participant space, edging toward an exit, etc. However, we have not studied these phenomena yet, and we do not have the empirical materials that would allow assertions that, and how, they work. Informal observation does not suggest that they are incompatible with our analysis. Still, it should be pointed out that 'purely verbal means' DO work for at least one class of conversations, i.e., those on the telephone. Furthermore, they work fully or partially in others, though not necessarily in all others. That is: there may be some conversations whose closing is accomplished solely by 'non-verbal means' (as when one of the parties has become involved in a side conversation, and his erstwhile coparticipant seeks to depart without interrupting). But in a range of others, conversational resources such as we have sought to describe supply some parts of the closing; and in still others, while there are 'non-verbal accompaniments' and consequences, the effective and strategic points in accomplishing the closing are managed by the use of practices like those with which we deal. Clearly, our analysis does not deal with all possible cases; but its relevance should not be over-restricted.

It will be noted in the above that we have set off the distinction between 'verbal' and 'non-verbal' in quotes. This is not the place to review the history and application of that distinction, or its usefulness. We use the terms here because of their use by the reader to whose comments we are reacting, and because of their status as common parlance in this area; we do not, however, thereby endorse the distinction.

including the moments after a 'final' good-bye, for reopening the conversation.[21] Getting to a termination, therefore, involves work at various points in the course of the conversation and of the closing section; it requires accomplishing. For the analyst, it requires a description of the prospects and possibilities available at the various points, how they work, what the resources are, etc., from which the participants produce what turns out to be the finally accomplished closing.

VIII

A few concluding remarks will be in point to try to specify the domain for which our analysis is relevant. What we are really dealing with is the problem of closing a conversation that ends a state of talk. It does not hold for members of a household in their living room, employees who share an office, passengers together in an automobile, etc., that is, persons who could be said to be in a 'continuing state of incipient talk'. In such circumstances, there can be lapses of the operation of what we earlier called the basic features; for example, there can be silence after a speaker's utterance which is neither an attributable silence nor a termination, which is seen as neither the suspension nor the violation of the basic features. These are adjournments, and seem to be done in a manner different from closings. Persons in such a continuing state of incipient talk need not begin new segments of conversation with exchanges of greetings, and need not close segments with closing sections and terminal exchanges. Much else would appear to be different in their conversational circumstances as compared to those in which a conversation is specifically 'started up', which we cannot detail here.

These considerations suggest that how a conversation is carried on in its course is sensitive to the placement of the conversation in an interaction episode or occasion, and that how an upcoming lapse in the operation of the basic features is attended to and dealt with by participants is sensitive to, and/or can accomplish, the placement of the conversation in its occasion. As it has been proposed that the problem of closing a conversation be shifted to ending its closing section, so ending an occasion (or interaction) can be seen to be located in some conversational episode. That participants attend as a task or as a piece of business to bringing the conversation to a close may have less to do with the character, organization,

---

[21] To cite but one example of this possibility:

B:	So uh, gimme a ring sometime
A:	yeah. A*l*right.
B:	Whatchu c'n do
A:	Yeah
B:	Tch! '*Kay*?
A:	O.K.
B:	A'right. Bye bye
	(1.0)
A:	Mnnuh He*ll*o?
B:	Yeah?
	(1.0)
A:	Uhm:::
	(1.8)
A:	Tch! hhehh hhh I didn't have anything in pu*ti*cular tuh say, I- I jus' fer a sekin' didn't feel like hanging up.
	etc.

structure, etc., of conversation *per se*, than with that of occasions or interactions; or, rather, it has to do with the organization of conversation as a constituent part of an occasion or interaction.

This kind of consideration can be overlooked if much of the data one is looking at is, as in the case of this paper, made up of telephone conversations, because there especially the occasion is more or less coterminous with the conversation; the occasion is constructed to contain the conversation and is shaped by its contingencies. Since, typically, the occasion ends when the conversation does, it appears that it is the conversation's closing that one is dealing with. But even in telephone conversations, in those cases in which the occasion has an extension beyond a single conversation, one may find that only that conversation which ends the occasion is brought to a close with the forms we have described (we have in mind situations in which a caller talks seriatim to several members of a family, for example).[22]

If these observations are correct and in point, then the observations we offered earlier about the articulation between conversation and ensuing actions, i.e., the preparation of actions geared to termination, are not passing observations. That there are geared actions required, and the possible need for preparing them, has to do with the OCCASION's ending, and it is as a part of conversation that the occasion may be ended. It is by way of the use of closing the conversation for ending the occasion that the use of a section to end the conversation may be appreciated, in a way similar to our appreciation of the use of a snack to end an evening or a get-together.

AFTERWORD

Of the papers which have drawn upon, criticized, developed, or been informed by "Opening Up Closings," three bear mention here. Jefferson (1973) develops quite independent phenomena (precise placement of talk, address terms, etc.) in sequential contexts she finds it relevant to characterize as "closing sections." Davidson (1978) uses the resources developed in this paper (as well as other resources) to render an analytic parsing of a particular case of a service encounter. Button (forthcoming) is most directly a development of the themes "opened up" in this paper; it begins as an investigation of the mechanisms by which "closings" which do not end their conversation come not to do so and he explores how closings come to have more in them, or do more, than closing alone. See also Clark and French (1981). Other aspects of our paper—the rationale of its enterprise, turn-taking, adjacency pairs, topic structure, etc.—have engendered discussion, criticism, etc., but those themes lead through a much more general literature in interaction analysis, sociolinguistics, and ethnomethodology, and cannot be usefully traced here.

---

[22] A simple distinction between face-to-face and telephone interaction will not do. We do not yet have any adequate technical account of these notions, which would specify the analytic dimensions of significant distinction. A variety of intuitive, plausible distinctions do not hold up. It should not be taken, from the text, that whereas face-to-face conversation can be either continuously sustained or have the character of a continuing state of incipient talk, telephone conversation invariably has the former character. That does not appear to be the case. And even if it were, it would be the distinction between these two modes, rather than that between face-to-face and telephonic, which would be relevant.

REFERENCES

ALBERT, E. 1965. " 'Rhetoric', 'Logic', and 'Poetics' in Burundi: Culture Patterning of Speech Behavior," *American Anthropologist* 66:6, Pt. 2, 40-41.

ATKINSON, J.M., and J.C. HERITAGE (eds.). Forthcoming *Structures of Social Action*. Cambridge: Cambridge University Press.

BUTTON, G. Forthcoming "No Close Closings," in: J.M. Atkinson and J.C. Heritage (eds.), *Structures of Social Action*. Cambridge: Cambridge University Press.

CLARK, H.H., and J. WADE. 1981. "Telephone Goodbyes." *Language in Society* 10:1-19.

DAVIDSON, J. 1978. "An Instance of Negotiation in a Call Closing," *Sociology* 12:1.

GARFINKEL, H., and H. SACKS. 1970. "On Formal Structures of Practical Actions," in: J.C. McKinney and E.A. Tiryakian (eds.), *Theoretical Sociology*. New York: Appleton-Century-Crofts.

GOFFMAN, E. 1961. *Encounters*. Indianapolis: Bobbs-Merrill.

———. 1963. *Behavior in Public Places*. New York: Free Press.

———. 1967. *Interaction Ritual*. Garden City, N.Y.: Anchor Books.

———. 1971. *Relations in Public*. New York: Basic Books.

———. 1975. Replies and Responses. *Centro Internazionale di Semiotica e di Linguistica, Working Papers and Prepublications* num. 46-57, serie C. Urbino, Italia: Università di Urbino. [Later published in *Language in Society* 5:257-313, 1976 and reprinted in *Forms of Talk*. Philadelphia: University of Pennsylvania Press, 1981.]

GOODWIN, C. 1981. *Conversational Organization: Interaction between Speakers and Hearers*. New York: Academic Press.

JEFFERSON, G. 1972. "Side Sequences," in: D.N. Sudnow (ed.), *Studies in Social Interaction*. New York: Free Press.

———. 1973. "A Case of Precision Timing in Ordinary Conversation: Overlapped Tag-Positioned Address Terms in Closing Sequences," *Semiotica*, IX:1.

MOERMAN, M. 1967. "Being Lue: Uses and Abuses of Ethnic Identification." American Ethnological Society, Proceedings of 1967 Spring Meetings.

———. 1970. "Analysis of Lue Conversation," I and II, mimeo.

PSATHAS, G. (ed.) 1979. *Everyday Language: Studies in Ethnomethodology*. New York: Irvington Publishers, Inc.

SACKS, H. 1967. Transcribed lectures, mimeo.

———. 1972a. "An Initial Investigation of the Usability of Conversational Materials for Doing Sociology," in: D.N. Sudnow (ed.), *Studies in Social Interaction*. New York: Free Press.

———. 1972b. "On the Analyzability of Stories by Children," in: J.J Gumperz and D.H. Hymes (eds.), *Directions in Sociolinguistics*. New York: Holt, Rinehart and Winston.

SACKS, H., E.A. SCHEGLOFF, and G. JEFFERSON. 1974. "A Simplest Systematics for the Organization of Turn-taking for Conversation," *Language* 50:696-735.

SCHEGLOFF, E.A. 1967. "The First Five Seconds: The Order of Conversational Openings." Berkeley: University of California Ph.D. dissertation, Sociology.

———. 1968. "Sequencing in Conversational Openings," *American Anthropologist* LXX:6.

———. 1970. The Social Organization of Conversational Openings, mimeo.

———. 1972. "Notes on a Conversational Practice: Formulating Place," in: D.N. Sudnow (ed.), *Studies in Social Interaction*. New York: Free Press.

———. 1979. "Identification and Recognition in Telephone Conversation Openings, " in: G. Psathas (ed.), *Everyday Language: Studies in Ethnomethodology*. New York: Irvington Publishers, Inc.

SCHENKEIN, J. 1972. "Towards an Analysis of Natural Conversation and the Sense of *Heheh*," *Semiotica* VI:4, 344-77.

———. 1978. *Studies in the Organization of Conversational Interaction*. New York: Academic Press.

Sociological Inquiry. 1980. Special issue on Language and Social Interaction, vol. 50, 3-4, edited by D.H. Zimmerman and C. West.

SUDNOW, D.N. (ed.). 1972. *Studies in Social Interaction*. New York: Free Press.

SYMBOLS USED IN TRANSCRIPTIONS

?	— indicates upward intonation
/ /	— indicates point at which following line interrupts
(n.0)	— indicates pause of n.0 seconds
( )	— indicates something said but not transcribable
(word)	— indicates probable, but not certain, transcription
but	— indicates accent
EMPLOYEE	— indicates heavy accent
DO	— indicates very heavy accent
::::	— indicates stretching of sound immediately preceding, in proportion to number of colons inserted
becau-	— indicates broken word
→	— points to the location of the phenomenon being discussed

ERVING GOFFMAN

Response Cries*

1.   To be all alone, to be a SOLITARY in the sense of being out of sight and sound of everyone, is not to be alone in another way—namely as a SINGLE, a party of one, a person not in a WITH, a person unaccompanied 'socially' by others in some public undertaking (itself often crowded), such as sidewalk traffic, shopping in stores, and restaurant dining.[1]

Allowing the locution 'in our society'—and, incidentally, the use of WE as a means of referring to individuals without specifying gender—it can be said that when we members are solitary, or at least assume we are, we can have occasion to make passing comments aloud. We kibitz our own undertakings, rehearse or relive a run-in with someone, speak to ourselves judgmentally about our own doings (offering words of encouragement or blame in an editorial voice that seems to be that of an overseer, rather than ourselves), and verbally mark junctures in our physical doings. Speaking audibly, we address ourselves as the sole intended recipients of our own remarks. Or, speaking in our own name, we address a remark to someone who isn't present to receive it. This is self-communication, specifically SELF-TALK. Although a conversation-like exchange of speaker-hearer roles may sometimes occur, this seems unusual: either we address an absent other, or we address ourselves in the name of some standard-bearing voice. Self-talk of one type seems rarely answered by self-talk of the other type. I might add that the voice or name in which we address a remark to ourselves can be just what we might properly use in addressing a remark to someone else, or what another might properly use in talking to us. It is not the perspective and standards that are peculiar, or the words and phrases through which they are realized, but only the fact that there are more roles than persons. To talk to oneself is to generate a full complement of two communication roles, speaker and hearer, without a full complement of role-performers; and which of the two roles—speaker or hearer—is the one without its own real performer is not the primary issue.

Self-talk could, of course, be characterized as a form of egocentricity—developmentally appropriate in childhood years, and re-appearing later only 'in

From *Language*, Vol. 54, 1978, pp. 787-815. Reprinted with permission of the Linguistic Society of America and Erving Goffman.

   * I have incorporated, without specific acknowledgment, a large number of suggestions, both general and particular, provided by John Carey, Lee Ann Draud, John Fought, Rochel Gelman, Allen Grimshaw, Gail Jefferson, William Labov, Gillian Sankoff, Joel Sherzer, and W. John Smith. I am grateful to this community of help; with it I have been able to progress from theft to pillage. Comments on broadcasters' talk are based on preliminary studies.

   [1] This easy contrast conceals some complications. A WITH—a party of more than one—can be solitary too, as when a lone couple picnics on a deserted beach. Strictly speaking, then, a SINGLE is a party of one present among other parties, whereas a solitary individual is a party of one with no other parties present.

certain men and women of a puerile disposition' (Piaget 1956:40). Common sense, after all, recommends that the purpose of speech is to convey thoughts to others; and a self-talker necessarily conveys them to someone who already knows them. To interrogate, inform, beseech, persuade, threaten, or command oneself is to push against oneself, or at best to get to where one already is, in either case with small chance of achieving movement. To say something to someone who can't hear it seems equally footless.

Or worse, self-talk might appear to be a kind of perversion, a form of linguistic self-abuse. Solitary individuals who can be happily immersed in talking to themselves need not seek out the company of their fellows—a convenience that works to the general detriment of social life. Such home consumption in regard to the other kind of intercourse qualifies either as incest or masturbation.

A more serious argument would be that self-talk is merely an out-loud version of reverie, the latter being the original form. Such a view, however, misses the sense in which daydreaming is different from silent, fugue-like, well-reasoned discussion with oneself—let alone the point (on which Piaget 1962:7 and Vygotsky 1962:19-20 seem to agree) that the out-loud version of reverie and of constructive thought may precede the silent versions developmentally. It misses, too, the fact that both the autistic and constructive forms of 'inner speech' are considerably removed from facially animated talk in which the speaker overtly gives the appearance of being actively engrossed in a spirited exchange with invisible others, his eyes and lips alive with the proceedings.

In any case, in our society at least, self-talk is not dignified as constituting an official claim upon its sender-recipient—which is true, incidentally, also of fantasy, 'wool gathering', and the like. There are no circumstances in which we can say *I'm sorry, I can't come right now; I'm busy talking to myself*. And anyway, hearers ordinarily do not REPLY to our self-talk, any more than to the words spoken by an actor on the stage, although they may REACT to both. Were a hearer to say, *What?*, that would stand as a rebuke to conduct, not a request for a rerun, much as when a teacher uses that response to squelch by-plays occurring at the back of the room; or, with a different intonation, it could mean that the self-talk had been misheard as the ordinary kind, a possibility which could itself induce a reply, such as *Sorry, I was only talking to myself*.

Indeed, our society places a taboo on self-talk. Thus it is mainly through self-observation and hearsay that one can find out that a considerable amount of this sort of thing goes on. Admittedly, the matter has a Lewis Carroll touch: the offense seems to be created by the very person who catches the offender since, it is the witnessing of the deed which transforms it into an improper one. (Solitary self-talkers may occasionally find themselves terminating a spate of self-talk with a self-directed reproach; but in doing so, they seem to be catching THEMSELVES— sometimes employing self-talk to do so.) In point of fact, the misdoing is not so much tied up with doing it in public as CONTINUING to do it in public. We are all, it seems, allowed to be caught stopping talking to ourselves on one occasion or another.

Expectedly, there are questions of frames and their limits. Strictly speaking, dictating a letter to a machine, rehearsing a play to a mirror, and praying aloud at our bedside are not examples of self-talk; but if others unexpectedly enter the scene of such solitary labor, we still feel a little uneasy and look for another type of work. Similarly, there are comedy routines in which the butt is made vulnerable by having to sustain a full-blown discussion with someone who is hidden from general view. And there are well-known comic gestures by which someone caught talking to himself attempts to transform the delict into a yawn, or into the just-acceptable vocalization of whistling, humming, or singing.[2] But behind these risible issues of frame is the serious fact that an adult who fails to attempt to conceal his self-talk, or at least to desist quickly upon the appearance of another person, is in trouble. Under the term verbal hallucination, we attribute failure in decorum here to 'mental illness'.[3]

Given the solitary's recourse to self-addressed remarks well into adult life, and given that such talk is obviously not merely a transitional feature of primary socialization (if, indeed, a natural phase of childhood development), one is encouraged to shift from a developmental to an interactional approach. Self-talk, when performed in its apparently permissible habitat—the self-talker all alone—is by way of being a mimicry of something that has its initial and natural provenance in speech between persons; this in turn implies a social encounter, and the arrangement of participants through which encounters are sustained. (Such transplantation, note, is certainly not restricted to deviant activity; thus a writer does it when he quotes, in the body of his own single sentence, an entire paragraph from a cited text—thereby pseudomorphically depositing in one form something that in nature belongs to another.)

With self-talk, then, one might want to say that a sort of impersonation is occurring; after all, we can best compliment or upbraid ourselves in the name of someone other than the self to whom the comments are directed. But what is intended here is not so much the mere citation or recording of what a monitoring voice might say, or what we would say to another if given a chance, but a stage-acted version of such a delivery, albeit only vaguely a version of its reception. What is set into the ongoing text is not merely words, but their animator also—indeed, the whole interactional arrangement in which such words might get spoken. To this end we briefly split ourselves in two, projecting the character who talks and the character to whom such words could be appropriately directed. Or we summon up the presence of others in order to say something to them. Self-talk, then, involves the lifting of a form of interaction out of its natural place, and its employment in a special way.

Self-talk described in this way recommends consideration of the soliloquy, long a feature of Western drama, although not currently fashionable.[4] An actor comes stage center and harangues himself, sometimes at enormous length,

---

[2] Nor should the opposite framing issue be neglected. A man talking to himself at a bar may cause the bartender to think him drunk, not peculiar; if he wants to continue drinking, he may suffer more hardship from the first imputation than the second. (In an instance reported to me, a bar-room self-talker, misframed as having had too much, temporarily solved this threat to his drinking rights by retreating to the tavern's telephone booth to do his self-talking.)

[3] I leave open the question of whether the individual who engages in verbal hallucination does so in order to create a disturbing impression, or does so in ignorance of the effects, or indifference to them, or in spite of concern about them. I leave open too the question of whether, in treating unabashed self-talk as a natural index of alienation, we have (in our society) any good grounds for our induction.

[4] It is never necessary in novels and comics, where the author can open up a character's head so the reader can peer into the ideas it contains; technologically, it is no longer necessary in the competing modes of commercial make-believe—movies and television. In these latter, a voice-over effect allows us to enter into the inner thoughts of a character shown silently musing.

divulging his inner thoughts on a pertinent matter with well-projected audibility. This behavior, of course, is not really an exception to the application of the rule against public self-talk. The soliloquizer is really talking to self when no one is around; we members of the audience are supernatural, out-of-frame eavesdroppers. Were a character from the dramatized world to approach, our speaker would audibly (to us) self-direct a warning: *But soft, I see that Jeffrey even now doth come. To the appearance of innocent business then*—and would stop soliloquizing. Were he to continue to self-talk, it would be because the script has instructed him to fail to notice the approaching figure whom all the rest of us have seen.

Now, if talking to oneself in private involves a mock-up of conversation and a recasting of its complementarity, then the production of this recasting on the stage, in the bloated format of a soliloquy, obviously involves a further insetting, and a transformation of what has already been transformed. The same could be said, incidentally, about a printed advertisement featuring realistically-posed live models whose sentiments are cast into well-articulated inner speech in broken-line balloons above their heads—providing a text that the other figures in the pictured world can't see, but we real people can, as distinguished from the continuous-line balloon for containing words that one figure openly states to another.

Here, I believe, is a crucial feature of human communication. Behavior and appearance are ritualized—in the ethological sense—through such ethologically-defined processes as exaggeration, stereotyping, standardization of intensity, loosening of contextual requirements etc. In the case under question, however, these transformations occur to a form of interaction, a communication arrangement, a standard set of participant alignments. I believe that any analysis of self-talk (or for that matter, any other form of communication) that does not attend to this non-linguistic sense of embedding and transformation is unlikely to be satisfactory.

2. These parables about self-talk provide entrance to a mundane text. First, definitions: By a SOCIAL SITUATION, I mean any physical area within which two or more persons find themselves in visual and aural range of one another. The term GATHERING can be used to refer to the bodies that are present. No restriction is implied about the relationship of those in the situation: they may all be involved in the same conversational encounter, in the sense of being ratified participants of the same state of talk; or some may be in an encounter while others are not, or are in a different one; or no talk may be occurring. Some, all, or none of those present may be definable as together in terms of social participation, i.e. in a WITH.

Although almost every kind of mayhem can be committed in social situations, one class of breaches bears specifically on social situations as such, i.e. on the social organization common to face-to-face gatherings of all kinds. In a word, although many delicts are SITUATED, only some are SITUATIONAL. We owe, to any social situation in which we find ourselves, evidence that we are reasonably alive to what is already in it—and furthermore to what may arise, whether on schedule or unexpectedly. If need for immediate action is required of us, we will be ready—if not mobilized, then mobilizable. A sort of communication tonus is implied. If addressed by anyone in the situation, we should not have far to go to respond, if not to reply. All in all, a certain respect and regard is to be shown to the situation at large. These demonstrations confirm that we are able and willing to enter into the perspective of the others present, if no more than is required to collaborate in the intricacies of talk and pedestrian traffic. In our society, then, it is generally taboo in public to be drunk, to belch or pass wind perceptibly, to daydream or doze, or to be in disarray with respect to clothing and cosmetics—and all these for the same reason. These acts comprise our conventional repertoire, our prescribed stock of 'symptoms', for demonstrating a lack of respectful aliveness in and to the situation; their inhibition is our way of 'doing' presence, and thereby self-respect. And the demonstration can be made with sound; audible indicators are involved as well as visual ones.

It is plain, then, that self-talk, in a central sense, is situational in character, not merely situated; its occurrence strikes directly at our sense of the orientation of the speaker to the situation as a whole. Self-talk is taken to involve the talker in a situationally inappropriate way. Differently put, our self-talk—like other 'mental symptoms'—is a threat to intersubjectivity: it warns others that they might be wrong in assuming a jointly-maintained base of ready mutual intelligibility among all persons present. Understandably, self-talk is less an offense in private than in public; after all, the sort of self-mobilization and readiness it is taken to disprove is not much required when one is all alone.

This general argument makes sense out of a considerable number of minor details. In a waiting room or on public transport, where it is evident that little personal attention to pedestrian traffic is required (and therefore less than a usual amount of aliveness to the surround), reading is allowed in our society, along with such self-withdrawal to a printed word as this makes possible. (Observe that reading itself is institutionalized as something that can be set aside in a moment, should a reason present itself—something that can be picked up and put down without ceremony. This definition does not hold for all our pleasures.) However, chuckling aloud to ourselves in response to what we are reading is suspect; this can imply that we are too freely immersed in the printed scene to retain dissociated concern for the scene in which our reading occurs. Interestingly, if we mouth the read words to ourselves, making the mouthings audible, we will be taken to be unschooled, not unhinged—unless, of course, our general appearance implies a high educational status and therefore no 'natural' reason for uncontained reading. (This is not to deny that some mumbled reading gives the impression that too much effort is invested in the sheer task of reading to allow a seemly reserve for the situation at large.)

In public, we are allowed to become rather deeply involved in talk with others, providing this does not lead us to block traffic or intrude on the sound preserve of others; presumably our capacity to share talk with one other implies we are able to share it with those who see us talking. So, too, we can conduct a conversation aloud over an un-boothed street-phone while either turning our back to the flow of pedestrian traffic or watching it in an abstracted way, and the words will not be thought improper. Even though our co-participant is not visually present, a natural one can be taken to exist, and an accounting is available as to where, cognitively speaking, we have gone. Moreover, this is a familiar place to which others can see themselves traveling, and from which we can be duly recalled, should events warrant.[5]

---

[5] I once saw an adolescent black girl make her male companion collapse in laughter, on a busy downtown street, by moving away from him to a litter can in which she had spied a plastic toy phone. Holding the phone up to her mouth and ear while letting the cord remain in the can—and then, half-turning as if to view the passing parade in a dissociated manner (as one does when anchored to an open telephone kiosk)—she projected a loud and lively conversation into the mouthpiece. Such an act 'puts

Observe also that we can, with some impunity, address words in public to a pet—presumably on the grounds that the animal can appreciate the affective element of the talk, if nothing else. In any case, although on these occasions a full-fledged recipient isn't present to reply to our words, it is clear that no imagined person or alien agency has captured our attention. On the other hand, to be seen walking down the street alone while SILENTLY gesticulating a conversation with an absent other is as much a breach as talking aloud to ourselves; it is taken to be evidence of alienation, just as much as its audible counterpart.

Finally, there are the words we emit (sometimes very loudly) to summon another into talk. Although such speaking begins by being outside of talk with actual others, its intended recipient is likely quickly to confirm—by ritualized orientation, if not by a verbal reply—the existence of the required environment, doing so before our utterance is completed.[6] A summons that is openly snubbed or apparently undetected, however, can leave us feeling that we have been caught engaging in something like talking to ourselves, and moreover very noticeably.[7]

To say that self-talk is a situational impropriety is not to say that it is a CONVERSATIONAL delict—no more, i.e., than any other audible breach of decorum, such as an uncovered, audible yawn. Desisting from self-talk is not something we owe our fellow conversationalists as such; i.e., it is not owed to them in their capacity as co-participants in a specific encounter, and thus only to them. Clearly it is owed to all those in sight and sound of us, precisely as we owe them avoidance of the other kinds of improper sounds. The individual who begins to talk to himself while in a conversational encounter will cause the other participants in the encounter to think him odd; but for the same reason and in the same way, those not in the encounter but within range of it will also think him odd. Here the conversational circle is not the relevant unit; the social situation is. Like a snail caught outside its shell, words are here caught outside of conversations, outside of ratified states of talk; one is saved from the linguistic horror of this fact only because the words themselves ought not to have been spoken. In fact, here talk is no more conversational than a belch; it merely lasts longer, and reflects adversely on a different part of personality.

So a rule: NO TALKING TO ONESELF IN PUBLIC. But of course the lay formulation of a rule never gets to the bone; it merely tells us where to start digging. In linguistic phrasing, 'No talking to oneself in public' is a prescriptive rule of communication.

---

on' public order in a rather deep way, striking at its accommodative close readings—ones we all ordinarily support without much awareness.

[6] A pet or a small child can be repeatedly summoned with a loud cry when it is not in sight, with some disturbance to persons in range; but a 'mental' condition is not ordinarily imputed. Typically it is understood that the words are merely a signal (a toy whistle would do) to come home, or to come into view to receive a message—but not to come into protracted conversation from wherever the signal is heard.

[7] Such an occurrence is but one instance of the deplorable class of occasions when we throw ourselves full-face into an encounter where none can be developed—as when we respond to a summons that was meant for someone behind us, or warmly greet a total stranger mistakenly taken to be someone we know well, or (as has already been mentioned) mistakenly reply to someone's self-talk. The standard statement by which the individual whom we have improperly entangled sets us right—e.g., *Sorry, I'm afraid you've . . .*—itself has an uneasy existence. Such a remark is fully housed within a conversational exchange that was never properly established, and its purpose is to deny a relationship that is itself required for the remark to be made.

The descriptive rule—the practice—is likely to be less neat, and certainly less available, allowing (if not encouraging) variously-grounded exceptions. The framework of normative understandings that is involved is not recorded, or cited, or available in summary form from informants. It must be pieced out by the student— in part by uncovering, collecting, collating, and interpreting all possible exceptions to the stated rule.

3. An unaccompanied man—a single—is walking down the street past others. His general dress and manner have provided anyone who views him with evidence of his sobriety, innocent intent, suitable aliveness to the situation, and general social competency. His left foot strikes an obtruding piece of pavement and he stumbles. He instantly catches himself, rights himself more or less efficiently, and continues on.

Therefore, his competence at walking had been taken for granted by those who saw him, confirming their assessment of him in this connection. His tripping suddenly casts these imputations into doubt. Therefore, before he continues, he may well engage in some actions that have nothing to do with the laws of mechanics. The remedial work he performs is likely to be aimed at correcting the threat to his reputation, as well as his posture. He can pause for a moment to examine the walk, as if intellectually concerned (as competent persons with their wits about them would be) to discover what in the world could possibly have caused him to falter— the implication being that anyone else would certainly have stumbled, too. Or he can address a wry little smile to himself, to show that he himself takes the whole incident as a joke—something quite uncharacteristic, something that can hardly touch the security he feels in his own manifest competency, and therefore warranting no serious account. Or he can 'overplay' his lurch, comically extending the disequilibrium, thereby concealing the actual deviation from normal ambulatory orientation with clowning movements, implying a persona obviously not his serious one.

In brief, our subject externalizes a presumed inward state, and acts so as to make discernible the special circumstances which presumably produced it. He tells a little story to the situation. He renders himself easy to assess by all those in the gathering, even as he guides what is to be their assessment. He presents an act specialized in a conventional way for providing information—a DISPLAY—a communication in the ethological, not the linguistic, sense. The behavior here is very animal-like, except that what the human animal seems to respond to is not so much an obvious biological threat as a threat to the reputation which it would ordinarily try to maintain in matters of social competence. Nor is it hard to catch the individual in a very standard look—the hasty, surreptitious survey sometimes made right after committing a fleeting discreditable deed. The purpose is to see whether witnessing has occurred and remedial action is therefore necessary; and this assessment itself is done quickly enough so that a remedy, if necessary, can be provided with the same dispatch as when there is no doubt from the start that it will be necessary.

However, instead of (or as a supplement to) engaging in a choreographed accounting that is visually available, our subject may utter a cry of wonderment, such as *What in the world!* Again, he renders readily accessible to witnesses what he chooses to assign to his inward state, and directs attention to what produced it; but this time the display is largely auditory. Moreover, if non-vocal gestures, in conjunction with the visible and audible scene, can't conveniently provide the required information, then self-talk will be the indicated alternative. An individual who suddenly stops in his tracks need only grimace and clutch at his heart if there is an open manhole at his feet; but the same stopping, consequent on his remembering that he was supposed to be someplace else, is more likely to be accounted for by words. (Presumably, the more obscure the matter, the more extended the self-remarks will have to be—and perhaps the less likely the individual will be to offer them.)

I am arguing here that what is part of the subject matter of linguistics, in some sense, can require the examination of our relation to social situations at large, not merely our relation to conversations. Apparently, verbalizations quite outside of conversations can play much the same role as a choreographed bit of non-vocal behavior. Together, they are like other situational acts of propriety and impropriety in that they are accessible to the entire surround, and in a sense designed for it. They are more like clothing than speech. But unlike clothing or cosmetics, these displays—whether vocal or in pantomime—are to be interpreted as bearing on a passing event, one with a limited course in time. (What we wear can certainly be taken as an indication of our attitude to the social occasion at hand, but hardly to specific events occurring during the occasion.) Necessarily, if unanticipated passing events are to be addressed, a marker must be employed that can be introduced just at the moment the event occurs, and withdrawn when concern for the event has ended.

4. I have argued that there is a prohibition against public self-talk, and that breachings of this rule have a display character—yet also that there are social situations in which one could expect self-talk. Indeed, the very force which leads us to refrain from self-talk in almost all situations might itself cause us to indulge in self-talk during certain exceptional ones. In this light, consider now in greater detail a few environments in which exposed self-talk is frequently found.

When we are 'informed' of the death of a loved one (only by accident are we 'told', since this verb implies that the news might be conveyed in passing), a brief flooding out into tears would certainly not be amiss in our society. As one might expect, it is just then that public self-talk is also sanctioned. Thus Sudnow (1967:141) describes the giving of bad news in hospitals:

> 'While no sympathy gestures are made, neither does the doctor withdraw from the scene altogether by leaving the room, as, for example, does the telegram delivery boy. The doctor is concerned that the scene be contained and that he have some control over its progress, that it not, for example, follow him out into the hall. In nearly all cases the first genuine interchange of remarks was initiated by the relative. During the period of crying, if there is any, relatives frequently "talk". Examples are: "I can't believe it", "It's just not fair", "Goddamn", "Not John...no..." These remarks are not responded to as they are not addressed to anyone. Frequently, they are punctuated by crying. The physician remains silent.'

The common-sense explanation here is that such informings strike at our self so violently that self-involvement immediately thereafter is reasonable—an excusable imposition of our own concerns upon everyone else in the gathering. Whatever the case, convention seems to establish a class of 'all-too-human' crises, to be treated as something which anyone not directly involved should still appreciate; they give us victims the passing right to be momentary centers of sympathetic attention, and provide a legitimate place for anything 'uncontrolled' we do during the occasion. Indeed, our utter self-containment during such moments might create uneasiness in others concerning our psychological habitat, causing them to wonder how responsive we might be to ordinary situated concerns directly involving them.

Not all environments which favor self-talk are conventionally understood to do so. For example, a podium speaker who suddenly finds that he has a page or line missing from his text, or a faulty microphone, will sometimes elect to switch from talking to the audience to talking to himself, addressing a full sentence of bewilderment, chagrin, or anger for his own ears and (apparently) his own benefit, albeit half-audibly to the room. Even in broadcast talk, when speakers lose their places, misplace their scripts, or find themselves with incoherent texts or improperly functioning equipment, they may radically break frame in this way, seeming suddenly to turn their backs on their obligations to sustain the role of speaker-to-an-audience. It is highly unprofessional, of course, to engage in sotto-voce, self-directed remarks under just those microphonic conditions which ensure their audibility; but broadcasters may be more concerned at this point about showing that some part of them is shocked by the hitch, and in some way not responsible for it, than about maintaining broadcasting decorum. Also, being the sole source of meaningful events for their listeners, they may feel that the full text of their subjective response is better than no text at all. Note that other social situations provide a speaker with an audience that is captive and concerned, and thereby encourage self-talk: drivers of buses, taxi, and private cars can shout unflattering judgments of other motorists and pedestrians when they have passed out of range, and feel no compunction about talking aloud to themselves in the presence of their passengers. After all, there is a sense in which a contretemps in traffic visibly and identically impinges on everyone in a vehicle simultaneously.[8]

The fact that drivers may actually wait until the apparent target of their remarks cannot hear them points to another location for self-talk, which is also suggested by the lay term MUTTERING. Frustrated by someone's authority, we can mutter words of complaint under our breath as the target turns away, out of apparent conversational earshot. (Here is a structural equivalent of what children do when they stick out their tongues, or put their thumbs to their noses, just as their admonisher turns away.) These sub-vocalizations reside in the very interstice between a state of talk and mere co-presence—more specifically, in the transition from the first to the second. Here function seems plain: in muttering, we convey that although we are now going along with the line established by the speaker (and authority), our spirit has not been won over, and compliance is not to be counted on. The display is aimed either at third parties or at the authority itself, but in such a way that we can deny our intent, and the authority can feign not hearing what we have said about him. Again, this is a form of communication that hardly fits the linguistic model of speaker and addressed recipient; here we provide a reply to the speaker that is displaced from him to third parties, or to ourselves. Instead of being the

---

[8] Of course, there will be occasions of equivalent license of non-verbal signs, both vocal and gesticulatory. In trying on a shoe, we can engage in all manner of grimaces and obscure soundings, for these signs provide running evidence of fit; and such information is the official, chief concern (at that moment) of all parties to the transaction, including the shoe clerk. Similarly, a sportsman or athlete is free to perform an enormous flailing about when he flubs; apart from other reasons for this license, he can be sure (if anyone can) that his circumstances are fully attended and appreciated by everyone who is watching the action. After all, such clarity of intent is what sports are all about.

recipient of our reply, the initial speaker becomes merely the object or target of our response. Like tongue-sticking, muttering is a time-limited communication, entering as a 'last word', a post-terminal dollop to a just-terminated encounter; it thus escapes, for incidental reasons, the injunction against persisting in public self-talk.

Consideration of self-talk in one kind of interstice recommends its consideration in others. For example, if we are stopped for a moment's friendly chat just before entering or leaving an establishment or turning down a street, we may provide a one-sentence description of the business we are about to turn to; this account serves as a rationale for our withdrawing, and as evidence that there are other calls upon our time. Interestingly enough, this utterance is sometimes postponed until the moment when the encounter is just ending, in which case we may mumble the account half-aloud and somewhat to ourselves. Here again is self-talk that is located transitionally between a state of talk and mere co-presence; again, self-communication is self-terminating, although this time because the communicator, not the hearer, is moving away. Here it is inescapably clear that the self-talker is providing verbal information to others present, though not using the standard arrangement—a ratified state of talk—for doing so.

Finally, it must be allowed that when circumstances conspire to thrust us into a course of action whose appearance might raise questions about our moral character or self-respect, we often prefer to be seen as self-talkers. If we stoop to pick up a coin on a busy street, we may well identify its denomination to ourselves aloud, simultaneously expressing surprise, even though we ourselves no longer need the information: the street is to be framed as a place of passage, not—as it might be to a child or a bum—a hunting ground for bits of refuse. If what we thought was a coin turns out to be a worthless slug, then we may feel urged to externalize, through sound and pantomime, that we can laugh at the fools we have made of ourselves.[9] Trying the door-handle of a car we have mistaken for our own, and discovering our mistake, we are careful to blurt out a self-directed remark that properly frames our act for those who witness it, advertising inadequate attentiveness in order to deny that we are thieves.

With these suggestions of where self-talk is to be found, we can take a second look at the conventional argument that children engage in it because they aren't yet socialized into the modesties of self-containment, the proprieties of persondom. Vygotsky, responding to what he took to be Piaget's position, long ago provided a lead ([1934] 1962:16):

'In order to determine what causes egocentric talk, what circumstances provoke it, we organized the children's activities in much the same way Piaget did, but we added a series of frustrations and difficulties. For instance, when a child was getting ready to

---

[9] Picking money off the street is, of course, a complicated matter. Pennies and even nickels we might well forego, if the doubt cast on our conduct is of more concern to us than the money. (We accept the small sums in change when paying for something in a shop, but there a money transaction is the business at hand.) Should another in our sight drop such a coin, we might well be inclined to retrieve and return it: we are allowed a distractive orientation to the ground we walk on, so long as this is patently in the interest of others. (If we don't retrieve our own small coins, then we run the risk that others will do so for us, and the consequent necessity of showing gratitude.) If the sum is large enough to qualify as beyond the rule of finders-keepers, we might quickly glance around to see if we've been seen, carefully refraining from saying or gesturing anything else. Covert also may be our act whenever we spy a coin of any denomination to see if any additional ones are not to be found.

draw, he would suddenly find that there was no paper, or no pencil of the color he needed. In other words, by obstructing his free activity we made him face problems.

'We found that in these difficult situations the coefficient of egocentric speech almost doubled, in comparison with Piaget's normal figure for the same age, and also in comparison with our figure for children not facing these problems. The child would try to grasp and to remedy the situation in talking to himself: "Where's the pencil? I need a blue pencil. Never mind, I'll draw with a red one and wet it with water; it will become dark and look like blue." '[10]

The implication is that, for children, the contingencies are so great in undertaking any task, and the likelihood so strong that they will be entirely discounted as reasonably-intentioned persons if they fail (or indeed, that they will be seen as just fooling around anyway), that they are always prepared to offer some voicing of what they are about. An adult attempting to learn to skate might be equally self-talkative.[11]

Some loose generalizations might be drawn from these descriptions of places for self-talk. First, when we address a remark to ourselves in public, we are likely to be in sudden need of re-establishing ourselves in the eyes and ears of witnesses as honest, competent persons not to be trifled with; and an expression of chagrin, wonderment, anger etc. would seem to help in this—at least establishing what our expectations for ourselves are, even if in this case they can't be sustained. Second, one could argue that self-talk occurs right at the moment when the predicament of the speaker is evident to the whole gathering in a flash, or can be made so—assuring that the utterance will come as an understandable reaction to an understood event; it will come from a mind that has not drifted from the situation, a mind readily tracked. The alien world reflected in hallucinatory talk is therefore specifically avoided; and so too is some of the impropriety of talking outside the precincts of a ratified conversation. Nor is 'understandable' here merely a matter of cognition. To quickly appreciate another's circumstances (it seems) is to be able to place ourselves in them empathetically. Correspondingly, the best assurance another can have that we will understand him is to offer himself to us in a version with which we can identify. Instead of thinking of self-talk as something blurted out under pressure, then, it might better be thought of as a mode of response constantly readied for those

[10] Piaget, as his reply (1962:3–4) to a reading of Vygotsky's MS suggests, apparently meant 'egocentricity' to refer to speech (or any other behavior) that did not take into consideration the perspective of the other in some way, and only incidentally (if at all) to speech not openly addressed to others, the latter being what Vygotsky described, and which I call 'self-talk'. Piaget's concept of egocentricity has led to another confusion, a failure to discriminate two matters: taking the point of view of the other in order to discover what his attitude and action will be, and accepting for oneself or identifying with the perspective of the other. The classic con operation illustrates how fully the first form of sympathy may be required and produced without leading to the second.

[11] Cook-Gumperz & Corsaro (1976:29) offer a more compelling account: 'We have found that children consistently provide verbal descriptions of their behavior at various points in spontaneous fantasy in that it cues other interactants to what is presently occurring as well as provides possibilities for plugging into and expanding upon the emerging social event.' The authors imply that if a fantasy world is to be built up during JOINT play, then words alone are likely to be the resource that must be employed, and an open recourse to self-talk then becomes an effective way to flesh out what is supposed to be unfolding for all the participants in the fantasy.

A purely cognitive interpretation of certain action-oriented, self-directed words ('non-nominal expressions') has also been recently recommended by Gopnik (1977:15–20).

circumstances in which it is excusable. Indeed, the time and place when our private reaction is what strangers present NEED to know about is the occasion when self-talk is more than excusable.[12]

5. It was suggested above that, when an unaccompanied man stumbles, he may present his case by means of self-talk instead of silent gesture. However, there is another route to the advertisement of self-respect. He can emit one or two words of exclamatory imprecation, such as *Hell!* or *Shit!* Observe that these ejaculatory expressions are nothing like the pointed shout of warning which one individual might utter to and for another—nor even like an openly directed broadcast to all in hearing, like a street-vendor's cry or a shriek for help. Talk in the ordinary sense is apparently not at issue. In no immediate way do such utterances belong to a conversational encounter—a ritually ratified state of talk embracing ratified participants—or to a summoning to one. First speaker's utterance does not officially establish a slot which second speaker is under some obligation to fill: there is no ratified speaker and recipient (not even imaginary ones), but merely actor and witness. To be sure, an interjection is involved; but it is one that interrupts a course of physical action, not an utterance.

When, unaccompanied, we trip and curse ourselves (or the walk, or the whole wide world), we curse TO ourselves; we appear to address ourselves. Therefore, a kind of self-remarking seems to be involved. Like the publicly tolerated self-talk already considered, imprecations seem to be styled to be overheard in a gathering. Indeed, the styling is specific in this regard: when no one is present in the individual's surround, the expression is quite likely to be omitted. If women and children are present, your male self-communicator is quite likely to censor his cries accordingly: a man who utters *Fuck!* when he stumbles in a foundry is likely to avoid that particular expletive if he trips in a day nursery. If it is apparent that only very close-by persons can see what we have just done (or failed to do), then whispered expletives are possible; if witnesses are far away, then shouted sounds will be required. 'Recipient design' is involved (to use Harvey Sacks' term), and so quickly applied as to suggest that on-going monitoring of the situation is being sustained, enabling just this adjustment when the moment arises which requires it. Of course, in any case we will have taken the time to encode our vocalization in the conventional lexicon of our language (which is likely to be the local one)—a feat that is instantaneously accomplished, even sometimes by bilinguals who, in addition, must generally select their imprecations from the language of their witnesses.[13] (This is not to say that bilinguals won't use a harsh imprecation from one language in place of a less harsh one drawn from the language in use; foreignness apparently serves as a mitigation of strength.) Significantly, we have here a form of behavior whose very meaning is that it is something blurted out, something that has escaped control; and so such behavior very often is and has; but this impulsive feature marks not the limits to which the utterance is socially processed, but rather the conventionalized styling to which it is obliged to adhere.

---

[12] Understandably, stage soliloquies occur only when the character's personal feelings about his circumstances are exactly what we members of the audience must be privy to, to be properly positioned in the unfolding drama.

[13] It would be interesting to know whether or not bilingual children who self-talk select the code likely to be employed by others in their presence.

It is plain that singles use imprecations in a variety of circumstances. Racing unsuccessfully to enter a turnstile before it automatically closes, or a door before it is locked for the evening, may do it; coming up to what has just now become a brick wall, we may exhibit frustration and chagrin, often with a curse. (Others, having formulated a possible reading of the precipitous rush we have made, can find that our imprecations are a way of confirming their interpretation, putting a period to the behavioral sentence we have played out, bringing the little vignette to a close, and converting us back to someone easily disattendable.) Precariously carrying too many parcels, we may curse at the moment they fall. When the horse we have bet on is nosed out at the finish line, we may damn our misfortune while tearing up our tickets; since our cause for disappointment, anger, and chagrin is amply evident, or at least easily surmisable, we have license to wail to the world. Walking along a wintry street that carries a record-breaking snow now turned to slush, we are in a position to cry *God!* in open private response—but as it happens, we do so just at the point of passing another—the cause of our remark and the state of our mind being perfectly plain and understandable. It might be added that the particular imprecations I have used so far as illustrations seem in our society to be the special domain of males: females, traditionally at least, use softer expressions. As is now well known, this gender convention is not impervious to rapid politically-inspired change.

Finally, I want to note that although imprecations and extended self-remarks can be found in much the same slot, do much the same work, and indeed often appear together—raising the question as to why they should be described seperately—judgment should be reserved concerning their equivalence. Other questions must be considered first.

6. The functioning of imprecations raises the question of an allied set of acts that can be performed by singles: RESPONSE CRIES, i.e. exclamatory interjections which are not full-fledged words. *Oops!* is an example. These non-lexicalized, discrete interjections—like certain unsegmented, tonal, prosodic features of speech—comport neatly with our doctrine of human nature. We see such 'expression' as a natural overflowing, a flooding up of previously contained feeling, a bursting of normal restraints, a case of being caught off-guard. That is what would be learned by asking the man in the street if he uses these forms—and, if so, what he means by them.

I am assuming, of course, that this common-sense view of response cries should give way to the co-ocurrence analysis that sociolinguists have brought to their problems. But although this naturalistic method is encouraged by socioling-uists, here the subject matter moves one away from their traditional concern. A response cry doesn't seem to be a statement in the linguistic sense (even a heavily elided one), purportedly doing its work through the concatenated semantic reference of words. A remark is not being addressed to another—not even, it seems, to oneself. So, on the face of it at least, even self-communication is not involved, but only a simpler sign process whereby emissions from a source inform us about the state of the source—a case of exuded expressions, not intentionally sent messages. One might better refer to a 'vocalizer' or 'sounder' than to a speaker. This, of course, is not to deny the capacity of a well-formed, conventionally-directed sentence to inform us about the state of the protagonist who serves as its subject, nor to deny that the speaker and protagonist can be the 'same'—for indeed, through the use of 1st person pronouns, they routinely are. But this latter arrangement brings us information through a message, not an expression. This route is fundamentally different from and less direct than the one apparently employed in response cries— even though, admittedly, such cries routinely come to be employed just in order to give a desired impression. Witnesses can seize the occasion of certain response cries to shake their heads in sympathy, cluck, and generally feel that the way has been made easy for them to initiate passing remarks, attesting to fellow-feeling; but they aren't obliged to do so. A response cry may be uttered in the hope that this half-license it gives to hearers to strike up a conversation will be exercised; but, of course, this stratagem for getting talk started could not work if an innocent reading were not the official one. Expectedly, the circumstances which allow us to utter a response cry are often just the ones that mitigate the impropriety of a different tack we could take, that of opening up an encounter by addressing a remark to an unacquainted other; but that fact doesn't relieve one of the necessity to distinguish between this fully social sort of comment and the kind that is apparently not even directed to oneself.

A response cry is (if anything is) a ritualized act in the ethological sense of that term. Unable to shape the world the way we want to, we displace our manipulation of it to the verbal channel, displaying evidence of our alignment to the on-going events; the display takes the condensed, truncated form of a discretely-articulated, non-lexicalized expression. Or, suddenly able to manage a tricky, threatening set of circumstances, we deflect into non-lexicalized sound a dramatization of our relief and self-congratulation in the achievement.

7.   Consider now some standard cries:

7.1.   THE TRANSITION DISPLAY. Entering or leaving what can be taken as a state of marked natural discomfort—wind, rain, heat, or cold—we seem to have the license (in our society) to externalize an expression of our inner state. *Brr!* is a standard term for wind and cold upon leaving such an atmosphere. (Other choices are less easily reproduced in print.) *Ahh!* and *Phew!* are heard when leaving a hot place for a cool one. Function is not clear. Perhaps the sounding gives us a moment to orient ourselves to the new climatic circumstances and to fall into cadence with the others in the room; these are not ordinarily taxing matters, and thus do not ordinarily require a pause for their accomplishment. Perhaps the concentration, the 'holding ourselves in' sometimes employed in inclement places (as a sort of support for the body) gets released with a flourish when we escape from such environments. In any case, we can be presumed to be in a state of mind that those already safe might well appreciate (for after all, weather envelops everyone in the vicinity), and so self-expression concerning our feelings does not take us to a place mysterious to our hearers. It appears that, unlike strong imprecations, transition displays in our society are not particularly sex-typed.

7.2.   THE SPILL CRY. Here the central examples *Oops!* and *Whoops!* are phonetically well-formed, although not in every sense words. They are as much (perhaps even more) the practice of females as males. Spill cries are emitted to accompany our having, for a moment, lost guiding control of some feature of the world around us, including ourselves. Thus a woman, rapidly walking to a museum exit, passes the door, catches her mistake, utters *Oops!*, and backtracks to the right place. A man, dropping a piece of meat through the grill to coals below, utters *Oops!*, and then spears the meat to safety with his grill fork.

On the face of it, the sound advertises our loss of control, raising the question of why we should want to defame ourselves through this publicity. An obvious possibility is that the *Oops!* defines the event as a mere accident, shows we know it has happened, and hopefully insulates it from the rest of our behavior—indicating that failure of control was not generated by some obscure intent unfamiliar to humanity, or some general defect in competence. Behind this possibility is another: the expression is presumably used for MINOR failings of environmental control. So, in the face of a more serious failure, *Oops!* has the effect of downplaying import, and hence implication as evidence of our incompetence. (It follows that, to show we take a mishap VERY seriously, we might feel constrained to omit the cry.) Another reason for (and function of) spill-crying is that, since a specific vocalization is involved, we necessarily demonstrate that at least our vocal channel is func- tioning—and behind this, at least some presence of mind. A part of us proves to be organized and standing watch over the part of us that apparently isn't watchful. Finally, and significantly, the sound can provide a warning to others present that a piece of the world has gotten loose, and that they might best be advised to take care. Indeed, close observation shows that the *oo* in *Oops!* may be nicely prolonged to cover the period of time during which that something is out of control.

Note that, when we utter *Oops!* as we slip on the ice, we can be making a plea to the closest other for a steadying hand, and simultaneously warning others to watch out; these circumstances surely open up our surround for vocalizations. When in fact there is no danger to oneself, we may respond to ANOTHER's momentary loss of control with an *Oops!* also—providing him with a warning that he is in trouble, a readied framework within which he can define the mishap, and a collectively established cadence for his anticipated response. That some sort of help for others is thus intended seems to be borne out by the fact that men seem more likely to *oops* for another when that other is a child or female, and thus definable as someone for whom responsibility can be taken. Indeed, when a parent plucks up a toddler and rapidly shifts it from one point to another, or 'playfully' swings or tosses it in the air, the prime mover may utter an *Oopsadaisy!*—stretched out to cover the child's period of groundlessness, counter-acting its feeling of being out of control, and at the same time instructing the child in the terminology and role of spill cries. In any case, it is apparent that *oopsing* is an adaptive practice with some survival value. And the fact that individuals prove (when the occasion does arise) to have been ready all along to *oops* for themselves, or for an appropriate other, suggests that when nothing eventful is occurring, persons in one another's presence are still nonetheless tracking one another and acting so as to make themselves trackable.

7.3. THE THREAT STARTLE, notably *Eek!* or *Yipe!* These response cries are sextyped (or at least so believed) for feminine use. Surprise and fear are stated—in lay terms, 'expressed'. But the surprise or fear are very much under control— indeed, nothing to be really concerned about. A very high open stairwell, or a walk that leads to a precipice, can routinely evoke *yipes* from us as we survey what might have been our doom, but from a position of support; we have had ample time to secure ourselves. A notion of what a fear response would be is used as a pattern for mimicry. A sort of overplaying occurs that covers any actual concern by extending, with obvious unseriousness, the expressed form which this concern would take. We demonstrate that we are alive to the fearsome implications of the event, but not overwhelmed by them—that we have seen the trouble and by implication will assuredly control for it, and are therefore in no need of warning; all of this releases others from closely tracking us. The moment it takes to say the sound is one we can use to compose ourselves. In a very subtle way, then, a verbal 'expression' of our state is a means of rising above it—and a release of concern now no longer necessary, coming after the emergency is really over.

Here an argument made earlier about multiple transformations can be taken up. Precipitous drops are the sort of things to which an individual can be very close without the slightest danger of falling over, or intent to do so. In these circumstances, it would seem that the imagery of accident would come to the fore, or at least be very readily available. It is this easily-achieved mental set that the threat startle seems to participate in. Thus the uncompelling character of the actual circumstances can be nicely reflected in the light and almost relaxed character of the cry. One has, then, given a warning-LIKE signal in dangerous-LIKE circumstances. Ritualization begins to give way to a copy of itself—a playful version of what is already a formalized version, a display that has been retransformed and reset, a second-order ritualization.

7.4. REVULSION SOUNDS, such as *Eeuw!*, are heard from a person who has by necessity or inadvertence come in contact with something contaminating. Females in our society, being defined as more vulnerable in this way than males, might seem to have a special claim on the expression. Often, once we make the sound, we can be excused for a moment while decontamination is attempted. At other times, our voice performs what our physical behavior can't, as when our hands must keep busy cleaning a fish, leaving only the auditory and other unrequired channels to correct the picture—to show that indelicate, dirty work need not define the person who is besmeared by it. Observe again that there is an unserious note, a hint of 'hyperritualization': often the contamination that calls forth an *Eeuw!* is not REALLY believed to contaminate. Perhaps only germ contamination retains that literal power in our secular world. So again, a protective-like cry is uttered in response to a contaminating-like contact.

8. So far, response crying has been largely considered as something available to someone who is present to others, but not 'with' any of them. If one picks accompanied individuals, not singles, the behavior is still to be found; indeed, response crying is, if anything, encouraged. So also, response cries are commonly made by persons in an OPEN STATE OF TALK, persons having the right but not the obligation to address remarks to the other participants; this is a condition that commonly prevails among individuals jointly engaged in a common task (or even similarly engaged in like ones) when this work situates them in immediate reach of one another. Examples follow.

8.1. THE STRAIN GRUNT. Lifting or pushing something heavy, or wielding a sledgehammer with all our might, we emit a grunt attesting the presumed peak and consummation of our fully-extended exertion. The sound seems to serve as a warning that, at the moment, nothing else can claim our concern—and sometimes as a reminder that others should stand clear. No doubt the cry also serves as a means by which joint efforts can be temporarily coördinated, as is said to be true of work songs. Observe that these sounds are felt to be entirely unintended, even though the glottis must be partially closed off to produce them, and presumably could be fully opened or closed to avoid doing so. In any case, it could be argued that the expression of ultimate exertion these sounds provide may be esentially overstated. I might add that strain grunts are routinely guyed, employed in what is to be taken as unserious way—often as a cover for a task that is reckoned as undemanding but may indeed require some exertion: another case of retransformation. Note too that strain grunts are employed during solitary doings that can be construed as involving a peaking of effort. The rise and falling away of effort contoured in sound dramatizes our acts, filling out the setting with their execution. I suppose the common example is the vocal accompaniment we sometimes provide ourselves on passing a hard stool.

8.2. THE PAIN CRY, *Oww!* or *Ouch!*[14] The functioning of this exclamation is rather clear. Ensconced in a dentist's chair, we use a pain cry as a warning that the drill has begun to hurt. When a finger is held firmly by the nurse, we *ouch* when the needle probing for a sliver goes too deep. Plainly, the cry in these cases can serve as a self-regulated indicator of what is happening—providing a reading for the instigator of the pain, who might not otherwise have access to the information needed. The meaning, then, may not be 'I have been hurt', but rather, 'You are just now coming to hurt me.' This meaning, incidentally, may also be true of the response that a dog or cat gives us when we have begun accidentally to step on its tail, although THAT CRY often seems to come too late. In any case, these are good examples of how closely a vocalizer can collaborate with another person in the situation.

8.3. THE SEXUAL MOAN. This subvocal tracking of the course of sexually climactic experience, a display available to both sexes, is said to be increasingly fashionable for females—among whom, of course, the sound tracing can be strategically employed to delineate an ideal development in the marked absence of anything like the reality.

8.4. FLOOR CUES. A worker in a typing pool makes a mistake on a clean copy and emits an imprecation; this leads to, and apparently is designed to lead to, a colleague's query as to what went wrong. A fully-communicated statement of disgust and displease can then be introduced, but now ostensibly as a reply to a request for information. A husband reading the evening paper suddenly brays out a laugh or a *Good God!*, thereby causing his wife to orient her listening, or even to ease the transition into talk by asking what it is. (A middle-class WIFE might be less successful in having her floor cues picked up.) Wanting to avoid being thought self-centered, intrusive, garrulous, or whatever—and consequently feeling uneasy about making an open request for a hearing in the particular circumstances—we act so as to encourage our putative listeners to make the initial move, inviting us to let them in on what we are experiencing. Interestingly, although in our society married couples may routinely breach many of the standard situational proprieties when alone together—this marking the gradual extension of symmetrical ritual license between them—the rule against persisting in public self-talk may be retained, with

---

[14] Solitarily experiencing a bout of intense pain, we sometimes follow its course with a half-moaned, half-grunted sound-tracing, as though casting the experience in a sort of dialogic form were a way to get through the moment and to maintain morale. We sometimes also employ such sound-tracings when witnesses are perceived present, producing in these circumstances a real scene-stopper—implying that our current, inner, acutely-painful state is the business everyone should be hanging on.

the incidental consequence that the couple can continue to use response crying as a floor cue.

8.5. AUDIBLE GLEE. A lower middle-class adolescent girl, sitting with four friends at a table in a crowded crêperie, is brought her order, a large crêpe covered with ice cream and nuts. As the dish is set before her, she is transfixed for a moment, and wonder and pleasure escape with an *Oooooo!* In a casino, an elderly woman playing the slots alongside a friend hits a twenty-dollar pay-off, and above the sound of silver dropping in her tray peeps out a *Wheee!* Tarzan, besting a lion, roars out a Hollywood version of the human version of a lay version of a mammalian triumph call.

9. It is important, I believe, to examine the functioning of response cries when the crier is a ratified participant of on-going talk—being a participant of a conversational social encounter, as opposed to a task-structured one. While walking along talking to a friend, we can, tripping, unceremoniously interrupt our words to utter *Oops!*, even as the hand of our friend comes out to support us; as soon as this little flurry has passed, we revert back to our talk. All that this reveals, of course, is that when we are present to others as a fellow conversationalist, we are also present to them—as well as to all others in the situation—as fellow members of the gathering. The conversational role (short of what the phone allows) can never be the only accessible one in which we are active.

So response cries can function in work encounters, and can obtrude into conversational ones. Now we move on to a closer issue. If these responses are to be seen as ritualized expressions—and some as standardized vocal comments on circumstances that are not, or are no longer, beyond our emotional and physical control—then there is reason to expect that such cries will be used at still-further remove, namely in response to a VERBALLY PRESENTED review of something settled long ago, at a place quite removed. A broker tells a client over the phone that his stock has dropped; the client, well socialized in this sort of thing, says *Yipe!* or *Eek!* (Jack Benny made a specialty of this response cry.) A plumber tells us what our bill will be, and we say *Ouch!* Indeed, response cries are often employed thrice-removed from the crisis to which they are supposed to be a blurted response: a friend tells us about something startling and costly that happened to him, and at the point of disclosure we utter a response cry—on his behalf, as it were, out of sympathetic identification and as a sign that we are fully following his exposition. In fact, we may offer a response cry when he recounts something that happened to someone ELSE. In these cases, we are certainly far removed from the exigent event being replayed, and just as far removed from its consequences, including any question of having to take immediate rescuing action. Interestingly, there are some cries which seem to occur more commonly in our response to another's fate as it is recounted to us (good or bad), than they do in our response to our own. *Oh, wow!* is an example.

We can play all these response games because our choice of vocalization allows the recipient, or rather hearer, to treat the sound as something to which a specific spoken reply is not required. To the plumber, we are precisely NOT saying: 'Does the bill have to be that high?'—such a statement would require a reply, to the possible embarrassment of all.

Having started with response cries in the street, our topic has moved into the shelter of conversations. But it should not be assumed from this that the behaviors in question—response cries—have somehow been transmuted into full-fledged creatures of discourse. That is not the way they function. These cries are conventionalized utterances which are specialized for an informative role; but in the linguistic and propositional sense, they are not statements. Obviously, information is provided when we utter response cries in the presence of others, whether or not we are in a state of talk at the time. That is about the only reason we utter them in the first place, and the reason they are worth studying. But to understand how these sounds function in social situations, particularly during talk, one must first understand the source of the prototypes of which they are designed to be recognizable versions. What comes to be made of a particular individual's show of 'natural emotional expression' on any occasion is a considerably awesome thing, not dependent on the existence anywhere of natural emotional expressions. But whatever is made of such an act by its maker and its witnesses is different from what is made of openly-designed and openly-directed communication.

10.   At the beginning of this paper it was argued that extended self-talk, if discovered, reflects badly on the talker. Then it was observed that elements in the situation can considerably mitigate the impropriety of talking to ourselves publicly—and that, in any case, we are prepared to breach the injunction against public self-talk when, in effect, to sustain this particular propriety would go even harder on our reputations. Much the same position could be taken with respect to interjected imprecations. In both cases, one can point to some hitch in the well-managed flow of controlled events, and the quick application of an ostensibly self-directed pronouncement to establish evidence—a veneer—of control, poise, and competency. Although response cries do not, on the surface, involve words uttered even to oneself—being IN PROTOTYPE merely a matter of non-symbolic emotional expression—they apparently come to function as means of striking a self-defensible posture in the face of extraordinary events, much as does exposed self-talk. However, one routine source of trouble in the management of the world is, interestingly enough, the management of talk itself. So again we have response cries, but this time ones that are constantly uttered.

First, there is the well-known filled pause (usually written as *ah* or *uh* or *um*) employed by speakers when they have lost their places, can't find a word, are momentarily distracted, or otherwise find they are departing from fluently-sustained speech. Response CRIES seems an awkward term for such unblurted subvocalizations; but they do, I think, function like response cries, if only in that they facilitate tracking. In effect, speakers make it evident that, although they do not now have the word or phrase they want, they are giving their attention to the matter and have not cut themselves adrift from the effort at hand. A word search, invisible and inaudible in itself, is thus voluntarily accompanied by a sound shadow—a sound, incidentally, that could easily be withheld merely by otherwise managing the larynx—all to the end of assuring that something worse than a temporary loss of words has not happened, and incidentally holding the speaker's claim to the floor.[15] (Interestingly, in radio broadcasting, where visual facial signs of a word search can't be effective,

---

[15] A case can be made that, in some English-speaking circles, the familiar hesitation markers are systematically employed in slightly different ways. For example, *uh* might be heard when the speaker had forgotten a proper name; *oh* might occur when he knew a series of facts, but was trying to decide which of them could be appropriately cited or best described for the hearers. The unfilled or silent pause participates in this specialization—giving one reason, alas, to think of it as a response cry, too. Here see the useful paper of James 1972.

the filling of pauses by a search sound or a prolongation of a vowel has much to recommend it; speakers are under obligation to confirm that nothing has gone wrong with the studio's equipment, as well as their own—the floor in this case being a radio station. If only inexperienced broadcasters frequently employ filled pauses, it is because professionals can manage speech flow, especially reading aloud, without the hitches in encoding which, were they to occur, would equally give professionals reasons to ritualize evidence of what was occurring.)

In addition to the filled-pause phenomenon, consider the very standard form of self-correction which involves the breaking-off of a word or phrase that is apparently not the one we wanted, and our hammering home of a corrected version with increased loudness and tempo, as if to catch the error before it hit the ground and shattered the desired meaning. Here the effect is to show that we are very much alive to the way our words should have come out; we are somewhat shocked and surprised at our failure properly to encode an appropriate formulation for the first time round, and the rapidity and force of the correct version seem to suggest how much on our toes we really are. We display our concern and the mobilization of our effort at the expense of smooth speech-production—electing to save a little of our reputation for presence of mind, over and against that for fluency. Again, as with filled pauses, one has what is ostensibly a bit of pure expression, i.e. a transmission providing direct evidence (not relayed through semantic reference) of the state of the transmitter, but now an expression that has been cut and polished into a standard shape to serve the reputational contingencies of its emitter.

11. Earlier it was suggested that imprecations were somewhat like truncated, self-addressed statements, but not wholly so. Later these lexicalized exclamations were shown to function not unlike response cries. Now we must try to decide where they belong.

Suppose that someone brings you the news that he has failed in a task you have seriously set him. Your response to the news can be: *I knew it! Did you have to?* In the styling I have in mind, this turn at talk contains two moves and a change of 'footing': the first move (uttered half under the breath with the eyes turned upward) is a bit of self-talk, or something presented in that guise—the sort of open aside which adults are especially prone to employ in exasperated response to children, servants, foreigners, and other grades who easily qualify for moments of non-person treatment. The second move (*Did you have to?*) is conventionally directed communication. Observe that such a turn at talk will oblige its recipient to offer an apology or a counter-account, locking the participants into an interchange. But although the recipient of the initial two-move turn will be understood to have overheard the self-addressed segment, he will have neither the right nor the obligation to reply to it specifically, at least in the sense that he does in regard to the conventionally communicated second portion.

Now shift from extended self-talk to the truncated form—imprecation: *Shit! Did you have to?* Given the same histrionics, one again has a two-move turn, with a first move that can't be answered in a conventional way. If the respondent does address the remark to this blurted-out portion, it will be to the psychic state presumably indexed by it—much as when we comfort people who have burst into tears, or when we upbraid them for loss of self-control. Or the respondent may have to venture a frame ploy, attempting to counter a move by forcing its maker to change the interpretive conventions that apply to it—as in the snappy comeback *Not here,* injected immediately after the expletive. In all this, and in the fact that standard lexicalizations are employed, *I knew it!* and *Shit!* are similar. However, although *I knew it* follows grammatical constraints for well-formed sentences, *Shit!* need not, even if one appeals to the context in order to see how it might be expanded into a statement. *Shit!* need no more elide a sentence than need a laugh, groan, sob, snicker, or giggle—all vocalizations that occur frequently, except in the utterances ordinarily presented for analysis by linguists. Nor, I think, does it help understanding very much to define *Shit!* as a well-formed sentence with *NP!* as its structure. Here, of course, imprecations are exactly like response cries. For it is the essence of response cries that they be presented as if mere expression—and not recipient-directed, proposition-like statements—were involved, at least on the face of it.

Imprecations, then, might best be considered not as a form of self-talk at all, but rather as a type of response cry. Unlexicalized cries have come to be somewhat conventionalized, and imprecations have merely extended the tendency, further ritualizing ritualizations. Since religious life already sets aside a class of words to be treated with reserve and ranked with respect to severity, response crying has borrowed them—or so it would seem.

Insofar as self-talk is structurally different from the normal kind, imprecatory utterances (like other response cries) are too, only more so. And because of this sharp, underlying difference between conventionally directed statements and imprecatory interjections, the two can be given radically different roles in the functioning of particular interaction systems; they serve close together, in complementary distribution and without confusion.

Consider tennis: during the open state of talk sustained in such a game, a player who misses an 'easy' shot can response-cry an imprecation loudly enough for opponents and partner to hear. On the other hand, a player making a 'good' shot is not likely to be surprised if an opponent offers a complimentary statement about him to him. (As these two forms of social control help frame his own play, so he will participate in the two forms that frame his opponents'.) But, of course, good taste forbids a player to address opponents in praise of his own efforts—just as they must allow him elbow room, and not reply directly to his cries of self-disgust. A player may, however, use directed, full-fledged statements to convey self-castigation and (when directed to his partner) apology. Response cries and directed statements here comprise a closely-working pair of practices, part of the ritual resources of a single interaction system. And their workings can be intermingled because of their structural difference, not in spite of it. Given this arrangement, it is understandable that a player will feel rather free to make a pass at ironically praising himself in statements made to opponents or partner, correctly sensing that his words could hardly be misframed as literal ones. (That he might employ this device just to induce others to communicate a mitigated view of his failure merely attests again to the various conveniences that can be made of forms of interaction.)

Just as response cries can form a complementary resource with conventionally directed statements, so they can with self-directed ones. For example, in casino craps, a shooter has a right to preface a roll, especially a 'come out', with self-encouraging statements of a traditional kind—directed to the fates, the dice, or some other ethereal recipient; this grandstanding (as dignified gamblers call this self-talk) sometimes serves to bring the other players into a cadence and peaking of attention. When, shortly, the shooter 'craps out', he is allowed a well-fleshed imprecation, coincidental with the dissolution of the table's coordinated involvement. So again we find complementarity and a division of labor, with self-talk located where collective hope is to be built up, and imprecatory response cry where it is to be abandoned.

12.1. DISCUSSION. Written versions of response cries seem to have a speech-contaminating effect, consolidating and codifying actual response cries—so that, in many cases, reality begins to mimic artifice, as in *Ugh!*, *Pant pant*, *Gulp*, and *Tsk tsk*; this route to ritualization is presumably unavailable to non-human animals.[16] This easy change is only to be expected: response cries themselves are by way of being second-order ritualizations, already part of an unserious (or less than serious) domain.

Here cartoons and comics are to be taken seriously. These printed pictures must present entire scenarios through a small number of 'panels' or frozen moments, sometimes only one. The cartoonist has great need, then, for expressions that will clearly document the presumed inner state of his figures, and clearly display the point of the action. Thus, if individuals in real life need response cries to clarify the drama of their circumstances, cartoon figures need them even more. So we obtain written versions of something that could be thought originally to have no set, written form. Moreover, cartoon figures portrayed as alone must be portrayed acting in such a way as to make their circumstances and inner states available to the viewer (much as real persons do when in the presence of others), and included in this situational-like behavior are response cries. (So also in the case of movies showing persons ostensibly alone.) In consequence, the practice of emitting response cries when alone is tacitly assumed to be normal, presumably with at least some contaminating effect upon actual behavior when alone.

12.2. A point might be made about the utterances used in response cries. As suggested, they seem to be drawn from two sources: taboo but full-fledged words (involving blasphemy and—in English—Anglo-Saxon terms for body functions) and from the broad class of non-word vocalizations ('vocal segregates', to employ Trager's term, 1958:1–12)—of which response cries are one, but only one, variety.

There is a nice division of linguistic labor here. Full-fledged words that are socially acceptable are allocated to communication in the openly directed sense, while taboo words and non-words are specialized for the more ritualized kind of communication. In brief, the character of the word bears the mark of the use that is destined for it; and we have a case of complementary distribution on a grand scale.

Non-words as a class are not productive in the linguistic sense, their role as interjections being one of the few that has evolved for them. (This is not to say that a particular vocal segregate can't have a very lively career, quickly spreading from one segment of a language community to others; the response cry *Wow!* is a recent example.) Many taboo words, however, are quite productive, especially in the tradition maintained in certain subcultures, where some of these words occur (if not

---

[16] The carry-back from the written to the spoken form is especially marked in the matter of punctuation marks, for here writing has something that speaking hasn't. Commonly used lexicalizations are: *underline*, *footnote*, *period*, *question mark*, *quotes*, and *parenthetically*. Written abbreviations (such as British *p* for *pence*) also enter the spoken domain. Moreover, there is a carry-back to the spoken form of the pictorial-orthographic form of the presumed approximated sound-effects of an action; *Pow!*, *Bam!* are examples.

function) in almost every syntactic position.[17] Furthermore, curse words are drawn from familiar scales of such words, and choice will sharply reflect (in the sense of display, negotiate etc.) the terms of the relationship between speaker and hearer; non-words don't function very effectively in this way.

Note that non-words can't quite be called part of a language. For example, there tends to be no canonical 'correct' spelling. When and where convention does begin to establish heavily a particular form and spelling, the term can continue to be thought of as not a word by its users, as if any written version must continue to convey that rough-and-ready effort at transcription is at work. (I take it here that, in our society, a feature of what we think of as regular words is that we feel the written form is as 'real' a version as the spoken.) Further, although we have efficient means of reporting another's use of an expletive (either literally or by established paraphrastic form), this is not the case with non-words. So, too, the voiced and orthographic realizations of some of these constructions involve consonant clusters that are phonotactically irregular; furthermore, their utterance can allow the speaker to chase after the course of an action analogically with stretches, glides, turns, and heights of pitch foreign to his ordinary speech. Yet the sound that covers any particular non-word can stand by itself, is standardized within a given language community, and varies from one language community to another, in each case like full-fledged words.[18] And the non-words of a particular language comply with and introduce certain of the same phonotactic constraints as do its regular words (Jefferson 1974:183–6). Interestingly, there is some evidence that what one language community handles with a non-word, other language communities do too.

On the whole, then, non-word vocalizations might best be thought of as semi-words. Observe that the characterization provided here (and by linguists) of these half-caste expressions takes no note that some (such as *Uh?* and *Shh!*) are clearly part of directed speech, and are often interchangeable with a well-formed word (here *What?* and *Hush!*); but others (such as the *uh* as filled pause) belong to a radically different species of action—viz., putatively pure expression, response crying. (Imprecations and some other well-formed interjections provide an even more extreme case, for exactly the same such word may sometimes serve as an ostensibly undirected cry, but at other times be integrated directly into a recipient-directed sentence under a single intonation contour.) Here again, one can see a surface similarity covering a deep underlying difference, but not the kind ordinarily addressed by transformationalists.

Apart from qualifying as semi-words, response cries can be identified in another way, namely as articulated free-standing examples of the large class of presumed 'natural expressions' or signs meant to be taken to index directly the state of the transmitter—some of which, like voice qualifiers, can paralinguistically ride roughshod across natural syntactic units of speech. Although gender differences in the basic semantic features of speech seem not very marked in our society, response cries and other paralinguistic features of communication are. Indeed, speech AS A

[17] Admittedly, even in these productive cases, taboo words are not entirely vulnerable to syntactic analysis. Saying that *the fuck* in a sentence like *What the fuck are you doing?* is adjectival in function, or that *bloody* in *What are you bloody well doing?* is an adverb, misses something of the point. Here specific syntactic location seems to be made into a convenience; somehow the intensifying word is meant to color uniformly the whole of the utterance in which it occurs (cf. Quang Phuc Dong 1971).

[18] Quine (1959:6) has an example: ' "Ouch" is not independent of social training. One need only to prick a foreigner to appreciate that it is an English word.'

WHOLE might not be a useful base to employ in considering gender differences, since it cancels sharp contrasts revealable in special components of discourse.

12.3. Earlier, I suggested that a response cry can draw on the coöperation of listeners—requiring that they hear and understand the cry, but act as though it had not been uttered in their hearing. It is in this way that such a form of behavior, ostensibly not designed for directed linguistic communication at all, can be injected into public life—in certain cases, even into conversations and broadcasts. In brief, a form of response perceived as native to one set of circumstances is set into another. In the case of blasphemous cries, what is inserted is already something that has been borrowed from another realm, semantic communication; so the behavior can be said to have been returned to its natural place, but now so much transformed as to be little like a native.

This structural reflexivity is, I believe, a fundamental fact of our communicative life. What is ritualized here, in the last analysis, is not an expression, but a self-other alignment—an interactional arrangement. Nor, as earlier suggested, is that the bottom of embedding. For example, when a speaker finds he has skated rather close to the edge of discretion or tact, he may give belated recognition to where his words have gone—marking a halt by uttering a plaintive *Oops!*, meant to evoke the image of someone who has need of this particular response cry, the whole enactment having an unserious, openly theatrical character. Similarly, in the face of another's reminder that we have failed in fulfilling some obligation, we can utter *Darn it* in an openly false manner—as a taunting, even insolent, denial of the imprecation we might normally be expected to employ. In brief, what is placed into the directed discourse in such cases is not a response cry, but a mocked-up individual uttering a mocked-up response cry. (All of this is especially evident when the cry itself is a spoken version of the written version of the cry, as when a listener responds to the telling of another's near-disaster by ungulpingly uttering the word *Gulp*.) So, too, the filled pause *uh*, presumably a self-expression designed to allow hearers to track speaker's engagement in relevant (albeit silent) production work, can apparently be employed with malice aforethought to show that the word does not follow (and is ostensibly the one wanted all along) is to be heard as one which the speaker might not naturally use (Jefferson, 192–4). In this case a 'correction format' has been used as a convenience, its work set into an environment for which it was not originally designed. Similarly, on discovering that he has said *April the 21st* instead of *May the 21st*, an announcer may (as one type of remedial work) repeat the error immediately, this time with a quizzical, speaking-to-oneself tone of voice, as though this sort of error were enough of a rarity to cause him to break frame; but this response itself he may try to guy, satirizing self-talk (and self-talkers) even as he engages in it, the transformation confirmed by the little laugh he gives thereafter, to mark the end to error-making AND playful correction.

The moral is that what is sometimes put into a sentence may first have to be analysed a something that could not occur naturally in such a setting, just as a solitary's self-comments may first have to be analysed as something found exclusively in social intercourse. And the transformations which these alien bits of speech undergo, when set into their new milieu, speak as much to the competence of ethologists as grammarians.

A turn at talk that contains a directed statement AND a segment of self-talk (or an imprecation or a non-lexicalized response cry) does not merely involve two different moves, but MOVES OF TWO DIFFERENT ORDERS. This is very clear, e.g., when someone in or out of a conversation finds cause to blurt out *Shit!*—and then, in apparent embarassment, quickly adds *Excuse me*, sometimes specifically directing the apology to the person most likely to have been offended. Here, patently, the first move is an exposed response cry; the second is a directed message whose implied referent happens to be the first. The two moves fit together nicely—indeed, some speakers essay an imprecation knowing that they will have a directed apology to compensate for it; but this fit pertains to how the two moves function as an action-response pair, self-contained within a single turn at talk, and not to any ultimate commonality of form. So, too, when an announcer coughs rather loudly, says *Excuse me* with greater urgency of tone than he likes, and then follows with a well-designed giggle: here we have a three-move sequence of sounded interference, directed statement, and response cry—the second move a comment on the first, and the third move a comment on the second move's comment. Any effort to analyse such strips of talk linguistically by trying to uncover a single deep structure that accounts for the surface sequence of words is destined to obscure the very archeological issues which the generative approach was designed to develop. A blender makes a mush of apples and oranges; a student shouldn't.

A student shouldn't, even when there is no obvious segmentation to help with the sorting. For now it is to be admitted that through the WAY we say something that is part of our avowedly directed discourse we can speak—ostensibly at least—for our own benefit at the same time, displaying our self-directed (and/or non-directed) response to what is occurring. We thereby simultaneously cast an officially-intended recipient of our proposition-like avowals as an overhearer of our self-talk. The issue is not merely that of the difference between what is said and what is meant—i.e. the issue of implicature; rather, the issue is that one stream of information is conveyed as avowedly-intended verbal communication, while the other is simultaneously conveyed through a structural ruse, i.e. our allowing witnesses a glimpse into the dealings we are having with ourselves. It is in this way that one can account for the apparently anomalous character of imprecations of the *Fuck you!* form. It might appear as if one person were making a directed verbal avowal to another by means of an imperative statement with deleted subject. But in fact the format is restricted to a relatively small list of expletives, such as *screw*; and none qualify as ordinary verbs, being constrained in regard to embedded and conjoined forms in ways that standard verbs in the elided imperative form are not (cf. Quang Phuc Dong).

Nor is this analysis of the unconversational aspects of certain conversational utterances meant to deny the traditional concept of transformation and embedding; rather, the power of the latter is displayed. Waiting with her husband and a friend for the casino cashier to count down her bucket of silver, a happy player says, *And when I saw the third 7 come up and stop, I just let out 'Eeeee'*. Here, through direct quotation, a speaker brings to well-circumscribed three-person talk what was, a few minutes before, the broadly accessible eruption of a single. This shows clearly that what starts out as a response cry (or, for that matter, as any sounded occurrence—human, animal, or inanimate) can be conversationally replayed—can be reset into ordinary discourse through the unlimited power of sound mimicry.

13. CONCLUSION. The public utterance of self-talk, imprecations, and response cries constitutes a special variety of impulsive, blurted actions—namely, vocalized ones. Our tacit theory of human nature recommends that these actions are 'purely expressive', 'primitive', or 'unsocialized', violating in some way the self-control and self-possession we are expected to maintain in the presence of others, providing witnesses with a momentary glimpse behind our masks.

However, the point about these blurtings is not that they are particularly 'expressive'. Obviously, in this sense of that word, ordinary talk is necessarily expressive, too. Naked feelings can agitate a paragraph of discourse almost as well as they can a solitary imprecation. Indeed, it is impossible to utter a sentence without coloring the utterance with some kind of perceivable affect—even if (in special cases) only with the emotionally distinctive aura of affectlessness. Nor is the point about segmented blurtings that they are particularly unsocialized, for obviously they come to us as our language does, not from our own invention. Their point lies elsewhere. One must look to the light these ventings provide, not to the heat they dispel.

In every society, one can contrast occasions and moments for silence with occasions and moments for talk. In our own, one can go on to say that by and large (and especially among the unacquainted) silence is the norm, and talk something for which warrant must be present. Silence, after all, is very often the deference we owe in a social situation to others present. In holding our tongue, we give evidence that such thought as we are giving to our own concerns is not presumed by us to be of any moment to the others present, and that the feelings which these concerns invoke in ourselves are owed no sympathy. Without such enjoined modesty, there could be no public life, but only a babble of childish adults pulling at one another's sleeves for attention. The mother to whom we would be saying *Look, no hands* could not look or reply, for she would be saying *Look, no hands* to someone else.

Talk, however, presumes that our thoughts and concerns will have some relevance, interest, or weight for others; and in this we can hardly avoid presuming a little. Talk, of course, in binding others to us, can also do so for protracted periods of time. The compensation is that we can sharply restrict this demand to a small portion of those present—indeed, often to only one.

The fugitive communications I have been considering constitute a third possibility—minor, no doubt, but of some significance if only because of what they tell us about silence and talk. Our blurtings make a claim of sorts upon the attention of everyone in the social situation—a claim that our inner concerns should be theirs, too; but unlike the claim made by talk, ours here is only for a limited time period of attention. Simply put, this invitation into our interiors tends to be made only when it will be easy for other persons present to see where the voyage takes them. What is precipitous about these expressions, then, is not the way they are emitted, but the circumstances which render their occurrence acceptable. The invitation we are free to extend in these situations we would be insane to extend in others.

Just as most public arrangements oblige and induce us to be silent, and many other arrangements to talk, so a third set allows and obliges us momentarily to open up our thoughts and feelings and ourselves, through sound, to whoever is present. Response cries, then, do not mark a flooding of emotion outward, but a flooding of relevance in.

There is linguistic point to the consideration of this genre of behavior. Response cries such as *Eek!* might be seen as peripheral to the linguist's domain; but imprecations and self-talk are more germane, passing beyond semi-word vocal segregates to the traditional materials of linguistics analysis. The point is that all three forms of this blurted vocalization—semi-word response cries, imprecations, and self-talk—are creatures of social situations, not states of talk. A closed circle of ratified participants oriented to engaging exclusively with one another in avowedly-directed communications is not the base; a gathering, with its variously-oriented, ofttimes silent and unacquainted members, is. Further, all three varieties of ejaculatory expression are conventionalized as to form, occasion of occurrence, and social function. Finally, these utterances are too commonly met with in daily life, surely, to justify scholarly neglect.

Once we recognize that there is a set of conventionalized expressions that must be referred to social situations, not conversations—i.e. once we appreciate that there are communications specifically designed for use outside states of talk—then it is but a step to seeing that ritualized versions of these expressions may themselves be embedded in the conventionally-directed talk to be found in standard conversational encounters. Appreciating this, we can then go on to see that, even though these interjections come to be employed in conversational environments, they cannot be adequately analysed there without reference to their original functioning outside states of talk.

It is recommended, then, that linguists broaden their net, to bring in uttering that is not talking, and to deal with social situations—not merely with jointly sustained talk. Incidentally, linguists might then be better able to countenance inroads that others can be expected to make into their conventional domain; for I believe that talk itself is intimately regulated and closely geared to its context through non-vocal gestures which are very differently distributed than the particular language and subcodes employed by any set of participants—although just where these boundaries of gesture-use ARE to be drawn remains an unstudied question.

REFERENCES

COOK-GUMPERZ, JENNY, and CORSARO, WILLIAM. 1976. Social-ecological constraints on children's communicative strategies. Papers on language and context, by Jenny Cook-Gumperz and John Gumperz (Working paper 46). Berkeley: Language Behavior Research Laboratory, University of California.

GOPNIK, ALISON. 1977. No, there, more, allgone: Why the first words aren't about things. Nottingham Linguistic Circular 6:15–20.

JAMES, DEBORAH. 1972. Some aspects of the syntax and semantics of interjections. Papers from the 8th Regional Meeting, Chicago Linguistic Society, 162–72.

JEFFERSON, GAIL. 1974. Error correction as an interactional resource. Language in Society 3:181–200.

PIAGET, JEAN. 1956. Le langage et la pensée chez l'enfant. 4th ed. Neuchâtel. [Trans. by Marjorie Gabain. New York: Meridian, 1957.]

———. 1962. Comments on Vygotsky's critical remarks concerning The language and thought of the child, and Judgment and reasoning in the child. (Appendix to Vygotsky, 1962 edition.) Cambridge: MIT Press.

QUANG PHUC DONG. 1971. English sentences without overt grammatical subject. Studies out in left field, ed. by A. M. Zwicky et al., 3–9. Edmonton: Linguistic Research, Inc.

QUINE, W. V. 1959. Word and object. New York: Wiley.

SUDNOW, DAVID. 1967. Passing on: the social organization of dying. Englewood Cliffs, NJ: Prentice-Hall.

TRAGER, GEORGE L. 1958. Paralanguage: a first approximation. Studies in Linguistics 13:1–12.

VYGOTSKY, LEV SEMENOVICH. 1962. Thought and language. Trans. by Eugenia Hanfmann and Gertrude Vakar. New York: Wiley.

JOHN J. GUMPERZ

The Retrieval of Sociocultural Knowledge in Conversation

It is a generally accepted premise of modern conversational analysis that to engage in and sustain a significant range of verbal encounters, participants must have both background information about the situation at hand and sociocultural knowledge, i.e., familiarity with the shared conventions governing the verbal categorization of the environment and the conduct of activities alluded to in the interaction. Study of the role of such extra-grammatical factors in verbal communication and their relationship to grammar has in fact become a major concern of modern research.

Existing theories visualize the relationships of sociocultural knowledge to grammar and speaking in one of two ways. There is the anthropological tradition of ethnography of communication in which sociocultural knowledge is seen as coded in the form of speech events. Such events are viewed in structural terms as time-ordered sequences of acts characterized by culturally specific values and norms which constrain both the content and form of what is said. The goal of speech-event analysis parallels that of grammatical analysis: to specify rules of appropriate language usage and interactive behavior in particular types of situations, and to show how such rules vary both cross culturally and across situations.

The second tradition, which derives from recent work in philosophy of language, frame semantics, and artificial intelligence, posits abstract semantic constructs variously called scripts, schemata, or frames, by means of which participants relate their knowledge of the world to what goes on in an encounter. The function of such interpretive frames is to fill in or supply information which is left unsaid or otherwise indirectly alluded to in the course of an encounter.

The two approaches differ both in theory and in analytical goal, yet they are similar in one important respect: both view sociocultural knowledge holistically in terms of a bounded set of categories. Our image of what these categories are derives from the way we visualize or *talk about* such culturally salient events or routines as rituals, ceremonies, games, interview sessions, court room interrogations, an evening at the restaurant, and the like. Where actual talk is analyzed, the aim is to produce ideo-typical descriptions, to set up typologies which can then be used to explain behavior in new situations.

Such structural analyses of events or interpretive frames have furnished definite proof that interpretation is always context bound and have illustrated the role of sociocultural variation and its linguistic correlates in interpretation. Yet any attempt to apply such ideotypical constructs in the study of everyday verbal interaction is certain to encounter serious problems. To begin with, although event labels are part of our everyday vocabulary and are regularly used when we talk

From *Poetics Today*, Vol. 1, No. 1, 1979, pp. 273–86. Reprinted with permission of *Poetics Today* and John J. Gumperz.

about modes of speaking, they are highly abstract in nature and on the whole poor descriptors of what is actually accomplished. When participants report on particular verbal encounters, they tend to do so by mentioning some item of content or by referring to what people were getting at or what they were trying to do. Event names in everyday talk are most often used metaphorically. Phrases like "we had a discussion" or "we had a chat" do not necessarily describe the activity of discussing or chatting.

Those sociologists and linguists who are centrally concerned with processes of everyday conversation in fact follow still a third separate academic tradition of enquiry which concentrates on the actual discourse mechanisms that serve to allocate turns of speaking, to negotiate changes in themes and focus and to manage and direct the flow of interaction, and which so far has made little use of notions like event and schema.

The picture of everyday conversation that emerges from this work is one of a dynamic interactive flow marked by constant transitions from one mode of speaking to another; shifts from informal chat to serious discussion, from argument to humor, or narrative to rapid repartee, etc. In other words, routines which when seen in speech-act terms might be considered as independent wholes, here serve as discourse strategies integrated into and interpreted as part of the broader task of conversational management.

The question arises: how are such shifts in perspective signalled linguistically in such a way as to enable all conversationalists to keep abreast of the flow of thematic progression and to predict what is intended? How are the signalling processes related to grammar, to the ethnographers' concern with language use and to the discourse analysts' concern with interpretation?

Sociologists have studied conversational management almost entirely at the level of content, in terms of lexical choice or speech-event function. What has been analyzed for the most part are everyday conversations where participants have similar sociocultural backgrounds. The analysis assumes, but does not attempt to demonstrate, that all participants are equally familiar with relevant strategies of verbal interaction.

My own concern in this paper is also with strategies of conversational management. But what I want to show is that such strategies are in large part specific to participants' sociocultural background and that differential control of such culturally specific strategies has important consequences for interpersonal and inter-ethnic relations, ethnic stereotyping and social mobility in modern urban societies. I further want to argue that the nature and functioning of sociocultural diversity at this level can best be revealed by detailed examination of the linguistic signalling devices or contextualization strategies used in conversational management and in signalling communicative intent.

I intend to demonstrate these claims by concentrating on a single situation, an excerpt from an interview-counselling session recorded in an industrial suburb in London. The participants are both educated speakers of English; one is a Pakistani teacher of mathematics, who although born in South Asia, has completed both his secondary school and university education in England. The other is a staff member of a center funded by the Department of Employment to deal with inter-ethnic communication problems in British industry. The teacher has been unable to secure permanent employment and having been told that he lacks communication skills for high school teaching, he has been referred to the center. While both participants agree on the general definition of the event as an interview-counselling session, their expectations of what is to be accomplished, and especially about what needs to be said, differ radically. Such differences in expectation are, of course, not unusual even where participants have similar cultural backgrounds. Conversations begin with an introductory phase where common themes are negotiated and differences in expectation adjusted. What is unusual about this situation is that the participants, in spite of repeated attempts of adjustment over a period of more than an hour, utterly fail in this negotiation. Our analysis concentrates on the reasons for this failure and shows how it is based on differences in linguistic and sociocultural knowledge.

Before we go into the actual tape it is necessary to give some background information about the theoretical assumptions that underlie our research. Even a casual inspection of a representative range of longer conversations shows that the maintenance of thematic progression in the face of regular changes in perspective involves more than mere choice of lexicon or choice of speech act. To the extent that we can speak of choice at all, it simultaneously affects several levels of communicative behavior: phonological, paralinguistic, prosodic, syntactic, lexical and non-verbal. Yet how these levels interact and how this interaction relates to the interpretation process, to cultural symbolism, and to normative constraints on discourse strategies are as yet poorly understood.

We begin by clarifying what is meant by differences in linguistic signalling mechanism. Clearly, we are not referring to grammatical rules such as might be discovered by the usual methods of contrastive analysis. Research in urban dialectology and in bilingual interference has shown that the linguistic differences that do occur in urban situations tend to be trivial from the point of view of grammar and rarely affect intelligibility at the level of propositional content of what is said. What we are dealing with are matters of usage which must ultimately be analyzed in comparative terms. But the common method of expressing usage distinctions statistically in terms of variable rules can tell us little about mechanisms of conversation management. Nor can we start simply by isolating time-bound episodes or events and contrast the codes used in them. That would be circular since one of the things we want to find out is how the transition among types of verbal activity or modes of speaking is signalled.

One way of solving the dilemma is to rely on ethnographic work to find out what kinds of interpretive differences do occur and determine whether or not these can be attributed to underlying interpretive processes. Our initial research strategy here follows that of Frederick Erikson who begins by seeking out what he calls certain gate-keeping situations, which are socially important in that they affect the life chances of the individuals studied, and which involve discourse requirements such that they are most likely to produce instances of the phenomena we are interested in studying. The interethnic counselling session is one such gate-keeping situation.

My analysis concentrates on what I have called *conversational inference*, that is, the participants' decoding of conversational intent. I use the term intent in the limited sense of intending to communicate where the conversation is going and how one needs to tie one's utterance to a previous speaker's moves so as to maintain thematic continuity. Analysis begins by locating time-bound sequences in a conversation which reveal evidence that participants show persistent differences in interpretation. We then build (a) on what we know about the outcome of the conversation and (b) on our understanding of relevant ethnically based contextualization processes to construct a theory of what it is about the inferential process that led to these differences in interpretation. Methods used for the discovery of contextualization cues have been described elsewhere. They rely partly on comparative analysis of a wide variety of ethnically homogenous in-group and ethnically mixed encounters, and partly on indirect elicitation procedures and role play experiments in which participants in a conversation, or others of similar background, listen to tape-recorded passages and are questioned to discover the perceptual cues they use in arriving at their interpretation.

To illustrate the procedure let us now turn to the first portion of our recording.

EXAMPLE 1

A — Indian male speaker
B — British female speaker

```
 1   A:   exactly the same way as you, as you would like
 2        ⌈to put on⌉
 3   B:   ⌊Oh no  ⌋     no
 4   A:   there will be some of   ⌈the⌉   things you would like to        .
 5   B:                           ⌊yes⌋
 6   A:   write it down
 7   B:   that's right, that's right (laughs)
 8   A:   but, uh. . anyway it's up to you (one second pause)
 9   B:   um, (high pitch). . well. .   ⌈I I Miss. C.⌉
10   A:                                 ⌊first of all ⌋
11   B:   hasn't said anything to me you see
          (pause, about 2 seconds)
12   A:   I am very sorry if  ⌈  she  ⌉  hasn't spoken anything
13   B:   (softly)           ⌊doesn't matter⌋
14   A:   on the telephone at least,
15   B:   doesn't matter
16   A:   but uh. . . .it was very important uh thing for me
17   B:   ye:s. Tell, tell me what it  ⌈is ⌉    you want
                                       ⌊umm⌋
19        Um, may I first of all request for the introduction please
20   B:   Oh yes sorry ⌉
21   A:               ⌊I am sorry
          (pause, about one second)
22   B:   I am E.
23   A:   Oh yes  ⌈(breathy) I see. . .oh yes. . .very nice⌉
23   B:          ⌊and I am a teacher here in the Centre  ⌋
24   A:   very nice⌉
25   B:          ⌊and we run⌉
26   A:                     ⌊pleased to meet you (laughs)⌉
27   B:                                                   ⌊different
28        courses (A laughs) yes, and you are Mr.?
29   A:   N.A.
30   B:   N.A. yes, yes, I see (laughs) Okay, that's the
31        introduction (laughs)
32   ?
33   A:   would it be enough introduction?
```

Note that apart from a few seemingly odd phrases the passage shows no readily apparent differences in linguistic code, yet the last section culminating in A's "Would it be enough introduction?" clearly suggests that something is going wrong. Normally one might explain this sort of utterance and the awkward exchanges that precede it in psychological terms as odd behavior, reflecting on participants' personal motives. But a closer examination of the interactive synchrony of the entire passage, as revealed in the coordination of speakers' messages with listenership or backchannel cues such as "um," "yes" or "no no" suggest that the problem is more complex than that.

Studies of interactive synchrony by Erikson and his collaborators, working primarily with non-verbal signs, have shown that in conversation of all kinds speakers' moves and listeners' responses are synchronized in such a way as to conform to a regular and measurable rhythmic beat. Most longer encounters alternate between synchronous or smooth phases exhibiting a high degree of coordination and phases of asynchrony which Erikson calls "uncomfortable moments." Our experiments carried on at Berkeley by Erikson, Gumperz and Bennett with ethnically mixed student groups reveal that the relationship of backchannel signals to speakers' utterances is closely related to interactional synchrony at the non-verbal level. In synchronous phases backchannel signals stand in regular rhythmic relationship to points of maximum information content in the speaker's message, as marked by stress and intonation contour. Asynchronous phases lack such rhythmic coordination. It has furthermore been noted that when participants are asked to monitor video or audiotapes of their own encounters, they have little difficulty in agreeing on the boundaries between synchronous and asynchronous phases. But when they are asked to interpret what was going on in these phases, their interpretations tend to differ. Conversational synchrony thus yields empirical measures of conversational cooperation which reflect automatic behavior, independent of prior semantic assumptions about the content or function of what was said and thus form useful starting points for comparative analysis of interpretive processes.

In interactions among individuals who share sociocultural backgrounds which are not marked by other overt signs of disagreement, asynchronous movements tend to reflect the initial negotiation transitions in verbal activity or routines such as we referred to at the beginning of this paper—unexpected moves by one or another participant—and are relatively brief. In our passage here, however, lack of coordination is evident throughout.

Note, for example, the placement of B's "oh no" (line 3). In a coordinated exchange this should appear shortly after A's verb phrase. Here it occurs after the auxiliary "like." Similarly B's "yes" (line 5) overlaps with A's "the." The same is true of B's "doesn't matter" (line 13) and A's "umm" (line 18) as well as elsewhere throughout the tape. In line 9, B shifts to a high pitched "um, well" and, as she is about to go into her message, A simultaneously sets in with "first of all."

In addition there are several premature starts, i.e., starts which lack the usual rhythmic interval, in lines 21, 23, 25, and in lines 8, 11 and 21 we find arhythmic pauses of one, two, and one seconds respectively.

Lack of coordination seems to increase rather than decrease with the progress of the interaction, culminating in several bursts of nervous laughter (line 25) which suggest that both participants are becoming increasingly ill at ease. Given what we know about conversational rhythm, such as synchrony, there is strong evidence for systematic differences in contextualization and interpretive strategies.

To find out what these differences are we must turn to content. The passage divides into roughly three sequentially ordered sub-episodes. These are distinct in manifest topic. But beyond that they also have semantic import in terms of the role relations and expected outcomes they imply, and can thus be seen as reflecting distinct activity types. In the first sub-episode B has just asked A for permission to tape record. Her request did not get recorded. The tape begins with A's response. B's request gives A the option either to agree or to refuse and further to explain or justify his decision. His words here indirectly suggest that he is agreeing and is taking advantage of his option to explain, to comment, on the importance of his problem. B, however, does not seem to understand what he's trying to do. Her "no, no" in line 3 suggests she is defensive about her request to record and her "that's right" in line 7 seems intended to cut short the preliminaries. In line 9, B attempts to lead into the interview proper. Her rise in pitch is of the type English speakers elsewhere in our comparative tapes use to mark shifts in focus or to introduce important new information. A's interruption here suggests that he either does not recognize or disagrees with her change in focus. Sub-episode 2, lines 9-17 then deals with what Miss C (apparently the person who originally referred A to B) has told B about his problem. In line 17, B's request reflects a renewed attempt to begin the interview proper. Here A responds with an asynchronous "umm" and then counters by asking for an introduction. The remainder of the passage then focuses on that introduction.

Looking in more detail at the process of speaker-listener coordination, we note that in 11, B simply ignores A's interruption. Her message is followed by an unusually long pause of 2 seconds. A's statement which follows that pause is marked by what, when compared to his preceding and following statements, is unusually slow rhythm and highly contoured intonation. There is stress on "very sorry" in line 12 and on "very important" in line 16. Listeners of English background who notice this shift in prosodic cues tend to dismiss it as rather minor. Many Indian English speakers, on the other hand, readily identify it as a sign of strong affect signalling that the speaker is very concerned about the fact that his case has not been explained. That prosodic cues act as signals of affect here, is born out by analysis of Indian English speakers' verbal interaction in a number of other encounters, as well as by several subsequent passages in the counselling situation. What we seem to be faced with is an ethnically specific signalling system where contoured prosody and slowed rhythm contrast with flattened contours and normal rhythm to suggest both special affect and personal concern.

Note, however, that B is either unaware of this signalling device or has decided to ignore it since she fails to respond appropriately. Her "doesn't matter" is rhythmically coordinated with A's sorry, which means that she is interpreting it as a formulaic excuse, rather than as a *preamble* to A's further statement. She then responds as A's continued "it was very important" with a "yes" spoken with normal intonation and without raising her pitch at all she attempts once more to begin the interview proper. When A then asks for the introduction, she counters with "oh yes sorry," whereupon A immediately, i.e., without the normal rhythmic interval, says "I'm sorry." Now B seems thrown off balance. She takes a full second to formulate her reply and it is easy to see why. Her own "sorry" indicates that she interprets A's preceding remark as implying she has been remiss, but when he himself then replies with "I'm sorry" he seems to be suggesting it is his own fault.

When B then gives her name in line 22, A replies with a very breathy and contoured "very nice." Indian English speakers who listen to the tape will readily identify this last as a formulaic utterance. It is the Indian English equivalent of Urdu "bahut acchaa" which is used as a backchannel sign of interest similar to our "O.K. go on." The breathy enunciation and contoured intonation are signs of polite emphasis. For English English speakers, however, the meaning is quite different. "Very nice" is used to respond to children who behave properly. In this situation moreover it might be interpreted as having sexual overtones. In any case, B ignores the remark and in line 15 attempts to shift the focus away from herself to talk about the center where she works. A, however, does not follow her shift in focus. His "pleased to meet you" focuses once more on her as a person. This is either intentional or it could be the result of his slowness in following her shift in focus. In any case, his laughing now suggests lack of ease.

B continues as if he hadn't spoken and then, when A laughs again, asks "and you are Mr. A?" When A then gives his name, she repeats it. Her subsequent laugh and her concluding statement: "Okay that's the introduction," indicate that she has interpreted A's original suggestion that they introduce each other as simply a request to exchange names, which, given her frame of reference, she regards as somewhat superfluous in this situation.

A's subsequent "would it be enough introduction" in line 33 however shows that he has quite different expectations of what the introduction was to accomplish. We can begin to see what these expectations are by examining the following exchange which takes place much later in the interview.

EXAMPLE 2

```
 1   A:   then I had decided because I felt all the
 2             way that whatever happened that was totally
 3             wrong that was not, there was no trace of
 4             truth in it. I needed teaching, I wanted
 5             teaching,    ⌈I want teaching⌉
 6   B:                    ⌊hu
 7   A:   I want to um um to waive   ⌈that⌉
 8   B:                              ⌊hu ⌋
 9   A:   ⌈condition⌉   so that by doing
10   B:   ⌊hu        ⌋
11   A:   some sort of training   ⌈language⌉   training
12   B:                           ⌊  hu   ⌋
13   A:   I can fulfill the condition and then I can
14             come back
15   B:   hu
16   A:   and reinstate in   ⌈teaching⌉   condition
17   B:                      ⌊  hu   ⌋
18   A:   this is what I had the view to write to
19             the Department of   ⌈Education and Science⌉   and
20   B:                           ⌊ yes I see            ⌋
21   A:   with the same view I approached
22   B:   Twickenham
23   A:   Twickenham as well as Oxbridge   ⌈University⌉
24   B:                                    ⌊  yes   ⌋
25   A:   as well as Ealing Technical College
26   B:   college
```

```
27  A:  and at the end they had directed me to
28          ⌈give⌉  the  ⌈best⌉  possible advice
29  B:     ⌊yes ⌋        ⌊yes ⌋
30  A:  by doing some sort of language course in
31          which I could best help, so I can be reinstated
32          and I can do something productive rather
33          that wasting my time    ⌈and⌉  the provincial and
34  B:                              ⌊yes⌋  I see, yes I understand
35  A:  the money and time
36  B:  Okay now the thing is Mr. A there is no course here
37          which is suitable for you at the moment
38  A:  this I had seen the   ⌈pro⌉  . . . prospectus  ⌈this⌉
39  B:                        ⌊yes⌋                    ⌊yes ⌋
40  A:  teacher's training  ⌈( )⌉
41  B:                      ⌊yes⌋  that's teacher's training
42          is for teachers who are employed doing language
43          training in factories
44  A:          per. . .perhaps perhaps there will be
45          some way out for you for to for to to
46          ⌈to help⌉  me
47  B:     ⌊to help⌋  there might be but I can't tell you now
48          because I shall have to, you see at the moment there
49          is no course sui. . . suitable for you   ⌈the⌉
50  A:                                               ⌊um ⌋
51  B:  Teacher's training course is run one day here, one
52          day there, two days here, two days there and these are
53          connected with a specific project
54  A:  I don't mind doing any sort of  |pro. . .project|  but
55  B:                                  |no but th. . . |
56          th. . . that's not suitable, I can tell you honestly
57          you won't find it suitable for you,  ⌈it won't⌉
58  A:                                          ⌊but    ⌋
59  B:  it is  ⌈nothing to do⌉   what you want
60  A:         ⌊but no it is  ⌋   not what actually I want I want
61          only to waive the condition, waive the condition
62          which I have been  ⌈restricted from the admission⌉
63  B:                        ⌊But you see it it               ⌋
64          would only be may five days a year, it's only
65          conferences, we don't have a teacher's training
66          course here
67  A:  nothing (looks at program)
68  B:  Yes, oh that's the RSA course
69  A:  Yes
70  B:  that's at Ealing Technical College, that isn't here
71  A:  But it's it's given here
72  B:  Yes that's  ⌈right ⌉  it's at Ealing Technical College
73  A:              ⌊it's it's⌋
```

A here has completed his story of experiences that led to his present predicament, and begins to explain what he wants. The phrase "I want to waive that condition" in lines 7 and 9 and his repeated use of the word "condition" in lines 13 and 16, are his references to the fact that he has been told that he needs additional communication skills. He then proceeds to ask to be admitted to a training course. When in line 36, B tells him that there is no course which is suitable for him, he disputes this by mentioning the Center's prospectus. Then in response to B's remarks in lines 51-53, he says "I don't mind doing *any sort of project.*" When B then insists that this would not be suitable, and is not what he wants, he says once more, repeating the same phrase twice, that all he wants to do is to "waive the condition." In other words, he wants another certificate, not more training.

From this, from our analysis of similar situations, and from our interviews with Asians in British industry, we can see that A, along with many others of similar background, views these counselling situations in terms which are similar to the way many Indians view contacts between government functionaries and members of the lay public in general. Following a type of cultural logic which is perhaps best illustrated in Louis Dumont, *Homo Hierarchichus,* these situations are seen as basically hierarchical situations in which the counselee acts as a petitioner requesting the counselor to facilitate or grant access to a position. It is the petitioner's role in such situations to plead or present arguments based on personal need or hardship (as in A's expressions of concern in example 1, line 12 ff.), which the functionary then either grants or refuses.

In the present case, having been told he lacks communication skills, A interprets this to mean that he needs to get another certificate to qualify for a new teaching post. What he wants to ask of B is to help him get such a certificate. Before he can make his request, however, he needs to find out what her position in the organization is so he can judge to what extent she is able to help him. This is what he wants to accomplish with his request for introduction. His awkward sounding comments are simply attempts at using indirect verbal strategies to get the information he needs.

Seen from this perspective, B's response is clearly insufficient. We know, for example, that although B is a trained teacher and does occasionally teach, her main function is that of assistant director of the center in charge of curriculum planning. In identifying herself as a teacher, she follows the common English practice of slightly understating her actual rank. Most of us would do likewise in similar situations. If someone were to ask me to introduce myself, I might say that I teach anthropology at Berkeley, but I would certainly not identify myself directly as a *full professor*, and list my administrative responsibilities. Anyone who needs this type of information would have to elicit it from me. To do so requires command of indirect strategies which could induce me to volunteer the required information, strategies which are dependent on socioculturally specific background knowledge. A's probes in lines 23, 24, 26, and 32 thus fail because he has neither the sociocultural knowledge to know what to expect nor the contextualization strategies to elicit information not freely offered.

What B's expectations are emerges from the following passage, extracted from a longer interview.

EXAMPLE 3

33 B: well tell me what you have been studying...
34 A: um...
35 B: up till now
36 A: um, I have done my M.Sc. from N. University
37 B: huh
38 A: I have done my graduate certificate in Education from
39   L. University. I had been teaching after getting that
40   teacher's training in H., in H.
41 B: Oh, so you have done some teaching.
42 A: Some ⌈I have done⌉ I have done some teaching
43 B: ⌊in H.   ⌋   I see
44 A: Um..I completed two terms...uh, unfortunately I had to
45   leave from that place because ⌈uh⌉ I was appointed only
46 B: ⌊oh⌋
47 A: for two terms
48 B: Oh so you didn't get to finish your probation, I suppose
49 A: (sighs) so that is uh ⌈ ⌉ my start was all right but later
50 B: ⌊oh⌋
51 A: on what happened it is a mi- a great chaos, I don't know
52   what where I stand or what I can do...um.⌈after   ⌉
53 B: ⌊and now you find⌋
54   you can't get a job
55 A: no this is not actually the situation. ⌈I ⌉ have not
56 B: ⌊oh⌋
57 A: completely explained ⌈my position⌉
58 B: ⌊yes, yes   ⌋
59 A: After um completing two um um terms of my probation ⌈teaching⌉
60 B: ⌊huh huh ⌋
61 A: I had to apply somewhere else. I, there was a job in the
62   borough, London borough of H., I applied and there that was
63   first application which I made and I got the job, but since
64   the beginning the teach- teaching situation was not suitable
65   for a probationary teacher.

B's request in line 33 is phrased in such a way as to focus on the substance of what A has been trained in. A responds first with an asynchronous "um" and then, following B's amplification, "up till now," he gives a list of his degrees starting with his first degree. B's "so you have done some teaching" stresses the "done" and is thus an indirect probe for more details on A's actual work experience. A's response to this probe is rhythmically premature and simply copies her phrase and the last part of her remark.

A's subsequent remark, "I completed two terms...," when interpreted in the context of what transpires later on, refers to the first of several probationary posts he has held. But at this point, he fails to make that clear. Instead, he hesitates slightly and goes on with, "unfortunately I had to leave that place because..." B's asynchronous "oh" in line 46 becomes understandable if we consider that being familiar with British education, she knows that probationary appointments are usually given for three terms. Given the way A presents his information she is justified in assuming, as her remark in line 48 implies, that something happened to cause him to be dismissed. When A attempts to correct her by saying "so that is, my start is all right," she interjects another surprised "oh."

Our interpretation that A is correcting B in line 49 is based on propositional content. His choice of words and his prosody are different from what an English English speaker might have used under the circumstances. English English speakers tend to signal corrections by a raise in pitch register, contrastive stress on the appropriate word, and/or some lexicalized transition like "no" or "I mean." A, however, uses his normal unaccented prosody. His initial unaccented "so" suggests (to English English speakers) that what he is saying follows from his previous remarks. At the end of line 51, however, with "I don't know where I stand," he shifts to contoured intonation. As in the case of lines 12-16 in example 1, we interpret this as a sign of affect or grave personal concern. Indian English speakers who listen to the tape state that this sort of phrase spoken as it is here gives them a more vivid impression of the speaker's real feelings than detailed semantic analysis. Thus we begin to see a systematic difference between Indian English and English English contextualization strategies. Whereas in English English, pitch register shift and stress placement conventionally signal matters of correction and emphasis which are part of normal information flow, in Indian English these prosodic features have additional expressive connotations and are used only in extraordinary circumstances.

Since B is unfamiliar with Indian English strategies, she fails to notice and goes on in normal intonation, "and now you find you can't get a job." Given his frame of reference A interprets this as a saying "you are not qualified to get a job," whereupon he comes in with the rude sounding, "This is not the actual situation" and goes on to insist on explaining his case in minute detail. Line 61 marks the beginning of his explanation, which lasts for more than half an hour. Throughout his narration, B makes regular attempts to get him to the point, and to concentrate on what she wants to know, that is: his teaching experience, the skills he has acquired, and what kind of training he needs to improve his skills. But she utterly fails to control the course of the interaction.

Returning now to theoretical implications, our data suggests that the dichotomy between linguistic signalling processes and social knowledge norms, which existing research traditions implicitly accept, breaks down when we go into the details of conversational inference. We can no longer see meaning as the output of an unilinear process in which sounds are transformed into meaningful sentences by application of grammatical rules and social norms determine the use of such meaningful sentences. Sociocultural conventions affect all levels of speech production and intepretation, from the abstract cultural logic that underlies all interpretation to the division of speech into episodes, to their categorization in terms of semantically relevant activities and interpretive frames; from the mapping of prosodic contours onto syntactic strings to selection among lexical and grammatical options.

This view of social knowledge is implicit in modern speech act theory and frame semantics. But work in this tradition has been limited by an unnecessarily diffuse view of extralinguistic knowledge as knowledge of the world and by its failure to consider the role of linguistic contextualization processes in retrieving information used in the processing of verbal messages. We can avoid some of the ambiguities inherent in frame semanticists' notions of meaning and intent by concentrating on what participants have to know in order to enter into conversation and to maintain thematic progression. This is essentially what sociologists concerned with conversational analysis have done. But in dealing with these problems we cannot assume that interpretive processes are shared. Only by looking at the whole range of linguistic phenomena that enter into conversational management can we relate what goes on in an interaction to participants' history and to their place in society at large.

MARILYN MERRITT

On the Use of *OK* in Service Encounters

In this paper I would like to do two things. First, I would like to report on my observations of some patterns in which *OK* is used. The patterns given are not, of course, exhaustive. Secondly, I would like to suggest an analysis that makes use of interactional concepts. I suggest that the implication is that such social interactional concepts need to be considered in the development of a viable way of talking about language use.

The analysis I am presenting here is based upon naturalistic observations of dialogic speech in one type of social context or situation. This is a context which I identify by the term 'service encounter'.[1] Briefly, by a service encounter I mean the situation of interaction between a 'posted' server and a second party (a customer) who invokes the server's participation as an operator of a 'serving post'. The serving post—in many cases, the cash register counter—is typically part of a larger 'service area' such as a store or a shop. Thus a buying and selling encounter between a customer and a server is a typical instance of a service encounter.

In looking at what people say in service encounters, it has been natural to focus on questions and responses to questions, as these comprise much of what goes on in service encounters. In doing so, I came to notice the occurrence of the word *OK*.

OK was referred to by Bolinger (1957) as an 'approbative'—defined in the dictionary as an act that is approving or assenting to the propriety of a thing with some degree of pleasure or satisfaction. *Webster's New International Dictionary of the English Language* (1928 edition) gives under the entry for *OK*: 'Correct; all right—chiefly put or indorsed on documents, bills, etc. to indicate approval'. The entry also suggests that the word is probably derived from the Choctaw *Okeh*, meaning 'it is so and not otherwise'.[2] *Webster's Third International Dictionary of the English Language* (1971 edition) makes no mention of the origin of the word. The entry lists its use as an adverb, synonomous with *all right* and *yes*, as in the sentence 'OK Doctor, I'll let you know'; and as a transitive verb, synonomous with *approve, authorize*, and *sanction*. Both these definitions corroborate Bolinger's designation.

My observations of the use of *OK* in service encounters are also largely corroborative. However, a closer look has led me to believe that a sense of approval or acceptance is often only part of what is being conveyed when the term *OK* is used. In particular, I argue that use of the term is attuned to punctuating interactional units within the encounter: move, turn, and stage.

I first noted that *OK* occurred in a particular position within the service encounter sequence, thereby characterizing what might be thought of as a pattern of usage. This pattern relates to the customer's initial request—occurring in the

From R. W. Shuy and A. Shunkal (eds.), *Language Use and the Uses of Language*, 1980, pp. 162–72.
Reprinted with permission of Georgetown University Press and Marilyn Merritt.

conversational slot I have elsewhere (Merritt 1976a:66, 70) called the 'customer start'—and the server's response or response slot.

The English language provides a number of lexical items with which to express affirmative response: *yes, yeah, yeh, yep, all right, OK, fine, right,* and so on. The differential use of these items in different contexts undoubtedly reflects degree of formality. However, at least in service encounters, there are patterns of variation that suggest another kind of distinction. As I have suggested elsewhere (Merritt 1976a,b) there are at least two major types of "customer starts": requests for information (as in "Do you sell bathing caps?") and requests for action (as in "Can I have a pack of Marlboros please?"). Correspondingly, there seems to be a dichotomy in the affirmative responses between *yes* items (*yes, yeah, yeh, yep, Umhmm*) and *OK* items (*all right, OK*). In particular, *yes* items seem to operate primarily as affirmative responses to requests for information, while *OK* items seem to operate more as affirmative or 'granting' responses to requests for action. Compare (1) and (2), for example, in which *yes* items occur, with (3), in which the server responds with an *OK* item.

(1) LIBRARY
     C: Do I reserve a book here?
  →S: Yes.

(2) GIFT SHOP
     C: Do you have lighters?
  →S: Yes. Over on the other side of the showroom.

(3) NOTIONS
     C: C'n I have two packs of Vantage Green?
  →S: OK (turns to get).

Frequently, if not typically, of course, these kinds of interchanges occur in sequence, as in (4), (5), and (6):

(4) SNACK TRUCK
     C: Do you have Marlboros?
  →S: Yeah. Hard or soft pack?
     C: Soft please.
  →S: OK (turns to get.)

(5) NOTIONS
     C: Hi, do you have uh size C flashlight batteries?
  →S: Yes sir.
     C: I'll have four please.
     S: Do you want the long life or the regular? See the long life doesn't last ten times longer than the regular battery. Usually lasts three times as long. Cheaper in the long run. These're eighty-eight. These're thirty-five each.
     C: Guess I better settle for the short life.
     S: How many you want?
     C: Four please.
  →S: OK (picks four and puts on counter). That's a dollar forty and nine tax, a dollar forty-nine.

(6) PHOTOGRAPHY STORE
     C: Do you stock polycontrast paper?
  →S: Yes we do. What size and quantity do you want?

    C: Twenty-five sheets, eight by ten, double weight.
→ S: OK (puts box on counter).

It may be that the *yes* items do occasionally occur in the response slot after requests for action (when they are accompanied by appropriate action). An example is given in (7).

   (7)   UNIVERSITY CAFETERIA
       C: Can I have one large cup of coffee black and one large cup of coffee with cream?
    → S: Um humm. (starts fixing)

However, I have observed no instances of *OK* on the response slot to a question of the "Do you have ____?" type. Rather, in the slot that is a response to the customer start, *OK* seems to be specialized as a response to a request for action. The actual satisfaction of a request for action, of course, is not a verbal response but the requested action itself (such as getting the pack of cigarettes, preparing the cup of coffee, etc.). This suggests that *OK* may have some special function as a signal or cue that the requested action is about to take place.

Initially, I hypothesized that *OK* might operate generally as an acknowledgement that it is the speaker's (that is, the person who said *OK*) "turn" (or present obligation) to take some action (getting the cigarettes, getting out the paper requested, etc.). In other words, the *OK* might signal approval of the request and intention to act on the request. It seemed, too, that the word *OK* might have a special role in bridging the transition from a verbal to nonverbal mode of interaction, much as the passing of a baton in a relay race bridges the transition from one person's running the race to a second person's running the race.

I began to notice, however, that the move immediately following the uttering of *OK* was not always nonverbal. This is illustrated in examples (8) through (11).

   (8)   SAVINGS BANK
       C: Do you sell government bonds?
       S: Yes, we do.
       C: I'd like one for fifty dollars please.
    → S: OK. Would you please fill out this application completely, sir.

   (9)   TICKET BOOTH, MOVIES
       C: Two please (pushing bill through window)
       S: Which picture?
       C: *American Graffiti.*
    → S: OK. That's five dollars.

  (10)   DEPARTMENT STORE, HOSIERY
       C: (approaches S with stockings, hands them to S)
       S: OK hon. That'll be one —
       C: (hands bill to S)
       S: — out of five.

  (11)   SNACK TRUCK
       C: (stands at window, S is turned away)
    → S: (S turns to C) OK. What do you want?
       C: Hot dog.

In every case, however, the next move (whether nonverbal or verbal) was made by the same speaker who said *OK* (in all these examples, the server), as predicted. Thus I modified my hypothesis, to wit:

> **Revised hypothesis.** In my materials *OK* items seem to operate generally as an acknowledgement that it is the speaker's (that is, the person who said *OK*) turn (or present obligation) to take some action — whether verbal or nonverbal — that is, to make the next move in the interaction. In cases where the next move is a nonverbal act, the *OK* item can be seen to be doing a kind of "bridging" between the verbal and the nonverbal. It anchors the nonverbal action in what has already gone on verbally, at the same time as it provides an expectation of something to follow.

The two patterns of use that have been examined so far involve the server's use of the term *OK* and its relation to the server's providing a requested service. Now let us consider examples in which it is the customer who says *OK*, as in (12) and (13).

(12)   JEWELRY
    (S has just shown C a necklace)
    C: Can you show me something else in that price range?
    S: Let me see what else I have (looking down). Here are two other pendants.
→C: OK. I'll take these two (pointing).

(13)   DEPARTMENT STORE, COSMETICS
    C: Can I have a bottle//o' the mint?//
    S: //What?   //What shampoo?
    C: The green.
    S: Which?
    C: The mint protein. Can I also see the conditioner?
    S: Which?
    C: The cucumber. Can I smell it?
    S: Sure (placing on counter).
→C: OK. I'll take both. That'll be charge.

In both cases, the customer seems to be not only expressing approval of the requested commodity, but also to be expressing satisfaction with having examined it. That is, he is expressing his having completed examination and his readiness to take the next move (in these cases, to decide whether to take the commodity or not, though in other cases the customer may defer this move pending examination of other commodities).

Now consider (14).

(14)   NOTIONS
    (C has been looking in rear of store at a selection of hair ties.)
    C: These're the only ones you have, right?
    S: Right.
→C: OK. Guess not. Thanks just the same.
    S: You're welcome.

Here the customer is expressly not approving of the requested commodity, but is satisfied with his examination of it. He then takes the next move to state his decision not to buy. By expressing his satisfaction with his examination of the commodity, he in a sense releases the server from any further obligation to continue to provide the requested commodity.

The use of *OK* to release the other party from the current obligation occurs also in examples (15), (16), and (17). In these examples, the requested commodity is not provided by the server but a reason is given. When the customer replies with *OK*, he gives an acceptance of that reason or account.

(15)　DELICATESSEN
　　　　C:　Do you have two dimes and a nickel for a quarter?
　　　　S:　(rings cash register, opens drawer) We don't have any dimes left.
　　→C:　OK. Thank you.

(16)　DRUG STORE
　　　　C:　Excuse me, I'm looking for Phisohex — do you have any?
　　　　S:　Should be over in aisle three under skin care.
　　　　C:　I already looked there. You wouldn't have any in stock, would you?
　　　　S:　No. If it's not on the shelf, we must be out.
　　→C:　OK. Thanks anyway.

(17)　UNIVERSITY CAFETERIA (the complete sequence of which example (7) is a segment)
　　　　C:　Can I have one large cup of coffee black and one large cup of coffee with cream?
　　　　S:　Um humm. (starts fixing)
　　　　C:　Make that black with sugar.
　　　　S:　You'll have to put your own sugar in. It's out.
　　→C:　Oh. OK. Fine.

In these cases, in which *OK* seems to be used by one participant to release the other participant, the release function can be interpreted as a special case of general or "ordinary" use of *OK*, as tentatively suggested in the "revised hypothesis" I have given. That is, since the *OK* speaker thereby obligates himself to take the next necessary move in the encounter, by so obligating himself he necessarily releases the other participant from any current obligation to continue his turn. Example (18) is another example of a "releasing" *OK*. In this case, it is not a commodity that has been requested but rather information as to its whereabouts.

(18)　NOTIONS
　　　　C:　Do you have Chanukah cards?
　　　　S:　Yeah, right back against the wall there. See the sign — Chanukah cards?
　　→C:　OK.

OK may also be used by the server to release the customer — in many cases, to express satisfaction with payment, as in (19).

(19)　NOTIONS
　　　　S:　OK. That'll be fifty, seventy-five, ninety cents altogether.
　　　　Coin
　　　　Cash register
　　　　Change
　　→S:　OK. Thank you.

Note that in (19), *OK* occurs twice. In (20), a similar term *all right* occurs in almost the identical pattern.

(20)   NOTIONS
      S: All right. That's twenty-five and two tax — twenty-seven.
      Sound of money
   →S: All right. Thank you.

The words *OK* and *all right* seem almost to punctuate the sequence. If they were in some sense punctuating or marking transition, the question arises as to what they would be marking transition between. I propose that the use of *OK* (and other *OK* items like *all right*) may signal a transition in stages or something like stages (perhaps 'phase' is a better word). Elsewhere (Merritt 1976a) I have suggested that service encounters typically are composed of four different stages: access, selection, decision, exchange, and closure. In (19) and (20), *OK* items are used twice in each sequence: first, at the point at which transition is being made from selection decision to exchange; and second, at the point at which transition is being made from exchange to closure. This suggests that *OK* does indeed function as a kind of bridging device, as proposed in the reversed hypothesis. However, it does not necessarily perform this function only between verbal and nonverbal phases of the encounter, but rather may occur at other possible transition points as well.

As a result of these observations I offer the following generalization. Use of the term *OK* has at least two possible functions: (1) that of signifying approval, acceptance, confirmation; (2) that of providing a bridge, a linking device between two stages or phases of the encounter. In these cases, use of the term *OK* seems to signify that the speaker suggests the termination of the phase that has just preceded and agrees to take the initiative in continuing with the next phase (or be satisfied with termination (as in (15) through (18)).

There are cases in which only the first, more traditionally asigned function seems to be operating, as in example (21).

(21)   NOTIONS (midway through the encounter)
      C: Yeah, but I wantta get//
      S: Yeah
      C: I wantta get colors —
   → S: Yeah you can mix the papers. OK. Whatever you wantta do.

But very frequently, as has been shown, both functions seem to be operating.[3] Consider the many occurrences of *OK* in the following service encounter (which is the entire sequence of which (21) is a part).

(22)   NOTIONS
      S: Whattaya lookin' for Miss? [Cough] ((maybe)) I can help you?
      C: Uh yeah. Christmas wrapping paper.
      S: All right. We'll show you. (Cash register slam.)
          Here you are. Right around here, Miss, look.
      C: Oh. OK.
      S: Around here.
      C: Oh I see.

S: Here's this ((inaudible)) and then we got uh different boxes here.

C: ((You don't carry)) the individual sheets.

S: All right.

C: Hmm.

S: And if you don't see anything individual, we'll sell these rolls, we'll break // a box for you.

C: Oh really?

S: We'll sell you one—you know what I mean. In other words, this is a dollar and a quarter for three, forty-five cents for one. Of course, this is Christmas wrap individual.

C: Yeah. OK. Good.

S: You can buy any of these individually. In other words, like—like one of these rolls you can have//

C: Un hunh.

S: . . . for forty-five cents a roll.

C: OK. Thank you.

(S goes back to serving post; C looks at paper)

S: You can break any of those boxes OK. Just take one roll out you want it.

C: ((OK)).

(S attends to other customer, a few minutes elapse)

C: You don't have any *yarn* ribbon, do you?

Ring

S: Yarn ribbon?

C: Unh hunh.

S: No. No yarn ribbon. Just uh—I forget—for wrapping packages?

C: Unh hunh.

S: No—we have what you see over here (walking away)

C: OK.

(a few seconds pass)

C: Is it ever possible to *mix* these tt-

S: Yeah. You can do whatever you want. You wantta—you can mix-em—whatever you wantta do.

C: The problem being that if I get one of these little boxes of bows I gotta make'em match (huh huh) same ((amount of)) paper.

S: Well—we're not breaking up the bows you know. 'Nother words you wantta take—a package of bows?

C: Yeah. But I wantta get//

S: Yeah.

C: I wantta get colors—

S: Yeah you can mix the papers. OK. Whatever you wantta do.

(several minutes go by, then C approaches the serving post)

C: (putting selections on counter) Two rolls.

S: All right. Ninety and forty-nine is//

C: Oh and I need some hair spray too.

((inaudible few seconds))

C: I'll come down and look. Go ahead and take his. (referring to next customer)

(after a few minutes)

S: OK. Anything else?

```
C:   That's all. Thank you.
S:   ((inaudible))
C:   Three o seven, three ten, three twenty-five. I'll put it in a bag for you.
Rattling
S:   OK. Thank you.
```

The notion that discourse and the significance of words as used should be studied within an interactional framework (utilizing interactional concepts such as move, turn, and stage (or phase)) has been suggested by Goffman (1964, 1971), Labov (1972), and others. The findings presented here about the use of *OK* in service encounters corroborate this notion, and hopefully contribute to a general understanding of the use of the word *OK*.

NOTES

This is a slightly revised version of the paper presented to the Fifth Annual Conference on New Ways of Analyzing Variation, Georgetown University, October 1976. I am grateful to Dwight Bolinger and William Labov for useful comments.

1. The notion of a service encounter is developed more fully in Merritt (1976a, chapters 1 and 3). See chapter 4 or Merritt (1976b) for a discussion of service encounter as it relates to the notions of discourse and speech event generally. Chapter 2 of Merritt (1976a) describes in detail the corpus from which the examples in this paper are drawn.

2. This suggestion is not supported by the well-known papers of Read (1963a,b) on the origin of *OK*. Read argues that *OK* began as a linguistically "faddish" way of abbreviating *all correct* (*oll korrect* = *OK*) in the late 1830s, and was later "boosted" by its association with the phrase *Old Kinderhook*, used in political campaign of 1840. Another researcher, Heflin (1962), argued against such an etymology of the word. The origin of *OK* is apparently not clearly resolved.

Though I shall not be concerned with word origin in this paper, it is interesting that the properties that have obscured the origin of *OK* are the very ones that make it interesting in terms of language use: "...It has been urged that *OK* was used in such a loose sense that it must have stood for something else besides *all correct*. But slang expressions are notoriously loose, and it should not be expected that either *OK* or *all correct* would be used in a strict sense..." (Read 1963a:13-14).

3. This raises, of course, the possibility of ambiguity of function for any given occurrence. In talking with servers, I have been told that in some service encounters there can be, indeed, ambiguity from this source. For example, one server, who sold jewelry and had to take stock out of a display case in order to show it to a customer, told me that when she had displayed an item and the customer said *OK*, it was not always clear whether the customer meant 'Yes, I'll take that one' or 'I'm finished looking at it (show me the next one)'. In a much more serious vein, an airline disaster of May, 1977 has been linked to the possible misunderstanding by one pilot of *OK* to mean 'confirmed; approved; go ahead and take off' rather than the intended 'that's all for now; I'll get back to you (when there is more information, when you're cleared for take-off)'.

This area of ambiguity is one that I hope to explore further in future research.

REFERENCES

BOLINGER, DWIGHT. 1957.   Interrogative structures of American English: The direct question. University, Ala.: University Press.

GOFFMAN, ERVING. 1964.   The neglected situation. In: The ethnography of communication. Special publication of the *American Anthropologist*, 66. Edited by John J. Gumperz and Dell Hymes.

GOFFMAN, ERVING. 1971.   Relations in public. Microstudies of the public order. New York: Basic Books.

HEFLIN, WOODFORD A. 1962.   'OK' and its incorrect etymology. *American Speech* 37:243-48.

LABOV, WILLIAM. 1972.   Rules for ritual insults. In: *Studies in social interaction.* Edited by David
Sudnow. New York: Free Press.

MERRITT, MARILYN WILKEY. 1976a.   Resources for saying in service encounters. Unpublished Ph.D.
dissertation. University of Pennsylvania.

MERRITT, MARILYN WILKEY. 1976b.   On questions following questions (in service encounters).
Language in Society 5:315-57.

READ, ALLEN WALKER. 1963a.   The first stage in the history of 'OK'. *American Speech* 38:5-27.

READ, ALLEN WALKER. 1963b.   The second stage in the history of 'OK'. *American Speech* 38:83-102.

Webster's New International Dictionary of the English Language. 1928. Springfield, Mass.: Merriam.

Webster's Third New International Dictionary of the English Language. 1971. Springfield, Mass.:
Merriam.

CAROL BROOKS GARDNER

Passing By: Streets Remarks, Address Rights, and the Urban Female

False facts.

The detour around the construction, the mud, the planks, Elena walking carefully on one of the planks, and one of the men yelling at her. Cupping his hands to his mouth, yelling. Another man laughing. Another man, stocky in his workclothes, throwing something at her that hadn't enough weight to carry itself to her—just a crumpled-up paper bag, a lunch bag.

False facts: they didn't really want to hurt her.

Didn't hate her.

Didn't want her dead.

False facts: the recitation of the weather around the country, the temperature recorded at all the airports. You believe it must mean something but it will not.

False facts: blood on instruments, no proof of pain. Proof only of blood.

—From Joyce Carol Oates
Do With Me What You Will

There is a norm of civil inattention between unacquainted persons in the large urban centers of America today, and the linguistic attendant of this civil inattention is silence.[1] The norm of civil inattention and silence may be breached by citizens in a number of ways and for a number of reasons. This study treats the type of breach that occurs as a result of what may be called a "street remark," that is, a comment in public taking place between the unacquainted. The occasion of concern here is the male-to-female street remark. But before treating this kind of street remark specifically, we should examine other occasions for street remarks in order to appreciate the context in which the male-to-female street remark occurs.

Not every contact between the unacquainted in public has a spoken feature, of course. There are possibilities for communication by affording extraordinary or insufficient proxemic space, for example. Or there may simply be a breach of the customary pattern of gaze; for civil inattention, this is making eye contact briefly from a distance of eight or ten feet, averting the eyes once contact is made, then raising them once more with a middle-distance focus to rest on a point slightly to the side of the passerby. Breaches of the gaze pattern happen when eye contact is not promptly broken or when gaze lingers too long upon some part of the passerby.

The act of walking past another person in a public place often involves features that are not breaches of civil inattention but constitute mere markers of the

From *Language and Social Interaction* (*Sociological Inquiry* 50:3-4, 1980), pp. 328-56. Reprinted with permission of University of Texas Press and Carol Brooks Gardner.

148

act. No extended contact takes place, yet some small notice has been served that human has come close to human.[2] These communicative features are paralinguistic and, occasionally, mechanical, and they occur with or without additional eye contact. Such paralinguistic and mechanical markers of public passage happen when both males and females pass, yet women in big cities note that they occur more frequently and with greater elaboration when lone persons of the opposite sexes pass each other. In such cases, it is usually the male who originates the marker. A young woman crossing a street in Manhattan, for example, finds her passage marked by the lone male occupant of a car: just as she comes level with the car, its horn gives two long, piercing blasts. As a young woman walks down Seventh Avenue, a large truck keeps pace with her and emits an air-braked noise—which sounds quite like a lip fart—every few feet; male laughter from the cab is also heard. Two youthful Puerto Rican bicyclists are waiting at a red light on the Upper West Side of New York; as a young woman crosses the street in front of them, they jingle their bike bells to the rhythm of her walk.

In addition to the mechanical signals that another person is passing, there is a group of physiological signals that are usually considered as occurring involuntarily or without awareness. These, too, take place with greater regularity and greater force when male passes female; again, the male is the originator of the marker. Physiological necessity may indeed play a role in their origin, yet gender-role prescriptions undoubtedly do so too. A woman walking down the street in an elegant Manhattan neighborhood watches a well-dressed middle-aged man coming toward her; as he passes her, he spits. Coming flush with a crew of watching construction workers, a young woman hears two of them belch heartily within a five-second period. A middle-aged white man gives the young woman approaching him an up-and-down glance of expressionless appraisal, rapidly takes out a handkerchief, and—as he comes within a foot or two of passing her—fruitily blows his nose.

Another class of the man-made markers of passage is differentiated from the previous class in that these markers are often contrived in nature. They are felt by passersby to be more "purposeful" or "intentional" than the preceding ones. For example, a young woman walking by St. Patrick's Cathedral in New York notes the four or five Puerto Rican youngsters who are seated on its steps and conversing in Spanish. Continuing their talk, they watch her attentively as she passes, and two of them shuffle their feet, the heels plainly audible against the steps. Their talk has not been available to her; the noise of their shoes has. Another young woman in New York prepares to pass a white male on the way through Bloomingdale's revolving door. He meets her eyes, they both come through their respective doors at the same time, and, as the male comes through, he drags his heels until he is a few steps past her. Passing a young hippie male coming out of a Fifth Avenue store, a young woman briefly notes him and his posture: his hands are stuffed deep into the pockets of his jeans. He gives her a brief up-and-down look and, as they pass, chinks the change in his pockets. A young white father wheeling his child in a stroller looks up and down at the young woman crossing Fifth Avenue opposite him. Eight feet away from her he gives stroller and child an extra hard push and lets it go—no hands!—and with one of his free hands begins patting his thigh and, at the same time, begins to whistle, continuing both activities until he and the woman have passed. Other men rhythmically tap some object at hand—a walking cane, a magazine, a gallery program—for a period demarcated by the civil inattention span, then cease their activity when civil attention ceases. These types of markers of passage thus salute civil inattention by obeying its boundaries and simultaneously undermine it by incorporating attention-getters such as gaze and noise into those boundaries.

Breaches of civil inattention that have a spoken component may occur on various accounts. One may confess ignorance and ask a stranger for time or for directions. One may request aid. The citizen also has the right to catch his or her fellow citizens out of role: looks may be pointedly given, conversations started, comments thrown. The man or woman who goes down the street in wedding gear, hopping on one foot, or carrying a couch will be obliged to take almost any intrusive look or comment in good spirits; he or she, by being out of the role of properly comported citizen, becomes an open person for the time being. Citizens caught in out-of-role pursuits are also required, and often are anxious, to provide explanations or respond to the looks and comments of passersby, thereby demonstrating that there is some reasonable gloss for what only appears to be an out-of-role pursuit or that there is an extenuating circumstance. In the cases just mentioned, these three urban Philadelphians explained to passersby, who met them with broad smiles and quizzical looks, that they were, respectively, on the way to a costume party, performing a fraternity initiation rite, and donating their old couch to some newlywed friends a few blocks away.

Another occasion for breaching civil inattention occurs when some obvious similarity exists between one passerby and another. This similarity makes a fiction of the anonymity of public life, and remarks may ensue. Persons with cars of the same make, children of the same age, dogs of the same breed are all licensed to give and receive street remarks when confronted by their doubles. Other types of breaches of civil inattention are open to falsification and exploitation (as, for example, the classical case of the young woman who drops a handkerchief or struggles when lifting a package in order to gain male aid and, eventually, acquaintance), but that of similarity is especially so. Citizens anxious to meet other citizens of whatever desirable class, age, or gender may simulate the evidence of an interest that this class, age, or gender will also be found to possess. Sometimes a person need only display the "similarity"; walking through the neighborhood inhabited by persons expected to have the similarity will accomplish the rest. One may sport a camera in order to suggest familiarity with photography, entitling one to speak to other camera-wearers and possibly receiving comments from others without cameras but who have knowledge. This use of "badges," as they may be called, announces some characteristic of the possessor that is usually unavailable to the public but that, once displayed, becomes a resource for focused interaction and conversation. In years past, one such resource was to carry a bestseller on the assumption that at least some of one's fellow citizens would have read it and could be relied upon to announce the fact. Nowadays, the efflorescence of the printed T-shirt and the well-appointed public jogger provide similar resources.

Finally, civil inattention may be breached when the citizen is accompanied by a person or animal in an open category, for example, a child or a dog. Those who are demonstrably different in appearance from their fellow citizens—the fat,[3] the handicapped, the ugly—often constitute adult open persons. Blacks and other racial minorities may also be spoken to as open persons, as may interracial couples, though their "openness" is said to have diminished considerably from what it was in the past.[4]

Thus far, I have said that women receive more, and more vigorous, markers of public passage than do males and that they are less frequently the originators of such markers. Now I would like to suggest that a women's public life is greatly different from a man's and that this difference comes in part from the manner in which she is treated in public by men. In urban areas women, especially youthful ones, are subjected to a free and evaluative commentary by men that is the lot neither of youthful men nor the prerogative of women to deliver if they so choose. This commentary does not deal solely with their appearance, though that is a common subject and a ready resource for men. There is evidence that women are open persons on the public streets, liable to receive street remarks at will, in much the same way that lower-status groups frequently are. It is not that these groups, women among them, are caught at being out of role and are reprimanded for it with public looks and comments. On the contrary, it is part of their roles as children, as blacks, as women, to be open to the public.

This is an important point to remember, since the force of many of the street remarks that women receive suggests that they are, in some way, acting out of role. A woman may not walk down the street carrying a couch, but she may as well be. Street remarks often accuse women of inferior looks, improper carriage or attire, inappropriate actions, and moral defects. It is not only unattractive, sloppy women who receive these remarks; it is also comely and well-groomed ones. These remarks are delivered by all classes and races of men, singly and in groups; sometimes they are spoken jokingly, sometimes they are spoken with vehemence and even accompanied by punches, tweaks, or blows. Much of this state of things could be better understood by examining the gender-role prescriptions of both the men who make these street remarks and the women who receive them. Men on the whole do not seem to realize that street remarks may be offensive to women; truly, they may not always be so. Many women, especially those with raised consciousnesses, do find male street remarks offensive or, at the least, intrusive. An explication of these male-to-female street remarks as instances of breaching civil inattention and attempting to initiate a state of talk will say something about the public nature of men and women—as well as about theories of symbolic communication that presume accurate mutual understanding of meaning and intention between the sexes.

Positive Constructions of the Male-to-Female Street Remarks

In by no means all time periods and cases have women taken offense at the male-to-female street remark. Indeed, traditional folk interpretations counsel women that street remarks are innocuously intended and flattering; they are the rewards due the woman who fulfills her female role requirements or they are the playful patter of the men she passes. The whistle is a type of shorthand street remark, and a 1961 newspaper column that asked women, "Do You Like to Be Whistled At?" received, for example, such positive answers as these: Whistles are expressions of approval, compliments, and "a perk-me-up to a girl" (quoted in Goffman, 1963, pp. 144–45n.).

Some years ago a *Glamour* magazine test ("Do You Act Like a Beauty?" 1969, pp. 138–39) gave its readers lessons in how to act responsibly beautiful. One of the items reads:

You're walking along the street and a workman whistles appreciatively at you. You:
a.   Ignore him.
b.   Tell him he's being pretty fresh.
c.   Call a cop.
d.   Smile in friendly acknowledgment and keep walking.

The correct answer is *d*.

Sociologists have also analyzed the positive possibilities of street remarks and whistles. Goffman (1963) writes:

> [I]n some Western communities there is the practice whereby a male communicates regard for the attractiveness of a passing female with whom he is unacquainted by whistling at her or greeting her with some other expressive sign. What follows is up to her. She can elect to act as if no relevant communication has occurred. Or she can elect to turn and ratify the comment by a friendly or hostile comment, in either case creating a momentary face engagement. (Apparently the more impersonally appreciative the whistle, that is, the more it can be construed not as a pickup, the more accepting the girl will be of it.) But in addition, she may smile visibly (so that the whistler knows his message has been appreciatively received), and at the same time look straight ahead so as not to allow for the collapse of separateness and the formation of an engagement. This latter tack represents, in effect, a collusion of both individuals against the rules of communication—an unratified breach of communication barriers. The breach is a slight one, however, since the person whistled at has been on the move away from the whistler and will soon be out of the range of engagement [pp. 144-45].

Goffman's analysis is instructive inasmuch as it places the responsibility for the breach on the woman, though it is in fact the male who is the invariable first mover. It is he who chinks the change in his pockets, whistles, or utters, as Goffman daintily says, "some other expressive sign." In some sense Goffman's analysis is an accurate one, for the woman's appearance is actually a first move of sorts, although it is one she cannot choose not to make. This fact, however, makes talk of the woman's choice in the street remark situation—however positively the remark may be construed—have a hollow ring.

The positive construction of street remarks is not a thing of the past; many men can state their street remarks so as to neutralize offense. A young woman crossing an urban Philadelphia street hears a male voice call out "Hey!" from across the street behind her; she does nothing, and the "Hey!" is repeated; she still does nothing and hears it repeated more insistently. The speaker crosses the street after her at last, saying plaintively, "Hey there! I *know* you not lookin' at me, but you sure are one *fine* woman!" Again, a young woman walks down the street in a black neighborhood in Philadelphia. A middle-aged black man approaches her and looks her over appreciatively: "Does your husband tell you how pretty you are?" he inquires of the woman, who wears no wedding ring. "Not often enough," she replies, and they exchange smiles. In these two cases, the men have supplied other information that defuses the possible offense of a street remark. In the first case, the man demonstrated, by his persistence and sincere tone, that regard for the woman's appearance was "all" he had in mind. In the second case, the man demonstrated the same by incorporating reference to the woman's married—and thus already taken—standing.[5]

Men also offer evidence, when confronted by women who are offended or hurt by a street remark, that they meant no harm. For the woman who counters a crude comment on her appearance with a pained look at the speaker, there is sometimes an apologetic assertion that he was only kidding. Again, when a woman shows pain a man may go out of his way to demonstrate that the offense was meant but meant for someone other than the offended woman. A woman walking past a crew of Manhattan construction workers on a windy day sees a worker punch his buddy illustratively on the arm and hears him call to her, "Lookit your hair! His hair looks better than yours!" She wheels and faces the speaker, speechless and hurt; it is clear from the expression on the speaker's face that he knows that he has hurt her, that he did not mean to, and that he does not know what to do. But he thinks of a way: seizing a third buddy, he says to the woman, "I didn't mean you, I was talkin' about *him*." He was not. Another version of the male assurance of harmless intent is reported by a rape victim who classes street remarks with rape as uninvited intimacies that women must suffer: "I turned around, and there were three nice-looking, long-haired young men, and I said, 'What *are* you doing?' [Then] they were quite crushed and seemed really put down. Then I said to them that when I walked around alone, I didn't want to have to worry about whether I was going to be attacked. I like being alone. I don't want to have to hold some guy's hand just to go down the street. They said goodnight to me very respectfully after that" (Russell, 1975, p. 168).[6] Respectful reversals of manner may also show the woman that male street remarkers, if they do not always envisage a positive response to their words, at least do not envisage a negative one.

Certain circumstances in the occurrence of the street remark offer male speakers the possibility for gallantry. If a street remark to an unknown woman is not always originally conceived of as a positive experience for the woman, there are sometimes ways in which a thoughtful male can make it so. Events of this sort often take place when a man looks appreciatively at or speaks appreciatively to a woman from behind—only to discover when he draws level with her that she is either not so attractive from in front or not so young as he had thought (and hence someone who has no right to be the possessor of an attractive posterior). A man so confronted commonly feels himself gulled. But his masking of this feeling may result in a positive encounter, if a brief one, for the woman and in the knowledge for the man that he has acted generously. An Englishwoman reports this case, which took place when her American mother visited Great Britain. Her mother, she writes, had lovely legs, "well-shaped with pretty ankles and neat narrow feet. The last time she was in England, a year before she died at sixty-five, she was walking across Grosvenor Square near the U.S. Embassy and an American sailor wolf-whistled at her from behind. She was pleased about this—'I'm afraid you're fifty years too late.' 'No, ma'am,' said the sailor; 'it's never too late with legs like those' " (Grenfell, 1976, p. 13).[7]

It is possible, however, for women simply to experience the pleasures of public regard, street remarks being one of these pleasures. When remarks can be construed impersonally, when they do not involve vulgar language, when they are unambiguously complimentary, when the speaker makes only the first remark and does not attempt another—then a woman may feel positive about being spoken to in public by an unknown man. Her positive feeling presumes that she is willing to overlook the asymmetry of public life and that she does not resent being constrained from answering back or from initiating remarks to attractive men herself. Her positive feeling also presumes that she can forget, at least temporarily, that this street remark is part of a class of markers that signals the passage of women more often than it does that of men and part of a class of utterances that are interactionally ambiguous for the woman and thus difficult to respond to. Still, some women do appreciate some public looks and remarks. This is shown in part by the testimony of American women who travel to countries where civil inattention is breached less often than in the United States, for example, to Great Britain. Once deprived of male citizens who ogle, a woman may miss the attention and in fact feel ignored.

Characteristics of Street Remarks

By noting some features of male-to-female street remarks, it is possible to understand why women do not uniformly construe these remarks positively.

When women write about male-to-female street remarks, they may emphasize that they are made to feel like objects as a result of these remarks (Tax, 1973, p. 30);[8] that receiving these remarks constitutes a landmark experience in their coming-of-age (Hennessey, 1970); that hearing male remarks may be the most memorable feature of some period or place in their lives (Rossner, 1966, p. 16);[9] and that they consider rape analogous to what takes place in the male-to-female street remark.[10] Men, as I will note, speak of playfulness, flattery, and the woman's provocation of public remarks. This disparity may in part be explained by the *double-entendre* nature of many remarks, which may seem a clever achievement to the male speaker but constitute an ambiguity impossible for the female recipient to respond to.

Cavan (1966) has written the obligation of the woman in a public bar to demonstrate that she is neither "open to all [n]or a solitary serious drinker, neither role having much moral status" (p. 180). Women in public, then, are obliged to show that they are neither accessible nor preoccupied, that they cannot be approached by every male, but that they can be won by some male. The characteristic sexual freighting of male-to-female street speech reproduces this ambiguity: it supplies a respectful semantic line that presumes the female is inaccessible and a disrespectful semantic line that presumes she is accessible. Often, especially when a group of males is involved, *double entendre* takes the form of one male's speaking not directly to a passing female, but in a manner that clearly indicates she is the subject of the talk and is the intended overhearer. Eye contact inappropriate to a conversation is used; the talk of the male is verbally to his fellows, but his gaze is focused on the woman.

There are obvious similarities between this kind of indirect speech and the black speech act of "signifying," but the main difference for white female speakers is that they are not allowed to take part as proper interlocutors and still maintain role requirements. For white street speakers, in fact, the woman is required not to ratify the male's attempt to gain the floor and initiate conversation. This is especially so in cases where *double entendre* is used, for—as only the covert subject of male conversation—a woman's attempt to become a ratified speaker in that conversation would be all the greater. Again, for white women, innuendo can, because of its veiled nature, be even more frightening than a direct sexual approach. A Southern woman speaks of walking in public past a group of observing men:

> As I walked past them it began.
> "Shore would like to have that swing in my backyard."
> "You want me to help you with your box, li'l lady?"
> "Hesh up, Alvin, that ain't nice. Don't you talk to her like that."

"I just want to help her with her box, thass all."

An explosion of mirth followed this riposte but it was quickly shushed by the man who had appointed himself my protector. There is always one Good Ole Boy in the lineup who takes on this role. Just as the minstrel show has an end man and a vaudeville team a top banana, any collection of Good Ole Boys has a Shucks Ma'am.

"Shucks, ma'am, he didn't mean to insult you. He just thinks yore mighty sweet, thass all."[16] [King, 1974, p. 79].

Other cases of *double entendre* may make props of actual or elaborated characteristics of the woman: one woman, holding a cat carrier with two cats in it, hears passing males talk in loud voices about the good-looking pussy they see; another woman feels a male gaze on her breasts, and hears one of the men she passes advise another that cantaloupes are now good eating in local markets. One effect of introducing topics taboo in polite conversation into public conversation is, and is meant to be, to embarrass the woman who cannot help but overhear them. Since the woman is only an overhearer and not a ratified speaker in the men's conversation, she is obliged to act as if she has not heard it in the first place; she is also obliged to act as if she had not heard it because there is a female tradition that to ignore male coarseness is a gender-role requirement. Finally, any clever reply a woman might make would open her to criticism for violating her feminine role propriety, since such a reply would be likely to include reference to, and certainly to ratify by recognition, sexual matters. The characteristic innuendo of many male-to-female street remarks also raises the more widespread sanction for males to assess female sexuality and propriety at will, transforming what ostensibly are business or service encounters, for example, into face-to-face engagements with sexual overtones. More generally still, many women experience a *double entendre* in everyday life, in focused as well as unfocused interaction, and at times when they least expect it. The potential for judging a woman's sexual propriety is thus always present in social life when she is in the age range considered sexually active; the occurrence of the *double entendre* in public life is therefore not unusual but simply consistent with a woman's general experience.

Another characteristic of street remarks is that they are often evaluative, and, ostensibly at least, evaluative in a positive way. Thus, male, and sometimes female, folk interpretations hold that these remarks are compliments. A proper compliment, however, is not given in public to the unacquainted, especially the unacquainted of the opposite sex, as male street remarkers do. Many men, moreover, prolong evaluations in ways that make it difficult plausibly to define the situation as complimentary: a man says "You're beautiful" to a young woman on a New York street, then follows her down the block repeating his evaluation every few seconds; a trio of Manhattan males clasp arms in a chorus line and break out singing "A Pretty Girl Is Like a Melody" at the sight of a young woman. When a woman responds with "Thank you," as in compliment etiquette among the acquainted, a man sometimes escalates into abuse. Or a man may speak of parts of her body that are normally not to be evaluated outside a bedroom, as reported in Babitz (1977, p. 15). Evaluations are not invariably positive ones, leading women who suspect that they are about to receive a street remark to fear it will be an insulting one. Then there are traditions of evaluation that encompass both positive and negative possibilities, such as the practice of rating women on a numerical scale. This emphasizes an aspect of street remarks that also leads women to fear them, namely, the variation between different street remarks within a certain time period.

Receiving first a five then a nine from different men within one day—and this happens—can be confusing to a woman, who may be made unsure about whether she is upholding the standard of femininity or degrading it.

A woman's appearance is, of course, a different entity from a man's. It is a part of every situation in which she finds herself; there are, in some sense, no dinners for which she does not have to dress. More, a woman's appearance is public information, addressed, as Goffman says, "to whom it may concern." Women may note that men delivering evaluative street remarks—even if they are positive—often fall below middle-class standards of dress, tidiness, and hygiene themselves. Women say they can more easily construe a street remark as complimentary if it comes from a well-dressed, attractive male of their own social class.[11]

An additional characteristic of street remarks is their construction of a woman's normal behavior as if it were out of role. As I have said, it is the right of every citizen, male or female, to remark in public upon the out-of-role behavior of persons not known to him or her personally. In male-to-female street remarks, however, men treat women acting within role as if they were breaking role constraints; many women consider that to react with anxiety or confusion to this is understandable.[12] For example: A woman walks down a Manhattan street with a Kleenex held to her nose, and a man says, "Whatsamatter, honey, you got a little cold? Aww . . . . " A young woman walks down a Philadelphia street on a windy day, her right hand held to her forehead to keep her headscarf in place; the young man approaching her raises *his* hand to his forehead and gives her a smart salute—a parody of the position that he wants her to believe she imitates. A young woman out in Manhattan on a chilly day hears a man say, "Whatsamatter with you. No stockings on a day like this." A young woman bicycling reaches down to roll up her pants leg and hears a passing motorist bellow, "Make sure you get it rolled up okay."

There is no sure way for a woman to pass down the street alone and not be commented upon. Accompanied by a man or a child, she furnishes evidence of proper in-role standing. But if she is alone, that standing is always in doubt and may be metaphorically spoken to by men. Indirect evidences of having, or having had, a man are also sometimes effective, such as being pregnant. Other types of accompaniment are ineffective, such as that of another youthful woman or women or that of an elderly male.

Still another characteristic of the male-to-female street remark is that it tests the woman's self-control. In form, many street remarks are attention-getters. Part of the ambiguity that results comes from the conventional requirements for civil inattention; that is, individuals are not supposed to be attentive to other individuals beyond certain limits. Too, traditionally prescribed female role behavior forbids women to speak to "strange males." Yet the overt form of a summons or attention-getter makes a claim on them, though it is a claim by an unacquainted person. Also, strangers do indeed have the right to make claims in certain situations, as when help is desired or some alarm is to be sounded. Women are therefore confronted by different reasons for breaking and maintaining frame: if they do choose to break frame, they are likely to find that they are the butt of a street remark instead of the recipient of a request for aid. A young woman walks past a New York stoop where she hears a man say sincerely, "Excuse me, miss." When she turns to see what he wants, he says, "You sure have got great boobs." A young woman sees a man roll down his car window and crackle a map with convincing helplessness; when she nears the car in response to his "Hey! Hey there!" he mutters obscenities to her. Passing a Philadelphia construction site, a young woman hears a slight cough, then a slightly louder cough, then a series of impressive coughs and a man say, "Hey! I'm dyin' of pneumonia—pneumonia I got!" She gives him a sheepish grin of sympathy and proceeds. A young woman walks past a group of young men, one of whom clears his throat lightly, then a bit more audibly, then a bit more audibly still, and, when she still does not respond, says, "What's the matter, you deaf?"[13]

A final problematic characteristic of the street remark for women is the occasional involvement of a split of functions for the men who utter it. This takes place in both single and group remarks, and it echoes an ambiguity that I have said is involved in many aspects of street remarks. Often when there are two or more males as speakers, a division of labor is presented for the female target: one male gives a respectful greeting, the other an evaluation vitiating the degree to which the woman can tell herself that she has received a simple bit of politeness and no more. Walking through Columbus Circle, a woman hears two hippies speak to her: the first exclaims, "Good morning, miss!" and the second chimes in, "Aw*right!*" and applauds softly. Walking by three welders on a university campus, a young woman hears the eldest say, "Good morning." She returns "Good morning" and immediately the youngest groans and says, "Ninety-nine." Sometimes one man will encompass both functions himself; he utters a first greeting remark and follows it with a second, evaluative one. Passing a grocery store where men are unpacking crates, a woman is greeted with "Good morning" by one worker. She turns her head and smiles, and he says, "Nice smile." At times, there is a frankly good guy/bad guy split when two men are involved. Walking past a street construction project, a young woman trips slightly. One black worker says sarcastically, "Oh, you don' wanna do *that*, now." She neither smiles nor replies, and a second black worker says brightly, "And how are you today?" Still she does not reply, and the first worker says contemptuously, "Miss Snot."

This split of functions leaves some women feeling confused and gulled: the second comment shows up the first as a sham, even if a woman attempts to consolidate the first definition by replying to it what it pretends to be. Knowledge that a street remark may turn out to be ambiguous in this way reduces a woman's opportunities for swift response, for she must choose the sense in which she is to take the remark, the greeting, or the evaluation. If she chooses the greeting, and if it has an abusive sequel, she has chosen to make the best of the man's rudeness; and this may happen not once, but ten times in a single day. Therefore the woman who tries to put the best face on street remarks may come to feel her good humor badly overworked.

Exploiting Breaches of Civil Inattention

The fact of the male-to-female street remark is in some respects an exploitation of the rules of civil inattention, since such remarks simultaneously require a woman (who is under greater role requirements to behave politely) to respond to an attempted opening and obliges a woman (who is also required to appear inaccessible to the public at large) to ignore it. In lower-level structural and formal ways, too, a woman becomes a participant in an exploitation of the rules of public order. I have shown, for instance, that there are tests of a woman's self-control in which a street remark masquerades as a summons for aid, information, or sympathy. There are many ways to work the situation that involve more complex tacks than an escalation to evaluative or second-move comments. For example, compliments are subject to certain rules in order to be taken sincerely within the frame of acquaintanceship in which they are customarily uttered. The parody of a compliment is not a compliment at all. Yet, in a male-to-female street remark, the parody of a compliment may be precisely what is given (and arguably—for the male, who is originating the breaching—all that is possible). Thus, the following three street remarks: A woman walks across campus and notes three men observing her. The first looks over, gives her a sincere smile, and says, "Nice nipples." She does not respond and hears his buddy say to him loudly, "I guess she doesn't like you." Again, a young woman walking in Philadelphia sees a young white approaching her from the opposite direction, watches him look her over approvingly and begin a traditional wolf whistle, and notes its transformation into the triumphal march from *Aïda*, which he continues to aim at her posterior for a full block. A black teenager approaches a woman in an underground subway passage. He is looking around sourly—his mind elsewhere, his expression says—and he is chewing the fingernail of his right index finger thoughtfully. With his free left hand he grabs the woman's breast as he passes, his eyes elsewhere, on more important matters. In these cases, the men violated three separate conditions—appropriate content, length, and degree of involvement—for giving a compliment.

In large urban centers, greetings are also only to be given to acquainted others, so that any street remark that simulates a greeting necessarily violates this constraint. Some males perform other parodies of greetings. Walking in Philadelphia, a young woman sees a black male approach her and hears him say, with a smile, "How the fuck are you?" She does not reply and continues on her way, but hears him yell, "How the fuck are you?" at her for two blocks from where he stands, finally yelling it at peak volume. This man violated the usual conditions for greetings not only by employing an obscene infix but also by failing to retire gracefully when his greeting was ignored.

Faced with situations that seem ambiguous on many grounds, women say they react in various ways. "Blocking" or "repressing" is mentioned, as is attempting to act as if "nothing is happening." Observing a woman who receives a street remark, one may note an increase in muscle tension, a too-fixed stare, eyes directed anywhere but at the male speaker, preenings and body checks, or the initiation of side involvements such as smoking—actions that are sometimes then used by men as resources for further comments.[14] Politicized women may see the obligation to act as if nothing is happening in order to maintain role requirements as fraudulent and an imposition; one has written of it as an obligation toward "autism" (Damrosch, 1975, p. 7).[15]

Another strategy women say they employ to deal with street remarks is to avoid—sometimes for years—the place where a particularly offensive remark has occurred. Women also say they avoid types of sites where they suspect street remarks are likely to occur and activities in which they feel remarks may ensue, such as bike riding. Or they say they may "be a block ahead of themselves" in terms of what is happening on the street. Women also report donning sunglasses so that men have less access to their reactions; adopting what they feel are "tough" and "businesslike" walks; avoiding what they feel is either too "provocative" or too casual dress;[16] and refraining from smiling while maintaining a serious, even "grim," facial expression.

Other women state specific maneuvers for transforming the street-remark situation into a comparatively harmless one. All involve the pretense of helplessness or incompetence, placing the offending male in a position of traditional chivalry and calling upon him to respond, out of his greater competence, with *noblesse oblige*. While this maneuver still relies on the male's being in a more powerful position, it is now the woman's initiative that has placed him there. A woman at an auto supply store who finds herself a target of pointed comments approaches a commentator and asks him for help, which she does not need, with her purchase; changing the footing of the situation, she finds the young man her willing adviser. Confronted by a leering attendant in a parking lot, a young woman trustingly approaches him and asks him the time; she receives a respectful answer and no further intrusion of gaze or comment. A teen-ager is followed by a man who delivers a monologue about her hair; she feigns deafness by making what she believes are appropriate noises, and the man apologizes to her. A woman approaching a construction site nods in a friendly manner to workers and greets them before they have a chance to speak. Male street remarks often put the woman in the position of ignoring what purports to be a greeting, a request for help, or a summons; women who use these tacks to defuse street remarks have effectively turned the tables on men and placed them in the very positions the women themselves fear. Exploiting breaches of civil inattention is thus a possibility for women as well as for men.

Men and Street Remarks: Socialization for Rejection

Women who answer back angrily to men who make street remarks often find that the man's next move is an escalation to a high level of verbal abuse. Male escalation after female reaction may in part be explained by the woman's having ratified an improper male attempt at getting the floor; when she does so, she changes the level of interaction, makes herself also an improper speaker, and formulates the pattern for the next turn.[17] Retaliation is not considered a feminine behavior. First, answering back constitutes a ratification of the interchange. The woman who has, up until that point, walked by as if she were unaware of the existence of male onlookers, has thereby not only ratified their offense but also exposed her own previous behavior as a fiction. Second, though some women are willing to dare a squelching remark, they seem unable to deal with the fact that a subsequent squelching remark (and then another) may be needed if the male chooses to take up the gauntlet. Small battles can be waged, then, up to perhaps one turn in length, but further escalation in this public context baffle the female verbal combatant. The reason for this may well be that, drawing again on traditional definitions of female privilege, she expects the male gracefully to withdraw.

Further, women are traditionally untrained for one of the ultimate consequences of verbal altercations, namely, physical altercations; when they choose to make a first move in a contest that, were it held among males, might easily come to blows, they may find that they are not qualified to make a second—and irremediable—one. Or they may make counterremarks more offensive than men would make. A final point is that the subject matter of a female remark to a male speaker would be, most appropriately, along the same lines of the male street remark, that is, a sexually humiliating remark or one that appraises his failure or success in achieving his gender-role expectations. In this case, however, the remarks would be members of two different universes, since males are not traditionally able to be humiliated sexually, at least not in the same way as females. Also, such remarks and such subject matter are not considered fit coming from a woman's mouth in private, much less on public streets. Women who say they do answer back report doing so only when they consider themselves in a safe situation where male retaliation is unlikely, when the remark is especially offensive, or when their mood is especially "bad."

Males thus serve notice that asymmetrical teasing (where the obligation to take the jest in good spirits can only be discharged by remaining silent or ignoring the remark) is the only possible form here. Furthermore, although asymmetrical teasing must be the case, the verbal content of the street remark often denies this. Women, allowed only nonresponse, are explicitly criticized for failing to respond; "What's the matter? Stuck up?" are familiar words. The accusation that a woman is displaying conceit is, of course, also an effort to find a response where none has occurred. It turns nonaction into action; considers that an offense; and responds accordingly. Other occasions may see men ignore women who answer back, breaking the frame and ending the breach after the street remark; they thereby transform the woman who has ratified their attempted intrusion upon herself a breacher of civil inattention.

One may say that there is more than one type of speech event taking place in the male-to-female street remark, depending upon whether one male or two or more males—a pair or group—is involved.[18] When one man is the speaker, any response on the woman's part, even if it is not angry or contemptuous, may elicit an escalation to hostility or even blows. It is with men in groups that the woman who responds will frequently hear male laughter, no matter what the nature of her response. The laughter may be analyzed as a relief move, and the need for such a move raises the question of what is at stake for males in street remarks.

The man who attempts to breach civil inattention by a male-to-female street remark is subject to as many definitional ambiguities as the woman who is its recipient. For him, the street remark may be a speech act whose function is to displace emotion toward women, and fear of rejection may be as relevant an emotion as hostility. There are several guards to a man's personal rejection when a woman resists the overture he presents. First, there is the impersonality of his remark—most remarks are stereotyped in nature, and all necessarily treat some aspect of a woman that is open to every other citizen in public. A man can therefore plausibly argue to himself, after a woman ignores him or sends him a withering glance, that since he made no personal overture, he can have suffered no personal rejection. Second, there is the brief nature of the street remark and the fact that it involves a moving linguistic target. By the time the man has risked a remark, a woman will have already passed by. Third, there are female gender-role constraints that, as the man must know, make it unlikely that a woman will counter with a hostile or embarrassing remark. Fourth, there is the street remark's use of innuendo and *double entendre*; this ensures that a man may hedge his bets whenever he chooses.

Yet there are simultaneously several features that ensure that the man, though he may not risk losing in any dangerous way, will always be rejected by the woman. Just as women are unlikely to respond in a hostile way, they are unlikely to respond positively; this too would violate their role requirements. By far the most frequent female reaction is ignoring the man or "acting as if nothing has happened." Men who make street remarks are thereby setting up the conditions for their own rejection. One possible positive reading of this ritual is its function as an informal means of socialization toward rejection by females. Street remarks may, in this way, furnish tests of expressive self-control for men as well as for women, socializing men for failure in more serious attempts to secure the attentions of women. The coda of laughter at the end of a street remark is not (or not merely) laughter at the woman, then, but also a sincere relief move for the man who has survived a mocked-up rejection with his ego intact. Too, the man who displaces anger or hostility in street remarks toward women he does not know may be less likely to display it in real-life situations. This explanation also makes comprehensible the habit of the street remark to treat women's normal behavior as if it were out-of-role behavior. Not only does this mimic the rules of justifiable breaches of civil inattention, but it provides an understandable topic for men socializing themselves toward female rejection: a woman's failure or success in winning status as a person worthy of rejecting males in the first place.

I have examined one instance of breaching civil inattention, the male-to-female street remark, and demonstrated characteristics of it that make it difficult for women to receive it positively. I have also argued that there are, for both men and women, possible functions of the street remark as tests of expressive self-control: women are taught to refrain from unseemly gender-role behavior in public and to accept the criticisms of men; men are socialized to maintain calm in the face of female rejection. From an examination of justifiable reasons for breaching civil inattention, I have concluded that the street remark is one that often treats women who are behaving within role as if they were behaving in an out-of-role fashion. That women are commonly so treated in public places, and that their appearance is a ready resource for public comment, demonstrates their very different public nature from that of men. Men, of course, are licensed to make the commentary and, in short, act as if public spaces were home territory for them in this respect. The presence of women on public streets thus has a positive function for men, who may use their presence to reassure themselves that public places are, in fact, not so anonymous after all. Nor are address rights the only rights men have toward women in public, for I have shown that there are a wide range of nonlinguistic markers that signal and comment upon a woman's presence. Taken together, and taken in the volume in which they may occur in large cities, street remarks and markers of passage help to explain why some women reasonably regard the city streets with what seems to others paranoia: a constant series of announcements of female status always seems a possibility. Although women are often disturbed by street remarks—if not by all of them, at least by some—the ways they report dealing with these remarks reinforce traditional definitions of the male as chivalrous and the woman as manipulative. Even if women respond, they are still in a position that is more subject to breaches of public order than is a man's. Men do find street remarks unobjectionable, for the most part, or consider them the woman's just deserts, and this highlights that their positive function for the male—a socialization effort that tests his ability to receive rejection—can involve as much risk as its function for the female, which is to learn to accept criticism in a properly passive way.

NOTES

Twenty University of Pennsylvania students and teachers (ten male and ten female) took part in the unstructured interviews that I speak of in the paper. My interviewees, I should note, were all white, so that this paper does not deal with black-male-to-black-female talk in public; this involves arguably different types of speech acts participating in a different verbal tradition.

1. The term *civil inattention* is Goffman's (1963, p. 84 and p. 95), and my usage of it follows his own. A recent work of Goffman's (1978) has supplied a careful statement of the assumptions and concerns of the solitary breacher of civil inattention, and a great many observations on more complicated breachings as well.

That talk is so warranted an event in large cities these days must be seen in light of other possibilities for behavior. First of all, life in smaller towns, in the South and Southwest, and in rural areas does not participate in the general haltness of speech of the big cities. If this is an American pattern, then, it is by no means generalized, and the American who travels even short distances can be sure of seeing variation. Second, certain neighborhoods within the large cities may themselves abide by different rules. Notable among these are black and Italian neighborhoods of New York and Philadelphia, where the street is conceived of as an extension of the home (a conception well described in Brown, 1965, p. 428).

2. Scheflen (1972, pp. 35–37) discusses such phenomena—though not specifically the signals I have spoken of—as markers of "territorial passage," concentrating more on the ethological interpretation. I should also note that the examples I have gathered all involve a female as the recipient of the marker and a male as the originator. Markers, though more delicate ones, do take place when male passes male, and markers are given by females too; a study of these would be welcome.

3. Millman (1980, pp. 9–10, p. 79, p. 85, pp. 184–85) gives examples of fat people open to public commentary.

4. For examples of public commentary on interracial couples, as well as on whites in black neighborhoods and blacks in the white South, see Gregory (1970).

5. It is noteworthy that both these examples involved black males. Some women are quick to say that they consider blacks in a different category when the question of feeling offense at street remarks comes up. Blacks are felt to be capable of remarks of greater offensiveness than whites but also of remarks that mitigate offense in ways that white males do not accomplish. It is arguable that, since street repartee is more a part of the black courting behavior than it is of white, blacks may in fact possess the greater skills in these situations that some white women feel them to. (For an instance of black-to-black street repartee that results in a legitimate acquaintance between two theretofore unacquainted persons, see Cooke, 1972, p. 40. Abrahams, n.d., pp. 31–32, presents instances of black males well versed in the art of "signifying," that is, making pointed *double entendres*, in this case about women they observe on the street. Black women are assumed by both authors to take these practices euphorically, and their freedom to make remarks in return is emphasized, though some black women I know feel the obligation to engage in repartee in return more of a burden than an opportunity to show off speech skills.) More than simply skills at street remarks, the men in these two examples may have had at stake the defusing of offense not for the white woman's gain, but for their own protection. By showing that they considered themselves no serious suitors, they thereby bypassed the possibility that they could be seriously refused on racial grounds or that they could constitute a racial threat to nearby white males.

6. Women's fantasies, when they have them, about the possible outcome of speaking back to male street remarkers often involve such immediate reversals of male affect. Several of these are presented in Medea and Thompson (1974, p. 73). The men that Medea and Thompson confront hypothetically always obediently turn tail and apologize or simply cower. I will suggest later that this is by no means the case in real life and that the innocuous intent of males is not the case everywhere.

7. In this same category, in which the undeserving receive praise, are incidents such as that of the woman I interviewed who believed herself to be flat-chested and reported as a compliment a man who passed her on the street and said in a heartfelt manner, "Nice tits!" A wheelchair-bound woman of my acquaintance counts each wolf whistle a compliment and an entré into normality.

8. At least half of the ten young university women with whom I spoke used the "object" simile, one saying that being spoken to freely on the street made her feel as though there were a placard in the window with her name and number for all to read. Eight of the ten young women spoke of male-to-female street remarks as "invasions of privacy." An extended analogy is also offered in Shear's "Free Meat Talks Back" (1976, pp. 38–39).

9. Nine out of the ten women interviewed remembered either the first time that a male gave them a street remark or had a "worst" or "most memorable" street-remark story. Two of these women also

offered street remarks that could be taken as compliments as "best" stories; in both cases, however, these were presented as exceptions that proved the rule.

10. See Medea and Thompson (1974, pp. 49–50) and Russell (1975, p. 168). Eight out of the ten women interviewed mentioned rape as having similarities with male-to-female street remarks.

11. There is a class element here, since traditional folk wisdom has it that only lower-class men deliver street remarks (in the interviews, men who admitted to making street remarks often charged this themselves). Women who believe that men of their own social class are delivering compliments when they deliver street remarks may therefore be protecting their class interests rather than their gender interests.

12. Men who treat women as if they were acting out of role thereby have also created a partial justification for their own behavior, for they are certainly allowed to breach the rules for civil inattention when they note a citizen out of role.

13. The entire category of required female self-control under male public attention-getters and summonses recalls those children's games where holding a pose or refraining from giggling is required; these are perhaps youthful training for purposeful adult ignorings of this sort. Inevitably, some women find that the attention-getter they have suspected of signaling a male-to-female street remark was actually sincere, as in the case of a woman who pointedly ignored a series of "Heys" only to discover later that the speaker was trying to return the fifty dollars in bills that had fallen out of her purse.

14. Collett and Marsh (1974) speak of women's performing "physically more difficult avoidance movements than men" on public streets (p. 10). Such movements involve, among other things, breast protection by torso turning and arm crossing. Their findings present another sort of feminine behavior that simultaneously achieves "nothing is happening" status and serves notice that women's bodies are to be protected even from an uninterested public at large.

15. The advice literature in feminist sources is more active, even spirited. (The basic position is represented by Lesbian Feminist Liberation: 1974.) Some women recommend yelling back, answering back, throwing rocks, copying down the names of men in company trucks and reporting them (Goldman, 1974, p. 5). An article furnishes an official complaint form to send to employers ("Wolf Hunting: Plan of Action," 1976); it also reports the availability of insulting cards to hand out to street remarkers ("This card has been chemically treated. In approximately 36 hours your prick will fall off"). Another woman reports throwing bags of garbage during New York's garbage strike; hawking phlegm from her throat and spitting; staring contemptuously at the man's crotch (Letter in *Ms.*, 1977, p. 12).

16. See Williamson (1971), where a feminist argues that women should affect "studied ugliness" in order to make their public life less traumatic. Her line of reasoning, however, is that clothes provoke disrespect and ill treatment by males in public. More careful sociological analysis of clothing, such as Wax's (1965), emphasizes the social construction that this is, for it is sociability, rather than sexuality, that is at the root of what women are supposed to present by their grooming. Thus, they are supposed to argue with their clothing that they are accessible to some men, but certainly not to all men, as Williamson's argument implies.

17. When men do not escalate to anger, they may use the woman's anger as a resource for still another remark. Colette and Willy's *Young Lady of Paris* reported an early example: "I've been out shopping for dresses and hats," her Claudine writes. "A man followed me and I had the unfortunate idea of sticking my tongue out at him. 'Oh, give that to me,' he said, and I'll know enough not to do that again" (1931, pp. 88–89). One woman interviewed reported that she and other teen-agers yelled back at cruising teen-age boys and were followed in turn by the boys for some time. Another woman reported saying, "Mind your own business," to which a man countered, "You're my business, honey"; she offered no topper of her own. That there is official male outrage at women's answering back is demonstrated by the story of a woman who lost her job on a newspaper for giving some firemen the finger after they had "made remarks about her legs, shouted 'Hey Baby,' etc." The official reason was that her reaction "casts a reflection on the objectivity of the paper" and that she "should have shown more feminine control," supplying informal support for the street remark as a test of expressive control. (Reported in *Majority Report*, Feb. 5–18, 1977.)

18. There is a considerable literature, both fictional and nonfictional, that emphasizes the sportive elements of the group street remark. Literature shows the street remark and "girl-watching," its eye-contact concomitant, as recreative. Examples can be found in Farrell ([1935] 1965, pp. 122–23); Pynchon (1973, pp. 32–34); Sillitoe ([1960] 1976, pp. 148–49). Factual writing shows it in a similar light (Cherry, 1974; Riemer, 1976). Sometimes sportsmen carry the imagery far, as in the case one of my male interviewees reported. The summer of the 1976 Olympics, male university students lined up on the roof of a fraternity house armed with a set of numeral ratings, which they held up in response to female

students passing by on the walk below. A second audience of males on the opposite side of the walk then applauded or booed the decision of the "judges."

REFERENCES

ABRAHAMS, R. D. "Negotiating Respect: Patterns of Presentation Among Black Women," *Journal of American Folklore*, 1975, *88*, pp. 58-80.
BABITZ, E. "My Life in a 36DD Bra, or the All-American Obsession." *Ms.*, June 1977, pp. 15-17.
BAKER, T., and JONES, R. *Coffee, Tea, or Me?* New York: Bantam Books, 1969.
BROWN, C. *Manchild in the Promised Land.* New York: Signet Books, 1965.
CAVAN, S. *Liquor License.* Chicago: Aldine, 1966.
CHERRY, M. *On High Steel.* New York: Ballantine Books, 1974.
COLETTE and WILLY. *Young Lady of Paris* (J. Whitall, trans.). New York: Albert & Charles Boni, 1931.
COLLETT, P., and MARSH, P. "Patterns of Public Behavior: Collision Avoidance on a Pedestrian Crossing." Mimeographed report, Department of Experimental Psychology, Oxford University, January 1974.
COOKE, B.G. "Nonverbal Communication Among Afro-Americans: An Initial Classification." In Thomas Kochman (ed.), *Rappin' and Stylin' Out.* Urbana: University of Illinois Press, 1972.
DAMROSCH, B. "The Sex Ray." *The Village Voice*, April 7, 1975, p. 7.
"Do You Act Like a Beauty?" *Glamour,* January 1969, pp. 138-39.
FARRELL, J.T. *Studs Lonigan.* New York: New American Library, 1965. (Originally published 1935.)
GOFFMAN, E. *Behavior in Public Places.* New York: Free Press, 1963.
GOFFMAN, E. *Relations in Public.* New York: Harper & Row, 1978.
GOFFMAN, E. "Response Cries." *Language*, 1978, *54*, 4.[Included in this volume.]
GOLDMAN, J. "Walk Down Any Street and Be a Prisoner of War." *Majority Report*, August 22, 1974, p. 5.
GREGORY, S. *Hey, White Girl!* New York: Norton, 1970.
GRENFELL, J. *Joyce Grenfell Requests the Pleasure.* London: Futura, 1976.
HENNESSEY, C. *I, B.I.T.C.H.* New York: Lancer Books, 1970.
KING, F. "The Good Ole Boy: A Southern Bell's Lament." *Harper's*, April 1974, pp. 78-82.
Lesbian Feminist Liberation, "Media: Of Ogling and TV News." *Majority Report*, October 3, 1974, p. 7.
Letter. *Ms.*, October 1977, p. 12.
MEDEA, A., and THOMPSON, K. *Against Rape.* New York: Farrar, Straus & Giroux, 1974.
MILLMAN, M. *Such a Pretty Face.* New York: Norton, 1980.
PYNCHON, T. *V.* New York: Bantam Books, 1973.
RICHIE, M. "A Paleness of Heart." *Harper's*, June 1973, p. 71-72.
RIEMER, J. " 'Deviance' as Fun: A Case of Building Construction Workers at Work." Paper presented at 71st annual meeting of American Sociological Association, New York, August 30 to September 3, 1976.
ROSSNER, J. *To the Precipice.* New York: Popular Library, 1966.
RUSSELL, D. E. H. *The Politics of Rape.* Briarcliff Manor, N.Y.: Stein and Day, 1975.
SCHEFLEN, A. *Body Language and Social Order.* Englewood Cliffs, N.J.: Prentice-Hall, 1972.
SHEAR, M. "Free Meat Talks Back." *Journal of Communication*, 1976, *26*, 38-39.
SILLITOE, A. *The Loneliness of the Long-Distance Runner.* London: Star, 1976. (Originally published 1960.)
SPRADLEY, J., and MANN, B. *The Cocktail Waitress: Woman's Work in a Man's World.* New York: Wiley, 1975.
TAX, M. "Woman and Her Mind." In Koedt, Levine, and Rapone (eds.), *Radical Feminism.* New York: Quadrangle, 1973.
WAX, M. "Themes in Cosmetics and Grooming." In M. E. Roach and J. B. Eicher (eds.), *Dress, Adornment, and the Social Order.* New York: Wiley, 1965.
WILLIAMSON, N. "The Case for Studied Ugliness." *Second Wave*, 1971, *1*, 10-11.
"Wolf Hunting: Plan of Action." *Majority Report*, September 4-17, 1976.

SECTION THREE

LANGUAGE AND SPEECH IN ETHNOGRAPHIC PERSPECTIVE

Dell Hymes conceived the term "ethnography of speaking" as a label for a particular anthropological approach to language and speech. Ethnography, as this concept has come to be used by anthropologists, involves both theory and method. Its aim is to elucidate the native point of view—of an event, an institution, or an entire community or society. Ethnography of speaking deals with the cultural organization of language use, in terms of both underlying conceptions and shared understandings about the role of language in social and cultural life and the structuring of actual speaking practices. Methodologically it combines several approaches, all aspects of the basic anthropological practice of participant observation in natural settings. Central to ethnography of speaking has been a focus on the variety of speech events that are found in a community, and their analysis in cultural, social, and linguistic terms. Attention to native concepts and labels is important to ethnography of speaking as to all ethnography. One salient aspect of ethnography of speaking has been its concern with artistic and symbolic properties of language and speech, as well as social interactional strategies. Analysis involves small as well as large verbal patterns, everyday and ordinary as well as formal and ritual speech, and the details and realities of face-to-face communicative behavior along with the underlying, ongoing social and cultural themes.

Much of ethnography of speaking has been cross-cultural in orientation, stressing the various ways in which people around the world differ in their use of the language. The papers by ELINOR OCHS and JOEL SHERZER are illustrative. In her study of Malagasy oratory, Ochs focuses on the relationship between speech styles and social structure, conflicts in speech norms, and the strategies and emergent qualities involved in actual performances. In his analysis of a Kuna story and its telling, Sherzer describes the various interpretations that are inherent in the story and the ways in which performers manipulate them strategically. Both of these papers stress the role of cultural beliefs in the structuring of verbal events, and the constant interplay between linguistic structure and sociocultural context.

RICHARD BAUMAN investigates the role of storytelling in dog trading in Canton, Texas. His approach involves a combination of social interaction and ethnographic perspectives. While of obvious importance to students of Western American folklore, his paper has significance that goes well beyond the analysis of narrative per se. Its discussion of lies, cons, and social structure link it to the work of ERVING GOFFMAN (Section Two), especially his concept of frame. The most broadly theoretical of the papers in this section is that of JUDITH T. IRVINE, who summarizes much research in sociolinguistics and ethnography of speaking concerning the dimensions of formality and informality in communication, proposing a useful, general overview. Drawing on her own research among the Wolof as well as recent published reports dealing with other societies, she shows the dynamic qualities of the formality/informality relationship, serving not only tradition, but also creativity and change.

The concept of ethnography of speaking goes hand in hand with that of communicative competence, which integrates linguistic competence with social, social interactional, and cultural competence. The acquisition and development of communicative competence involves learning to produce and perceive functionally meaningful linguistic distinctions and to master rules for language use. BAMBI B. SCHIEFFELIN's study of a social relationship among the Kaluli of Papua New Guinea, and the verbal interactions associated with it demonstrates the way in which the acquisition of linguistic competence and the acquisition of social competence are intertwined.

SELECTED BIBLIOGRAPHY

BAUMAN, R., and SHERZER, J. (eds.). 1974. *Explorations in the Ethnography of Speaking.* New York: Cambridge University Press.

GUMPERZ, J.J., and HYMES, D.H. (eds.). 1964. *The Ethnography of Communication.* Washington, D.C.: American Anthropologist. Special publication no. 66.

————. 1972. *Directions in Sociolinguistics: The ethnography of communication.* New York: Holt, Rinehart & Winston.

HYMES, D. 1974. *Foundations of Sociolinguistics: An ethnographic approach.* Philadelphia: University of Pennsylvania Press.

ELINOR OCHS

A Sliding Sense of Obligatoriness:
The Poly-Structure of Malagasy Oratory

MAJOR MODES OF SPEAKING

The notion of oratory on the plateau area of Madagascar must be understood in terms of local notions of speaking. Generally, there are two major modes of speaking. The first is called *resaka*. *Resaka* can be loosely defined as informal conversation. Elders describe it as *teny andavanandro* ('everyday talk') or *teny tsotra* ('simple talk'). The second major mode of speaking is *kabary*. *Kabary* is ceremonial speech, what we might call oratory.

Kabary contrasts with *resaka* in a number of ways. First of all, whereas *resaka* is characteristic of informal situations, casual encounters, *kabary* is characteristic of formal situations. For example, most ceremonial events—circumcisions, marriages, deaths, bone-turnings—include oratory performed in the *kabary* mode. The use of *kabary* can itself create formal situations, such as in the expression of thanksgiving by a guest to his host at the end of a visit.

Secondly, one who uses the *kabary* mode must *manolaka ny teniny* 'wind his words'. That is, he must speak in an allusive manner. Elders say that *kabary* differs from *resaka* in that the former requires that the speaker draw circles around an idea (*miodidina*) where the latter does not. In both *resaka* and *kabary*, winding speech is highly valued. But in *kabary*, it is obligatory, whereas in *resaka* it is merely preferred.

Winding speech entails more than simply speaking in a roundabout manner. It demands that the speaker have command of a large repertoire of stylistic devices. He must, for example, use numerous *ohatra* ('examples, comparisons') in presenting his talk. And beyond this, he must know a range of *ohabolana* ('proverbs') appropriate to specific topics. Requiring the most skill are *hainteny*, passages of extended metaphor. These *hainteny* focus on the habits of plants and animals in the local environment. A skilled orator uses *hainteny* to allude to some corresponding human behaviour. For example, in expressing his humble status, an orator might use the *hainteny*:

> *Ary indrindra, indrindra fa toy ny tsimbotry miaraka amin-adrisa aho, ka tsy tompon-dia fa mpanaraka! Tsikirity momba fody, tsy tompon-dalana fa mpanohy dia . . .*

And especially, especially: Like the tiny grasshopper going with adult grasshoppers am I, so not a leader of the journey but a follower! The midget bullfinch about the cardinal, not a maker of roads but a continuer . . .

From *Language in Society*, Vol. 2, 1973, pp. 225-43. Reprinted with permission of Cambridge University Press and Elinor Ochs.

All of the genres used in creating winding speech are *entin-drazana*, traditional speech ways given to the present generation by the ancestors. And, traditionally, any member of the community who assumes the role of orator must have competence in these traditional forms. Certainly today, when people say of another "Yes, he speaks Malagasy well," they mean that person knows how to wind his speech through example, proverb and natural metaphor.

A third important difference seperating *kabary* from *resaka* is that *kabary* performances are governed by rules which are in theory known and understood by most members of the community. Of course, there are systematic rules which govern everyday talk, particularly routines such as greetings, partings, excusing oneself and so on, but these rules are both less explicit and less interesting to members of the community; and furthermore, they cover a less extended piece of discourse. Rules of *kabary* performance, on the other hand, are a frequent point of departure for long discussions by local elders, particularly during the ceremonial season, when *kabary* are given several times a week in different villages.

Kabary as a focal point of tradition and as a focal point of artistic expression is, then, regarded with keen interest. It is not uncommon to see groups of elders evaluating the skills and approaches of speechmakers following a *kabary* performance. A speechmaker who pleases his audience is rewarded with praise such as: "He is a very sharp speechmaker." "He is prepared." "He is a true speechmaker, a child of his father." His words are said to be 'well arranged' and 'balanced'. His performance is described as 'satisfying'. But it is rare for all elders to agree completely in their evaluations. Typically, some elders consider a speechmaker as able, while others consider him as merely a student of the *kabary*, as yet unaccomplished. Evaluations are based on both skill in handling winding speech and on one's ability to follow certain rules governing the sequence and content of particular oratory. Differences in evaluation reflect different ideas as to what these rules in fact are.

The focus of this presentation will be on the argumentative aspects of *kabary* structure. One particular *kabary* performance has been selected for analysis, the *kabary vodiondry* or marrige request *kabary*. This *kabary* provides some of the richest material on structural disagreement. It is considered by elders to be the most difficult *kabary* to perform. It is a source of endless post-performance talk. But, further, talk about the *kabary* structure appears in the *kabary* itself. It is characteristic of marriage request *kabary* that they be *mafana* ('heated'), that is, with disagreements.

THE MARRIAGE REQUEST KABARY

Let us consider first the basic structure of all *kabary* performances. These structural features are not a source of disagreement. Elders agree that they are essential to any performance. *Kabary* always require a minimum of two speechmakers. The performance must be a dialogue. The speechmakers are said to *mifamaly* ('answer one another'). Answering is considered as a privilege of all listeners. A *kabary* which permits no answer is, in the words of one speechmaker, the speech of a dictator. Normally, a speechmaker closes his remarks with a request for those listening to reply, to continue the talk:

> *Hianareo no hanohy maito, hanohy ny tapaka sy hanentina ny madilana. Araka ny fitenenana io dia hoe: Raha misy tsy feno io, dia fenoy izay!*
>
> It is you (plural) who are to continue the link, to breach the gap, and to darn the hole. As the expression says: If there is something not complete in this talk, then complete it!

The speechmaker is requesting that those listening comment on his speech. Generally, he is soliciting their support. In these circumstances, absence of an answer is a serious insult indicating that the speechmaker is not supported by other participants present. Typically, even if there is disagreement, an answer will be supplied.

The *kabary vodiondry*, or marriage request *kabary*, requires two speechmakers, one representing the family of the girl, the other representing the family of the boy. Great care is taken to recruit able orators, for the *kabary* is difficult to complete. Traditionally, an elder kinsman from the father's line is requested to speak for the family. It often happens, however, that no elder is qualified within the family to perform this *kabary*. In these cases, it is necessary to hire a semiprofessional speechmaker in the area. In all cases, the speechmaker must be male. Women are excluded from this role. They are considered to have less tact and subtlety than men—both essential qualities in *kabary* performances. Women cannot be relied upon to always maintain respect despite disagreement, they say. They tend to be hotheaded and openly express anger or hostility (Keenan, 1974).

The marriage request itself takes place in the village of the girl's father. Typically a courtyard is cleared and decorated with sisal leaves. Long tables are placed at either end of the area. It is at these tables that elders of both families sit and face one another. Elders of the girl sit at one end; elders of the boy at the other. The main speechmakers sit with these elders.

The day of the marriage request finds kinsmen and neighbors of the girl's family gathering together in the family's village waiting for the arrival of the boy's family. As the latter approach, no official notice is taken until their speechmaker initiates a series of requests to enter the village. The speechmaker representing the girl's family consults elders on either side of him. If it is agreed that the speechmaker has performed this step of the *kabary* adequately, then he and those he represents may enter the area reserved for the request *kabary*. Otherwise, they must wait, and the speechmaker must repeat his efforts.

This general pattern continues throughout the performance of the *kabary*. It is the boy's speechmaker who initiates each step of the *kabary* and the girl's speechmaker who responds with an evaluation. He may agree with the words of the first speechmaker. He may approve his handling of that step and urge him to proceed with the next step to be completed. Or, on the other hand, he may indicate that the other's words are not *ara-dalana*, according to tradition. There is an error in his *kabary*. When a speechmaker responds as such, he is said to *manao fandrika*, 'make traps'. Before the *kabary* can continue, the speechmaker from the boy's side must do one of two things. Either he must be able to justify his handling of the *kabary*, show that no error has been made or he must admit his error. A speechmaker who successfully defends his approach is said to *manala fandrika*, 'open the trap,' that is, free himself from the trap. A speechmaker who admits error is said to be *voa fandrika*, 'caught in the trap'. He must correct his error by first repeating the relevant step in the correct manner and secondly paying a small fine to the girl's family.

The privilege of making traps rests only with the speechmaker for the girl's family. The boy's speechmaker cannot make traps in his own right. As in all formal requests, the party who does the requesting is considered to be inferior to those to whom the request is directed. And one means of persuading the latter is for the requestor to exaggerate this inequality. It is typical, for example, for the speechmaker for the boy to criticize himself severely, while exhalting the virtues of the other speaker. In this sense, the boy's speaker is willing to be 'caught' in a trap a few times, as this indicates to all present that he is truly inferior to the speechmaker he faces. Traps and fines demonstrate the humility of the boy's family and their respect for the family of the girl.

To accomplish the request, the requestors must please those to whom the request is put. To please the requestors must proceed through the *kabary* in a manner acceptable to this party. And acceptability always rests on whether or not the speechmaker spoke *ara-dalana* 'according to tradition'.

But what does it mean to speak *ara-dalana*? This question is the fly in the ointment. Knowledge of traditional speech norms is not widespread. There are very few men who can recall, for example, the lengthy format of *kabary* performed several generations back. The relative unavailability of this information has two interesting consequences: First of all, such knowledge is prized. One who is knowledgeable in this area is not simply a *ray amandreny* ('elder') but a *tena ray aman-dreny* ('true (wise) elder'). Familiarity with traditional speech norms can, then, enhance one's personal status in the community.

It takes no great stretch of the imagination to realize that *kabary* performances serve these personal ends of the speechmaker. They are platforms for exhibiting knowledge of the traditional oratory. In the marriage request *kabary*, the speechmakers are concerned not only with the matter at hand, the marriage contract. They are greatly concerned with maintaining or enhancing their status as *tena ray aman-dreny*. The making and breaking of 'traps' must be seen in this light. The speechmaker for the girl's family may display his knowledge by indicating errors or gaps in the oratory of his adversary by making traps. The boy's speechmaker, on the other hand, shows his skill by successfully freeing himself from these traps and by generally proceeding with as few errors as possible. The speechmaker for the boy is then in a bind. He needs to admit a few errors to be a successful 'requestor', to show honor to the girl's family. But, as a speechmaker and elder, he does not wish to be trapped too often lest his status suffer. A consequence of this is that a *kabary* performance may break into a heated debate over the point of what constitutes speaking *ara-dalana*.

The issue is further complicated by the fact that even outside the performance arena, elders do not agree on rules for traditional oratory. In interviews, some speechmakers claimed that there were seven steps to the marriage request *kabary* and that proverbs were not part of traditional oratory. Others said that there are twelve steps and that proverbs are a critical element in all *kabary*. Still other elders representing the traditional approach would say that there are three important parts to accomplish in the marriage request *kabary*. We cannot say that there is even a unified ideal of the marriage *kabary*. This means that when speechmakers approach the performance setting, they may bring different conceptualizations of what constitutes a *kabary*. In the three marriage request performances which this

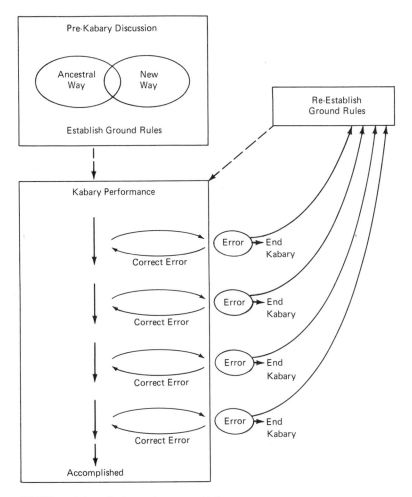

FIGURE 1.   Schematic of a marriage request kabary.

ethnographer witnessed and recorded, this was the case. Each speechmaker expected to perform a *kabary* which did not coincide with the other's expectations.

THE FIRST MAJOR POINT TO BE ESTABLISHED IN THIS PAPER IS THAT THERE IS NO ONE UNIFIED CONCEPT OF THE *kabary* SHARED BY ALL MEMBERS OF THE SPEECH COMMUNITY.

Speechmakers base their concept of *kabary* on a variety of sources. Some rely on pamphlets sold weekly in local town markets. These pamphlets focus on one or two types of *kabary* performances, advising would-be speechmakers on oratorical technique. Typically these pamphlets guarantee immediate personal success if the reader adheres to the suggested format: "The book will help you considerably in your ability. And remember that those who eagerly read books must become clever in the *kabary*, even those who are not able at all" (preface to *Kabary Malagasy araka ny Fomba Tranainy sy Vaovao* by Randria, Joseph). But this literature is limited to those who can read well and memorize passages to impress listeners.

More typically, *kabary* lore is passed down orally from one knowledgeable elder to some younger man interested in maintaining these speech ways. In some households as well, there are journals written by male elders and passed on to succeeding generations. Among other items, these journals contain notes on *kabary* format, proverbs appropriate to particular *kabary* and so on (Bloch 1968). The best of traditional speechmakers will incorporate a bit from market pamphlets, a bit from what they learned as a child observing *kabary* performances, a bit from these journals and so on, to produce a rich *kabary*. To consider the structure of the marriage *kabary* as commonly shared is to ignore this variation. Traditions which are passed on through families differ from the gospel of the market literature. And then, traditions between families vary. Finally, we have to consider individual variation (personal style), particularly in the case of the semi-professional speechmaker, who sifts through a number of sources to determine 'the structure'.

Given that notions of what is obligatory in a *kabary* vary, let us return to a point made earlier. To successfully accomplish the marriage request, the speechmaker for the boy must proceed through the *kabary* without making serious errors which he cannot correct. He must somehow free himself from the traps set by the girl's family. BUT, IF THE NOTION OF OBLIGATORY RULE IS NOT FIXED, WHAT CONSTITUTES AN 'ERROR'? Here is the crucial point which dominates these *kabary* performances. The actual structure of any one performance depends on how this issue is resolved.

Let us now turn to the performances themselves and examine behaviour which demonstrates that the notion of obligatory rule and therefore of error is variable.

VARIATION AND ITS HANDLING

1.   *Pre-kabary Discussions*.   That notions of *kabary* structure differ is well-recognized by members of the community. To avoid major conflicts on this subject in the actual request performance, the families of both the boy and the girl meet beforehand, often together with the delegated speechmakers. (In traditional times, the speechmakers were not revealed to one another until the actual performance.) In these discussions, a compromise is worked out between what the girl's family expects to be the *kabary* and what the boy's family expects. They establish at this time what are to be the ground rules for the performance. In this way, the possibility of direct loss-of-face, of open confrontation in the performance is greatly reduced. When the boy's speechmaker begins the actual request *kabary*, he frequently refers back to these arrangements. In the request which took place in the village in which the ethnographer lived, the first words of the approaching speechmaker were:

> If the program has changed then we will go back, but if there are no changes then we will proceed as agreed.

And the speechmaker for the girl answered:

> The program has not changed from our agreement.

What constitutes an error then is relative to these pre-arranged ground rules.

2.   *Arguments in Kabary*.   In fact, the ground rules are typically never conclusively formulated and agreed upon, and so arguments do appear in the request performance. In the request *kabary* contrived for my benefit by professional speechmakers, these critical arguments were not apparent. But in the actual request *kabary* where the speechmakers represented the interests of different families, arguments over ground rules were maintained from beginning to nearly the end.

The arguments as to why an error had been made or, conversely, as to why an error had not been made are precisely the stuff out of which great speechmakers are made. At these points in the *kabary*, the skill of the orator is tested, and all rhetorical devices are called into play. In order for the *kabary* to proceed, one side has to convince the other that it is correct. The orator appeals to emotion—what the young couple want, what the family want, what the ancestors wanted—and to what he considers to be a fact, that is, what he considers to be the ground rules established by both families. As one of these major dialogues mushrooms, reference to pre-*kabary* discussions becomes more frequent. Lengthy accounts as to what each side said at that time are recounted. For example:

> Girl's speechmaker: We asked for but did not see that which was decided at the meeting arranged by you together. But this is what was heard then by us: "How should this business at Ambano (village of girl) be? Will there be a real *kabary* or...? This is an affair of the family and the father's name, so we will give blessing to one another according to the way they (the girl's family) do it." Then the people there said: "Hah! This will be a big *kabary* sir. We will answer one another until the sun sets." We can not hide sir, so this was heard by us. So now here are your words. The words of the speechmakers understood by us. What was agreed by you then (is not done now). So lest we are deceived... A *kabary* was given by us and a *kabary* is expected to be heard by us. (From *kabary* at Ambano.)

3. *Adherence to Contrastive Approaches*. In appealing to 'fact', the speechmaker goes beyond reference to the consensus established previously by both sides. He singles out one particular approach as the one he believes in and follows. In all three of the request *kabary* I witnessed, two major approaches to handling the *kabary* were referred to. One approach was referred to as *fomban-drazana*, the 'ancestral custom', and the other was termed *lalana vaovao*, the 'new way'. It is not simply that some speechmakers know less than others. Some speechmakers positively prefer the new way over the ancestral format.

This distinction is particularly striking between speechmakers of different generations. Many of the younger speechmakers are anxious to complete this ceremony with as little fuss as possible. They have been exposed to the French system of education, and many hold jobs in local towns. Whereas traditionally, these affairs are to be handled with subtlety and indirectness (winding speech), in terms of *lalana vaovao*, they are to proceed in a simple and straightforward manner. Some advocators of the *lalana vaovao* actually want to avoid performing the *kabary* altogether, rather to substitute a friendly discussion. The gulf between the two approaches is a source of bitterness for some traditional speechmakers:

> Today the people speak more directly than the ancestors. Because the people before took care to preserve relationships. Today people just say directly the faults of others, challenge the other. The ancestors could not 'answer' like that. But rather, they made circles around the thought.

> In the request (*kabary*) it is not good to speak directly... But today the *kabary* is already direct. If you speak directly, the *kabary* is a child's *kabary*, and there is no

respect and honor, because it is a *kabary* of those of equal status. But when you request something then the other must be above. The two speechmakers, the one bringing the girl's family's speech and the one from the boy's family—the girl's speaker must be superior from the beginning to end and the boy's speaker beneath.

Structural variation, then, can be a consequence of not only regional, familial and individual approaches, but of generational differences as well. Or, to state it in another way, variation in the structure of oratory can be a consequence of the degree of contact and identification with local European culture. There are several examples in different *kabary* which link the simple, direct approach with contemporary, European attitudes. For example, in the *kabary* done in the village where I lived, a very old speaker on the girl's side commented:

> Yes, sir. When those who were victorious over the Malagasy arrived, they entered— the white-skinned ones. The place changed. Things were not done according to the ancestors, of the time of the grandfather and the grandmother. The character and the custom changed from then on. The respect, gratitude among kinsmen changed. The changes were said by that able young man... And when those able now speak, they say: Civilization progresses. But this civilization was not made known to me in schools with roofs, for I went to schools with no roofs...We (on the girl's side) are not able to open the path for you without greeting you. However, when you all arrived, you did not knock on the door. So we are a bit shocked, sir, for you come, as they say: "The past was different but today trousers are worn." We are not knowledgeable in civilization, for we went to schools without walls...

Similarly, a younger man in another *kabary* performance who represented the boy's interests commented throughout the *kabary*:

> As I said, sir, the ways of the ancestors are referred to, but I am born later, so—the marriage request should be nothing more than a visit, to be done according to what one can do.

In a third *kabary*, the two families actually parted during the performance over precisely this difference. The boy's family, though originally from a small village about 200 kilometers south of the capital, lived at the present time in the capital itself. Those who had come to represent the family were professional men and government officials. The main speechmaker knew nearly nothing of the ancestral approach, and the girl's speaker could not accept this. As members of the boy's party hastened to their Peugeot, the mother of the boy approached the girl's speechmaker and said:

> I ask that the guilt be lifted from me for we are strangers and not bold to confront all of you in this discussion which just passed. That is, the speech was made simple, because these children are in a hurry, and you know that this particularly causes errors. And the reason we made mistakes was because some had made a long journey from Antananarivo, and these people are FUNCTIONARIES, doing all sorts of work, West, East, waiting (for the ceremony).

The split was inevitable where the two sides reckoned their social position in terms of different skills—one set oriented towards urban life and another oriented towards the more traditional rural society. Differences in generation and differences in degree of culture contact cannot be considered apart from one another, for it is the younger generation which in general is more exposed to European ways. As free rice land becomes scarcer, younger men are forced to look for employment in towns near their ancestral village.

The presence of these two approaches—the 'new way' and the 'ancestral way'—in all three of the request *kabary* attended, however, cannot be explained exclusively in terms of urban/rural or generational differences. In each of the *kabary*, the 'new way' was championed by the speechmaker for the boy's family. This was no coincidence. It is highly advantageous to the boy's side to advocate a simple and straightforward performance. In pre-*kabary* discussions, the boy's family typically tries to streamline the format as much as possible. If the two families can agree upon a simple approach, there is less chance of falling into 'traps'. In the 'new way' the opportunity to err is reduced as the number of obligatory terms to be included is fewer. Thus, the probability of the request being completed successfully is greater in theory if the simpler approach is used.

But, as mentioned, the agreement reached by the two families is never conclusive. Though speechmakers refer to the 'new way', notions of what constitutes its obligatory structure are no more unified than are those underlying the 'ancestral way'. In all three *kabary* performances, speechmakers representing the boy's family had intended to perform a far more simple *kabary* than was demanded then and there by the girl's speechmakers. And, of course, on the other hand, the speechmakers representing the girl's family were, in all three cases, 'shocked' (*mahagaga*) that the speech of the other orator was much simpler than what had been agreed on.

What constitutes an error or trap depends on what each side considers to be the compromise agreement made between the 'new way' and the 'ancestral way'. Roughly speaking, we could say that even the simplest of approaches would include such items as:

1. Asking permission to enter and speak (asking blessing from girl's family, asking guilt to be lifted from speaker).
2. Hymns and prayer by boy's speaker.
3. Greetings.
4. The request.
5. Offering of brideprice (*vodiondry*).
6. Statement of confidence from the boy (*manome toky*).
7. Blessing by girl's family (*tso-drano*).

4. *A Sliding Sense of Obligatoriness.* When a speechmaker from the girl's family points out an error in the speech of the other orator, he refers to those items of the 'ancestral way' which both families agreed to include in the performance. For example:

> Excuse me. And it shames me to speak to you all and the repetition makes this heavy... We do not want to drag out this affair, is that correct? And if by chance we speak like this... We brothers-in-law talked to one another this morning. And these were their words: "THE WAYS OF THE ANCESTRAL VILLAGE COMPLETELY WILL BE ACCOMPLISHED BY ME AND THERE IS NOTHING TO PREVENT THIS AT ALL." (*Kabary* at Antsirabe.)

or, in the *kabary* done in the village where the ethnographer lived:

> But having just arrived, you brusquely made the request. This is not both our program.
> This is not both our program. This is a ceremony of happiness, a time to remember. It
> is not just a taking of the spouse without a proper request. So if you are still to request,
> proceed with ALL THE CUSTOMS, sir, so that we understand. (*Kabary* at Namoizaman-
> ga.)

Similarly, speechmakers on the boy's side often defend themselves by pointing out
that the program arranged by the families was to be simple. Typically, the
speechmaker states that he is not expected to perform the particular item demanded
by the other orator. For example:

> Excuse me, sir, but here is grandfather, Ingahy Ratsimba, who says (to us): "We hoped
> to hear a *kabary*, and hoped for a long talk." The discussion is already in motion.
> Furthermore, when we arrived, we asked that a blessing be given by you for the new
> household. But, to go back to what we discussed two months back, we decided then
> not to hurry and to have a few people only to take care of this business. So we came—
> just a few of us. We ask for prayer and blessing to be from you. And these are still
> needed by us, because we want descendants. And it is known that these things bring
> goodness to a household. BUT THE *kabary* OF THE ANCESTORS, WE DO NOT DO AT ALL,
> NOT EVEN A BIT. (*Kabary* at Ambano.)

But, as mentioned previously, the speechmaker for the boy has a difficult
time. On the one hand, he is willing to admit to a few errors to appear inferior. On
the other hand, he is not willing to admit to a great number of errors or fundamental
errors lest his reputation and the reputation of the family he represents suffer. When
a point is reached in a request *kabary*, where the boy is unwilling to admit to an error
or when he is incapable of correcting an error, reliance on these two approaches is
strongest. The two sides become polarized—one dedicated to ancestral custom, the
other to the simple approach with which he is most familiar.

The fourth major point, then, in support of *kabary* structure as variable rather
than fixed is that STRUCTURAL RIGIDITY IS A FUNCTION OF FACTORS AFFECTING THE
kabary PERFORMANCE. Attitudes towards what is obligatory appear to be less a
function of some fixed ideal than of the way the *kabary* is proceeding. Each side
becomes more grounded in their approaches as the tension mounts. This is true
particularly when one side or both sides feel that ample respect is not being given to
them, for example, if the boy's orator speaks too simply, as if he were on an equal
level with the girl's family.

The polarization of attitudes towards *kabary* procedure can be correlated with
an increased use of personal reference terms which emphasize the differences
between the two sides. Thus, in controversial exchanges, speechmakers make
distinction such as:

REFERENCE TO BOY'S SIDE		REFERENCE TO GIRL'S SIDE
Hianareo	⟵⟶	*Izahay*
(You, plural)		(We, exclusive of addressee)
Mpangataka		*Mpanome*
(Requestors)		(Givers)
Mpaka		*Mpamoaka or Mpandefy*
(Takers)		(Senders off)

Vahiny	*Tompon'draharaha*
(Guests, Strangers)	(Hosts)
Mpiteny	*Mpipaino*
(Speakers)	(Listeners)
Reni-vohitra*	*Ambanivohitra**
(Town)	(Country)

* Only in *kabary* at Antsirabe.

In these parts of the oratory where notions or obligatoriness are more rigid, there is a wealth of information about norms of speech use. To a much greater extent than in other parts of the *kabary*, speechmakers talk about what OUGHT to be done instead of simply doing it. That is, for example, instead of greeting the other family, a speechmaker states that one ought to greet one another at this point in the *kabary*. Here sources to justify performance procedure are repeatedly brought to bear. The words of the ancestors, of family elders, of the Bible are considered as standard source material. Together, these utterances amount to a metalanguage that refers to the structure of the discourse in process. It is talk about talk. Here are some extracts from different request *kabary* which exemplify the metalanguage and the heavy use of source material:

From the *kabary* at Antsirabe, girl's speaker:

> However, there is only one real way of bringing this. In speaking, it is all right to let a few things go by. But it is pointed out by me to you that the speaking manner before these people—I can not ignore it, particularly the head speaker. For children, errors must be corrected. The speechmaker just said: "I speak simply," but this is not THE WAY AT ALL, even for the marriage, not at all...

> You said before "According to THE WAYS OF THE ANCESTRAL VILLAGE, the gate has been opened." This is true. The right to speak has been given. That was not thought by me, but it is the WAY OF THE ANCESTORS.

From the *kabary* at Ambano, girl's speaker:

> I do the *mialan-tsiny* (lifting of guilt) for it is the way *of the ancestors up until now*.

> We all did not create this, for it is the *Lovan-tsofina* (oral legacy) performed by ALL OUR ELDERS.

> The respect to God is already finished by us. WE CONSULTED IN A HIGH VOICE TO BE HEARD, FOR IT IS NOT TO BE DONE SIMPLY.

> If the WAYS OF THE ANCESTORS are looked at, then there must be a big *kabary*, to be answered by one another, in the way called *kabary ifanaovana* (*kabary* done by each other). It is not to arrange words to defeat one another, nor to give away a child. If there is to be this kind of *kabary*, we ought to continue answering one another, and we ought not to say: 'Isn't the *kabary* finished with this blessing?'... And if there is a *kabary* still to be done, then REFER TO THE SOURCES WHICH I REFER TO. The talk done by you has been supported by the way of: THE WORDS OF THE ANCESTORS LEFT BY THE ELDERS, for though the religious part of the *kabary* is finished, the prayers and blessings yet remain. That is my word.

But, if the request is to be completed, if a marriage is desired, then this diversive rigidity must be transformed into a flexible alliance. How is this accomplished?

CASE 1:   In the *kabary* at Namoizamanga (a small rural village where the ethnographer lived) the tension was reduced by the intervention of the father of the girl, who had not spoken previously. He urged his family to allow the other speechmaker to proceed. This encouragement was supported by members of the audience, who shouted comments such as: "Discuss it easily, and so not make additional talk!" Then the boy's speechmaker stated that he was in agreement with the girl's family. The speechmaker for the girl allowed it to continue but made the comment that the present program was not the one which had been considered previously but a new one. New ground rules were assumed but never made explicit.

CASE 2:   In the *kabary* at Ambano (a village of nobles, just outside of a large town), the two sides decided to reformulate the ground rules when nearly the whole *kabary* had been given. At that point it was asked by the girl's family whether the 'new way' or the 'words of the ancestors' were to be used. As the boy's speaker could not perform the traditional request, the new way was adopted, much to the disappointment of the girl's family. One member of the family added the words: "I have seen many requests, sometimes as *mpaka* (takers of the girl) and sometimes as *mpamoa* (givers of the girl), but not one like this one." This reconciliation was encouraged as well by the father of the girl and by the pastor who sat on the girl's side.

CASE 3:   The *kabary* which took place in Antsirabe, a large town with a significant French population, was the most interesting of all the *kabary* in terms of conflict resolution. As mentioned previously, the boy's family lived well over a hundred kilometres away in the capital, whereas the girl's family lived in Antsirabe, close to the ancestral village. Whereas the girl's family had recruited someone from the ancestral village itself to speak for them, the boy's family had delegated someone who had spent most of his life in the city. He was an extremely poor speaker: He could not correct any error he made. He could only apologize with words, when what was expected was, at least, a small monetary offering as compensation. He was so unskilled that elders afterwards could find little of interest in his speech to argue about. It was humiliating to the boy himself. He ran off, soon followed by the remainder of the family. The elders of the girl simply could not accept this display of ineptitude. It was not a *kabary* at all in their eyes.

But, because both families wanted the marriage finalized, the girl's family sent the brother and father of the girl to beg the boy and his kin to return. They did, on the condition that the request *kabary* would not be continued. This interruption of the *kabary* was intensely displeasing to the elders, as the ancestors always required that the *kabary* be *tanteraka*, 'completed, accomplished'. It was the duty of speechmakers to continue each other's words until the finish. When the groom's family returned, however, the two families simply prayed together and ate with one another. Acting as if the 'traditional' ceremony had been completed successfully, both sides proceeded to the local church to ratify the partnership in the eyes of Christianity.

In all three cases, it was some member of the girl's family who restored the relationship between the two families. It is a violation of one of the major interactional norms to cause someone loss of face in a direct encounter. As it is the girl's speechmakers who put the other speaker on-the-spot (by making traps), it is primarily their responsibility to prevent total humiliation. Of course, as seen in Case 3, sometimes the attacks go too far. Nonetheless, it is up to them to bend, to soften their stance, so that the request can be accomplished.

As the *kabary* winds down, as some sort of vague consensus is reached again, attitudes towards obligatory approaches change as well. Whereas in the height of controversy each speechmaker talked of 'only one way', of the 'new way', or of the 'ancestral way', with the ease of tension the comments become suddenly transformed into statements such as:

> *Samy manana ny fomba.*
> Everyone has his customs.
>
> *Samy manana ny fitondrana.*
> Everyone has his own way of bringing the speech (performing the *kabary*).
>
> *Samy manana ny heviny daholo.*
> Everyone has his own ideas.

It is made explicit that there is more than one way to perform the request *kabary*. The tremendous range in attitude towards what ought to comprise this *kabary* indicates once again the SLIDING SENSE OF OBLIGATORINESS. Within one *kabary* performance, participants go from extreme parochialism to an attitude of laissez-faire.

The identification of a family with one set of rules is advantageous as long as its status depends upon proving a particular point. But when the particular point begins to threaten the overall purpose of the ceremony, it is dangerous to continue stressing what divides the two families. After all, the purpose of the ceremony is to unite the two families through contract of marriage.

The move towards greater unity, towards identification with, rather than separation from, the other family is expressed in a number of ways. First, as seen above, both groups are, at least, willing to tolerate each other's attitudes towards the *kabary*. Secondly, terms of personal reference encompass both sides and cease to distinguish one from the other:

(1) First of all, there is reference to *isika*, the inclusive 'we' form, or *-ntsika*, the inclusive 'our', as in

> *Vita ny naharantskika.*
> OUR business TOGETHER is completed.
>
> *Fetim-pifaliana fetin'ny mariazy...Nonolotra adidy izahay fa ny mariazy no hijerentsika azy, tompoko.*
> A ceremony of happiness, a ceremony of marriage. We (exclusive) performed our duty, but it is the marriage which will be witnessed by US ALL.

(2) Secondly, the speechmakers once again refer to one another as *mpinaotra*, 'brothers-in-law'.

(3) Thirdly, the families call one another *havana*, 'kinsmen', for they are no longer *vahiny*, 'strangers'.

(4) In addition, terms of reference which apply generally to many people are used, such as *olom-belona* 'living people', *samy*, 'everyone' and so on.

Aside from the use of cohesive terms of reference, proverbs are used heavily to emphasize the ties between the families. For example, in Case 2, the father of the girl intervened several times to remind those present:

> *Maty iray fasana, velona iray trano.*
> Dead we dwell in one tomb, living we dwell in one house.

This proverb refers to the fact that both families come from the same ancestral homeland and have rights to the same tomb. As in death they will remain together, so in life they should be bound together. The proverb was repeated several times by others at a later moment in the *kabary*. Other proverbs were used in a similar manner by the pastor in this *kabary*:

> *Tana-kavia sy havanana: izay didiana maharary.*
> Villages to the right and left: the one which is cut off is made to suffer.
>
> *Trano atsimo sy avaratra: izay tsy mahalena hialogana.*
> Houses to the south and north; that which doesn't leak will protect the other.

The two sides become solidly united when the young girl is brought into the performance arena from a room where she has been waiting. She is seated next to her bridegroom, and together elders from both families give *anatra*, 'advice' to them:

> "So now: From this day forth, you both will begin... It is said by ALL OF US ELDERS HERE, that you are no longer children but adults, to begin a household..."

The giving of advice, then, allows elders from both families to act as a single group. Those who are already elders face those who are on the brink of becoming elders.

The final unifying idiom which is present is the 'will of God'. It is mentioned that after all, it is up to God and not to those present to decide if the marriage should take place. They put the matter in His hands. This attitude is present from the beginning, when a prayer beseeching God's favour is offered. The prayers again constantly make reference to what unites the families. Here is an excerpt from a prayer made at the beginning of the *kabary* at Antsirabe (Case 3).

> Happy is our heart, God, to consult with, to thank you God who created the foot and the hand. We give respect to you God the Father and the Son and Holy Ghost. That which is done by us here, God, to bring together these two children who have come of age, let them have descendants, and don't let their destinies conflict, for all are the same in the palm of your hand. We elders are bound here God, and it is known by you that we are *one* in blood. Even though coming from distant parts of the earth which differ, we are ONE BLOOD joined here (our homeland), called Anjanampara. Even if we are runaway children, so living at different places, we are still joined here again ONE BLOOD at this time today. God the creator, we request you, if there are incorrect words, if there are things not in accordance with You, forgive us, God. And let it please be that this done by us will bring honour to Your name alone. The name of Jesus Christ the Saviour is requested by us to make us good, from this time forth. Amen.

The final prayer thanks God for His protection and requests that He strengthen the family:

> "Let there be mutual love of ALL THE FAMILY."

5. *Match of Wits vs. Successful Alliance.* The final bit of evidence in support of the variability in notions of obligatoriness in *kabary* comes from backstage comments from participants who are not the delegated speechmakers. When the families move from a narrow, rigid attitude to a more flexible and broadminded one, it becomes apparent that the request *kabary* is primarily a match of wits among elders. It is the most developed art form in the culture and a source of great delight and interest to all participants. But when the verbal jousting begins to threaten a desirable alliance, the players lose their audience support.

In the *kabary* at Antsirabe (Case 3), I left the tape recorder running long after the boy's family had left the area. As soon as it was clear that the elders had made a shambles of the situation, the women dominated the next stage of action. They spoke firmly about what had gone wrong and exactly what needed to be done. They sent the father and the brother of the girl quickly to bring the others back. But even further, the women openly declared this affair to be the folly of men. Here are a few representative comments:

> The point is this: the affair of the elders is nothing, but the marriage is something which affects us all.
>
> The elder's affair is a loss, our gathering before here, so let us not repeat the affair of the elders.
>
> You know, when elders get together they can not bottle up their mouths... So, because of this, when the handling of the elders is not liked by you, then do not butt in, for if you butt in...
>
> Why did the boy go away? The thing of the elders and the wedding are two different things.
>
> So we should say to them (the boy's family): Don't gather the elders for we are not to be confused by the affair of elders. That is simple...
>
> Let the elders have one kind of talk and the wedded couple another. Let the elders agree with one another here. But the wedding must be done as arranged.

The adherence to or abandonment of particular structural principles form part of the strategy of this verbal match. But the rules of the game are constrained by rules of the larger ceremonial event. The speechmakers are not allowed to 'play to win', for to win their game may mean losing the alliance. The players must be constantly reminded that the securing of descendants is the end desired by those gathered. And when this end is threatened, many are willing to throw all the rules out the window. THE RULES ARE IMPORTANT ONLY IN SO FAR AS THE PARTICIPANTS ALLOW THEM TO BE IMPORTANT.

We have presented five substantial properties of the request *kabary* which show that rules governing its structure are neither commonly shared nor rigidly adhered to:

(1) The necessity of pre-*kabary* discussion to iron out differences in attitudes towards sequence and content of the *kabary*.

(2)   The arguments which inevitably appear in the *kabary* itself over what the ground rules are, as established in (1).

(3)   Reference in the *kabary* to two distinct approaches to performing the *kabary*: the 'ancestral way' and the 'new way'.

(4)   The tremendous range in adherence to obligatory rules by speechmakers, the fact that rigidity in approach is related to tension between the two families: When the tension is reduced, there is tolerance and acceptance of many approaches.

(5)   The fact that when the *kabary* threatens the possibility of alliance between the two families, many are willing to reject the importance of all the rules and to see it as diversion for elders and not to be taken seriously.

What constitutes the procedure of any single marriage request *kabary* can not be predicted *a priori*. The structure and content of the oratory is dependent upon what each family brings to pre-*kabary* discussions: local, familial, individual styles, what ground rules are established at that time, the interpretation of these ground rules in the *kabary* itself, the emotional climate of the performance, and so on. It is characteristic for the performance not to proceed smoothly. We find false starts and repetitions. We find the more direct language of everyday speech along with the more highly valued allusive speech way. We find minor participants shouting out stage directions to speechmakers: "Speak louder!" "Look at us!" "The other one should be saying that!" "Don't argue!" In fact, it is the partial unpredictability of the oratory that stimulates most of the talk which occurs. It is, in part, what makes a particular performance *mafana*, 'heated', rather than *matsatso,* 'flat'.

REFERENCES

BLOCH, M. 1968.   Astrology and writing in Madagascar. In J. Goody (ed.), *Literacy in traditional societies*. Cambridge: Cambridge University Press.

KEENAN, E. 1974.   Norm-makers, norm-breakers: Uses of speech by men and women in a Malagasy community. In J. Sherzer and R. Bauman (eds.), *The ethnography of speaking*. London and New York: Cambridge University Press, 125-43.

JOEL SHERZER

Strategies in Text and Context:
Kuna *kaa kwento*

Kaa kwento, "the story of the hot pepper," is told among the Kuna Indians of Panama. The Kuna Indians are a group of tropical forest agriculturalists who inhabit a string of island-villages along the northeast coast of Panama (San Blas) and a few small villages in the interior Darien jungle. This analysis of *kaa kwento* begins with one telling or performance of the story. This telling is discussed in some detail and compared with other performances of *kaa kwento*. Both the story and the events of which the telling of the story is the central part are analyzed in order to demonstrate the interplay between the significance of *kaa kwento* and the contexts in which it is performed. An important feature of the structure of *kaa kwento* is that it lends itself to multiple interpretations; this feature can be understood as functional in Kuna social and cultural life when situated in the actual contexts in which it is exploited.

The version of *kaa kwento* that is reproduced here was recorded on February 18, 1971, in the gathering house of the island-village of Mulatuppu, San Blas. It is told by Mastayans, one of the *saklas* (chiefs)[1] of Mulatuppu, to a group of men. More particularly, it is told to an elderly, well-known *sakla* from the village of Achutuppu, who at the time was visiting Mulatuppu for several days in order to chant Kuna tradition in the gathering house. Mastayans, together with a group of Mulatuppu men, is keeping the visiting *sakla* company and entertaining him in the gathering house on this morning, as is required by Kuna custom. Were there no visitor, the gathering house would be locked and most of the men of the village, including the *saklas*, would be off working in the jungle mainland or fishing. Mastayans announces that he will tell *kaa kwento* if the visiting *sakla* will serve as his *apinsuet* (responder). The visiting *sakla* agrees and does so, participating in the performance of *kaa kwento* by ratifying each line with an affirmative grunt, a *teki* (thus it is), a repeated word or phrase, a comment, a laugh, or a question.[2] The structure of the telling of *kaa kwento* is thus Mastayans as teller, the visiting *sakla* as addressee-responder, and the group of men in the gathering house as audience. This communicative structure (sender—receiver-responder—audience) is a very common Kuna one, characteristic of events ranging from the most ritual and ceremonial to the most informal and everyday.

From *Journal of American Folklore*, Vol. 92, pp. 145-63, 1979. Reprinted with permission of American Folklore Society and Joel Sherzer.

[1] I use the Kuna term *sakla* throughout in order to avoid the connotation of chief as powerful authoritarian figure. The Kuna *sakla* is rather a specialist in tribal tradition who, by means of verbal artistry and rhetoric, convinces, advises, and offers guidance.

[2] In the translation of the performance of *kaa kwento* provided below, the visiting *sakla*'s comments are set off with brackets.

Here is an English translation of *kaa kwento*, as told by Mastayans. The line division is based on both an intonation pattern characteristic of lines in Kuna storytelling and the set of line initial and line final phrases, words, and particles particular to Kuna storytelling.[3]

1. I am going to tell you *kaa kwento* then.
2. I will do so as if speaking to you as my responder.
3. Now this story was told to me by the *sakla* of Mammimullu, Mantipaytikinya; he was once teaching me a little of this *kaa kwento*.
4. It was true.
5. There was once a *muu*; a *muu*.[4]
6. This *muu* was the owner of a plum tree; the *muu* was the owner of a plum tree.
7. There was once this *muu* who was the owner of a plum tree, and before, when it produced fruit, it was possible to gather a lot.
8. It was possible to gather up to four baskets.
9. Then one day this plum tree which used to produce four baskets went bad.
10. The fruit of the plum tree fell down.
11. When the owner of the fruit tree went to see it, all the fruit had fallen.
12. "It is not possible to gather it," said the *muu*.
13. She said: "Why did my plum tree go bad? Its fruit does not get ripe for me."
14. "Since the fruit will not get ripe for me, who can it be that touches my fruit?" the *muu* meditated.
15. Then one day the *muu* got a boy to watch over the plum tree.
16. The *muu* said to the boy: "Grandson,[5] you will watch over my plum tree; you will take care of my plum tree."
17. "Here you will watch over my plum tree, to see who is touching my fruit."
18. The grandson said "all right."
19. Then he sat on top of the tree, watching from there.
20. Now he watched over the fruit sitting there; like the *muu* told him;
[visiting *sakla*: Who could be touching her fruit?]
    yes: in order to see who could be touching her fruit.
21. Then, when she awoke, the *muu* went to see.
22. When she got there, she saw that her fruit had fallen again.
[visiting *sakla*: It had still fallen again.]
23. The *muu* said to the grandchild: "Did you see the person who caused the fruit of my plum tree to fall? Did you see?"
24. He replied: "No, I didn't see anyone; I didn't see anyone"; "All right" she said to him.
25. Now, "All right" she said, "then tonight you will watch for me again; tonight you will watch for me again."
26. "You will look well; who could be touching the fruit of my plum tree?"
[visiting *sakla*: The boy.]
27. The boy remained seated.

---

[3] See Dell Hymes, "Discovering Oral Performance and Measured Verse in American Indian Narrative," *New Literary History*, 8 (1977), 431-57.

[4] As will be discussed below, the Kuna word *muu* has three meanings: grandmother, old woman, and midwife. I have retained *muu* in this translation in order to maintain the ambiguity.

[5] The boy is sometimes referred to and addressed as "boy," sometimes as "grandson." Since Kuna kin terms are frequently used to address nonkin, usage of these terms in the text should not be understood as necessarily implying kin relationships.

28. The *muu* went back to her house.
29. The owner of the plum tree is in the house sleeping.
30. Then, next day she awoke again; she went to ask again.
31. She asked again, she saw again, the fruit of the plum tree had fallen again.
32. Then she asked the grandson again: "Did you see; the fruit of my plum tree, who touched it, did you see?"
33. "No, I didn't see anyone," he replied.
34. The *muu* got very furious: "He didn't watch well for me"; the *muu* got angry.

[visiting *sakla*: angry, "You didn't watch."]

35. "I see that you are not watching," she said to him.
36. Then the *muu* decided to finish the boy off.[6]
37. "He doesn't pay attention to me," she said: "I'll finish him off."
38. Then the *muu* dug the earth.

[visiting *sakla*: The earth.]

39. She dug the earth; four meters deep she dug; the *muu* dug in the earth.
40. Then the *muu* threw a ring down into the earth.
41. And she said to the grandchild, "My ring fell; go get it for me."
42. Then the boy stood a ladder inside the earth.
43. Then the grandson descended, below the earth.
44. And when he had descended, when he began to look for the ring, she grabbed the ladder and pulled it up.

[visiting *sakla*: Impossible to climb up again.]

45. Impossible to climb up again; how can you climb up again? It's straight.
46. Then she covered all the earth, cover, cover, cover; well, closed.
47. The grandchild died;

[visiting *sakla*: He died.]

   he died; inside the ground.
48. Now the grandchild who was there had a mother; he had a father as well.
49. Then they searched; "Where could our son have gone?" they said.
50. The mother searched, "Where could my grandchild have gone? Where could my son have gone?"
51. As she did not find him, she went to the *muu*'s to ask; "Have you seen my son?" she asked.
52. "No, I have not seen him," she said to her; "I have not seen him; it's true."
53. Then the mother cried for her little boy, the father cried for his little boy.
54. Then little by little they forgot;

[visiting *sakla*: Forgot.]

   after a lot of time had gone by, they forgot.

[visiting *sakla*: The *muu* forgot?]

55. The mother forgot; the *muu* of course knew because it was she who buried him in the earth.

[visiting *sakla*: She surely knew.]

56. She surely knew.
57. The mother cried for her little boy.
58. Then, she cried, after a time little by little she forgot. She remembered and forgot again; then it didn't make any difference.
59. Now she also had a daughter; it was her brother who died.

---

[6] This translates the Kuna verb *opeloe*, literally, "to cause to end."

60. When they would eat, the boy would tell his sister to go (and get hot pepper); around the house of the *muu* there was something growing.
61. It grew on top of the earth of the burial, something very small grew.
62. Then it got bigger and the *muu* wondered what it was.

[visiting *sakla*: What was growing?]

63. It kept slowly growing, growing, growing; then it produced fruit.
64. And the fruit that it produced got ripe, and it was pepper.

[visiting *sakla*: Pepper.]

65. Pepper.
66. Thus the *muu* was the owner of a pepper plant, and the pepper plant belonged to the *muu*.
67. The pepper plant produced much fruit.
68. The boy who died, when he ate, would say to his sister:
69. "Sister, go to the *muu*'s to ask for a little pepper for me; I want to eat with pepper."
70. She would go to ask for it.
71. She would say to the *muu*: "I want a little of your pepper."
72. The *muu* said "all right," the *muu* would go to get pepper for her.
73. Then one day while eating, she went to ask again.
74. She said to the girl "You go and pick the pepper," and she went to pick the pepper.

[visiting *sakla*: To the *muu*'s.]

75. She always would go to pick it at the *muu*'s; the *muu* was the owner of the pepper plant.
76. Then a person began to speak inside the earth to the girl who was picking the pepper.
77. "Little girl," it said; "little girl," the pepper spoke.

[visiting *sakla*: Below the earth it spoke.]

78. Below the earth a person spoke; "little girl," it said.
79. She heard that it said "little girl."
80. Someone is calling her.
81. The pepper frightened her and she went back to her mother's.
82. She said to her mother, "I was picking pepper and someone called me.
83. From below the pepper he called me: 'little girl' he said to me; I got frightened" she said.

[visiting *sakla*: Frightened.]

84. Her mother was surprised.

[visiting *sakla*: Surprised.]

85. She said to her, "Let's go so that you listen."
86. So the mother herself went also in order to listen.
87. Then when the girl picked the pepper it called again.
88. "Little girl, little girl," it was calling.

[visiting *sakla*: Such calling.]

89. Yes, such calling; the father thus realized and the mother thus realized that their son who had been killed was heard here.
90. So, it was the fault of the owner of the pepper plant.
91. Then they began to dig; in order to see what was inside the earth.
92. The person who was inside called and they dug with a shovel, with a digging stick.

93. He called: "Over here is my head."
[visiting *sakla*: Over here.]
94. "Over here are my feet"; one could hear the person speaking.
95. Then they dug slowly, slowly, slowly.
[visiting *sakla*: The mother is digging.]
96. The mother is digging up her son.
97. Then the boy is there.
98. The boy who took care of the plum tree and whom the *muu* had buried came back to life again.
[visiting *sakla*: So they caught the *muu*.]
99. They had caught the *muu*.
100. The boy came out of the ground.
[visiting *sakla*: He'll tell about the *muu*.]
101. Then he was asked, "Why did this happen to you?"
102. So he explained.
103. "I was walking about here and the *muu* placed me here to take care of her plum tree.
104. And seeing that I did not take good care of her plum tree, the *muu* dug the earth.
105. The *muu* threw me into the earth.
[visiting *sakla*: She threw the ring.]
106. She threw the ring.
107. Now the *muu* buried me in the earth, and there grew the pepper plant, and from there I called you," he said.
108. It is true.
109. By now the boy had grown up, he was already a young man.
110. "As for the *muu*, I'll kill her," he said.
111. Then, the boy having come out on top of the ground went away, he went up to heaven.
112. He went up to heaven in a plate.
113. He took a golden hook
114. It seems that he asked his father for it.
115. Having returned here, he went to the *muu*'s.
116. The *muu* already knew.
117. The *muu* was seated beside the fireplace trembling with fear.
118. Then the boy grabbed her with the hook; he did it to the *muu*. *Mok.*[7]
119. Then he carried her away again; he carried the *muu* with the hook.
120. He rose with her.
121. He pulled her in the plate.
122. To *sappi pirkwen*, that is Sodom.
123. Sodom is a very dangerous place where there is much fire.
124. There are many carbonized *ikwa* trees; there are many carbonized *paila* trees.
125. There the *muu* was dragged to the middle of the fire; the *muu* was completely toasted.
126. For this reason our ancestors said, "If on this earth a *muu* buries a bird, she will be thrown in that place.
127. The *muus* will be carried to a place which is known as *pursipu* where there are many burning trees, where there are many ashes; there are punished the *muus*.

---

[7] *Mok* is an onomatopoetic particle, used in narration.

128.   Those who in this world do not know how to take care of birds; those who bury birds.
129.   There they are left"; that is why our ancestors chanted thus.
130.   That is what he told me.
131.   Up to here I have told you a little.

POSSIBLE CONTEXTS FOR PERFORMANCE
OF KAA KWENTO

It is necessary to begin this exploration and explanation of *kaa kwento* by contrasting the performance reported on here with other possible performances and by viewing this event in relation to a more total Kuna ethnography of speaking.

Kaa kwento, like other Kuna *kwentos* "tales" or "stories," can be performed in two different ways in two different contexts for two different purposes:

(1)   A *kwento* can be spoken by *saklas* or other knowers of the stories, typically in the Kuna gathering house but also in one's own home, for example, to young children. In such performances of *kwentos*, there is a focus on entertainment, amusement, play, and humor.

(2)   A *kwento* can be chanted by Kuna *saklas* in the gathering house, usually in the evening, to an audience of men and women. The chanting of *kwentos* is practiced in the eastern portion of San Blas, which includes Mulatuppu. Inhabitants of the western portion of San Blas do not feel that it is appropriate to chant *kwentos* and criticize those who do so. While a chanted *kwento* may be pleasing, amusing, or humorous to the listeners, the ultimate purpose of all chanting is to illustrate proper and improper modes of behavior and to call on the community to follow the former.

Further examination of these two ways of performing *kwentos* is necessary for an understanding of the problem posed in this paper. *Kwentos*, when performed in spoken form for amusement in the gathering house, are told on days when people do not work (holidays, or days when there is an interdiction on work because of an eclipse, and so forth), when there is a *sakla* visiting from another village and men sit around the gathering house with him, or just before the evening chanting of *saklas*. The *kwentos* are a diversion for the pleasure and amusement of those present—a small group of men during the daytime or the gradually gathering group of men and women at night. *Kwentos* are told in colloquial Kuna, in the style appropriate for gathering-house narration. This linguistic variety and style are easily understood by all Kuna. The focus is on the play and humor of narration. The narrator alternates fast and slow, loud and soft speech, imitates voices and sounds, and tries to make his audience laugh. The audience, especially a single person in it at whom the story is directed, asks questions and makes humorous comments. There is much laughter.

Kwentos are one of a number of genres, topics, or themes that can be chanted in the gathering house by *saklas*. Others are tribal myths, legends, and history; reports of personal experiences, including dreams; and advice, to particular individuals, groups of individuals, or the community at large. There are regional and individual differences in practice and attitude in San Blas with regard to what topics are appropriate for *saklas'* chanting. Inhabitants of the western portion of San

Blas criticize those of the east for chanting biblical themes, non-Kuna history (for example about Christopher Columbus and Simon Bolivar), personal dreams, and *kwentos*. Chanting is a most serious affair. The subject matter is drawn on by the *sakla* for the purpose of his moral instruction to the audience. The performance is in the form of a ceremonial dialog between two *saklas* in which one chants verse by verse, the other responding *teki* (thus it is) after each verse. The linguistic variety is phonologically, syntactically, and semantically distinct from colloquial Kuna. In this style, metaphors abound. It is the mark of a good *sakla* to use not only conventional, traditional metaphors, but to elaborate and develop them in personal and appropriate ways. The *sakla* states and stresses his moral as he chants. After the *sakla*'s chant, there is an interpretation in colloquial Kuna by an *arkar* (*sakla*'s spokesman). This interpretation explains the message of the chant. The interpretation of the chant, by both *sakla* and *arkar*, is thus part of the structure and strategy of its performance.

The performance of *kaa kwento* analyzed here is an interesting case with regard to these two Kuna ways of performing *kwentos*. The *kwento* is spoken and told primarily for amusement, on the occasion of a visit of a well-known *sakla* from another village. But the visiting *sakla* takes on the role of *apinsuet* (responder), as he might in a chanted version of the *kwento*. And while there is no *arkar* interpretation, the teller, Mastayans, does provide a short moral, using a metaphor, or at least an allusive term, as part of the end of the *kwento*. The special properties of this particular performance of *kaa kwento* are important to the analysis of its strategic structure and are discussed below.

It is useful to place the distinction between two ways of performing *kwentos* (spoken and chanted) within the larger system of Kuna discourse. The three principal Kuna ritual-ceremonial discourse types are the chanting of *saklas*, the incantations of curing and magical control, and the shouting of puberty festivals, each in a particular linguistic variety and style quite distinct from colloquial Kuna and, especially in the case of the latter two, not intelligible to nonspecialists.[8] The addressees of curing and magical and puberty festival discourse are objects, which are believed to understand the linguistic variety involved. The efficacy of these texts resides in convincing the object to perform an act or acts, either after having heard the text or simultaneous to the hearing of the text. There is no interpretation and none is necessary since the object-addressees understand the language of the text. On the other hand, the chanting of *saklas* is addressed to humans, the audience that is present and expected to listen to the performance. The *arkar*'s interpretation is for them and is needed both because of the metaphorical language of the chants and because of the belief that reformulation and repetition are needed in order to drive home the message. Spoken *kwentos*, like reports and personal narratives recounted in the gathering house, are in colloquial Kuna. There is no formal interpretation as part of the performance. None is needed since the message is clear and easily understood by all those present and no allusive message is involved.

[8] See Joel Sherzer, "*Namakke, Sunmakke, Kormakke*: Three Types of Cuna Speech Event," in *Explorations in the Ethnography of Speaking*, ed. Richard Bauman and Joel Sherzer (Cambridge: Cambridge University Press, 1974), pp. 263-82.

THE STORY AND INTERPRETATIONS

Kaa kwento, as recounted by Mastayans, is a seemingly simple narrative that shares features with other stories and myths found in South America as well as all over the world. It contains good deeds and evil deeds, punishments and rewards, deaths and a rebirth, and a moral. In terms of diffusion, the probable source of *kaa kwento* is the singing bone or speaking hair motif of European folktales, now widespread in Latin America.[9] It is most interesting that this motif has reached a tropical forest Amerindian society and become well integrated into its social and cultural life and its speaking practices. As rich as *kaa kwento* is with regard to narrative development and symbolic oppositions—features that no doubt add to its role as a story told for amusement and entertainment—it does not provide an internal interpretation of the narrative development or symbolic oppositions, thus making it most useful for Kuna *saklas*, in that they can develop an interpretation of their own choosing as part of the structure of the telling.

When chanted in the Kuna gathering house, *kaa kwento* can be given various interpretations by the *sakla* and the *arkar*. These interpretations can be both general and particular and they can be opposed or in contradiction to one another. At the most general level the text can have to do with proper behavior and ways of treating other people. At a more particular level, it can have to do with the raising and care of young children. At a still more particular level, it can have to do with the care of babies, especially at birth, by midwives. And at the most particular level, it can have to do with what to do with babies who are born, in one way or another, socially inappropriate—twins, albinos, those with birth defects, or the products of an illegitimate relationship. Contradictory interpretations result from differing points of view taken with regard to the issues involved in the care and treatment of babies, children, or people in general.

A clue to the possible interpretations of *kaa kwento* and its place in Kuna verbal life is provided by the moral offered by Mastayans at the end of his narration on this particular morning in 1971 (lines 126-129).

> For this reason our ancestors said, "If on this earth a *muu* buries a bird, she will be thrown in that place. The *muus* will be carried to that place that is known as *pursipu* where there are many burning trees, where there are many ashes; there are punished the *muus*. Those who in this world do not know how to take care of birds; those who bury birds. There they are left"; that is why our ancestors chanted thus.

The word *sikkwi* (bird) had not appeared in the story, and what the *muu* had buried was a boy. But *sikkwi* is a euphemism for baby, and when Kuna babies die, as distinct from adults, they are buried in their house in the village, by the midwives if the death is at birth. Adults, on the other hand, are buried in the cemetery outside the village.

---

[9] I am grateful to Roger Abrahams for pointing this out to me. See Lutz Mackensen, *Der Singende Knochen* (Helsinki: Folklore Fellows Communication No. 49, 1923) and Stith Thompson, *The Types of the Folktale* (Helsinki: Folklore Fellows Communication No. 184, 1961), Type 780 *The Singing Bone* and Type 780B *The Speaking Hair*.

With this useful hint, *kaa kwento* can be examined in greater detail, starting with the ways in which the text is open to multiple interpretations. First there is the question of whether there is a need or purpose for interpretation at all, and what the nature of interpretation might be. Put another way, can the story be taken point by point for what it is with no meanings other than the actual characters and actions described or are these to be viewed as somehow symbolic of or representative of something else?

With regard to possible interpretations, there are first the most general interpretations: what are the reasons for or the meanings of the punishments and rewards, of both the *muu* and the boy? That is, what is the significance of the story, taken as a whole? Then there are particular, local interpretations—details in the narrative whose significance is not overtly explained in the text itself. Another way to look at these is as features of the text where there is a choice such that the overall general structure of the text (not its interpretation) would not change if another choice had been made. Examples are: why the title *kaa kwento* (the story of the hot pepper) and not *sirwer kwento* (the story of the plum tree) or *muu kwento*? Why does the *muu* have a *sirwer* tree and not a coconut tree, banana tree, or *ikwa* (wild fruit) tree? Why does a pepper plant grow up where the boy is buried and not a coconut, banana, orange, or *sirwer* tree? Why does the tree belong to a *muu* and not a father, mother, or grandfather? And why a boy and not a girl?

Understanding of some aspects and details of the story depends on explaining certain Kuna linguistic, social, and cultural presuppositions, presuppositions that are not stated explicitly and overtly in the text, but that are essential to it.[10] Discussion of these presuppositions shows the necessity of placing the text in the context of the language, society, and culture of which it forms a part. At the most general level of the plot, there are the punishments and rewards. The boy is punished for not properly caring for the *sirwer* tree, but later comes back to life. The *muu* is punished for having buried the boy. The boy is punished in this world, and the *muu* is punished in the afterworld. The Kuna believe that individuals are rewarded and punished in the afterworld for their good deeds and misdeeds in this world. The rewards and punishments are often appropriate to the individual's role in society. It is interesting to consider just what the boy is punished for. He was asked by the *muu* to watch over the *sirwer* tree. It is common Kuna practice to hire someone to take care of a possession. However, a *sirwer* tree is very unimportant in the Kuna tree-plant ranking system. It is owned, but its fruit is free for anyone to take, in any quantity, at any time.[11] So the *muu* had no right to try and protect her fruit. Furthermore, it is never made clear what happens to the fruit—if the tree is merely old and no longer productive, if someone actually comes and takes the fruit, or if the boy is somehow responsible. Nor is it clear exactly who the boy is and what

---

[10] On the importance of narrative presuppositions for an understanding of American Indian discourse, see Sally McLendon, "Cultural Presuppositions and Discourse Analysis: Patterns of Presupposition and Assertion of Information in Eastern Pomo and Russian Narrative," in *Linguistics and Anthropology* (Georgetown University Roundtable on Languages and Linguistics, 1977), ed. Muriel Saville-Troike (Washington, D.C.: Georgetown University Press, 1977), pp. 153-89.

[11] See James Howe and Joel Sherzer, "Take and Tell: a Practical Classification from the San Blas Cuna," *American Ethnologist*, 2 (1975), 435-60.

his relationship is to the old woman, the *muu*. The word *muu* has three meanings in Kuna and all are potentially relevant to an understanding of *kaa kwento*: (1) old woman, (2) grandmother, (3) midwife. The *muu* kills the boy by burying him. Although it is appropriate to bury dead infants on the spot, the boy in question was neither dead nor an infant; so burying him was a misdeed. The pepper plant that grows up on the spot where the boy was buried gives the story its title—*kaa kwento*. The pepper is hot and is used as a condiment in food. According to the Kuna system of ranking plants and trees, *kaa* is owned, but the owner must give an asker permission to pick some if needed for a meal. This is why the boy's sister asks for and obtains permission from the *muu*. The plate and golden hook used by the boy are part of a complex of objects believed by the Kuna to exist in the afterworld for their use. The *muu*'s eternal place of punishment, Sodom, is clearly borrowed from Christian tradition, but it is given a Kuna name as well—*sappi pirkwen* or *pursipu*—and is full of trees from the Kuna environment.

The complexity and richness of the text are further elucidated by examining it in terms of the symbolic oppositions found by Lévi-Strauss to be pervasive in tropical forest, South American mythology.[12] Thus the drama between the *muu* and *machi* (young boy) running through the story opposes age to youth and female to male. The two plants in the story—the *sirwer* (plum) tree and the *kaa* (hot pepper)—oppose unproductive and unripe to productive and ripe, and sticky and sweet to hot and spicy. It might be argued that *muu* is to *machi* as *sirwer* is to *kaa*, that is, old, unproductive, weak, and falling on the one hand and young, productive, powerful, and rising on the other. Furthermore, according to the Kuna tree-plant ranking system described above, *sirwer*/*kaa* opposes relatively wild (nature) to relatively owned (culture). Since the *sirwer* is not eaten as part of a Kuna meal and the *kaa* is, and since *kaa* is used almost exclusively with cooked food, *sirwer*/*kaa* also opposes raw to cooked.

The narrative development relates these various oppositions and introduces others, which it also relates to them. The story is essentially about misbehavior and punishment for misbehavior and life and death. In brief, because the *sirwer* lacks life, the *muu* asks the *machi* to find out who is causing the problem (misbehaving toward it). Because the *machi* does not properly protect the *sirwer* (misbehaves), he is punished with death; the *muu* kills him. The *muu* dies on this earth but comes back to life in heaven. The *machi* comes back to life on this earth and goes up to heaven to punish the *muu* for *her* misbehavior. In the course of this narrative development, the opposition up-above/down-below is introduced. The fruit of the *sirwer* tree falls down, the *machi* is buried underground. The *kaa* grows up out of the ground, the *machi* comes out because of it and after it, and the *machi* goes up to heaven to punish the *muu*.

These textual explanations and explorations enable us to understand the plot of *kaa kwento*, in general and in detail, including some of its potential symbolism. They do not, however, reduce the text to unambiguous interpretation; rather they make the various possibilities for interpretation more interesting and intriguing, denser and richer. Thus we know why the *muu* is punished in the text. But what does this symbolize? Are there circumstances under which the *muu* would have been justified in killing the *machi*? Following the clue provided by Mastayans' offered

[12] See *Mythologiques* (Paris: Plon, 1964-1971).

moral: was the *muu* punished for killing a baby born with some kind of defect (should a birth defect be taken as unseriously as failing to care for a *sirwer* tree)? Or was the *muu* punished for failing to see that there really was no defect or that it was minor (to fail to care for a tree that anyone is permitted to pick from is not a defect)? There are a variety of points of view among the Kuna on how to deal with birth defects just as there are on other subjects. Texts such as *kaa kwento* enable leaders such as *saklas*, symbolic moralists who are expected to take public positions in metaphoric language, to exploit a single plot in several ways. Furthermore, the same story can be used to justify and symbolize various points of view.

MASTAYANS' PERFORMANCE OF *KAA KWENTO*

Let us return to the actual performance of *kaa kwento* that I recorded. The strategy and structure of this telling must be understood from several intersecting perspectives. First there is a story, told for amusement. Mastayans' telling of the story entertained the assembled group and especially the visiting guest of honor.

Second, Mastayans' inclusion of a moral using allusive language and stating explicitly that "our ancestors chanted thus" relates this entertaining telling to the more serious telling that might occur if this story were performed chanted.

The conversation between Mastayans and the visiting *sakla* that follows the telling of *kaa kwento* deals with precisely the fact that this same story can be chanted. Mastayans opens (line 3) and closes (line 130) his telling by giving credit to his teacher, Mantipaytikinya, a *sakla* from the village of Mammimullu, with whom he has been studying. He points out (line 3) that "he was teaching me *a little*" and (line 131) "I have told you *a little*" (italics mine), formulaic understatements used by ceremonial leaders, which indicate that more is known—more known by Mastayans himself, more known by his teacher, Mantipaytikinya of Mammimullu, and more known by the ancestors. Not only do these statements give credit to his teacher, they serve as well to remind the audience that Mastayans himself is a knowledgeable and diligent *sakla*, one who gains prestige for himself and his village by traveling to other villages to study with venerable traditional specialists. Mastayans, by combining elements of an amusing, entertaining telling (first perspective) with an allusive moral indicating potential for serious chanting and framing devices characteristic of ritual-ceremonial discourse (second perspective), leads us to a third perspective with regard to structure, strategy, and, ultimately, interpretation, one that is relevant to this particular occasion. The immediate message of Mastayans in performing this story on this day is to announce to a well-known visiting *sakla* and to his own village that "I Mastayans am a knowledgeable *sakla*, one who studies with others to learn the traditions of our ancestors and performs them for my own village by chanting in the gathering house."

Mastayans utilizes the rich and intricate potential of *kaa kwento* to the fullest. He tells it well and it is well appreciated by the audience. Although he provides a moral, he never, any more than the text itself, takes a stand on the crucial issues raised in the story. *Muus* should treat babies well, but what does this mean? What does treating well or not treating well entail? His moral is just as open to multiple interpretation as the story that led to it. Mastayans is indeed a knowledgeable *sakla*, a clever political leader.

FURTHER CONSIDERATIONS

Understanding of the structure and significance of *kaa kwento* depends on placing it in its Kuna context, in two senses:

(1) an explanation of the linguistic, cultural, and social presuppositions necessary for an appreciation of the laconicity of the narrative and of the potential for alternative interpretations inherent in it;[13]

(2) a focus on the performance of *kaa kwento*, in actual Kuna settings, in which various analyses and interpretations are offered by the performers themselves as part of the strategy and structure of the performance.

From the point of view of Kuna ethnography of speaking, it is possible to view *kaa kwento* in terms of a particular constellation of components of speech.[14] Thus:

SETTING: gathering house; morning, afternoon, or evening.

PARTICIPANTS: *saklas*, *saklas'* spokesmen, audience of gathered men or men and women.

ENDS: amusement, social control, demonstration of personal knowledge.

ACT SEQUENCE: story, responses, interpretation.

KEY: playfully, humorously, seriously.

INSTRUMENTALITIES: spoken colloquial Kuna, chanted gathering house Kuna.

NORM OF INTERACTION: verse and then response, audience comment and laughter.

GENRE: *kwento*.

This constellation of components is a set of resources that are exploited by Kuna individuals as part of the dynamic, emergent structures and strategies of everyday communicative life. Thus, in the performance of *kaa kwento* focused on here, Mastayans utilizes this particular constellation of components of speech in a unique way for his own personal reasons of the moment. The dynamic structure of the event relates the backdrop and ground rules of Kuna speaking practices to the details of interactional life on that particular day. In a sense, Mastayans' clever exploitation of *kaa kwento* can be compared to such small, strategic bits of verbal behavior in our own society as name-dropping (for example: "You'll never guess who I saw at the club today?"), in which social interactional moves are achieved by reference to a prestigious person or place. But the Kuna way to be clever with language, to gain prestige and acquire recognition, is typically through long verbal

---

[13] Careful examination of the text in relation to Kuna language, culture, and society suggests still other analyses and interpretations. One interesting one, which has not been discussed because it is not offered by the Kuna as part of their performance of the story, has to do with Kuna social organization and residence rules. The Kuna are matrilocal; a man after marriage goes to live in the house of his wife. The *muu* in *kaa kwento* does not live in the same house as the boy; that is, she might be the mother of the father of the boy, but not of the mother. It might be argued that she is punishing her son, lost according to Kuna residence rules, by killing his son. According to such an interpretation, the *muu* would be reacting against the rules of Kuna social organization; the story would be a reminder not to do so.

[14] See Dell Hymes, "Studying the Interaction of Language and Social Life," in *Foundations in Sociolinguistics* (Philadelphia: University of Pennsylvania Press, 1974), pp. 29-66.

performances, whether these are memorized texts or verbal structures developed during performance.

The approach taken to *kaa kwento* is structuralist in that it is concerned with the structural properties of the story. But these structural properties are not viewed as static organizational features or underlying abstract logic. Rather, the dynamic structure of the text is focused on by analyzing the story in relationship to the contexts in which it is performed, in terms of the potential for openness of interpretation, and in terms of the ways in which this potential is exploited during performance. This approach is consistent with trends in recent or poststructuralism, which are concerned with dynamic, rhetorical aspects of texts and text-context interrelationships.

Lévi-Strauss, in his extensive study of tropical forest South American mythology, investigates myths that share such features with *kaa kwento* as relations between young and old and men and women, the interplay between life and death, and the origin of plants. But *kaa kwento*, as recorded here, has a narrative development and especially a moral that is completely different from the interpretations given by Lévi-Strauss. As analyzed here, the story has to do essentially not with raw and cooked and nature and culture, but rather with how to treat people, especially babies at birth. No doubt at a more abstract level, the occurrence in the story of such basic oppositions as male/female, young/old, productive/unproductive, and life/death is related to the significance and interpretation the Kuna themselves provide. These are the elements that set the stage and weave the intrigue that lead to the moral. They contribute to the potential of the text for openness and multiplicity of interpretation.

Since his primary interest is in abstract, logical structures of myths, independent of particular cultures or societies, Lévi-Strauss' method is to look at similar myths in many societies, the increasing breadth of comparison and contrast leading to the positing of more and more abstract structures. There is no doubt about the validity of searching for underlying or abstract structures of myths or stories; this is in part what analysis is all about. But at the same time it is important to insist on principled ways of relating posited underlying constructs to actually performed events. With regard to the Kuna we are in a privileged position in that they themselves posit underlying structures or meanings in the form of interpretations of the symbolism of the text and its message and—the most important point—they do so as part of its very performance, for an audience to hear, learn from, and criticize. This is not to say that an outside analyst should simply record and repeat Kuna-performed interpretations. But further and deeper analysis should relate in principled ways to Kuna performers who themselves are involved in the analytical process.

Many of the myths that Lévi-Strauss studies are etiological, their significance or point being reported as an explanation of the origin of fire, cooking, plants, or death. *Kaa kwento*, as I recorded it and as interpreted by the Kuna in their performance of it, is not etiological, but either entertaining, rhetorical, or both. Lévi-Strauss' etiological myths look to the past in order to explain the origin and reason for the present. *Kaa kwento* looks to the past (not mythical in the Kuna sense) in order to call for a particular mode of behavior in the future. Thus, in spite of its possible etiological origin (in diffusional terms), Kuna *kaa kwento* is now at its core thoroughly rhetorical and political. As has been shown here, in the particular performance I recorded, the teller, Mastayans, uses *kaa kwento* for two rhetorical-political aims:

(1) to argue for a particular mode of behavior, by means of an entertaining telling;
(2) to convince his immediate audience, especially the visiting *sakla*, that he, Mastayans, is a good *sakla*, that is, a knower and performer of Kuna tradition.

It is difficult if not impossible to compare *kaa kwento* with the myths that form the basis of Lévi-Strauss' study or with similar myths reported by other collectors or analysts of South American Indian mythology, since *kaa kwento* was recorded and analyzed in the context of performance. The others are reported essentially as summaries of referential content, outside their performance context, and rhetorical purpose is rarely mentioned. However, comparison of *kaa kwento* with similar stories in other American Indian societies does support the notion, already pointed out by T.T. Waterman in a careful 1914 study of many North American Indian folktales, that referential content is independent of the point or explanation provided by particular societies, groups, or occasions.[15] Although Waterman did not study actual performances of tales, his insistence on the separability of content and explanatory element or moral points to a potential for the use of tales in the rhetoric of performance, in which morals are developed and stressed independently of particular referential contents. The concept of potential for rhetorical use, inherent in a text, is similar to Kenneth Burke's notion of "literature as equipment for living."[16] Thus the same or similar story can have quite different interpretations or purposes in different societies. Even within a single society it is possible for the same story to be structured differently by different groups. The Hopi are a well-documented American Indian case of this. Fred Eggan reports that "it soon became apparent that the origin legends of the same clan from different villages showed major contradictions and that even within the same village the stories of associate clans did not always correspond.[17] In a recent paper, Nancy Parrott Hickerson reviews the Hopi situation:

> There is, in fact, no body of Hopi tribal mythology—there is simply the mythology of the several Hopi clans. These clan traditions are related to one another—there is a common geographical setting, and a basic similarity as major events of creation and important supernatural figures recur. However, the mythology tells, especially, of events and places which bear on the properties, prerogatives, ceremonial responsibilities, and political claims of the individual clans.[18]

Lévi-Strauss has the Hopi case among others in mind when he writes: "La même population, ou des populations voisines par le territoire, la langue ou la culture, élaborent parfois des mythes qui s'attaquent systématiquement à tel ou tel problème en envisageant, variante après variante, plusieurs manières concevables de la

---

[15] "The Explanatory Element in the Folk-tales of the North American Indians," *Journal of American Folklore*, 27 (1914), 1-54.

[16] Kenneth Burke, "Literature as Equipment for Living," in *The Philosophy of Literary Form*, rev. ed. (New York: Vintage Books, 1957), pp. 253-62.

[17] Fred Eggan, *Social Organization of the Western Pueblos* (Chicago: University of Chicago Press, 1950), p. 79.

[18] Nancy Parrott Hickerson, "The 'Natural Environment' as Object and Sign," *The Journal of the Linguistic Association of the Southwest*, 3 (1978), 39.

résoudre."[19] But notice that *kaa kwento* resolves its problems in various ways within the same text, or rather, leaves open to interpretation possible solutions to the problem, and, ultimately, leaves open just what the problem is.

With regard to *kaa kwento*, although no studies of this singing bones motif exist that provide contextual information about societal interpretation, function, and purpose as I do here, we can speculate, in the Waterman and Burkean sense, on the basis of the way similar stories are reported and classified in collections of Amerindian folktales. Relatively similar stories are found among the Umotina of the northern Mato Grosso and among the Zuni of the North American Southwest. The Umotina have a myth in which a couple buries a boy and afterward from his corpse grow various crops, including pepper.[20] In a Zuni myth, two brothers bury their grandmother, and on the spot where they bury her, a hot pepper plant grows up.[21] Both of these stories are reported as if explaining the origin of hot pepper. Quite the contrary, of course, in the Kuna story, in spite of its title,[22] which is perhaps evidence of diffusion from groups in which it is used etiologically.

I do not find it strange that the same story or myth can be open to various interpretations as a strategic, structured part of its performance. This seems a natural feature of a nonliterate, American Indian society, in which discourse is central to social and political life. The openness of structure of *kaa kwento* is particularly well suited to the Kuna gathering in which individuals, especially *saklas* and other political leaders, gain prestige, jockey for position, and convince others on the basis of creative, adaptive, strategic use of speech.

It seems useful, by way of summary, to place this study within a paradigm of possible ways of going about the analysis of literature in nonliterate societies:

(1) Literature is studied in and for itself, abstracted from its use or sociocultural context, perhaps becoming grist for various textual mills—linguistic, structuralist, and so forth.

(2) Literature is seen as a reflection of some other aspect of the life of the people who produce and perform it, an aspect claimed to be more basic—social organizational, economic, psychological, and so forth.

(3) Literature is viewed in relationship to contexts provided by the society and culture in which it is found, and attention is paid to the functions and situations of performance.

While the approach developed here falls most clearly within number 3, it moves along a continuum that ranges from structuralist to ethnomethodological. The former approach is oriented toward abstract structures and tends not to be interested in concrete contexts. For the latter, context is the focus of analysis and the text is secondary. Careful attention to both text and context, their intersection and interaction, is crucial to an understanding of Kuna *kaa kwento*.[23]

---

[19] Claude Lévi-Strauss, *Le Cru et le Cuit* (Paris: Plon, 1964), p. 338. The Hopi case is discussed on p. 339.

[20] Kalervo Oberg, *Indian Tribes of Northern Mato Grosso, Brazil* (Smithsonian Institution, Institute of Social Anthropology, Publication No. 15, 1953), pp. 108-109.

[21] Frank Hamilton Cushing, *Zuni Folk Tales* (New York: Putnam, 1901), pp. 175-84.

[22] For the significance of titles, see Dell Hymes, "Myth and Tale Titles of the Lower Chinook," *Journal of American Folklore*, 72 (1959), 139-45.

[23] Research for this paper was supported by NSF, NIMH, the University of Texas Institute of Latin American Studies, and a Guggenheim Fellowship. R. Bauman, J. Howe, I.C. Lieb, D. Sherzer, and B. Stross offered insightful criticism.

RICHARD BAUMAN

"Any Man Who Keeps More'n One Hound'll Lie to You": Dog Trading and Storytelling at Canton, Texas

The coon hunter and the trader, like their compatriots elsewhere in the American expressive landscape, have constituted a presence in Texas folk tradition, and their tales and exploits have captured the attention of Texas folklorists from J. Frank Dobie to Américo Paredes. Dobie (1946) for example, adapted two tall tales of coon hunting in his sketch, "The Cold-Nosed Hounds," while Mody Boatright (1965:96) recorded a coon-dog story attached to Gib Morgan, the legendary oil driller. One of the core episodes in the saga of Gregorio Cortez, which Américo Paredes has chronicled, is a crooked horse trade carried off by Gregorio's brother, Román (Paredes 1958:37-39). In contemporary Texas the horse trader may have been pushed off the scene by the tractor, and the coon hunter may ride around in a $8,000 pickup, but the traditions of the sharp trader and the hound-dog man have lost none of their vigor in the East Texas area around Canton.

Canton, Texas is a small town of approximately three thousand people, located about sixty miles east and a little south of Dallas. Its principal claim to fame is that, on the Sunday preceding the first Monday of every month, Canton becomes the scene of a large and very popular trading fair. The average attendance is about twenty thousand—perhaps double that on Labor Day. The fair draws traders and dealers from as far away as New York, California, Oregon, and Minnesota.

First Monday at Canton—for so it is still called, though the action has shifted to Sunday in accommodation to the modern work week—fits into a long tradition of American trade days. From the beginning, an important commodity in the trading that went on during First Mondays was horses and mules. Professional horse and mule traders were called "jockies"; hence, "Jockey Day" and "Hoss Monday" are other names for the occasion, and "jockey ground" or "jockey yard" designate the area in which the trading was conducted (Sartain 1932:253). Numerous local histories and personal documents testify to the high degree of interest and excitement generated by the action on the jockey ground during the height of the trade days in the nineteenth and early twentieth centuries. But, as horses and mules declined in importance with the mechanization of Southern agriculture, First Monday trade days declined as well, to the point that very few now remain. Still, some trade days have been in continuous existence since they began, while other have been revived, reincarnated as flea markets.

Revised from a longer paper in R. D. Abrahams and R. Bauman (eds.), *And Other Neighborly Names: Social Process and Cultural Image in Texas Folklore*, 1981, pp. 79-103. Reprinted with permission of University of Texas Press and Richard Bauman.

Though an occasional mule or two is still hauled to Canton for trade, and a considerable amount of domestic poultry is sold there as well, where animals are concerned, coon dogs are the real focus of interest during First Monday. This dog trading was an early feature of Canton First Monday. No one seems to know precisely when it began but my oldest informants, who are past eighty, remember it from their earliest visits to Canton. In 1960, a few years before the general trading left the courthouse square for separate grounds, the dog trading was moved to its own site across the highway from the main area, down on the river bottom. The dog grounds and dog trading are not part of the Chamber of Commerce operation. The grounds are privately owned, and the dog trading generally has a very different tone from the flea-market atmosphere across the road.

First, whereas many of the flea-market dealers and public are women, the people on the dog grounds are almost exclusively men. Again, the flea market attracts many urban types—as well as townspeople from surrounding towns. On the dog grounds one sees mostly rural people: farmers, hunters, more blacks, more people of lower socioeconomic status generally. The activity on the dog grounds begins in earnest on Friday night, when people begin to gather, set up tents and campers, stake out their dogs, drink, play cards, shoot dice, talk dogs, go off into the surrounding countryside to hunt, and generally have a good time.

At the peak of the trading there are hundreds of hunting dogs of all kinds on the dog grounds, though coon-hounds are clearly predominant. Some coon-dog men are as serious as other dog fanciers about breeding, standards, registration, papers, and the other trapping of "improving the breed." Most dealing in dogs at this level involves fancy stud fees, careful records, big money—into the thousands of dollars for a top dog. Many hound-dog men, however, are far more pragmatic. They just want good, working hunting dogs, and cannot afford to pay a great deal of money for them. These men tend to be less careful about the niceties of breeding, record keeping, and so on; they are satisfied with whichever dogs get together behind the shed, breeding old Handy to old Ready. This is the group of dog traders that comes to Canton, and as a group they tend not to be highly regarded by the serious coon-dog breeders or by the townspeople in general. One citizen of Canton described dog traders to me as people for whom "making a living gets in the way." Some are professional dog jockies; most are amateurs. Their motivations for coming to Canton are various and often mixed. Some come to get "using dogs," while others just like to "move their dogs around" or "change faces." The professionals come to make some money, but many traders just want the activity to pay for itself—i.e., to pay for the trip and for the dogs' feed.

The dominant reasons for coming to Canton, though, are to get together with other hound-dog men to talk about dogs and hunting, and to trade for its own sake, as recreation. For the majority of traders at Canton the economic motive is far from the top of the list; dog trading for them is a form of play, a contest of wits and words. Some men actually keep one or two dogs around at any given time just to trade, and, not surprisingly, these are usually rather "sorry" dogs, "old trashy dogs that ain't worth a quarter for nothin'." One trader put it this way: "My experience is, I'll be in Canton in the morning, be there Sunday all day, I've got a dog trade always. Reason I want to go because a man's gonna meet me there and demonstrate his dog and I'm gonna take mine. Course the one I'm gonna take ain't much of a dog . . . Now and then I get a good dog, then I get one that ain't worth bringin' home, but still it's trade that I like to do."

In other words, Canton is "where the action is" (see Goffman 1967). Of course, no dog trader is averse to making some money, and one of the stated goals of any swap is to "draw boot"—i.e., to get a dog and some cash for for your dog. One man told me that his fellow traders would "trade with you for ten when ten's all they got in their dog, then they'll make five on your dog." These are small sums, though. In most cases cash profit stands as a token of having played the game well; it is a sweetener that enhances the encounter. It is also true that many of the transactions at Canton are straight cash sales; but the dynamic of these transactions is the same in all essentials as trading, and they are considered to be and labeled trades.

When I asked what brought him to Canton, one old trader, who has been coming to First Monday for more than seventy years, replied, "Well, I enjoy trading and enjoy seeing my old friends." For him, as for most others on the dog grounds, the essence of First Monday is trading and sociability. I propose in the remainder of this paper to explore some of the interrelationships between the two activities. In the course of the analysis I hope to demonstrate how traditional narratives of the kind studied primarily by folklorists and the personal narratives of special interest to linguists and sociologists can be productively studied within a unified framework, based on these genres' coexistence in the repertoires and performances of those who tell them. The formal and functional interrelationships among these stories within the institution of dog trading can best be uncovered by an analytical perspective that merges the concerns of folklore and sociolinguistics, to the enrichment of both.

As a point of departure, let us consider the following two excerpts from dog-trading encounters at Canton. The first involves two participants: John Moore, a black man in his early forties, and Mr. Byers, a white man in his early fifties. John Moore has the dogs, and Byers has just walked up to look them over.[1]

BYERS: He strike his own fox? [I.e., can he pick up the fox's trail by himself?]
MOORE: He strike his own fox. Strike his own fox. Clean as a pin, strike his own fox. [Pause.] And he'll stand to be hunted, he'll stand to be hunted [Byers interrupts—unintelligible]. What is that?
BYERS: He run with a pack good?
MOORE: Oh yes, oh yes. And he'll stand . . . he'll stand three nights out a week. He has did that and took off—ain't seen him waitin' behind that. [Unintelligible.] He'll stand three nights out a week. I've known that to happen to him. [Pause.]

           I try to be fair with a man 'bout a dog. Tell the truth about a dog, tell you what he'll do. If there's any fault to him, I wanna tell the man. If I get a dog from a man, if there's any fault to him, I want him to tell me.

           I bought . . . we bought some puppies from a man, we asked him, said, "they been vaccinated?" Said, "now we gonna buy the puppies," say, "now if they been vaccinated, we wanta know if they ain't." Say, "now, what we's gettin' at, if they ain't been vaccinated distemper's all around." We wanted 'a vaccinate 'em.

           And he swore they were vaccinated and after we bought 'em they died, took distemper and died. Then he told a friend o' ours, he say he hate that he didn't tell us that the dogs, the puppies, wasn't vaccinated.

           See, and I begged him, "I tell you somethin' man, we gonna buy the puppies, gonna give you a price for 'em," I said, "but there's one thing we just wanta know if they been vaccinated." And then turned right around . . . then turned right around and told the man that they hadn't been vaccinated. And here I begged him, "I'm beggin' you, gonna buy the dogs, puppies, at your price."
BYERS: I traded two good coon dogs for two Walker dogs [a breed of hounds] [Moore: Mmm hmm] supposed to be good fox dogs.

MOORE:	Mmm hmm.
BYERS:	Sumbitches wouldn't run a *rabbit*.
MOORE:	You see that?
BYERS:	Boy, I mean they wouldn't run nothin'.
MOORE:	I tell you for...what is your name?
BYERS:	Byers.
MOORE:	Mr. Byers, this here is John Moore, everybody know me here. I can take you to some people in here any day—I'm talkin' about some rich, up to date people—I have sold dogs to, and they'll tell you....I'm talkin' 'bout for hunnerd dollars, sold some hunnerd dollar dogs, seventy-five dollar dogs, fifty dollar...I haven't got a dog over there for fifty dollars. You can't raise one for that, 'cause a sack o' feed down there where we live cost you four fifty for fifty pounds, what we feed the hounds on, we feed the hounds on, and then we get scraps from that slaughter pen to put in. And if I tell you somep'n 'bout a dog i'm not gon' misrepresent him. Not gonna misrepresent him.

You see that little ol' ugly gyp [bitch] there? She'll git in the thicket....We was runnin' the Fourth o' July, I think it was, runnin' a big grey fox. Across the road runnin' right down 'side this culvert, oh, 'bout like that [unintelligible]. You've seen it where, that's what, briar, you know, you know briar up under there, you know, know what I'm talkin' 'bout—these ol'...where...got them stickers on, 'bout like that [holds up his finger], 'bout that size, got that runner, big runner to 'em. And just had the place solid.

And we had a fox under there, and got him under there 'bout three o'clock, and he stayed there till it got daylight, he stayed under there to daylight. The road on east side o' that place.

And daylight come and them ol' feet comin' out from under round there drove her all buggy. He just walked in them briars. Place he could get in, you'd just see him every while just walkin', just walkin'. You could hear that gyp now smell that fox. He got him hot, he just walk in them briars.

That little gyp come up in now, and she come up, man, there, like this fox, far like to the middle o' this pickup, quite that far—come out, shot out from under there, wasn't long before she come out just sprawled on her belly.

There she is, right there. There she is right there. [To dog:] Yeah, come over here.

(Recorded Canton, Texas, July 31, 1971)

In the second encounter there are three participants, only two of whom are heard in this excerpt: Homer Townsend and Herman Smith. Townsend's son is interested in Smith's dogs, but his father does the talking.

TOWNSEND:	Will them ol' dogs you got catch a rabbit?
SMITH:	Yeah.
TOWNSEND:	Really get up there and catch one.
SMITH:	Yes sir. I'd buy another one that'll outrun 'em.
TOWNSEND:	Well, a man told me while ago they wouldn't hardly *run* a rabbit.
SMITH:	I tell you what I'll do. I'll take the man out here and *show* him. That's all I can do...that's the *best* way, is to take him out and show him. I'll buy another 'un that can run with 'em...uh, keep 'em or sell 'em or buy another 'un that could run with 'em, see....
TOWNSEND:	[Interrupts:] He's interested in some dogs, some greyhounds, and, uh, that man says they wouldn't hardly run a rabbit.
SMITH:	[Angrily:] I'll *show* you! That's all I can do. You know me, I don't *lie* about these dogs. I tried 'em out, see, I tried them dogs out before I ever bought 'em, see. And I do the *coon* dogs thataway. I wouldn't give a dime for nary a dog I didn't know on this ground until I hunted him.

I sold one last...uh...summer and the man asked me what I'd take. I said, "I won't even price him till you go huntin'." I said, "I sell mine in the *woods*!" And when we went huntin', he treed three coons. Come out, and he said, "Whatcha want for that dog?" I said two-fifty. And he went countin' out them twenty dollar bills.

I got a little ol' gyp out there I've had three years. And she's three years old— she's been treein' coons ever since she was a year old! And she's still in my pen! And I got one o' her puppies mated to that 'un yonder...that's the one over there. Took him out the other day, just started trainin' him, you know.

That's the reason I got them greyhounds, 'cause I can see 'em, see? I can't hear a thing outta this ear. I gotta go with somebody and they got a bunch of trash and....No, somebody got one to run with 'em, I'll buy 'em this morning.

TOWNSEND: [Leaving:]   Well, we'll talk to you a little bit...after awhile.
SMITH: [Loudly:]   I'll take 'em out here and *show* you! That's the way I am. I don't lie about these dogs. I ain't...I don't believe in it.

I bought a dog here 'bout three or four months ago down here from an ol' man and ended high nigh walkin' him! And he was tellin' me about that dog, trainin' young dogs and this 'n' that, and I give him thirty dollars for it, and I *give* him to that little boy down there. That hound don't tree. I *give* him to him. I wouldn't lie to him, I *give* it to him! I don't lie about it. I'll buy 'em on the tree or sell 'em on the tree, I don't care about the money. I don't lie about these dogs. You hear anything very long and you'll say it's all right, you know what I mean?

(Recorded by Donna West, Canton, Texas, November 1, 1970)

For our purposes, two features stand out from these excerpts. First the participants clearly devote a considerable amount of interactional attention to the issue of truthfulness and lying; and, second, one of the devices they resort to in addressing this issue is telling stories. Anyone who is at all familiar with hound-dog men, coon hunters or otherwise, will feel no surprise at hearing they have some involvement in lying and storytelling.

To an audience familiar with coon hunters, the association between lying and coon hunting is so well-established that it constitutes an expressive resource for performance. As summed up for me with artful succinctness by a Texas coon hunter, "any man who keeps more'n one hound'll lie to you." One type of lying associated with coon hunting, and of longstanding interest to folklorists, is the tall tale, the traditional tale of lying and exaggeration. Hunting has always been a privileged domain for tall tales: *The Types of the Folktale* (Thompson 1961) established the hunting tale as a special subgroup of tales of lying (types 1890–1909), and the standard American tall-tale collections are full of hunting windies (see Baughman 1966: types 1890–1909 and motifs X1100–1199, with references therein).

By contrast, the more common story of personal experience, told straightforwardly as truth, contextualizes the tall tale; it contributes to the humorous effect by establishing a set of generic expectations that the tall tale can bend exaggeratedly out of shape. The effect is reciprocal, of course: The obvious exaggeration of the tall tale creates an aura of lying that colors the "true" stories as well.

When we juxtapose the personal narrative and the tall tale, there are actually two dimensions of "lying" that become apparent. First, the unusual but not impossible events of the former are transformed into the exaggeratedly implausible events of the latter. Thus tall tales are lies, insofar as what they report as having happened did not happen, nor could have happened.

There is more, though. The tall tale is usually told in the third person, which distances it somewhat from the narrator, and contrasts with the characteristic use of the first-person voice in the personal narrative. A common feature of tall-tale style, however, is also the use of the first person (Brunvand 1978: 136–137), either directly ("I had an old coon dog that would go out in the woods. . . .") or as a link between the narrator and the third-person protagonist ("I knew an old boy, he had him a coon dog. . . ."). When the first-person voice is employed a second dimension of "lying" comes into play. The use of the first person brings the tall tale closer to personal narrative; it allows the story to masquerade for a while as a "true" personal narrative, until the realization that what is being reported is impossible shatters the illusion. In other words, these first-person tall tales are what Goffman calls "fabrications," "the intentional effort of one or more individuals to manage activity so that a party of one or more others will be induced to have a false belief about what it is that is going on" (1974:83). What appears to be going on is an account of actual events; what is really going on is a lie masquerading as such an account—hence, a double lie. The man who tells such a tale in the third person is a liar; the man who tells it in the first person is a tricky liar, a con man. Thus two potential dimensions of "lying" enter into the expressive ambience of coon hunters: outright lies and fabrications.

As suggested, however, traditional tall tales are not very common at Canton. Even without them, though, the aura of lying persists around the personal dog stories because, although recounted as true, they are susceptible to creative exaggeration, another dimension of "lying," for at least two major reasons. First, like all natural sociable interaction, the encounters of coon hunters are at base about the construction and negotiation of personal identity. In them sociable narratives are a vehicle for the encoding and presentation of information about oneself in order to construct a personal and social image (Bauman 1972). In Watson and Potter's apt formulation, "social interaction gives form to the image of self and the image of the other; it gives validity and continuity to the identifications which are the source of an individual's self-esteem" (1962:246). The way to establish that you are a good coon hunter is to show that you have good hounds, and are thus knowledgeable about quality dogs—even more so if you have trained them yourself. Thus, because hunting stories are instruments for identity building, for self-aggrandizement (Labov and Waletzky 1967:34), there is a built-in impulse to exaggerate the prowess of one's dogs with hyperbole ("When he trees, hell, if you ain't give out, you're plum gonna get him of starvation before he comes away from there"), or by selection (omitting mention of the faults of a dog you're bragging on) as a means of enhancing one's own image (cf. Gilsenan 1976:191). This tendency toward "stretching the truth," as it is often called, has been widely reported in men's sociable encounters (see, e.g., Bauman 1972; Bethke 1976; Biebuyck-Goetz 1977; Cothran 1974; Tallman 1975). It is one more factor that gives hound-dog men the reputation of being liars.

The other factor which promotes the expressive elaboration of the hound and hunting story is that, whatever its referential and rhetorical functions, it also constitutes a form of verbal art. That is, it is characteristically *performed*, subject to evaluation, both as truth and as art for the skill and effectiveness with which it is told (Bauman 1977:11). The esthetic considerations of artistic performance may demand the embellishment or manipulation—if not the sacrifice—of the literal truth in the interests of greater dynamic tension, formal elegance, surprise value, contrast, or other elements which contribute to excellence in performance in this subculture. "Stretching the truth," of course, which chiefly exaggerates and selects, is not exactly the same as the outright lying of the tall tale. Nevertheless, although the two activities can be terminologically distinguished to point up the contrast between them, they are usually merged; and the term "lying," in an unmarked sense, is used to label both (see the figure below). Fabrication, our third analytically distinguished type of lying, has no folk label.

[outright] lying   stretching the truth

     For these reasons, then, some expectations of lying attends the telling of these stories about special dogs and memorable hunts. Realizing this, the tellers frequently resort to various means of validating their accounts. These range from verbal formulas like "I guarantee," to the testimony of witnesses (as in the above story), to offers to demonstrate the dog in action. One man concluded a lengthy story about the hunting prowess of his hound with:

> You don't believe it, take and let your dogs run a coon loose, and I'll lead her, anybody tonight, anybody got their damn good cold-nose dogs, and if she don't run that coon and tree that coon, it's gonna be somethin' that ain't never happened. She'll run that sumbitch till by god, she'll tree that sumbitch.

(Recorded Canton, Texas, August 1, 1971)

Despite these attempts at validation, the expectation persists that hound-dog men will lie when talking about their dogs.

     Hunting tall tales and ordinary dog stories do not exhaust the repertoire of storytelling at Canton. The special character of First Monday for the hunters who attend is that it is an occasion for dog trading; not surprisingly, then, trading itself constitutes an important conversational resource for those who gather there. Like the hunting tall tales, some of the trading stories are traditional fictions, part of the national—even international—treasury of lore about shrewd trades, deceptive bargains, gullibility, and guile. Still more common, though, are personal narratives about trades in which the teller himself was involved. Some of these, interestingly, are about being taken. Dog trading is, after all, a contest, and even the canny trader can be bested occasionally, as in the following account:

A: That's that little Trigg [a breed of hound] I's tellin' you about.
B: I bought one o' them one time, Cal, was the funniest thing I got in. When I swapped for 'er, and give some money, in Texarkana, old boy said, "I guarantee 'er." Said, "She's one of the finest coon dogs I've ever had in the woods in my life." I carried that dog home, I pitched 'er out, first thing she hit was a deer. I think the day or two later, I finally found 'er. And I mean she wouldn't run *one* thing on Earth but a deer, not anything. So I carried 'er back to Texarkana and just give 'er away. Yessir, and *five* minutes after the boy drove off with that dog, a guy drove up and said, "Do you know where I can find a deer dog anywhere for sale?"
C & D: [laugh.]
B: I'll bet he hadn't got two mile outa town, when . . .
D: [interrupting:] Outa town, dog and all?

B: Yeah. Ain't no tellin' what he'd give for the dog, and she was perfect. I mean she was a straight deer dog. Wouldn't run nothin' else. But that's my luck.

(Recorded Canton, Texas, August 1, 1971)

In this story, the teller loses out not once, but twice. He is victimized by being lied to outright by another trader—note the inevitable preoccupation with lying—and then compounds the problem by giving away the deer dog, worthless to a coon hunter, moments before he is presented with a golden opportunity to sell it at a handsome profit. Still, he is philosophical about it; he introduces the story as the *funniest* experience he has had with Trigg hounds, and chalks up the whole experience to luck.

While admitting that one has been taken in a trade might seem to expose one to some risk of losing face, the risk is apparently offset by the reportability and performance value of a good story. And, after all, it did take an outright lie on the trader's part to accomplish the deception. Moreover, any trader worth his salt has plenty of stories about how he bested someone else in a trade by the exercise of wit, cleverness, or deception. The same man who lost out twice on the deer dog told the following story, recounting a classic example of the short con, a fabrication *par excellence*.

Last time I went over to Canton, I had a dog I called Blackjack. He was just about as sorry a dog as I ever had owned. He wouldn't do nothin' but eat. Take him huntin' and he lay out under the pickup.

So I decided I'd take him over to Canton, and I did, and I met a friend of mine over there, named Ted Haskell, out o' Corsicana. I told Ted, I said, "now, you go up that alley up yonder and meet me 'bout half way where they's tradin' dogs yonder, and then we'll introduce ourselves. You...we'll...sell this dog, and I'll give you half what I get outa it."

I met ol' Ted, and he says, "well, ol' Blackjack," he says, "I haven't had a coon race since I sold him," he says, "where'd you get him?"

"I got him over to Palestine."

"Well, I declare, I wisht I had him back," he says, "what are you askin' for him?"

I said, "I'll take thirty dollars."

Well, they began to gather 'round and listen and listen. We kept talkin' 'bout him. He'd brag on Blackjack. And finally, an ol' boy eased up and called me off and says, "I'll give twenty dollars for him." And I said, "well, pay me."

Well, he paid me; course I told Mr. Haskell mighty glad I'd met him, and he turned and went one way, and I went the other way, and we met at the pickup and divided the money. I come home, and he come back to Corsicana.

So I'm sure that man felt about like I did when I bought him, 'cause he wasn't worth carryin' a-huntin'.

(Recorded by Thomas A. Green, Blooming Grove, Texas, May 31, 1968)

Stories like this one manifest a significant ambivalence about lying and other swindles, especially about lying—whether outright lying, stretching the truth, or fabrication—in conducting the trading itself. As indicated, dog trading is viewed by the confirmed traders as a game of strategy in which, like many other games of strategy, deception occupies a central and accepted place. There is a long tradition in American folklore and popular literature of admiration for the shrewd trader, from the Yankee peddler to the Southern horse trader, who makes his way through the world by wit and words (Dorson 1959:47–48; Ferris 1977; Green 1968, 1972). The numerous entries in Baughman's *Type and Motif-Index of the Folktales of England and North America* (1966) under K134, Deceptive horse sale (or trade), as well as such literary pieces as the horse trade in Longstreet's *Georgia Scenes* or the recent popular collections of horse-trading tales by Ben Green (1968, 1972), suggest that Americans enjoy hearing about shrewd traders and therefore, at some level at least, accept their crooked dealings (cf. Boatright 1973:146). The interplay between the trader's verbal skill in trading and his verbal skill as a storyteller is probably significant here; the two are complementary aspects of his overall image as quick-witted and shrewd, one who manipulates men and situations—whether trading encounters or social gatherings—to his own advantage. Good traders are not reluctant self-publicists; one Canton regular told me with obvious pride: "I'll tell you what you can do. You can put me right out there on that road, barefooted, if it wasn't too hot, and before I get home, I'll have a pair of shoes, I want to tell you."

Nevertheless, whereas chess, for example, is unequivocally and only a game, in which such strategic deception as may occur is completely contained within the play frame, dog trading is not so unambiguous. While trading is certainly engaged in as play by many of the participants at Canton, the play frame is almost never overtly acknowledged. The only instances I observed that were openly marked as play were framed by such obviously inappropriate offers as five dollars plus a toothless old dog for a proven hound in prime condition. Otherwise, the public construction placed upon the trading encounter depicts it as a serious business transaction, and it is *always* susceptible to being understood as such by one or both participants. Here is the crux of the matter. The traditional American ideal demands, if not absolute honesty in business transactions, at least the maintenance of the public fiction that the participants are telling the truth (cf. Simmel 1950:314). Thus lying does not accord with the public construction of a dog-trading transaction, nor is it consistent with the actual understanding of those who consider a dog trade straight business, not a game. The trader who lies about a dog during the conduct of a trade may see himself and be seen by some other traders as a master player, gulling the marks as they deserve; but he may also be despised as a swindler who cheats honest people. No harm is done by telling stories about shrewd or crooked trades—indeed, such accounts may be relished for their performance value—but actually hoodwinking someone is a different matter. It makes the difference between Goffman's benign and exploitive fabrications (1974:87,103).

Having explored the relationship between lying and storytelling among the dog traders at Canton to this point, we can now return to the excerpts from the trading encounters with which we began our exploration. The strong preoccupation with lying and storytelling that characterizes both encounters should be relatively more comprehensible in light of the preceding discussion.

The strategy that emerges from the expectations and conventions of dog trading is that one should take pains during an actual transaction to *dispel* the aura of lying that surrounds it. The most direct means of doing so is by explicit insistence on one's truthfulness and by disavowal of lying. In the encounters under examination, both John Moore and Herman Smith employ this means of establishing their trustworthiness. John Moore volunteers early in the enounter: "I try to be fair with a man 'bout a dog. Tell the truth about a dog, tell you what he'll do. If there's any fault to him, I wanna tell the man." And then, employing the powerful rhetorical device of identification (Burke 1969:20-23), Moore puts himself in Byers' position: "If I get a dog from a man, if there's any fault to him, I want him to tell me." A little later, to validate the information he is providing about his dogs, he insists: "If I tell you somep'n 'bout a dog, I'm not gon' mispresent him. Not gonna misrepresent him." In the second encounter, Herman Smith is rather seriously challenged by Homer Townsend; he reiterates with some vehemence throughout the encounter, "I don't lie about these dogs!" These are all disclaimers of outright lying or of stretching the truth by selection or distortion. I have not recorded or observed any instances in which a participant disavowed pulling off a fabrication, though it is conceivable that such disavowals might occur.

For our purposes, perhaps the most interesting means by which the dog traders seek to establish and substantiate their identities as honest men is in telling stories. If we examine these stories, we see that they are closely related to the sociable narratives discussed earlier in this paper—specifically, to personal narratives about the performance of particular dogs and to personal narratives about trading experiences.

Three narratives appear in the excerpt from the first trading encounter, two told by John Moore and one very minimal one told by Mr. Byers. Moore clearly tells his first story, about being victimized in a trade by buying some puppies which the seller falsely assures him had had their shots, as a rhetorical strategy to convey his negative attitudes toward a trader who would tell an outright lie about a dog. By implication he emphasizes his own trustworthiness in a context where trickery and deceit are widespread. Moore's central rhetorical purpose is to distance himself from dog traders who lie, and his story is obviously and strongly adapted to that purpose. Much of his narrative is given over to establishing this polarization (Labov 1979) between the dishonest trader and Moore himself, as customer. The trader's lie is doubly destructive because it was both unnecessary, since Moore was going to buy the dogs whether or not they had had their shots, and cruel, since it resulted in the death of the dogs. Moore gave the trader ample and repeated opportunity to tell the truth, but he remained firm in his lie; and everyone suffered as a result, even the liar himself, since the death of the puppies brought him remorse ("he hate that he didn't tell us . . . ").

Byers too has been taken in a trade. He comes back with his account of having traded once for two dogs that were supposed to be good fox dogs and then discovering that the "sumbitches wouldn't run a *rabbit*." This story establishes that he has already been victimized at least once in a trade and, by implication, that he does not intend to let it happen again. Since he is not the one whose honesty is on the line, however, having no dog to trade, his story is rather minimal—just long enough to make his point, without attempting to be strongly persuasive. Still, there is not a clause in his narrative that lacks a clearly evaluative element.

Moore goes on to reaffirm his *bona fides* by mentioning his satisfied customers, including "some rich, up-to-date people." Then, picking up on Byers' apparent interest in fox dogs, Moore points out a fox dog among his own string, and proceeds to tell an extended story about her prowess in a recent hunt in order to build up her credentials—a sales pitch in narrative form. Stories of this kind are especially motivated during trading transactions because one cannot tell from merely looking at a dog what its hunting abilities are. Straightforward enumeration of the dog's qualities could also get the information across, but corroborating narratives, convincingly told, may add verisimilitude to the seller's claims. Hence the usefulness of combining such narratives with additional claims to honesty, as

Moore does both directly and by telling his story about a dishonest dog trader in order to distance himself from such practices. As the one offering the dogs, Moore has to tell stories that are persuasive enough to establish both his honesty, as in the first story, and the dog's quality, persistence, toughness, etc., as in the second. In sociable interaction there is no immediate negative consequence if your audience does not accept the truth of your story; in trading encounters, others must accept your story sufficiently to be persuaded to *act* on it, hopefully by trading for or buying your dog.

The second excerpt contains two stories, both told by Herman Smith, the man with the dogs. Townsend has rather seriously challenged him with offering dogs that won't perform. Smith accordingly counters with a story to demonstrate that, far from being willing to risk a customer's dissatisfaction or skepticism, he would actually *refuse* to conclude a sale until the dog has proven itself in the woods. This is not just honesty, it's superhonesty. Smith's second story is in the same vein: having been taken in by an unscrupulous trader who lied about the treeing ability of a dog, Smith would not himself stoop to selling the worthless hound, but gave it away to a little boy. Any man who gives dogs to little boys can't be all bad. Here is another instance of extreme polarization between the dishonest trader and the honest man: the unscrupulous trader places profit over honesty, while Smith values honesty over profit ("I don't care about the money. I don't lie about these dogs"). Just so there is no question about his own honorable values, he repeats the relevant points again and again.

Honesty	—over Profit
I wouldn't lie to him.	I *give* him to that little boy down there.
I don't lie about it.	I *give* him to him!
I don't lie about these dogs.	I *give* it to him!

Interestingly, however, this story compromises one of Smith's earlier claims to Townsend—that he himself tries out all the dogs he acquires before buying them. If he had done so in this case, he would not have had a worthless dog fobbed off on him. But it is more important to tell an emphatic story for its rhetorical effect than to worry about a minor inconsistency like this. Should Townsend pick up on it, however, this inconsistency could undermine Smith's claims to scrupulous honesty.

Close formal comparison of the stories told during trading with their counterparts in sociable interaction must be reserved for a later paper. However, this second story of Smith's is so closely parallel to the story of the deer dog, discussed earlier in the paper, that even a brief comparison highlights certain significant differences generated by the differing contexts in which they occur and their respective functions in these contexts.

In both stories the narrator acquires a dog from someone who lies to get rid of it and then, discovering that the dog does not perform as expected, gives it away. The story of the deer dog, told for entertainment in sociable interaction, is connected to the discourse that precedes it solely by the fact that the dog in question was a Trigg hound, and the previous speaker had pointed out a Trigg in his own string of dogs. No more is needed for the story to be appropriate in this sociable context. The extra twist at the end of the story, in which a customer appears for the dog immediately after it has been given away, makes the tale unusual and endows it with entertainment value; there is credit to be gained, as a performer, in telling it. The event sequence consists of six principal episodes, most of which have subepisodes:

(1) trading for the dog in the expectation that it was a coon dog; (2) taking it home; (3) taking it on a disastrous trial hunt, in which it turns out to be a deer dog; (4) having to search for the now apparently worthless dog; (5) returning to Texarkana to give it away; and (6) being approached by someone looking for a deer hound exactly like the one just given away. The evaluative dimension of the story serves to highlight the reportability of the experience, the humor and irony of the situation.

Herman Smith's story, however, is more strongly motivated and rooted in its conversational context. Smith's prospective customers are leaving, apparently because they don't believe his dogs are any good, and he is very concerned to establish his trustworthiness as a dog trader. The narrative line of the story is minimal: (1) trading for the dog; (2) discovering that it won't perform as promised; and (3) giving it away. More important by far is the rhetorical impact. The rhetorical power of the story resides in the fact that, unlike the unscrupulous trader, Smith spurned the opportunity to swindle someone else with a worthless dog; instead, he gave it away to the little boy. This is the point that he emphasizes most strongly in his story. Most of the work of the narrative, the thrust of its heavy evaluative dimension, aims at a polarization between the dishonest trader and the honorable narrator. Note, however, that this story, like those of John Moore and Mr. Byers, does also involve a trader who is not as honest as Smith presents himself to be, one who lies outright about a dog. Thus we come full circle: the very story that is told in the course of a trading encounter to dispel any suspicion of the trader's dishonesty reinforces the aura of lying that surrounds trading in general. Any man who keeps more'n one hound'll lie to you.

Dog trading at Canton First Monday brings together and merges two important figures in American tradition, the hunter and the trader. Both are strongly associated with storytelling as subjects and performers, and both are major exponents of the widely noted American predilection for expressive lying. Since at least the time when a distinctive body of American folk humor first emerged in the early years of the American republic, the hunter and the trader have occupied a privileged place in American folklore. Dog trading at Canton is a thriving contemporary incarnation of this American folk tradition; the tall tales and personal narratives of its participants place them in unbroken continuity with the generations of hunters, traders, and storytellers that have given American folklore some of its most distinctive characteristics.

NOTES

[1] Pseudonyms are employed throughout this paper to protect the privacy of individuals. The representation of spoken language is, frankly, intended to have more expressive than linguistic accuracy in a strictly formal sense. I am more interested here in the narratives as oral literature than as dialectological data. No words have been added or deleted, no grammatical constructions "corrected," no eye-dialect introduced, but I have been concerned to convey that this is a record of language in a spoken, not a written mode, and to preserve something of the quality (however vague and impressionistic that term may be) of the oral discourse. To this end, I have selectively employed a variety of devices, some of them in themselves conventions for representing oral speech in print (e.g., "gonna," "'bout"), some of them attempts to capture certain features of local pronunciation as employed by the speakers (e.g., "sumbitch," "hunnerd"). I have avoided, however, certain renderings of pronunciation that tend to evoke most readily features of negative stereotype, most notably "d-" for "th-" as in "dis" and "dat." Above

all, I would emphasize that no pejorative connotation of any kind is intended by the mode of presentation I have employed.

For a valuable and provocative discussion of these issues, see Preston 1982.

BIBLIOGRAPHY

BAUGHMAN, ERNEST W. 1966. *Type and motif-index of the folktales of England and North America.* The Hague: Mouton.

BAUMAN, RICHARD. 1972. The La Have Island general store: Sociability and verbal art in a Nova Scotia community. *Journal of American Folklore* 85:330-43.

———. 1977. *Verbal art as performance.* Rowley, Mass.: Newbury House.

BETHKE, ROBERT D. 1976. Storytelling at an Adirondack inn. *Western Folklore* 35:123-39.

BIEBUYCK-GOETZ, BRUNHILDE. 1977. "This is the dyin' truth": Mechanisms of lying. *Journal of the Folklore Institute* 14:73-95.

BOATRIGHT, MODY C. 1965. *Gib Morgan, minstrel of the oil fields.* Dallas: SMU Press. (Orig. pub. 1945.)

———. 1973. The oil promoter as trickster. In *Mody Boatright, folklorist.* Ernest Speck, ed. Austin: University of Texas Press. (Orig.pub. 1961.)

BRUNVAND, JAN. 1978. *The study of American folklore,* 2nd ed. New York: Norton.

BURKE, KENNETH. 1969. *A rhetoric of motives.* Berkeley and Los Angeles: University of California Press. (Orig.pub. 1950.)

COTHRAN, KAY L. 1974. Talking trash on the Okefenokee Swamp rim, Georgia. *Journal of American Folklore* 87:340-56.

DOBIE, J. FRANK. 1946. The cold-nosed hounds. In *The pocket* Atlantic. New York: Pocket Books.

DORSON, RICHARD M. 1959. *American folklore.* Chicago: University of Chicago Press.

FERRIS, BILL. 1977. *Ray Lum: Mule trader, an essay.* Memphis: Center for Southern Folklore.

GILSENAN, MICHAEL. 1976. Lying, honor, and contradiction. In *Transaction and meaning: Directions in the anthropology of exchange and symbolic behavior.* Bruce Kapferer, ed. Philadelphia: Institute for the Study of Human Issues.

GOFFMAN, ERVING. 1967. Where the action is. In *Interaction ritual.* New York: Doubleday-Anchor.

———. 1974. *Frame analysis.* New York: Harper Colophon.

GREEN, BEN K. 1968. *Horse tradin'.* New York: Knopf.

———. 1972. *Some more horse tradin'.* New York: Knopf.

LABOV, WILLIAM. 1979. A grammar of narrative. Lecture presented at the University of Texas at Austin, October 10, 1979.

———, and DAVID FANSHEL. 1977. *Therapeutic discourse.* New York: Academic Press.

———, and JOSHUA WALETZKY. 1967. Narrative analysis: Oral versions of personal experience. In *Essays on the verbal and visual arts.* June Helm, ed. Seattle: University of Washington Press.

MORRIS, CHARLES. 1946. *Signs, language and behavior.* New York: Braziller.

PAREDES, AMÉRICO. 1958. *With his pistol in his hand.* Austin: University of Texas Press.

SARTAIN, JAMES ALFRED. 1932. *History of Walker County, Georgia,* vol. 1. Dalton, Ga.: A.J. Showalter Co.

SIMMEL, GEORG. 1950. *The sociology of Georg Simmel.* Kurt Wolff, trans. and ed. Glencoe: Free Press.

TALLMAN, RICHARD. 1975. Where stories are told: A Nova Scotia storyteller's milieu. *American Review of Canadian Studies* 5:17-41.

THOMPSON, STITH. 1955-1958. *Motif-index of folk-literature,* 6 vols. Bloomington: Indiana University Press.

———. 1961. *The types of the folktale,* 2nd rev. ed. Helsinki: Folklore Fellows Communication no. 184.

TOELKEN, BARRE. 1979. *The dynamics of folklore.* Boston: Houghton Mifflin.

WATSON, JEANNE, and ROBERT J. POTTER. 1962. An analytical unit for the study of interaction. *Human Relations* 12:245-63.

JUDITH T. IRVINE

Formality and Informality
in Communicative Events

Formality and its opposite, informality, are concepts frequently used in the ethnography of communication, in sociolinguistics, and in social anthropology to describe social occasions and the behavior associated with them. This paper examines the usefulness of those concepts in description and comparison. What might one mean by *formality*, in terms of observable characteristics of human social interaction? How might formality correspond to the cultural categories with which other peoples describe their own social occasions? Are the relevant distinctions best formulated as dichotomy (as the contrast formality/informality might suggest), or as a continuum ranging between two poles, or as something more complex? Do whatever distinctions we decide are involved in formality/informality apply to every society? Will the same kinds of behavioral differences, or the same kinds of cultural categories, emerge everywhere?

I pose these questions in an attempt to further the development of a more precise analytical vocabulary, particularly for the ethnography of communication, which has perhaps invoked those concepts most often (although their relevance is not limited to that field). We now have a small number of case-history descriptions of ways of speaking in particular speech communities. But the terms in which those descriptions are made are often vague, lacking in explicit analytical content, too close to our own folk categories—inadequate for cross-cultural comparison, or even for description itself. Many anthropologists (and I include myself) have used terms such as formality without defining them or thinking about their definitions, simply assuming that the meanings are clear, when in fact the usages are vague and quite variable.

My object, then, is to give our usages more substance and to explore how they might then better serve cross-cultural comparison. I shall first consider what has been meant by formality and informality in the recent literature—that is, what various authors seem to have intended those terms to describe. The literature I draw upon comes mainly from sociolinguistics and the ethnography of speaking although some works in other fields will be cited as well. I shall then restate these various senses of formality in what I hope is a more explicit fashion and argue for the usefulness of the more detailed formulation for comparison, both within and between speech communities. A third section of the paper attempts a more extended comparison; it examines the formality of certain social occasions in two African societies, the Wolof and the Mursi, and compares them with a third society, the

From *American Anthropologist*, Vol. 81, 1979, pp. 773-90. Reprinted with permission of the American Anthropological Association and Judith T. Irvine.

Ilongots of the northern Philippines. The fourth, and final, section, asks whether the cover term formality remains useful at all.

The last section also considers some broader issues in social theory to which these terms and concepts relate. Actually, this is the larger object of the essay. Refining an analytical vocabulary is not simply a matter of improving the quality of empirical data; the terminology also reflects and incorporates more general assumptions about the nature of the social order. To discuss the descriptive and analytical vocabulary, therefore, is also to address those assumptions.

WHAT HAS BEEN MEANT BY FORMALITY IN THE LITERATURE

A look at some recent literature in sociolinguistics, the ethnography of speaking, and related fields (e.g., Gumperz and Hymes 1972; Bauman and Sherzer 1974; Sanches and Blount 1975; Fishman 1968; Bloch 1975; Kirshenblatt-Gimblett 1976; papers in *Language in Society; Working papers in Sociolinguistics*) suggests three principal senses of formality, which are potentially confused with each other. These different senses have to do with whether the formality concerns properties of a communicative code, properties of the social setting in which a code is used, or properties of the analyst's description.

For instance, many authors use formality in the sense of an increased structuring and predictability of discourse. Here, formality is an aspect of code, such that the discourse is subject to extra rules or some greater elaboration of rules. In this vein, for example, Bricker (1974:388) and Gossen (1974:412), both writing on the Maya, and Fox (1974:73) who writes on the Rotinese, all describe "formal speech" as marked by special structuring—notably redundancy, and syntactic or semantic parallelism. Others have emphasized the predictability of structured discourse; they have argued that a "formal style" reduces the variability and spontaneity of speech (see Joos 1959 and Wolfson 1976). For example, Rubin's (1968) paper on bilingualism in Paraguay discusses formality in terms of limitations on the kinds of behaviors that are acceptable and on the amount of allowable variation (conceived as deviation from a norm).

Other authors use formality/informality as a way of describing the characteristics of a social situation, not necessarily the kind of code used in that situation. The relevant characteristics of the situation may have something to do with a prevailing affective tone, so that a formal situation requires a display of seriousness, politeness, and respect. For instance, Fischer (1972), describing ways of speaking among Trukese and Ponapeans, discusses the use of "respect vocabulary" and "formal etiquette" as displays of politeness marking a formal situation. In Fishman's (1972:51) discussion of "lecturelike or formal situations," formality seems to be understood as the opposite of levity and intimacy. Ervin-Tripp (1972:235), too, relates formality to politeness and "the seriousness of such situations." Not all authors agree on just what formality means about a situation, however. Rubin (1968) lists formality as a situational variable separate from "degree of intimacy" and "degree of seriousness." For Labov (1972:113), formality of situational context is what makes a speaker pay increased attention to his or her speech.

Finally, many authors use formal to refer to a technical mode of description, in which the analyst's statement of the rules governing discourse is maximally explicit. Although most linguists apply this sense of formality (as "explicitness") only to the statements made by an outside observer,[1] some anthropologists also apply it to a people's own analysis of their social order. When Murphy (1971:159), for instance, speaks of "the formal, conscious models of society held by its members," he refers to those conceptions of society and behavior that informants can present in explicit verbal statements. For other anthropologists the explicit statements need not be verbal; see Leach's (1965:15–16) discussion of nonverbal ritual as a way in which social structure, or a people's ideas about social structure, are made explicit and "formally recognized."

These three senses of formality have often been merged or interrelated. For example, when formality is conceived as an aspect of social situations, it is common to extend the term to the linguistic varieties used in such situations, regardless of what those varieties happen to be like otherwise. Formal and informal pronouns are a case in point. Their formality lies in what they connote about a social setting in which they are appropriately used; they do not necessarily differ in the number or elaboration of syntactic (or other) rules governing their use.

Some authors go further, blending all three senses of formality and arguing that formal descriptions are most suitable (or only suitable) for the more structured discourse that occurs in ceremoniallike formal situations. Here, one wonders whether it is not just the use of the single term formal for a kind of description, a kind of discourse, and a kind of situation that makes the three appear necessarily related. Discourse that is spontaneous is still rule-governed, as linguists working with syntax have been at pains to point out; indeed, a major effort of linguists in the past 20 years has been to show how and why rules of grammar permit the utterance and comprehension of sentences that have never occurred before. Explicit formulation of those rules cannot, therefore, be limited to specially rigidified or redundant discourse. So, with Halliday (1964), I would seek to avoid confusing the technical sense of formality (explicitness of the observer's description) with senses that concern the behavior and conceptual systems of the people described.

Still, some ways of interrelating different senses of formality are potentially fruitful. Maurice Bloch (1975) has recently argued, for instance, that code structuring and situational formality are causally related, so that increased structuring of discourse necessarily brings about increased politeness and a greater display of respect for a traditional, normative social order (and perhaps a coercive political establishment). That argument has various antecedents in social anthropology, although they are less clearly articulated and do not give particular attention to speech. One such forerunner is Durkheim's conception of ritual, as expressing and confirming the solidarity of the group and constraining the individual to conformity. A related matter, too, is the widespread view in structural-functional anthropology that connects structure with norm and tradition, and with order, coherence, and stability—a view of structure as essentially static.

Bloch's argument is an important one and I shall return to it later. Now, however, the point is that these basic questions about structure and action in discourse can be addressed only if the relevant variables are first disentangled. Arguments that do so (such as Bloch's) are much more useful than those that merely slide from one sense of formality to another, leaving implicit the connection between formal situations and frozen, rigidified speech (or other behavior).

FOUR ASPECTS OF FORMALITY
THAT APPLY CROSS-CULTURALLY

Leaving aside questions of causal relationships for now, I will restate, in a more detailed way, what considerations one may have in mind when describing social occasions as formal or informal. A search of some available ethnographic evidence, inadequate as it is for the purpose—and filtered as it is through ethnographers' descriptive vocabularies—suggests that the discourse aspect and the situational aspect of formality should be broken down into finer distinctions. Four different aspects of formality emerge that seem to apply to a wide variety of speech communities, perhaps to all. The four kinds of formality often co-occur in the same social occasion though not always (hence their presentation as separate variables).

Increased Code Structuring

This aspect of formality concerns the addition of extra rules or conventions to the codes that organize behavior in a social setting. Although I focus on the linguistic, any code (such as dress, gesture, or spatial organization) can, of course, be subject to degrees of structuring. It is important to recognize, however, that a social occasion involves many codes that operate at once, and the degrees of structuring that they variously display may differ. Even within the linguistic code one should distinguish among the various levels of linguistic organization that may be subject to the additional or elaborated structuring, such as intonation (including pitch contour, meter, loudness, and speed of talk), phonology, syntax, the use of particular sets of lexical items, fixed-text sequences, and turn taking. Increased structuring need not affect all these aspects of linguistic organization equally or at the same time.[2] Some speech events formalize different parts of the linguistic system and so cannot be lined up on a simple continuum from informality to formality.

For instance, among the Wolof[3] there are two distinct speech events, *woy* ("praise-singing") and *xaxaar* ("insult sessions"), which differ from ordinary conversations in their structuring of intonational patterns (among other things). But different aspects of intonation are affected. In praise-singing, the pitch contour of utterances is more structured than in ordinary talk but meter remains relatively loose; in insult sessions, meter is strictly regulated (with drum accompaniment), while pitch remains loose. It would be impossible to say that one form of discourse is more formalized than the other, although one could say that both are more formalized than ordinary conversation (and less formalized than some types of religious singing, which structure both pitch and rhythm).

Similarly, among the Yoruba, two speech events, both associated with the Iwi Egungun cult celebrations, formalize different aspects of the discourse (Davis 1976). In one event, speakers use highly structured utterances, often fixed texts, on conventional topics, whereas turn taking among speakers is unpredictable, with much of the interest for the audience residing in the speakers' competition for the floor. In the other type of speech event, turn taking is quite strictly regulated (as though in a play), but the topics can be creative and novel. The formalization of discourse here cannot be thought of as just a progressive rigidifying and restriction on creative potential. Instead, what is involved is a focusing of creativity onto a certain aspect of talk, which is highlighted because other aspects are redundant and predictable.

Code Consistency

A second kind of formalization involves co-occurrence rules. At many different levels of linguistic organization and in other avenues of communicative expression as well, speakers select from among alternatives that have contrasting social significance. Co-occurrence rules provide for the extent to which these choices must be consistent. In the kinds of discourse that ethnographers have labeled more formal, consistency of choices (in terms of their social significance) seems to be greater than in ordinary conversation, where speakers may be able to recombine variants to achieve special effects.

For example, among the Wolof, differences of pitch, loudness, and speed of talk (as well as other discourse features) may connote something about the speaker's social rank: high pitch, high volume, and high speed all suggest low social rank, while low pitch, low volume, and a laconic slowness suggest high social rank. Sometimes a speaker can mix choices (e.g., high pitch + low volume + low speed seems to indicate baby talk, used by adults to address infants; for some other mixes and their uses, see Irvine 1974); but in some kinds of discourse—which one might call the more formal—choices for each discourse feature are consistent in their social connotations.

Another example comes from Friedrich's (1972) paper on Russian pronouns. Friedrich notes that usage of the second-person pronouns *ty* and *vy* (for singular addressee) can be consistent or inconsistent with facial expressions. More formal situations are characterized by greater consistency—as opposed to "ironic" uses that combine the pronoun *vy* (usually called the formal pronoun) with a contemptuous expression ("paralinguistic *ty*"). Similarly, Jackson (1974:63) indicates that among the Vaupés Indians, "language-mixing"—for example, the use of Tuyuka words in a conversation that is syntactically Bará (and Bará in the rest of the lexicon)—is likely to occur only in informal discourse. In settings that she calls "more formal," co-occurrence rules are stricter so that the social connotations of lexicon and syntax are consistent (connotations of longhouse and descent-unit identity).

Because many authors describe co-occurrence violations with terms such as *irony*, *levity*, *humor*, or *local color*, it appears that some of what is meant by the "seriousness" of formal situations is actually a matter of behavioral consistency and adherence to a set of co-occurrence rules that apply to these situations and not to others. As Ervin-Tripp remarks (1972:235), co-occurrence rules are especially strict in formal styles of discourse "because of the seriousness of such situations."

But why should co-occurrence rules and "seriousness" be linked? Perhaps the clue lies in the fact that code-switching and code inconsistencies are so often used as distancing devices—ways of setting off a quotation, making a parenthetic aside, mimicking someone, or enabling a speaker to comment on his or her own behavior (see Goffman 1961; Irvine 1974; and the code-switching literature summarized in Timm 1975). By code inconsistency the speaker can detach himself from the social persona implied by one type of usage and suggest that that persona is not to be taken quite "for real"; the speaker has another social persona as well. Code inconsistency, then, may be a process of framing or undercutting one message with another that qualifies it and indicates that in some sense, or from some point of view, it doesn't really count (cf. Bateson 1972; Goffman 1961, 1974). In contrast, the code-consistent message has to count; it has to be taken "seriously" because no alternative message or social persona is provided. Each aspect of the speaker's behavior shows the same kind and degree of involvement in the situation.[4]

Invoking Positional Identities

A third aspect of formality has to do with the social identities of participants in a social gathering. More a property of the situation than of code *per se*, it concerns which social identity (of the many that an individual might have) is invoked on a particular kind of occasion. Formal occasions invoke positional and public, rather than personal, identities (to use a term proposed by Mead [1937] and applied to speech events by Hymes [1972]).[5] Public, positional identities are part of a structured set likely to be labeled and widely recognized in a society (that is, it is widely recognized that the set of identities exists and that persons X, Y, and Z have them). Personal identities, on the other hand, are individualized and depend more on the particular history of an individual's interactions. They are perhaps less likely to be explicitly recognized or labeled and less likely to be common knowledge in the community at large.

This aspect of formality is involved in what many authors have interpreted as the formal event's emphasis on social distance (as opposed to intimacy) and respect (for an established order of social positions and identities). For example, Albert (1972), writing on the Burundi, distinguishes two speech events that she calls formal and informal visiting. Formal visiting requires an open acknowledgement of differences in social rank, and it usually occurs between persons whose positions are clearly ranked in a publicly known, apparently indisputable sense (such as feudal lord and vassal). Formal visiting is characterized by other aspects of formality as well: special structuring and planning of the discourse; use of formulas; special stance; and "seriousness" (which I take to imply some constraints on topic, intonation, facial expressions, and gestures, and consistency of these with social rank).

Because positional identities and formal (structured) discourse go together in the example just cited, one might suppose that this type of social identity is necessarily invoked by the structuring of discourse and need not be considered an independent variable. But another part of Albert's description suggests otherwise. Here, Albert discusses a speech event she calls "semiformalized quarreling," a "symbolic fight" between persons who represent the bride's and groom's families at a wedding. It seems that the major factor contrasting "semiformalized quarreling" with other (unformalized) quarreling is that the identities of the participants are positional rather than personal. True, enough information is not really given to know whether there are also differences in the organization of discourse in these two kinds of quarrels. But Albert's statement that there is always a great danger that the symbolic fight might become a real fight suggests that the major difference between them lies less in the organization of the discourse than in whether it applies to personal identities.

Of course, societies can be compared as to what social identities are structured in this positional (or formal) sense; and, within a society, communicative events can be compared as to which positional sets are invoked and the scope of the social relations organized in them. For instance, among the Wolof, kinship positions, although publicly known, organize relations among a smaller group of persons than do society-wide identities, such as caste. An individual Wolof man is patrilateral cross-cousin to only a certain group of people, and that identity is relevant only to his interaction with them, whereas his caste identity is relevant to his interaction with everyone. Whether the identities invoked in a Wolof communicative event are society-wide or not has consequences for many aspects of the participants' behavior. It is convenient to say that the wider, or more public, the scope of the social identities invoked on a particular occasion, the more formal the occasion is, in this third sense of the term.

Emergence of a Central Situational Focus

A fourth aspect of formality concerns the ways in which a main focus of attention—a dominant mutual engagement that encompasses all persons present (see Goffman 1963:164)—is differentiated from side involvements. Probably all conversations display this differentiation to some extent. Jefferson (1972) shows that even ordinary conversations between two persons clearly mark off certain sets of utterances as side sequences and distinguish them from the main, or focal, sequence. When a social gathering has a larger number of participants, however, it may or may not be organized around a central focus of attention that engages, or might engage, the whole group. An American cocktail party, for example, is usually decentralized, with many small groups whose conversations are not meant to concern the gathering as a whole; but a lecture is centralized even if members of the audience mutter asides to each other during the lecturer's performance.

The emergence of a central focus of attention for a social gathering parallels the process of focusing mentioned above for aspects of code. Participation in the central, focal activity is regulated and structured in special ways. For instance, it may be that only certain persons have the right to speak or act in the main sequence, with others restricted to the side sequences. In the main sequence, speech is governed by constraints on topic, continuity, and relevance that do not apply (or not to the same extent) in the side sequences (cf. Ervin-Tripp 1972:243).

This focusing process can be seen at work in the organization of events at a Wolof naming-day ceremony. Much of the ceremony involves decentralized participation: the guests sit in small groups, chatting and eating. At various points, however, a *griot* (praise-singer) may start shouting bits of praise-poems in an effort to capture the attention of the crowd and establish a focus of attention for his performance. If he succeeds, the situation changes character, altering the patterns of movement and talk for all participants, and bringing caste identities (rather than more personal relations) into the foreground.

Similarly, David Turton (1975), in his writing on the Mursi of southern Ethiopia, distinguishes among three kinds of political speech events according to criteria that seem to resemble this focusing process. Turton calls the difference between "chatting," "discussion," and "debate" in Mursi society a difference in "degree of formality": what the more formal events entail is a process of setting off a single central (onstage) speaker from his audience, by spatial arrangements and verbal cues. Only men of certain age-grades may speak in the main (focal) sequence; other persons are relegated to the audience or to side sequences.[6] In this way, central activities and central actors are differentiated from peripheral activities and actors.

For any society, that only certain kinds of activities and actors will be able to command center stage can be expected. At the least, the activities must be ones that all participants recognize as relevant to them. Because these distinctions are made by the participants themselves in the ways they direct their attention and in the ways they do or do not perform, the organization of a formal occasion must reflect ideas that the participants hold about their own social life. In this sense a people's own analysis of its social order is intrinsic to the emergence of a central situational focus, the fourth aspect of formality, just as it was intrinsic to the explicit labels for, and public knowledge of, positional identities.

A CROSS-CULTURAL COMPARISON:
WOLOF, MURSI, AND ILONGOT
POLITICAL MEETINGS

I have suggested that these four aspects of formality may apply universally—that all speech communities may have social occasions that show different degrees of formality according to each of these criteria or combinations of them. These four aspects of formality are useful for comparing communicative events within a given sociocultural system, as the previous examples are meant to illustrate. But how might communities differ with respect to formality and informality in social occasions? For cross-cultural comparison both the similarities and the differences among societies need to be seen in some systematic fashion. Using the definitions of formality here proposed, one can say that speech communities may differ: (a) in the specific details of each variable or aspect of formality (e.g., what social identities are available, or precisely which linguistic phenomena are subject to additional structuring?); (b) in the ways the four aspects of formality combine or are interdependent; (c) in additional factors that correlate with formality in a given community (that is, when formality in one or all aspects is greatest, what other characteristics will the social occasion display in that community?).

To show how such differences might work and what kinds of factors might explain them, I shall compare in more detail two societies, the Wolof and the Mursi (from Turton 1975), with respect to the organization of political discourse and action. Each of these African societies has special speech events concerned with politics, including some events that are more formal than others. In other respects the two societies are quite different. The Wolof have a large-scale, complex organization of castes and centralized political authority, with a strong emphasis on social rank and inequality. The Mursi are a small-scale society, with an acephalous political system, and recognize no fundamental differences in rank other than those based on sex and age.

The comparison between Wolof and Mursi will be supplemented with a comparison with a third society, the Ilongots of the northern Philippines (from Rosaldo 1973), that shows certain resemblances to each of the other two. This part of the discussion will allow me to return to some earlier questions about relations between formality and political coercion.

Wolof and Mursi Political Speech Events

Both the Wolof and the Mursi distinguish more formal political "discussions" or "meetings" (*methe* in Mursi, *ndaje* in Wolof) from casual "chat" about political topics. The more formal events contrast with the chats in all four of the ways that are being discussed.

First, the more formal events show a greater degree of structuring, both in spatial arrangements and in the discourse. Spatially, the Wolof participants are arranged according to rank; within this arrangement the speaker in the focal sequence stands (near the center) while others sit (or stand around the sidelines). The Mursi participants are spatially arranged by age-grades, with the focal speaker standing separately and pacing back and forth. In the discourse, in both societies each speaker opens with conventional phrases. Among the Wolof there are also conventional interjections by griots in the audience, and sometimes special repetitions by griots acting as spokesmen for high-caste speakers.

The more formal events also show greater consistency in the selection among alternative forms in all communicative modes. Among the Wolof, a speaker's movements, gestures, intonation, amount of repetition, and degree of syntactic elaboration are all consistent with his social rank, particularly his caste (and so will differ according to whether he is a griot or a noble, for instance), whereas in informal chatting he might vary one or more of these modes for special purposes. Among the Mursi, although Turton gives few details, it appears that the successful speaker is one who performs in a manner fully consistent with the social image of a wise elder. The speaker's movements should be forceful but he should not show "excitement," repetitiousness, or "unintelligible" enunciation—from which I infer that there are co-occurring constraints on gesture and facial expression, intonation, rapidity of speech, choice of phonological variants, and the organization of his discourse.

In the more formal events in both societies there is a single main focal sequence, in which participation is specially regulated: only certain persons really have the right to speak "on stage," and that right has to do with their publicly recognized social identities. Among the Mursi, these positional identities involve sex and membership in particular age-grades; among the Wolof, they involve generation, caste, and tenure of labeled political offices.

There are, however, some clear differences between formal meetings of the Wolof and of the Mursi, differences that concern the organization and nature of participation among those persons who have the right to speak onstage. One difference lies in the regulation of turn taking. In Wolof meetings turn taking is relatively highly structured; the order of speakers may be announced at the beginning, or there may be a person who acts as a master of ceremonies. That is, there is usually one person who has the right to control the order of speakers in the focal sequence. In Mursi meetings, however, speakers compete for turns, and interruptions are frequent. A speaker may not be able to finish what he wants to say before the audience or another speaker interrupts him.

Another contrast concerns the nature of the speaking roles themselves. Among the Wolof, the more formal a speech event is (according to any of the four criteria, and depending on whether or not the occasion is explicitly concerned with politics), the more likely it is that the speaking roles will divide into complementary sets, associated with high and low social rank. That is, even among those who participate in the main sequence of discourse, participation is differentiated into two asymmetric roles. All levels of linguistic organization show this differentiation. There will always be some participants who speak louder, at higher pitch, with more repetitive and more emphatic constructions (usages that connote low social rank), while other participants speak more softly, at lower pitch, with fewer emphatic constructions, and so on (usages that connote high social rank). This asymmetry of speaking roles is always a concomitant of formality in Wolof speech events. But I call it a concomitant because one would not want to say it is part of a *definition* of formality that might apply cross-culturally, since the Mursi speaking roles, for instance, seem to be more symmetrical. Among the Mursi there are no structured differences among speaking roles at political meetings. Even the behavioral differences between speaker and audience are fewer than among the Wolof because the Mursi audience interrupts and interjects loud comments in a way that the Wolof audience would not.

What aspects of social or political organization, which (as has been noted) are quite different for the two peoples, might be reflected in the differing organization of their formal speech events? One possible explanation for the Wolof asymmetry of speaking roles is that Wolof society shows a greater degree of role differentiation altogether. But that is not a sufficient explanation for a contrast in speech-event organization that is qualitative, not quantitative (asymmetry vs. symmetry, not really as a matter of degree). Rather, I think the explanation lies in the Wolof preoccupation with rank and hierarchy, as opposed to the Mursi outlook, which is more egalitarian—the only structured inequalities being sex and age. The rural Wolof view society as composed of complementary unequal ranks where the upper has a natural right to command the lower.[8] Political decisions are culturally seen as initiated and decreed from above, by a recognized leader; the role of followers is only to advise and consent.

As a result, Wolof village political meetings are convened not for the purpose of decision making but for announcing decisions made from above and answering questions about them. The complementarity of ranks is the source of the asymmetrical speaking roles; the centralization and autocracy of political authority is the source of the master of ceremonies's right to determine the order of speakers. There is no competition among speakers for the opportunity to express opinions, since the expression of opinions and counterarguments is not the purpose of the meeting. Among the Wolof the expression of opinion and the exercise of debate go on in private, as does the leader's decision-making process.

Mursi political meetings, in contrast, are convened for the express purpose of decision making, by consensus, about future collective action. Each man of sufficient age has an equal right to participate in the consensus and to try to influence what consensus will be reached.

From the differences between Wolof and Mursi formal political meetings, however, it is not logical to conclude that political decision making is *actually* despotic among the Wolof and democratic among the Mursi. Wolof leaders need consensus support for their decisions, or their followers may fail to cooperate or may abandon them for other leaders. Conversely, for the Mursi, Turton notes that the decisions arrived at in formal meetings are sometimes such foregone conclusions that they were not reached during the course of the meeting at all. Private lobbying is as much a factor in some Mursi decisions as it is in the Wolof decision-making process.[9]

The differences between Wolof and Mursi formal political meetings do not reflect differences in the actual decision-making process so much as they reflect contrasts between what can be shown onstage and what happens offstage. The formality of the meetings has to do with what can be focused upon publicly; and it is in this sense that formality can often connote a social order, or forms of social action, that is publicly recognized and considered legitimate (regardless of whether political power actually operates through that public, formal social order or not).

The organization of these meetings reflects political ideology, therefore, but it does not necessarily reflect political actuality.

Ilongot Political Meetings

We have seen that the Wolof and Mursi political meetings are both more formal, in all respects, than ordinary conversation about political matters. But is one *kind* of meeting more formal than the other? If so, does the more formal kind place greater restrictions on its participants' political freedom, as Bloch (1975) suggests? These questions are addressed more easily by turning from the Wolof and Mursi to a third society, the Ilongots of the northern Philippines (as described by Rosaldo 1973), among whom both kinds of meetings are found. One Ilongot subgroup holds political meetings that, in certain ways, resemble the Mursi *methe*; another subgroup holds meetings that resemble the Wolof *ndaje*. Many aspects of language and cultural context remain the same for both Ilongot subgroups, however. For this reason, whatever difference the form of the meeting might make should emerge more clearly than it did in the initial comparison of Wolof and Mursi.

According to Rosaldo, the Ilongots are an acephalous, egalitarian society in the process of being incorporated into a larger Philippine national polity that is both more hierarchical and more authoritarian. This process has not affected all Ilongot communities equally, however; it has gone much further among coastal communities than it has inland. Ilongots are divided, therefore, into two subgroups, the "modern" and the "traditional," which contrast in a number of ways (and see themselves as distinct). Among other things, the two subgroups differ in their conceptions of how a political meeting should be organized. Like the Mursi, traditional Ilongots hold meetings in which there is no master of ceremonies. Speakers compete for the floor and interrupt each other frequently. Like the Mursi, too, speaking roles are relatively undifferentiated. Although some men "speak for" others, no one is bound by what another says, and the relevant parties may also speak for themselves. Modern Ilongots, on the other hand, disapprove of interruptions. In their meetings a master of ceremonies calls on speakers one by one; and the people he calls on are "captains," who speak on behalf of their "soldiers" (men from their respective localities). The soldiers, who remain silent, are considered bound to uphold what their captain says. In the regulation of turn taking and differentiation of complementary behavioral roles, therefore, modern Ilongot meetings have come to resemble the Wolof meetings described above.

As among the Wolof, this centralized type of meeting coincides, for the modern Ilongots, with a new ideological emphasis on rank and authority. The connection is surely not accidental. In fact, one of the interesting things about the Ilongot example is its implication that the kinds of political meetings seen among the Wolof and Mursi actually correspond to two very basic kinds of political ideology that are widely found in societies around the world.[10]

But which kind of meeting is more formal? The modern Ilongot meeting has a more centralized focus of attention: only one person speaks at a time, and the differentiation of central from peripheral participants is apparently maintained throughout, unlike the traditional meeting (Rosaldo 1973:204–205). In one sense, therefore, the modern meeting seems to be the more formal (that is, in terms of the fourth aspect of formality listed in this article). Yet, the opposite is suggested by linguistic aspects of the discourse. Oratory in traditional meetings displays much more linguistic elaboration and redundancy, such as repetitions of utterances and parts of utterances, reduplicative constructions, formulaic expressions, and so on. Modern Ilongot oratory lacks those elaborations although it does have a few stylistic conventions of its own. So, in terms of linguistic structuring (the first aspect of formality), the traditional meeting is the more formal. The Ilongots themselves perhaps recognize that linguistic elaboration when they call modern oratory "straight speech" and traditional oratory "crooked speech." From an analytical perspective, therefore, one could not say that one type of meeting is altogether "more formal" than the other. The two are just formalized in different ways. For the Ilongots, at least, the two ways seem to be complementary (and hence, mutually exclusive). Rosaldo suggests (1973:220) that much of the linguistic elaboration and redundancy in traditional oratory is a matter of maintaining continuity and relevance in the central sequence of utterances, and keeping that sequence distinct from peripheral discourse. Linguistic elaboration, in other words, is a way of organizing speakers' access to the floor, in the absence of a master of ceremonies; it is his functional equivalent in this respect, and one would not expect to find both extreme linguistic elaboration and extreme centralization in the same communicative event.

Because the various aspects of formality are not maximized on the same social occasions, formality/informality is not a single continuum, at least not for the Ilongots. Therefore, if one type of meeting somehow restricts the political freedom of its participants more than the other, it is not formality in general that brings restrictions, but only one aspect of formality (either centralization of attention or increased structuring of code). That the more elaborated, redundant oratorical style is found, among the Ilongots, in the less authoritarian political system suggests that increased code structuring (the first aspect of formality) is not necessarily an instrument of coercion manipulated by a political leadership. As Rosaldo comments (1973:222), "Linguistic elaboration, and a reflective interest in rhetoric, belongs to societies in which no one can command another's interest or attention, let alone enforce his compliance." In contrast, the centralization of attention in modern Ilongot meetings, with a master of ceremonies who not only prevents interruptions but determines which persons may be central speakers and which only peripheral, is the more restrictive of political expression, at least for some participants. Defined as peripheral, the Ilongot "soldiers" are not allowed to speak at the meeting at all. Their opportunities for creative statement are virtually nil.

Yet what the Ilongot "soldier" can or cannot do onstage in the meeting tells little about what he might do offstage. That the captain speaks for his men does not show whether he is a tyrant or a mere figurehead. As among the Wolof and Mursi, the formal organization of political meetings among the Ilongots is more directly related to political ideology—conscious models of the way society ought to work, as held by its members—than to the way political decisions are actually made. It is not clear, therefore, that either kind of meeting has a coercive effect on its participants in the long run, although the modern Ilongot meeting does seem to restrict some participants' opportunities for creative expression during the meeting itself.

In sum, the argument that formalizing a social occasion reduces its participants' political freedom can hold true only in limited ways. (a) Only certain aspects of formality (particularly the fourth, centralization of attention) are relevant to it; structuring of the linguistic aspects of the discourse (the first aspect of formality) is less relevant. (b) Not all participants are necessarily affected. (c) Possibly, formalization is coercive only if a society's political ideology, which the formal meeting's organization expresses, is authoritarian. (d) Finally, any restrictions on participation in formal meetings do not necessarily apply to other contexts, which may be the ones where political decision making actually occurs and where political freedom is, therefore, more at issue.

"FORMALITY" AS A CONCEPT IN SOCIAL THEORY

Formality and Social Stasis

The foregoing discussion has concerned relations between formality (of social occasions) and political coercion. But there remains a broader kind of constraint: the force of tradition. Does formalizing a social occasion inevitably tend to reinforce a normative, traditional social order (regardless of whether that tradition prescribes an authoritarian political leadership)? Does formality always imply rigidity, stability, or conservatism?

To address those questions, the various aspects of formality must be distinguished from each other, since formality represents not just one, but several dimensions along which social occasions can vary. Not all aspects of formalization necessarily concern the public social order at all. The structured discourse of poetry, for instance, does not automatically have a special relationship to the social establishment. It need not have a public audience or a public subject matter. Nor do the ways in which the discourse in poetry is structured necessarily have to be traditional ways. If formality in speech events reflects, and in that sense supports, a traditional social system, it is the other aspects of formality that do so, not the structuring of discourse in itself. With the other three aspects of formality, the relation to an established public social system is more evident, since the social occasions that could be called formal in these respects would be those that invoke social identities and modes of participation that are publicly recognized and considered appropriate.

Certainly, these occasions concern the publicly known social system; they may even call attention to it. What is not quite so clear is whether they therefore *reinforce* it. By mentioning a thesis, for instance, one does in a certain sense support it, more than if it were allowed to fall into oblivion; but mentioning it does not mean that one agrees with it. Calling attention to something can also be a way of altering it—as when a rite of passage calls attention to an individual's social identity in order to transform it into another. Some anthropologists have argued that it is the very formality of such ritual occasions, which minimize personal histories and focus on the relevant social relationships, that makes the creative transformation possible (see, for example, Douglas 1966:77–79).[11]

Now it might be objected that the transformation of social identities that goes on in a rite of passage, although a kind of creativity, is a superficial kind in that it operates only *within* a traditional system. It is not the same thing as change in that system, to which formalization might still be inimical. But formalization can be thought inimical to change only if one has a certain view of the social system to which formal occasions call attention—a view that the social system is monolithic, that the structure of a society prevents its members from conceiving of alternatives, and that all members of society have exactly identical conceptions of the social order. If members' political ideologies, for instance, differ, there can scarcely be a situation in which such differences become more apparent than in formal meetings whose organization, as we saw for the Wolof, Mursi, and Ilongot, is ideologically based. This ideological clash is just what happens among the Ilongots, when people from coastal ("modern") communities and people from inland ("traditional") communities have to hold joint meetings. When, on such an occasion, the Ilongots found they did not agree on how a meeting should be run, assumptions about how and why meetings are organized could not be left unquestioned. They had to be discussed (and, one gathers, some accommodation reached; see Rosaldo 1973:219). That is, the process of formalization forces the recognition of conflicting ideas and in so doing may impel their change. (There is also, of course, the inverse situation, in which a group with internal conflicts tries to avoid holding the formal meetings that might oblige those conflicts to be faced. Stability and communal harmony are thus achieved by *not* formalizing. See, e.g., the Israeli *moshav* described by Abarbanel 1975:152.)

The Ilongot example represents an acculturative situation, where the ideational conflict comes about because new ideas are introduced from outside. I do not want to suggest, however, that outside influence is necessary before formalization can induce change. To the extent that ideas about the social order vary according to the social position of those who hold them, any social system will generate differences of opinion, and that is quite apart from the possibility that the ideas themselves might be ambiguous, contradictory, or indeterminate. The point is that formalization does not automatically support stability and conservatism unless the social relations it articulates are fully agreed on by everyone and admit no alternatives. Whether that is the case depends on the particular social relations and on the cultural system in question; it is not implicit in the analytical concept of formality itself.[12]

Is "Formality" Useful as a Cover Term?

The various aspects of formality distinguished in this paper concern quite different kinds of social phenomena. Some concern properties of code while others concern properties of a social situation; some focus on observable behavior while others invoke the conceptual categories of social actors. For purposes of description and analysis, all such matters can and should be considered separately. But their separation in a research strategy does not mean that they are all fully independent variables. In fact, they must be interdependent, to the extent that cultural definitions of social situations and social identities must have a behavioral content.

This interdependence is something that social actors can exploit by altering their behavior to bring about a redefinition of the situation and of the identities that are relevant to it. The Wolof griot (praise-singer) who tries to capture the guests' attention at a naming-day ceremony illustrates this process (see the section on the emergence of a central situational focus). If he succeeds in attracting the attention of all the guests, a situation that began as a multifocused gathering coalesces into a single all-encompassing engagement; and, in consequence, positional identities whose scopes are wide enough to include all persons present will be invoked. Normally, caste identities are the relevant ones, especially since the griot is acting in accordance with his own caste specialization. Because high-caste persons in general owe largesse to griots, invoking caste identities places high-caste guests under obligation to reward the praise-singer even if the words of his performance do not mention them. (Some high-caste Wolof report that in the hope that they will not have to pay, they pretend not to notice the griot unless he already has a large audience.)

In this example, the Wolof naming-day ceremony, the third aspect of formality (positional identities) is entailed by the fourth (emergence of a centralized situational focus). In fact, it is reasonable to suppose that centralization is always likely to entail positional identities if a large number of persons are present, because positional identities are the ones that are widely recognized and that organize people on a systematic and broad scale. Similarly, the third aspect of formality is also entailed by the second (code consistency), because the sociolinguistic variants among which the speaker selects usually express categorical, not individual, identities. Complete code consistency would mean, for instance, that a Wolof man who uses an intonational pattern associated with griots (extreme speed, loudness, high pitch) will consistently express griot identity in all other aspects of his behavior as well (syntax, posture, movements, and so on). Little scope would be left for individuality.

Yet, if there are certain ways in which the various aspects of formality are interdependent, there are other ways in which they are not. In the first place, the entailments just mentioned do not seem to be reversible. Thus no. 4 entails no. 3, but no. 3 does not have to entail no. 4. The griot can invoke caste identities even when privately addressing a single high-caste individual, and he can do so simply by declaring, "I am a griot." Although some of his intonational and gestural usages must be consistent with this statement if it is not to sound like a joke, not all of them need be. For instance, his speed of talk might be slow, unlike the rapid tempo normally associated with griots. By such means he can distance himself enough from the griot role to make some personal comment on it, even if he still intends caste identities to define the situation and to suggest his interlocutor's course of action.

Finally, there is no intrinsic reason why code consistency, positional identities, or centralization (no. 2, 3, or 4) should entail a change in the degree of structuring to which a code is subjected (criterion no. 1) or vice versa. Linguistic aspects of discourse in poetry are structured, for instance, but a poem's subject matter can be entirely private. Moreover, code switches and code inconsistencies in poetry are frequent and can contribute significantly to the poem's special effect. The first aspect of formality seems, therefore, to be independent of the other three; and this was also suggested by the Ilongot example, in which the same event cannot maximize both linguistic structuring (formality no. 1) and centralization (formality no. 4).

Is there, after all this, any sense in which all four aspects of formality are related—a sense in which *formality* remains useful as a cover term? I think there is, but it is so general that it is not very useful as an analytical tool. The only thing all four criteria have in common is that all of them concern the degree to which a social occasion is systematically organized. This sense of formality as "degree of organization" has some resemblance to Goffman's (1963:199) definition of formality/informality as "tightness"/"looseness." The thrust of my argument, however, is that being organized in one way does not necessarily mean being organized in other ways to the same degree or at the same time. In fact, the various ways in which a communicative event is organizable may be complementary or even antithetical, rather than additive.

I suspect, therefore, that it is appropriate in few instances to speak of "formality" generally without specifying more precisely what one has in mind. Otherwise, there is too great a risk of mistaking one kind of formality for another or assuming that kinds of formality are really the same. That an ordinary English word has multiple meanings—as we have seen in its multiple uses in the sociolinguistic literature—does not make those meanings essentially homogeneous, nor should we unwittingly elevate this word's polysemy to a social theory. As Leach has remarked (1961:27), "We anthropologists . . . must reexamine basic premises and realize that English language patterns of thought are not a necessary model for the whole of human society."

NOTES

Acknowledgment. I am indebted to Ben Blount, Dell Hymes, Joel Sherzer, Maurice Bloch, and David Turton for their helpful comments on an earlier version of this paper.

1. The application is made except insofar as the linguist acts as his or her own informant and so combines the roles of observer and subject.

2. Actually, to equate the relevant aspects of code structuring with addition of or elaboration of existing rules presents some problems. The notion seems to apply well enough to examples such as the Wolof insult sessions described in the section *Increased Code Structuring*, because speech rhythms in those sessions must not only conform to the usual metric principles of stress and length in ordinary speech but be further organized to fit a precise and repetitive drum rhythm. But it is not clear that redundancies of meter, rhyme, or syntactic parallelism in poetry should always be interpreted in terms of addition of rules. For instance, Sherzer's (1974) description of Cuna congress chants proposes that syntactic parallelism and redundancy are achieved by retaining underlying representations, i.e., by *not* following the usual transformational rules that would zero out redundant noun phrases and verb phrases. This suggests that the special aesthetic structure of chants is achieved by using fewer rules, rather than more. Yet, how do the rules of chanting provide for the fact that the usual reductions are not to occur? Is there any assurance that this provision is not best analyzed via extra rules that reinsert the redundant forms, since that analysis might better conform to general principles of markedness (if the chants are to be considered as marked discourse forms)? A similar problem arises for types of Western poetry in which, it is sometimes said, structuring of meter and rhyme is accompanied by syntactic and semantic "poetic licence." This argument suggests that extra structuring in one aspect of the discourse might be accompanied by loosening of structure in another. It is not clear, however, that "licence" is really the appropriate conception of poetic syntax and semantics. The issues here are complex and they reach far beyond the scope of this paper.

3. Since my fieldwork was conducted in rural areas of the Préfecture de Tivaouane, when I speak of "the Wolof" I can, of course, mean only the villages I have myself observed and the extent to which they may be representative of Wolof villages more generally. This caveat is necessary because "Wolof" as an ethnic category now includes a numerous and diverse population, urban as well as rural, elite as well as peasant. I believe my comments here apply to the *Communautés Rurales* (Senegalese rural administrative units) in the core regions of Wolof occupation; they do not necessarily apply to urban Wolof.

4. See Goffman's discussion (1963:198–215) relating formality/informality to degree of involvement in a situation.

5. Other authors describe a similar distinction in somewhat different terms. Geertz (1966), for example, speaks of the "anonymization of individuals" in cermonialized interaction.

6. For another example, see Tyler's (1972) paper on the Koya of central India. A number of behavioral differences, including lexical choices, differentiate central from peripheral actors in Koya formal events.

7. The occasions I refer to are public meetings conducted in rural villages or *Communautés Rurales*. Increasingly, Wolof call these meetings by the French term *réunion*, which (in Senegalese usage) distinguishes them more definitively from casual encounters than does the Wolof term *ndaje*.

8. I leave aside the relation of the priesthood (*Imams* and *marabouts*), which ranks highest in a religious sense, to political decision making.

9. On this point, Turton comments (personal communication) that "although the Mursi do indeed see their debates as decision-making procedures, I am less and less convinced that, from the point of view of the outside observer, they should be thus characterized."

10. I do not mean to suggest that these two societal types, if types they are, exhaust all possibilities of political ideology and organized political discussion; our own society probably fits neither. Nor, on the basis of materials presented in this paper, do I propose to match such types to points on an evolutionary scale. That two forms of political discourse have a certain historical relationship among the Ilongots does not mean they will have the same relationship everywhere.

11. See also Firth (1975) on "the *experimental* aspect of [formal] oratory" in Tikopia (emphasis in original). Firth argues that public meetings and formal oratory emerge in Tikopia under conditions of crisis and social change, not during periods of stability. The Tikopia *fono* (formal assembly of titled elders) cannot be dismissed as merely a reactionary reaffirmation of a threatened tradition. It is also a means of publicly exploring important issues, and a way for Tikopia leaders to find out whether a new proposal is likely to be acceptable (1975:42–43).

12. Sally Falk Moore (1975:231) makes a similar point: "It is important to recognize that processes of regularization, processes having to do with rules and regularities, may be used to block change or to produce change. The fixing of rules and regularities are as much tools of revolutionaries as they are of reactionaries. It is disastrous to confuse the analysis of processes of regularization with the construction of static social models."

REFERENCES CITED

ABARBANEL, JAY 1975 The Dilemma of Economic Competition in an Israeli Moshav. *In* Symbol and Politics in Communal Ideology. Sally Falk Moore and Barbara Myerhoff, eds. pp. 144–65. Ithaca: Cornell University Press.

ALBERT, ETHEL 1972 Cultural Patterning of Speech Behavior in Burundi. *In* Directions in Sociolinguistics. John Gumperz and Dell Hymes, eds. pp. 72–105. New York: Holt, Rinehart and Winston.

BATESON, GREGORY 1972 Steps to an Ecology of Mind. San Francisco: Chandler.

BAUMAN, RICHARD, and JOEL SHERZER, eds. 1974 Explorations in the Ethnography of Speaking. London: Cambridge University Press.

BLOCH, MAURICE, ed. 1975 Political Language and Oratory in Traditional Society. New York: Academic Press.

BRICKER, VICTORIA 1974 The Ethnographic Context of Some Traditional Mayan Speech Genres. *In* Explorations in the Ethnography of Speaking. Richard Bauman and Joel Sherzer, eds. pp. 368–88. London: Cambridge University Press.

DAVIS, ERMINA 1976 In Honor of the Ancestors: The Social Context of Iwi Egungun Chanting in a Yoruba Community. Ph.D. dissertation, Brandeis University.

DOUGLAS, MARY 1966 Purity and Danger. Baltimore: Penguin.

ERVIN-TRIPP, SUSAN 1972 On Sociolinguistic Rules: Alternation and Co-occurrence. *In* Directions in Sociolinguistics. John Gumperz and Dell Hymes, eds. pp. 213–250. New York: Holt, Rinehart and Winston.

FIRTH, RAYMOND 1975 Speech-making and Authority in Tikopia. *In* Political Language and Oratory in Traditional Society. Maurice Bloch, ed. pp. 29–44. New York: Academic Press.

FISCHER, JOHN 1972 The Stylistic Significance of Consonantal Sandhi in Trukese and Ponapean. *In* Directions in Sociolinguistics. John Gumperz and Dell Hymes, eds. pp. 498–511. New York: Holt, Rinehart and Winston.

FISHMAN, JOSHUA 1972 Sociolinguistics: A Brief Introduction. Rowley, Mass.: Newbury House.

FISHMAN, JOSHUA, ed. 1968 Readings in the Sociology of Language. The Hague: Mouton.

FOX, JAMES 1974 "Our Ancestors Spoke in Pairs": Rotinese Views of Language, Dialect, and Code. *In* Explorations in the Ethnography of Speaking. Richard Bauman and Joel Sherzer, eds. pp. 65–85. London: Cambridge University Press.

FRIEDRICH, PAUL 1972 Social Context and Semantic Feature: The Russian Pronominal Usage. *In*

Directions in Sociolinguistics. John Gumperz and Dell Hymes, eds. pp. 270–300. New York: Holt, Rinehart and Winston.

GEERTZ, CLIFFORD 1966 Person, Time and Conduct in Bali: An Essay in Cultural Analysis. Yale Southeast Asia Program, Cultural Report Series, No. 14. New Haven.

GOFFMAN, ERVING 1961 Encounters: Two Studies in the Sociology of Interaction. Indianapolis, IN: Bobbs-Merrill. 1963 Behavior in Public Places. New York: Free Press. 1974 Frame Analysis. New York: Harper and Row.

GOSSEN, GARY 1974 To Speak with a Heated Heart: Chamula Canons of Style and Good Performance. *In* Explorations in the Ethnography of Speaking. Richard Bauman and Joel Sherzer, eds. pp. 389–413. London: Cambridge University Press.

GUMPERZ, JOHN, and DELL HYMES, eds. 1972 Directions in Sociolinguistics. New York: Holt, Rinehart and Winston.

HALLIDAY, MICHAEL 1964 The Users and Uses of Language. *In* The Linguistic Sciences and Language Teaching. Halliday, McIntosh, and Strevens, eds. London: Longmans. (Reprinted in Fishman 1968, pp. 139–69.)

HYMES, DELL 1972 Models of the Interaction of Language and Social Life. *In* Directions in Sociolinguistics. John Gumperz and Dell Hymes, eds. pp. 35–71. New York: Holt, Rinehart and Winston.

IRVINE, JUDITH 1974 Strategies of Status Manipulation in the Wolof Greeting. *In* Explorations in the Ethnography of Speaking. Richard Bauman and Joel Sherzer, eds. pp. 167–91. London: Cambridge University Press.

JACKSON, JEAN 1974 Language Identity of the Colombian Vaupés Indians. *In* Explorations in the Ethnography of Speaking. Richard Bauman and Joel Sherzer, eds. pp. 50–64. London: Cambridge University Press.

JEFFERSON, GAIL 1972 Side Sequences. *In* Studies in Social Interaction. David Sudnow, ed. pp. 294–338. New York: Free Press.

JOOS, MARTIN 1959 The Isolation of Styles. Monograph Series on Languages and Linguistics 12:107–13. Washington, D.C.: Georgetown University. (Reprinted in Fishman 1968, pp. 185–91.)

KIRSHENBLATT-GIMBLETT, BARBARA, ed. 1976 Speech Play. Philadelphia: University of Pennsylvania Press.

LABOV, WILLIAM 1972 Some Principles of Linguistic Methodology. Language in Society 1:97–120.

LEACH, EDMUND 1961 Rethinking Anthropology. London: Athlone.

LEACH, EDMUND 1965 Political Systems of Highland Burma. Boston: Beacon Press.

MEAD, MARGARET 1937 Public Opinion Mechanisms Among Primitive Peoples. Public Opinion Quarterly 1:5–16.

MOORE, SALLY FALK 1975 Epilogue: Uncertainties in Situations, Indeterminacies in Culture. *In* Symbol and Politics in Communal Ideology. Sally Falk Moore and Barbara Myerhoff, eds. pp. 210–39. Ithaca: Cornell University Press.

MURPHY, ROBERT 1971 The Dialectics of Social Life. New York: Basic Books.

ROSALDO, MICHELLE Z. 1973 I Have Nothing to Hide: The Language of Ilongot Oratory. Language in Society 2:193–224.

RUBIN, JOAN 1968 Bilingual Usage in Paraguay. *In* Readings in the Sociology of Language. Joshua Fishman, ed. pp. 512–30. The Hague: Mouton.

SANCHES, MARY, and BEN BLOUNT, eds. 1975 Sociocultural Dimensions of Language Use. New York: Academic Press.

SHERZER, JOEL 1974 Namakke, Sunmakke, Kormakke: Three Types of Cuna Speech Event. *In* Explorations in the Ethnography of Speaking. Richard Bauman and Joel Sherzer, eds. pp. 263–82. London: Cambridge University Press.

TIMM, L. A. 1975 Spanish-English Code-Switching: El Porqué y How-Not-To. Romance Philology 28:473–82.

TURTON, DAVID 1975 The Relationships Between Oratory and the Exercise of Influence Among the Mursi. *In* Political Language and Oratory in Traditional Society. Maurice Bloch, ed. pp. 163–84. New York: Academic Press.

TYLER, STEPHEN 1972 Context and Alternation in Koya Kinship Terminology. *In* Directions in Sociolinguistics. John Gumperz and Dell Hymes, eds. pp. 251–69. New York: Holt, Rinehart and Winston.

WOLFSON, NESSA 1976 Speech Events and Natural Speech: Some Implications for Sociolinguistic Methodology. Language in Society 5:189–210.

BAMBI B. SCHIEFFELIN

Adɛ: A Sociolinguistic Analysis
of a Relationship

Recent studies have documented the importance of a variety of paralinguistic phenomena such as intonation, voice quality, volume, and pitch in conversation. These phenomena, which Gumperz (1977) has called contextualization cues, are used by adults in signaling how communicative acts are to be interpreted. The appropriate use of and response to contextualization cues in connection with a linguistic proposition presupposes that one has certain kinds of linguistic and sociocultural knowledge. There remains, however, the question of how children acquire this knowledge which is necessary to correctly interpret, respond to, and produce socially appropriate interactional sequences. As a step toward understanding this process, I will discuss how children in one society learn about making and responding to requests based on a strategy of appeal.

The data are taken from ethnographic fieldwork among the Kaluli people, a traditional, small-scale society on the Papuan Plateau, Papua (New Guinea). The observations of everyday interactions and the transcriptions of tape-recorded spontaneous conversations which I will draw upon are part of a larger study on the development of communicative competence reported elsewhere (B.B. Schieffelin, 1979a, 1979b, 1984).

Young children learn about requests based on appeal in the context of a particular relationship between siblings. The relationship is marked by the term *adɛ* and may be characterized as one in which an older sister "feels sorry for" her younger brother, and acts toward him in an unselfish and nurturing way. It is one of the most important relationships in Kaluli society.

The correct use of the term *adɛ* is important in evoking the *adɛ* relationship. Because this relationship is developed between brothers and sisters, it is instructive to first describe the differences in form and use between kin terms used for brother (*ao*) and sister (*ado*) and the term *adɛ*. Then we examine the different aspects of the *adɛ* relationship in the contexts in which it is used in family interactions and see how children are taught to respond to requests based on appeal. We then present the difficulties all children have in using the *adɛ* term appropriately. Finally a myth is presented which adds another level of significance about the relationship within Kaluli culture.

Siblings: Terms of Reference and Address

From the time they are small, siblings spend a great deal of time together, eating, bathing, playing, and sleeping in the same house. Only when they are 7 or

This paper is excerpted from "How Kaluli children learn what to say, what to do, and how to feel," unpublished Ph.D. dissertation, Columbia University, 1979. Field work (1975-1977) was supported by Wenner-Gren Foundation for Anthropological Research and the National Science Foundation.

229

8 years old do they begin to form more independent relationships with same sex peers and spend less time around the house with the younger children. Throughout their time together in the gardens and walking around in the bush, brothers and sisters develop a sense of shared experiences in relation to everyday routines, associating actions and events with particular places and each other. A whole world of associations develops for the child in the context of times spent together with siblings.

In these everyday interactions, brothers and sisters have available a number of names that they use in both address and reference. The selection of one or another of these names may depend on a particular aspect of the relationship that the speaker wants the listener to attend to at that moment. In addition to proper names, siblings use reciprocal names having to do with shared food, namesake names, affectionate names, teasing names, relationship and kin terms.

The Kaluli kinship terms for brother and sister are relatively uncomplicated in that they do not indicate sex of speaker, age in relationship to speaker or whether the relationship is full or half. The kin terms for brother and sister are:

nao	'my brother'	nado	'my sister'
gao	'your brother'	gado	'your sister'
ene ao	'his/her brother'	ene ado	'his/her sister'

The first and second person possessive prefix (n-, g-) and the third person possessive pronoun *ene* are part of the kin term. In address, the terms are used (first person) with or without the unbound possessive pronoun, e.g., *ni nado!* ('my sister') or *nado!*

In reference, the possessive pronoun is always used with the kin term, e.g., *gi gao* 'your brother'.

Kin terms are used often and in a wide variety of social situations:

1.   In greetings, used exuberantly and reciprocally, proper names can be used with them, e.g., *nao!* or *nao* Wanu!
2.   In everyday talk when reporting an event, e.g., "I saw *gi gado* 'your sister' at the stream."
3.   In making inquiries after an individual, e.g., "Where is *ni nao* 'my brother'?"
4.   After hearing a report of a sad event from a sibling, used following an expressive word to express compassion, e.g., "*heyɔ, nao* 'alas, my brother'."
5.   As attention-getting devices in conversations, or as openers.
6.   In any situation in the assertive modality, e.g., in sequences with *ɛlɛma* to teach greetings, calling out, and in establishing identities and relationships between children. (B.B. Schieffelin 1979a).
7.   In requests as an address term when the speaker is either demanding something or asking in a neutral way, e.g., "*nao*, hand me the ax."

Sibling terms may be extended to a variety of individuals beyond the immediate family. Classificatory brothers and sisters both in and out of the village are called by these same sibling terms, and the range of usage that has been described applies to them as well.

Adɛ: A Relationship Term

I became aware of another term that could refer to siblings during transcription of taperecorded family interactions.

(1)　Mɛli (24.3) was with her mother and brother Seligiwo (7.). There was a large bushknife on the floor near the little boy.[1]
(as Mother leaves room, to Mɛli):

He will accidentally cut himself.
Stay here and watch over *adɛ*.

This term *adɛ* was not reported in E.L. Schieffelin (1976:52-58) in his discussion of Kaluli kin terms and other terms of address and reference. When I asked about the word *adɛ* adults could not explicate the meaning, but would point to sisters, and their younger brothers. When asked what two siblings called each other, or how they referred to each other, Kaluli adults gave proper names or kin terms, but never the term *adɛ*. This term was used in everyday family interactions and yet the Kaluli were unable to talk about it in response to my questions as they could about kin terms.

Consequently my analyses were based on the spontaneous occurrences of the *adɛ* term that were taperecorded in different contexts with different speakers.[2] Two major sociolinguistic rules formulated by Ervin-Tripp (1972) and Gumperz (1967) were used to describe the rules of the use of the *adɛ* term and kin terms for siblings, as well as the *adɛ* relationship itself. The first rule is alternation, where there is a choice between alternative ways of speaking which involve social selectors. The factors determining the choice of terms used in reference and address will be discussed here. Following the selection of the alternate, co-occurrence rules were determined for paralinguistic phenomena (volume, voice quality) and linguistic forms (expressive terms, speech acts).

The Use of *adɛ* in Address and Reference

Unlike the kin terms for brother and sister (and all other kin terms) which take a possessive prefix or pronoun, *adɛ* cannot be possessed. That is, on the morphological level it functions quite differently from other kin terms. In address one says *adɛ*; **nadɛ* or **ni adɛ* is never said. Nor can one refer to someone else as **gadɛ* or **ene adɛ*. The term *adɛ* does not conform to the rules of marking possessive or referential relationships as do all other kin terms and special names.[3]

Adɛ is different pragmatically as well. In contrast to the variety of speech acts and speech events in which speakers use kin terms, *adɛ* is very restricted. In fact, it cannot be used in any of the situations listed as appropriate for the sibling terms. In family interaction, in address, it is not used frequently.

There is only one type of social situation in which it is appropriate to use the *adɛ* term in address. When one is begging for something or wants someone to feel sorry and fulfill a request, it can be used as a vocative in the modality of appeal. In addition *adɛ* is limited in register; in keeping with the appeal modality it must be used with a soft plaintive voice, which the Kaluli call *gesiab* 'makes someone feel sorry'. Older children and adults use *adɛ* in address to make requests based upon appeal. Sisters use it reciprocally with each other; brothers use it with their sisters. However, brothers would never use it between themselves, and instead would use *nao* 'my brother' when begging for something.

In reference only adults use the term *adɛ* and only to refer to their own children (or grandchildren). They address one child and refer to the other as *adɛ*. While *adɛ* is usually used between cross-sex siblings (older sister/younger brother), a mother will occasionally use the term to refer to a relationship between her sons when they are both under 6 years of age. After that the *adɛ* term is not used. Thus, there is continuity with later adults usage, since men do not call each other *adɛ*.

The situation between sisters is different. Mothers use the *adɛ* term to speak to one and refer to the other until they are 12 to 15 years old or no longer under the control of the mother. Sisters, as adults, continue to use this term with each other when asking for help or requesting special objects.

In addition, unlike the wide range of people one can call brother or sister (classificatory siblings both in and out of the village), *adɛ* is used to refer to and address a limited number of individuals, only those siblings with whom one has grown up.

The referential use of *adɛ* can be illustrated in this way:

Addressee	Referent	
	Older Sister	Younger Sibling
Older Sibling		*adɛ*
Younger Sibling	*adɛ*	

Thus there must be two people who are in the appropriate relationship with each other in order for the term to be used. In addition we see that the *adɛ* term is RECIPROCAL—that is, mothers can address an older sibling and refer to a younger sibling as *adɛ*, or address a younger sibling and refer to an older sister as *adɛ*.

Given its particular linguistic and sociolinguistic characteristics, it appears therefore that *adɛ* is not a kin term but a context-specific relationship term. It is used only to evoke the *adɛ* relationship.

While the *adɛ* relationship develops within the brother/sister relationship, it is not "given" by virtue of shared substance or genealogy like the brother/sister relationship (E.L. Schieffelin 1976:55). The brother/sister relationship is INDEPENDENT OF SITUATION—a child is a brother or sister whether walking in the forest, playing, or sleeping. The *adɛ* relationship is taught and evoked only under particular circumstances, and is SPECIFIC TO SITUATIONS in which a person needs something and appeals to someone to feel sorry for him. These situations in which *adɛ* is used both impart meaning to and become part of the meaning of the relationship being created.

The kin terms "brother" and "sister" do not have the specific "feeling components" in them that *adɛ* has. Kin terms are general, used for a range of different speech events, speech acts, interactions and moods. They are too diffuse to have the strategic and rhetorical force of *adɛ*. The meaning of *adɛ* is situationally specific, that of nurturing and giving out of feelings of compassion.

Because the kin term meanings are independent of situation, they would not be as effective rhetorically as *adɛ* in evoking the specific feelings the mother is both creating and drawing on every time she uses the term. The choice of a lexical item is "constrained by what the speaker intends to achieve in a particular interaction as well as by expectations about the other's reactions and assumptions" (Gumperz 1977:196).

Creation of the *adɛ* Relationship

In a family with two young children the usual situations arise in which the *adɛ* relationship can be created by the mother. In ongoing interactions the mother will secure the attention of the older child (most often a girl, 2 to 4 years of age) and tell her to either terminate or initiate a specific activity with her younger sibling, referring to the infant as *adɛ*. This procedure is predictable in that the mother uses a consistent set of contextualization cues. She will stop what she is doing and focus her attention on the two children. Her facial expression will show concern. She will use an expressive word meaning 'have pity' (*wɔ*) or 'feel sorry for (someone else)' (*heyɔ*), and her voice will have a soft plaintive quality *gesiab* 'make someone feel sorry.'[4] She will speak to the older child softly and slowly, creating an ambiance of intimacy, appeal, and compassion. WHAT the mother says (message content) will tell the child how to act. How the mother says it (message form) will communicate to the child how she is to feel. The way in which the mother speaks, her voice quality, use of expressive words and *adɛ* (contextualization cues) provide the expressive model for the child: that one should have feelings of compassion and feel sorry for a helpless infant.

In these interactions, by using the term *adɛ* in reference, the mother is helping to create and develop a set of motivations and assumptions for the older child, informing her how to act as well as how to feel. In addition, since two children are always involved, she is creating "structures of expectations" (Tannen 1979) for the younger one, showing how acting in an appealing or begging way will elicit compassion and assistance. Given that similar situations recur in which mothers repeatedly use this formulaic set of contextualization cues, the appropriate mood and behaviors are presented in and as a unified scenario. The relationship is being created as both partners learn their roles. And, as additional children come into the family, the roles of younger and older sibling are played out between different members. Children learn both to beg and to "feel sorry" and give.

To observe the behaviors and attitudes that constitute the *adɛ* relationship, we look at situations that regularly occur in which children between 2 and 4 years of age and their younger siblings learn to recognize *adɛ* interactions and act appropriately in them. There are four components to the *adɛ* relationship: mothers repeatedly tell their children how not to treat *adɛ*, to share or give objects to *adɛ*, to take care of *adɛ*, or simply to be with *adɛ*.

How Not to Act

Given their energy, curiosity, and lack of social knowledge, 2- to 4-year-olds will sometimes interact with their younger siblings in ways which the mother views as inappropriate. They may play too roughly, tease them with objects, bother them while they are nursing. Reprimands to the older child take the following form:

(2)   Mɛli (26.) is playfully offering my rubber sandal to her brother Seligiwo (9.).

> ¹ Mother→Mɛli→>Seligiwo: You take! *ɛlɛma.*⁶
> (waving sandal at baby)   ² gu/gu there!/
> (as baby reaches, Mɛli pulls sandal away)
> ³ Mother→Mɛli: No, what's this?
> *heyɔ* ('feel sorry'), one doesn't do that to *adɛ.*

In these contexts the mother ties the two children together verbally by speaking to the older child and referring to the younger one. Her consistent manner of appealing to the older child to "feel sorry' is conveyed by the quality in her voice (*gesiab*) and the expressive *heyɔ*. Feeling sorry is associated with the *adɛ* relationship and how one must act with a younger helpless sibling. Children between 2 and 4 years receive many negative directives, such as "don't disturb *adɛ*" (who is asleep), "don't take *adɛ* outside" (it's cold), and "don't tease *adɛ*" (*dikidiɛsabo*).

Giving and Sharing

Besides telling the other child what *not* to do, mothers make explicit what children *ought* to do in the *adɛ* relationship. One of the most important things a child has to learn is when to give things. Mothers frequently ask the older child to share food or give an object to a younger child who is whining for it, or showing some interest.

(3)   Mɛli (32.2) is playing with one of my rubber sandals. Seligiwo (15.) squeals.

Mother→Mɛli: Give *adɛ* the other one. (Mɛli doesn't)

(4)   Abi (31.2), Mother, and sister Yogodo (5½ yrs.) are eating ginger. Abi drops his.

Mother→Abi: I'll look for it, you wait.
Mother→Yogodo: Yogodo!
Yogodo→Mother: Yea?
Mother→Yogodo: Give your ginger to *adɛ.*
Yogodo: I'll break my ginger in half and give.
Mother→Abi→>Yogodo: Yogodo, I want ginger, *ɛlɛma.*

Example 4 is a good illustration of how speakers switch between the term *adɛ* and the proper name when asking for food. After Mother appeals to Yogodo to give ginger to *adɛ*, Yogodo agrees. Mother tells Abi to ask for ginger, using Yogodo's proper name. The *adɛ* term is not used because it is not appropriate with *ɛlɛma*, which is assertive. Furthermore, since Yogodo has already agreed to give it, she does not have to be made to "feel sorry" and give.

In many cases the older child will comply when asked to give something to the younger one. However, there are times when the younger child has begged and the mother has verbally intervened on the behalf of the younger child, using *adɛ*, and the older child still does not want to give. Here the mother may physically intervene and take the desired object from the older child, leaving that child to have an angry temper tantrum. It is important not to frustrate a young child who has begged for something.

In the examples above, the younger child is over one year old. The pattern of giving within the *adɛ* relationship has been encouraged from early on. In the next example we see in more detail one way in which this is done. The mother herself provides the model of the behavior that she wants her children to follow.

(5)   Wanu, a boy (29.), baby sister Henga (2.), 5½ yr. sister Binaria, and Mother. Wanu is holding an uncooked crayfish.

> ¹ Mother→Wanu: *wɔ*, after cooking let's give
> it to *adɛ*, to Henga.
>
> ² huh?/
>
> ³ After cooking, let's give it to Henga.
>
> ⁴ ɛm?/
>
> ⁵ To Henga.
> ⁶ Binaria→Wanu→>Mother: Yes, *ɛlɛma*.
>
> ⁷ No!
>
> (Other talk, 1 min. 20 sec.)
> ⁸ Mother→Wanu: To *adɛ*, after it's cooked
> I'll give it to *adɛ*.
> (holding out crayfish)   ⁹ this?/
> ¹⁰ Yes, for *adɛ*, I'll cook it for *adɛ*.
> (still holding out crayfish)   ¹¹ this?/
> ¹² Yes. (Wanu gives crayfish to Mother)
> (Mother cooks crayfish; other talk
> 2 min. 10 sec.)
> (Mother has cooked crayfish; Wanu sees it)   ¹³ to me!/
> ¹⁴ Mother→Wanu: *wɔ*, I'm giving to *adɛ*.
> I'm giving it to *adɛ*.
> ¹⁵ (Offering Wanu a piece): You eat this.
> ¹⁶ Binaria→Mother (whining): *wɔ*, to me.
> ¹⁷ Mother→Binaria: You eat something else!
> ¹⁸ Binaria→Mother: *wɔ*, to me.
> ¹⁹ Mother→Binaria: *wɔ*, I'm giving it to
> *adɛ*. You'll eat spinach. I'm giving it to
> *adɛ*.
> (Wanu tries to grab a piece of crayfish)
> ²⁰ Mother→Wanu: You've had enough!
> The head is mine. It (the meat) I'm
> giving to *adɛ*.
> (loudly, to Mother)   ²¹ *don't give to *adɛ*!/
> ²² Mother→Wanu: *wɔ*, I'm giving to *adɛ*,
> to Kobake, she's hungry.

Mother first introduces the idea of giving the crayfish to the baby (line 1). She uses the expressive (*wɔ* 'feel sorry') and the *adɛ* term followed by the baby's name, Henga, associating the two. Binaria (line 6) tells Wanu to agree, but he refuses. A little later Mother brings it up again (line 8), using the *adɛ* term and saying "I'll give it to *adɛ*." Using the first person present tense of the verb *give*, (instead of the imperative form), she tells Wanu how she will act, rather than commanding him to give. She is trying to get him to agree to her behavior, which of course depends on his giving up the crayfish, which he does. Wanu requests the cooked crayfish, to which his mother responds plaintively (line 14) "I'm giving it to *adɛ*." However, she offers Wanu a piece. Binaria, who was not offered any, appeals to her mother and this elicits a sharp refusal. After Binaria's second appeal (line 18), Mother switches modality and responds by appealing on behalf of the baby. After claiming the head for herself, she tells the others she is giving the meat to *adɛ*. Wanu protests and uses a pragmatically inappropriate utterance (line 21). To this his mother responds with an expressive, the *adɛ* term, the name Kobake, which is used for newborns (the baby is 2 months) and the reason, "she's hungry." Actually the mother's last utterance (line 22) has four reasons in it: *wɔ* 'feel sorry', the *adɛ* term itself, the special name for newborns (who are the most helpless and to be pitied), and hunger. The idea here is that sharing with and giving to the younger child is an important component of the relationship; one should anticipate desires as well as fulfill explicit requests. Again, the specific contextualization cues of voice quality, prosodic contours, and expressive words are used when speaking to the older child. When a child does comply, reward is not explicit. The happiness of the infant is pointed out, the *adɛ* relationship has been fulfilled and is its own reward.

While in the majority of instances of the use of *adɛ* older children are asked to act with regard to the younger one, the reverse also happens. Thus reciprocity in the *adɛ* relationship is encouraged between siblings when the older one is a girl.

Nurturing and Caregiving

Another important aspect of the *adɛ* relationship is that of nurturing and caregiving. Mothers frequently ask their older daughters to help in child-minding activities (their sons are prevailed upon much less frequently). Daughters are asked to "watch over *adɛ*," "check on the location of *adɛ*," "bring food to *adɛ*," or "draw water for *adɛ*'s bath."

(6)   Mɛli (32.2) and her mother are at home; Seligiwo (15.) has just walked out of the house.

[1] Mother→Mɛli: Go see about Seligiwo,
go see about *adɛ*.

[2] no/

[3] He'll go to Bambi's house.

[4] okay/

(Mɛli goes to see where he is)

Again, these requests are always made in a plaintive voice, appealing to the older child using the *adɛ* term to refer to the younger one. In this example, as in others, after the initial request with a proper name (to refer to the younger child); if compliance is not forthcoming the mother repeats the request, this time using the *adɛ* term.[6] This adds rhetorical force to her request, and implicitly adds the reason why the child should do as the mother says. This tactic is not restricted to asking older children to act in caring ways toward a younger child. There are occasions when the mother wants the younger one to take the older one into consideration as well. However, when children do not comply, there is little the mother can do but give up her attempts and drop the issue.

When making requests mothers want their children to feel compassion and be moved, to act of their "own free will." This is what responding to appeal is about, and how it differs from responding to an assertive demand. The ability to respond to someone who needs help, to respond out of compassion, is instilled from the earliest age, as soon as there are two children. Mothers use *adɛ* as a way of putting children in a particular role relationship with one another, which makes it harder for one child (in the presence of the mother) to refuse to fulfill the wishes of another, especially of a younger child.

Togetherness

The final aspect of the *adɛ* relationship that emerged from the analysis of family interactions involves a notion of togetherness.

(7) Mother is settling Mɛli (30.2) and Seligiwo (13.) down together.

Mother→Mɛli: Sit on here, then.
Adɛ and you together sit on this.
(to Seligiwo)   sit on this/
                                                 we two sit/

Young children are repeatedly involved with siblings in situations having a number of important features in common. These situations have to do with acting out of feelings of compassion. The content of the mother's message is consistent: either prohibiting one child (usually the older one) from hurting or distressing the younger one, or urging the older one to act in a positive way (sharing, helping, giving objects, being together) toward the younger one. These messages constitute the prescriptions for how one is to act in the *adɛ* relationship. The concomitant contextualization cues in association with the message content provide the expressive model for how one is supposed to feel toward the younger sibling, on whose behalf the mother acts to express what he himself may not yet be able to. In fact, the mother is (in REFERENCE) adopting the very stylistic devices that the children will later use (in ADDRESS) when they are older and appeal to siblings to "feel sorry."

Children's Use of the *adɛ* Term

In examining contexts in which children are acquiring socio-cultural know-ledge we must consider the child's use of the *adɛ* term as well as the mothers' modeling strategies. Because of its special usage in restructed contexts, children must learn when it is appropriate to use the *adɛ* term instead of a kin term for the correct interactional effect. Once the term is selected, the appropriate modality and speech acts that co-occur with it must be used.

Young children often make requests based on appeal and when doing so frequently use the expressive *wɔ* 'have pity'. (They never use the form *heyɔ* which is used when the speaker wants the listener to feel sorry for someone other than the speaker.) Young children correctly use *wɔ* before a vocative, usually a proper name, in begging and appealing for objects. However, in these requests, the *adɛ* term is used infrequently. When it is used, it is always to address someone who in another context could be appealed as to as *adɛ*. In other words, children never use the term with their parents, or young cousins, but only those siblings with whom it could be appropriate. Thus the addressee is always appropriately selected.

Where young children make errors is in other aspects of use. For one, the modality is incorrect in that children use *adɛ* in an assertive way with loud voices and not in the modality of appeal. In addition, they use it in situations that are not appropriate, when not eliciting sympathy or compassion. Finally, they use *adɛ* with inappropriate speech acts. Let us examine some examples of children's use of the *adɛ* term and the response of mature speakers to them.

(8)   Abi (31.2) is playing with a large tree nut, a wild almond.

(calling to his sister 5½ yrs.)   ¹ *adɛ! look at my wild almond!/
² Mother→Sister: "Sister! Look at my wild
almond sister!"

Abi is correct in his choice of addressee—that is, in some situations his older sister would be called *adɛ*. However, this was not one of them. The modality is incorrect, as Abi was assertive, calling out, using *adɛ* in an exuberant way as a vocative, which is inappropriate with *adɛ* (as Wanu did in example 5, line 21). While his syntax is correct, his speech act, a directive "to look" as constructed, is socially inappropriate. And in repeating his utterance, which both Abi and his sister can hear, the mother provides a model of the appropriate way to say that particular speech act, using the kin term "sister." We know that Abi's use of *adɛ* is not appropriate in this context since his mother changes what he in fact has said.⁷ In addition, an examination of the transcripts reveals no occasions on which adults and older children use *adɛ* in an assertive way, or with this type of speech act. In this situation, as in others, he would have been correct had he used the kin term *nado* 'my sister', since he was not evoking what is special to the *adɛ* relationship.

Adults know the correct usage of the *adɛ* term and the meaning of the *adɛ* relationship. They do not support a child's innovative use of either the term or the relationship. By insisting upon and maintaining the restricted context of usage, mothers define, reshape and guide the child's own emerging interpretation of events.

(9)   Mɛli (28.3) is playing a peeking game with her brother Seligiwo (12.).

Seligiwo (babbling): *adɛadɛadɛadɛ*, etc.
(to Seligiwo)   ¹ *say *adɛ*!/
(Seligiwo continues to babble)
(to mother)   ² that one is saying/mother/that one
                                                     is saying/mother/(he) says
                                                     "*adɛ*"/
³ Mother→Mɛli: Yes, he says
"my sister Mɛli."
(to mother)   ⁴ (he) said "*adɛ*"/

Like their mothers, young girls tell even younger chidren what to say in ongoing interaction. Responding to her brother's babbling, Mɛli tells him to "say *adɛ*!"

Her mother, who is not attending to what the children were doing, makes no comment. While Seligiwo continues to babble, Mɛli reports his speech to her mother (line 2). Her mother's response provides the correct model of what Mɛli was supposed to hear: *nado* 'my sister', not *adɛ*. In providing the adult model which the child is expected to learn, the mother recasts the infant's babbles into what is socially possible in that situation, as well as what is socially correct. In doing this, she informs Mɛli of what it is that she should be hearing, which is "my sister Mɛli." *Ado*, which can be used with a proper name, greets a particular person, while *adɛ*, which cannot be used with a proper name, suggests a particular relationship. The term *adɛ* cannot be used in a playful situation, such as the one in which Mɛli and her brother are involved. Mɛli used *adɛ* inappropriately: one does not use *adɛ* in an assertive way or with *ɛlɛma*, and one does not say *adɛ* outside of the appropriate speech act.

Examples 8 and 9 illustrate the consequences of violations of what Cook-Gumperz and Gumperz (1976) call co-occurrence expectations. The situation and the mood of the interaction set up the mother's interpretation. The term *adɛ* used by the child without the appropriate combination of message content and contextualization cues becomes unacceptable in the situation and the mother therefore reinterprets the child's utterance to match co-occurrence expectations.

Errors in the child's use of *adɛ* were treated differently by the mothers from those made in the use of other linguistic forms. For example, if the child applied the wrong proper name or kinship term to someone, the mother would provide the correct name or kin term, followed by a directive to repeat it (*ɛlɛma*). However, when the child used *adɛ* in the wrong speech situation, modality, or speech act, the mother provided the correct model of what to say (as in examples 8 and 9) but did not ask the child to repeat the correct form. Mothers were consistent in their own use of the *adɛ* term and repeated the correct form and way of speaking after the child's inappropriate use, not calling attention to the error or making it as explicit as they had done with the misapplication of other names and terms.

From longitudinal data it appears that the use of the term *adɛ* is not mastered before the age of 3 years. While children make requests based on appeal (using the appropriate expressives and voice quality), they in fact do not use the term *adɛ* as part of the request. The three children applied the term to someone who could be *adɛ* in the right situation. But all failed to use it with the correct demeanor, modality, speech act, and situation. Both Abi and Wanu used the expressive term *wɔ* with the *adɛ* term, but in each case other co-occurrence rules were not met. Most of the time *adɛ* was used in address, which is correct, but in a few instances it was used in reference, which is not correct for children in any case.

By the age of 5 years children are using *adɛ* correctly to address their siblings when making requests based on appeal. Speakers would use the term only when putting pressure on someone to comply. Older children never use it in reference, which is correct. When a girl uses *adɛ* in address, requests are made to either a younger sibling or an older sister, whichever one has what she wants.

While older children use the *adɛ* term correctly, with the appropriate interactional force, it does not always bring the desired effects, as mothers often determine how interactions with young children will be resolved.

(10) Wanu (24.1) is eating a crayfish and his sister Isa (8 yrs.) wants some. Mother is nearby.

¹ Isa→Wanu (whining): wɔ, me, Wanu.
² Mother→Wanu→>Isa: You eat!
  ɛlɛma = (you don't eat!)

                                                ³ you eat!/

⁴ Isa→Wanu (whining): Wanu, head to me.
⁵ Mother→Wanu→>Isa: Which one?! ɛlɛma.
⁶ Isa→Wanu: adɛ, half to me.
⁷ Mother→Wanu: Eat!
  (Isa whines)
⁸ Mother→Isa: Don't take his!

We have just examined different situations in which children are learning about the adɛ relationship as an example of some of the processes involved in the acquisition of sociocultural knowledge necessary to make socially appropriate linguistic propositions. We have looked at the ways in which mothers teach their young children about the adɛ relationship by repeatedly shaping their expectations and assumptions through the use of formulaic, culturally specific, and situationally restricted messages which co-occur with a consistent set of contextualization cues. In addition we have seen that in a number of situations the child applies the restricted adɛ term too broadly in terms of speech acts, demeanor, and situation. Instead of explicitly correcting the child, the mother repeats the "correct" way of talking in that situation. In looking at the role of "interpretation" we have seen that there are socially and situationally appropriate ways to interpret the babblings of an infant. In all of these social situations the message the child gets is consistent. Doing and feeling are interconnected. Both linguistic proposition and contextualization cues must be socially appropriate in order to effect communication.

The adɛ Relationship in Myth

So far what we know about the adɛ relationship is from its use in family interaction where the inappropriate treatment of adɛ was one important source of information about what constituted that relationship and what it meant. Because the Kaluli could not talk about the relationship it had to be observed in order to understand its meaning and to construct the rules of appropriateness governing the use of the term. However, other sources of ethnographic information are available, and these too exploit the absence or violation of the relationship as a way of elucidating its significance.

From the use of adɛ in song we know that it is extremely powerful in evoking sadness and crying when people sing about "having no adɛ" (Feld 1979, chaps. 3 and 5). It is one of the most profound cultural and sentimental relationships, and outside of marriage, the most important male/female relationship for adults. Another source of information about adɛ is myth, where we are presented with an adɛ relationship, and the consequences of its violation. The Kaluli do not say that the following myth is about the adɛ relationship, but about a boy who turned into a bird, and the origin of crying. It was collected and transcribed by S. Feld (see Feld 1979).

Once upon a time there was a young boy and his older sister; they called each other adɛ. One day they went off together to a small stream to catch crayfish. After a short time the girl caught one; her younger brother as yet had none. Looking at the catch he turned to her, lowered his head, and whined, "*Adɛ*, I have no crayfish." She replied, "I won't give it to you; it is for my mother."

Later, on another bank of the stream she again caught one; her younger brother was still without. Again he begged, "*Adɛ*, I have no crayfish." Again she refused, "I won't give it to you; it is for my father." Sadly, he continued to hope for a catch of his own. Then finally, at another bank, she again caught a crayfish. He immediately begged it, whining, "*Adɛ*, I really have nothing." She was still unwilling; "I won't give it to you; it is for my older brother."

He felt very sad. Just then he caught a very tiny shrimp. He grasped it tightly, and when he opened his palm it was all red. He then pulled the meat out of the shell and placed the shell over his nose. His nose turned a bright purple-red. Then he looked at his hands. They were wings.

As she turned and saw her brother become a bird the sister was very upset. "Oh, *adɛ*," she said, "I'm sorry; don't fly away." He opened his mouth to reply but what came out was not words but a high falsetto cooing cry of the *muni* bird. He began to fly off. His sister was in tears at the sight of him and cried out, "Oh, *adɛ*, I'm sorry, come back, take the crayfish, you eat them all, come back and take these crayfish." Her calling was in vain. The boy was now a *muni* bird and continued to cry and cry.

We explore the cultural themes of this myth as a way of stating some of the significant aspects of the *adɛ* relationship for the Kaluli. This provides a larger ethnographic perspective to what in fact the mother is trying to create in this relationship between her children. Feld (1979, chap. 1) analyzes this myth in terms of major cultural themes, one of which is the theme of food, hunger, and reciprocity. In establishing the *adɛ* relationship in daily interactions, the passage of food is frequently from older sister to younger brother. The younger brother comes to feel "owed" and begs what the sister has. The older sister has been taught to respond to this type of appeal and give, while demanding little in return. Thus to deny her younger brother is a serious breach of the expectations he has about the *adɛ* relationship. In the myth we see the consequences of the breach of expected *adɛ* behavior. The young boy begs food from his older sister. Both the child's utterance, "*Adɛ*, I have no crayfish" (his situation) and his voice quality are aimed at making the sister feel sorry for him and give. However, each request is refused, as the sister places other family members before her younger brother. This entire sequence, in fact, runs contrary to all norms of Kaluli social practice, especially in light of the expectations created by mothers teaching their children about *adɛ*. In denying food to her younger brother, the older sister breaks a basic rule. Building on the work of E.L. Schieffelin (1976), Feld explores another theme, that of sorrow, loss, and abandonment. Kaluli deeply fear loneliness. No companionship, no assistance, no one to share food with, is perhaps the most awesome human state. Loneliness is seen as nonassistance, the condition of being without relationship. Schieffelin emphasized the basic Kaluli urge to share with others. "As human relationships are actualized and mediated through gifts of food and material wealth, so these things come to stand for what is deeply felt in human relationships" (1976:150). And, as Feld points out, "it thus makes sense that Kaluli equate breakdowns in reciprocity assistance, sharing . . . with vulnerability, loss, abandonment, isolation, loneliness, and ultimately death" (1979:15). The fact that the older sister consistently denies her younger brother food signals the fact that he has no *adɛ*, no one in the relationship of giving to his request based upon appeal. No one feels sorry for him, no one is moved by his situation. As Feld further suggests, "for the boy hunger becomes isolation; denial of the expected role becomes abandonment. The anxiety is both frightening and sad; at once the boy is diminished to a non-human state" (1979:15).

Feld takes up a number of other important cultural themes in his analysis of the myth, but one particularly relevant to this discussion is the importance of birds to the Kaluli. They perceive children to be like birds, with their high-pitched voices and repetitive vocalizations; children must not eat certain birds, lest they never speak. In addition, the Kaluli believe that birds are *ane mama*, spirit reflections of their dead. In the case of actual or symbolic death, one is reduced to the state of a bird. Thus the consequences of the breach of the *adε* relationship is that the boy turns into a bird, and his crying is the origin of weeping (see Feld 1979 for further discussion about the use of *adε* in song).

Thus the significance of the *adε* relationship is not limited to something between children, or a strategy the mother uses to get her older daughters to assist with the younger children. By creating the *adε* relationship in childhood, where events and associations are largely out of the control of the young individuals, the mother provides a very meaningful, lifelong relationship for her children's siblings, one in which appeals will not be refused, and one which gives meaning throughout their lives.

NOTES

[1] Children's ages are given in months and weeks unless otherwise indicated. 24.3 is 24 months, 3 weeks. Transcription conventions follow Bloom and Lahey (1978). Child speech is on the right side and adult speech and all contextual information is on the left. Examples in Kaluli with interlinear glosses may be obtained by writing to the author.

[2] A total of 97 occurrences in 83 hours of taperecorded family interactions form the basis for this analysis.

[3] An exception to this is in funerary sung texted weeping, where the *adε* term may be used with possessives (Feld 1979, chapters 3 and 5).

[4] See Feld 1979, chapter 3 for a discussion of *gesiab* in the context of song.

[5] Kaluli mothers tell their young, language-learning children what to say in on-going interaction using the directive *εlεma*, 'say like that'. This is reported in B.B. Schieffelin 1979a and in press. The transcription convention for multiparty talk with *εlεma* is as follows: Single arrow → indicates speaker→addressee; double arrow →> indicates speaker→addressee→>addressee. For example, in line 1 Mother wants Mεli to say to Seligiwo "you take!"

[6] In address, speakers always use *adε* as a first in making a request; it is never used to escalate or add force to a request, as it is in reference.

[7] According to my Kaluli assistant the use of the term is *mahagali siyo* 'not quite right'. This is different from *hala siyɔ* 'mispronounced' or *togode siyɔ* 'incorrectly said' (grammatically).

BIBLIOGRAPHY

BLOOM, L. and LAHEY, M. 1978. *Language development and language disorders*. New York: J. Wiley and Sons.
COOK-GUMPERZ, J. and GUMPERZ, J. 1976. Context in children's speech. Working Paper #46. Language Behavior Research Laboratory, University of California, Berkeley.
ERVIN-TRIPP, S. 1972. On sociolinguistic rules: Alternation and co-occurrence. In *Directions in sociolinguistics: The ethnography of communication*, ed. J. Gumperz and D. Hymes. New York: Holt, Rinehart and Winston.

FELD, S. 1979. Sound and sentiment: Birds, weeping, poetics and song in Kaluli expression. Ph.D. dissertation, Indiana University.

GUMPERZ, J. 1967. On the linguistic markers of bilingual communication. In *Problems of bilingualism*, ed. J. Macnamara. *Journal of Social Issues* 23:48-57.

———. 1977. Sociocultural knowledge in conversational inference. In *Linguistics and anthropology*, ed. M. Saville-Troike. Georgetown University Round Table on Languages and Linguistics. Washington, D.C.: Georgetown University Press.

SCHIEFFELIN, B. B. 1979a. Getting it together: An ethnographic approach to the study of the development of communicative competence. In *Developmental pragmatics*, ed. E. Ochs and B. B. Schieffelin. New York: Academic Press.

———. 1979b. A developmental study of word order and case-marking in an ergative language. Papers and reports in child language development 17. Linguistics Department, Stanford University.

———. 1984. How Kaluli children learn what to say, what to do and how to feel. New York: Cambridge University Press.

SCHIEFFELIN, E. L. 1976. The sorrow of the lonely and the burning of the dancers. New York: St. Martins Press.

TANNEN, D. 1979. What's in a frame? Surface evidence for underlying expectations. In *Discourse Processes*, Vol. 2. New Directions, ed. R. Freedle. Norwood, N.J.: Ablex.

SECTION FOUR

SOCIAL BASES OF LANGUAGE CHANGE

All living languages are constantly undergoing change, and change can be observed at different linguistic levels, including phonology, morphology, syntax, and semantics. Some changes are motivated by social forces among a particular group of speakers. Other changes are influenced by time or abrupt changes in society and technology. A most important aspect of the study of linguistic change is the careful and precise description of what features of language are changing, and in what ways. The papers in this section concentrate on grammatical structure, vocabulary, pronominal choice, and language choice. Linguistic change involves a dynamic intersection of internal linguistic processes with various social and cultural factors.

JOHN BAUGH's paper examines linguistic variation for the Black English copula in Harlem, the Sea Isles, and Jamaica. He discovers a high degree of linguistic continuity in these disparate Black English communities. All languages vary to some degree, and Baugh's work demonstrates that quantitative variable analyses can illuminate instances of linguistic stability, that is, in addition to the well-established tradition that examines linguistic change. CHRISTINA BRATT PAULSTON deals with a much researched topic within sociolinguistics: variation in second-person pronominal usage in Western European languages. She uses a combined social interactional and ethnographic approach in this study of an aspect of language change in Sweden.

Bilingualism and other manifestations of languages in contact have attracted much attention in the last decade. The last two papers in this volume deal with quite different types of contact situations in two different parts of the world. SUSAN GAL investigates language choice, including code-switching, in a bilingual (German and Hungarian) community in Austria. Her concern with changing patterns of language

245

use reveals significant differences in men's and women's speech (see the very different approaches taken by Trudgill and Gardner in Sections One and Two respectively). One of the most dramatic instances of language contact, along with linguistic variation, is the pidginization and creolization of language. GILLIAN SANKOFF and SUZANNE LABERGE describe some grammatical aspects of the development of New Guinea Tok Pisin, from a lingua franca pidgin into a creole language. Their discussion is based on the premise that the social and communicative functions of a language are related to both its structure and the ways in which it changes.

SELECTED BIBLIOGRAPHY

HYMES, D.H. (ed.). 1971. *Pidginization and Creolization of Language*. New York: Cambridge University Press.

LABOV, W. 1972. *Sociolinguistic Patterns*. Philadelphia: University of Pennsylvania Press.

LEHMANN, W.P., and MALKIEL, Y. (eds.). 1968. *Directions for Historical Linguistics*. Austin: University of Texas Press.

VALDMAN, A. (ed.). 1977. *Pidgin and Creole Linguistics*. Bloomington: Indiana University Press.

WEINREICH, U. 1953. *Languages in Contact*. The Hague: Mouton.

JOHN BAUGH

A Reexamination of
the Black English Copula[1]

INTRODUCTION

All facets of Afro-American behavioral research have obvious social implications. Undoubtedly, the catalytic impact of the civil rights movement has influenced this social orientation. In the case of linguistics, however, some of the most significant theoretical advances of our time can be linked directly with Black English Vernacular (BEV) research. In spite of the fact that scholars have typically approached BEV in a delicate and diplomatic manner, controversies rage at both professional and lay levels with regard to the viability and legitimacy of BEV research. This is not surprising because BEV is a stigmatized dialect and as such represents a highly personal and consequently emotional topic. Though there are strong social concerns, and in some instances social consequences, involved in BEV analyses, affiliated linguistic issues also continually crop up. As a result we are forced to review the limitations, appropriateness, and social applicability of contemporary introspective linguistic theories. The present discussion, although rooted in a socially important topic, will stress linguistic concerns. This is not to suggest that the social aspects of BEV are being dismissed as unimportant, merely that they are not of primary concern here.

The present analysis reexamines the nature of copula variation in BEV and is cast in the tradition of the earlier copula research by Labov (1969) and Wolfram (1974). This analysis differs from previous examinations, however, in that more constraints have been introduced and the Cedergren-Sankoff computer program for multivariant analysis has been employed.

The data are from the Cobras, an adolescent peer group that was interviewed by John Lewis ("KC") as part of Labov's earlier BEV research. Having conducted fieldwork of my own in a Los Angeles BEV community, I am aware of the stifling effect that the interview can have on the vernacular corpus. After reviewing Lewis's interview, however, I feel that the authenticity of the data is clear. At this point, let it suffice to say that Lewis showed an acute ethnosensitivity in all of the interviews that he gathered. Although these data are synchronic, the present analysis reveals some diachronic implications as well. To my knowledge, this investigation represents one of the first times that multivariant analysis has been used with regard to BEV for historical purposes.

[1] I am grateful for comments on earlier versions of this chapter from Gillian Sankoff and William Labov.

Linguistic Variation and Linguistic Theory

When the variable rule was first introduced (Labov, 1969), the full potential of variable analysis for linguistic purposes could not be known. That its potential has been gradually maturing is seen in the works of Trudgill (1971), G. Sankoff (1974), Cedergren and Sankoff (1974), Wolfram (1974), Lavendera (1975), and others. In a sense one might view variable analysis as traditional in linguistic research; after all, what could be more natural or traditional than entering the speech community, gathering a corpus, reviewing the corpus for paradigms, and reporting the nature of linguistic systematicity wherever it is found? In spite of this traditional orientation, however, influential linguists have stressed the theoretical restrictions imposed by nonideal corpora. As a result systematic variation—henceforth variation—has typically been viewed as free variation. In this instance it will be most beneficial to review affiliated theoretical and methodological concerns as they relate to BEV.

This research on BEV differs from the more formal research in linguistics because the latter analysis is usually inductive. Depending on one's theoretical perspective, this can be seen as a blessing or a curse. Whereas the evolution of formal linguistic research has resulted in a condition where many scholars turn to themselves as informants, there are few, if any, trained linguists whose intuitions about BEV are reliable for descriptive purposes. Another difficult choice must therefore be made. Should we strive to train speakers of Nonstandard English to become linguists so that they can then introspect about their language, or should we strive to enhance our empirical methodologies? Unquestionably, the only feasible alternative available to BEV is to continue with the empirical tradition. In training nonstandard speakers to become introspective linguists we would inevitably bombard their native intuitions with preconceptions to the point where the validity of these intuitions would be questionable.

What, then, does this have to do with linguistic theory? Quite simply, when we look at advances in linguistics, we see that the methodologies employed in introspective research are not generally applicable even in the first approach to a language. In turn, the scholar who is interested in BEV and in related social concerns finds that contemporary methodologies and theories are often not suited to the task. This is not a new point by any means; Hymes has repeatedly indicated that we must take ethnographic considerations into account when conducting linguistic investigations, simply because ethnographic factors DIRECTLY affect the language (cf. Hymes, 1962).

Returning to the special needs confronting BEV, then, there is an obvious need to enhance inductive methodologies. One could argue that these empirical needs have been in existence for many years, but in the case of BEV there seems to be a sense of urgency, a desire to rectify methodological inadequacies quickly. Unfortunately, the recognition of methodological and theoretical inadequacies does not lead immediately to rapid reassessment and revision. Nevertheless, significant strides are being made on several linguistic fronts and the resulting innovations can now be applied or reapplied as necessary. At this point in linguistic evolution, that is, with the maturation of variable research, it is safe to say that the incorporation of variable phenomena is a requisite for thorough descriptive purposes. And the greatest value lies in identifying the most significant constraints on these phenomena. A related concern must focus on what is meant by the term "Black English." In this chapter, for the sake of brevity, this issue is not treated in depth; Black English is used to refer to the vernacular dialect, namely, the dialect that is native to most working-class black Americans and that reflects the usage of "some or all of the features which are distinctive [in the colloquial dialects of these black Americans]."[2]

If we refine the accuracy of variable rules in the linguistic realm, the structural relations between Standard English (SE) and BEV will become clearer. In turn, such findings will bear directly on educational issues such as bidialectalism and linguistic-dialectal interference. Furthermore, the common concerns associated with English research in general must be considered. Given that BEV is structurally similar to SE, it stands as an important point of structural contrast and as such provides an excellent basis for comparing aspects of language change, language acquisition, and concepts of competence, both "linguistic" and "communicative" (cf. Hymes, 1974).[3] At present, linguistics is able to address these highly emotional topics with a high degree of objectivity. When valid linguistic correspondences or differences can be revealed, we can hope to approach social and educational concerns with a higher level of accountability. I am suggesting that wherever systematic linguistic relationships can be identified, no matter how large or how small, those relationships should ultimately be addressed. To the extent that a given linguistic phenomenon cannot be examined or substantiated at the level of the informants within a speech community, one should question the legitimacy of the description.

The final point that I would like to make with regard to linguistic theory and variable linguistic phenomena is a personal one and closely related to BEV concerns generally. Many scholars who have little or no formal linguistic training have used the nonstandard speech of Afro-Americans as an indicator of communicative deprivation, cognitive limitation, and the like (cf. Bereiter and Engelmann, 1966). Although this is fallacious from a linguistic perspective, the nature of contemporary introspective linguistic methodology is coincidentally such that it implicitly supports the elitist perspective that assumes BEV to be an "inferior" dialect. I am not advocating as a moral obligation that we enhance empirical methods; rather, it would seem that BEV and many other stigmatized dialects throughout the world cannot be accurately described for social, educational, or other purposes until the descriptive limitations of introspective research are clearly exposed.

Field Methods

We have seen that there is a definite need to reestablish strong contacts in the speech community; it is equally important to recognize that the task of the fieldworker, especially the urban fieldworker, is difficult and often precarious, and requires an intimate ethnosensitivity to the speech community and to one's informants. This may seem to be an added burden, but in those instances where inductive evidence is the only legitimate source of data social obstacles are unavoidable.

[2] I have expanded Fasold's (1969) definition in an effort to incorporate an implicit interactional dimension into the definition. It is, after all, the interactional component that Bloomfield has identified as instrumental in defining the speech community (cf. Bloomfield, 1933, p. 42).

[3] This does not imply that we should stay at the level of analyzing purely linguistic constraints. Rather, I suggest that we take full advantage of an accurate linguistic statement prior to incorporating constraints that cannot be defined with the same accuracy as linguistic phenomena.

Scanning the BEV literature written over the past decade, one is struck by the fact that much of the descriptive emphasis is focused on younger members of the community, with the data usually having been gathered by strangers (i.e. outsiders to the community) in unfamiliar surroundings. Efforts to justify these limited procedures have been based on the claim that children tend to be less formal than adults, and that, consequently, for descriptive purposes, the vernacular corpora of children represent the purest BEV forms. Such procedural limitations have been discussed before (cf. Wolfram, 1974; Mitchell-Kernan, 1971) and need not be further discussed here. However, the role of the BEV fieldworker needs to be reviewed more carefully.

The role of the fieldworker should be stressed if for no other reason than the accuracy of a final empirical analysis, but for BEV the significance of the fieldworker is critical. Ironically, there has been minimal concern—at least in the overwhelming majority of BEV research—with the importance of data gathering. It has been as if the desire to describe the language has taken precedence over the need to ensure the accuracy of the corpus. Effective fieldwork can—and must—be carried out on Black English at all social levels. But the gathering of the vernacular of the city streets is fundamental for an accurate view of social, historical and educational issues.

As has been mentioned, most of the data used in this study were gathered from the Cobras by John Lewis (KC), who is an excellent fieldworker for BEV. Lewis, a black man, has lived through many of the same experiences as the Cobras, and is therefore intimately familiar with native topics of interest; he was able to argue with informants without social difficulty. These special skills were particularly useful because the Cobras lived in a situation where the ability to handle oneself in verbal confrontations was highly prized. Thus, Lewis's own verbal skill clearly increased his effectiveness as a fieldworker. Throughout these data, two factors seemed to enhance Lewis's interviews: his intimate understanding of his informants' social perspectives, and his close contacts with the Cobras in a variety of social situations—not merely in the interview.

The study of BEV has been plagued by shortcuts in the field and quiet dismissals of many adult informants for social reasons alone. Undeniably, the task of gathering BEV data is often difficult and this too is a social fact, but if we intend to address BEV in a traditionally sound manner, then we must enhance our field methods in general. Like KC, we must be able to take the time to gain the trust of several representative informants.

THE BEV COPULA: A BRIEF REVIEW
OF PREVIOUS RESEARCH

Before moving on to current analysis, let us review the implications of previous copula research. Although a variety of works on the copula have emerged in broader contexts, the present remarks are intended primarily with BEV and West Indian Creole (WIC) examinations in mind. In early statements of the creole position, Bailey (1965) and Stewart (1969) proposed that BEV had a zero copula. Although arguments for a zero copula, with emphasis on zero, have since been seen as greatly overstated, Bailey and Stewart established the importance of looking closely at the

African and WIC roots of contemporary BEV.[4] Examining black–white linguistic relationships with emphasis on the creolist position, Stewart reviewed the grammatical relationship between SE and white nonstandard dialects in opposition to BEV and Gullah, and found that the auxiliary had unique and similar markings in both Black dialects. In addition, examining another distinctive BEV feature (*be*), he questioned the possibility of European (Irish) influence:

> But if that is the origin of the Negro-dialect use of *be* (i.e., borrowed by Negroes, let us say, from Irish immigrants to North America), then why is it now so wide-spread among Negroes but so absent from the still somewhat Irish-sounding speech of many direct descendants of the Irish immigrants [1969, p. 16]?

For the purpose of the present discussion, concern necessarily concentrates on the historical influences that affect copula variation. But dialect borrowing need not be restricted to a single contact group. The Irish presence as indentured laborers and their subsequent role as slave overseers could easily explain the dialectal contact. Nevertheless, the creolist position appears to be quite strong as well. It is quite possible and even likely that contemporary BEV dialects contain linguistic influences from both the Irish and the West Indians (cf. Traugott, 1972). These historical issues, although relevant to the current discussion, will be presented in greater detail at a later point in the chapter.

Labov (1969) found variation in the copula to be the result of a series of grammatical and phonological rules that were parallel to those of colloquial deletion in SE. Deletion in BEV was possible only in environments where contraction was possible in SE. Furthermore, the variable constraints on the contraction and deletion rules were parallel except for the phonological effects which opposed the deletion of a vowel to the deletion of a consonant. Labov's initial analysis has been confirmed and reduplicated in several studies (e.g., Legum et al., 1971; Wolfram, 1969; Mitchell-Kernan, 1971).[5] Carrying the research further by building on the work of Labov, as well as aspects of his own research in Detroit, Wolfram (1974) examined the nature of copula variation in a comparison of white and black Southern speech.

But, although these studies have led to a synchronic understanding of copula variation, numerous historical questions still remain unanswered. Recognizing the complexity of the diachronic issues that surround this particular problem, Fasold (1976) proposes an alternative historical solution that takes both the creole and SE origins into account. Citing evidence from Botkin's narratives (1945) as a structural point for historical reference, as well as the contemporary works of Labov, Stewart, and his own previous discussion of the phenomena (1972); Fasold posits that the copula may have originally been omitted as a grammatical feature because of BEV's African and creole origins, but that this deletion was later transformed into a phonological rule. Furthermore, his argument suggests that the transition from initial grammatical constraints to more current phonological conditionings could

---

[4] Again, we must appreciate that their remarks came at a time when the social atmosphere was such that the "awareness level," if you will, of many blacks was such that African origins were not only palatable but preferred.

[5] A number of other works centering on the copula have treated it in broader linguistic and social contexts, for example, Day's work on the Hawaiian Creole (1972) and Ferguson's multilingual comparative survey on the absence of the copula (1971).

have taken place with minimal changes in the surface forms. We will return to Fasold's position shortly, but for the moment, let us say that his argument seems quite plausible given the strength of the arguments that have been presented from both sides of the diachronic debate.

THE PRESENT ANALYSIS

The Cobra data are excellent from a synchronic standpoint owing to the handling of the data and the Cobra's collective command of BEV. But significant strides have also been made beyond the realm of field procedures: It is, appropriately, the advanced analytic techniques that have been developed by Cedergren and Sankoff, (1974) that now provide the necessary tools to look at these variable phenomena in more detail (cf. Griffin et al., 1973).

The Sample

These data were gathered in the mid-1960s. Since that time, some of the Cobras have ended up in jail or been killed or wounded in urban disputes. Most of the members are now in their mid to late twenties and, as far as I know, are still living in and around Harlem. I should also point out that KC did not record all of the 26 taped conversations of which the analyzed corpus is composed. Some of the interviews were conducted by Clarence Robins,[6] and some of the group interviews were successfully conducted by combinations of black and white investigators. For the most part, however, it was KC and the Cobras.

During the mid-1960s the primary concern of the Cobras was the defense of their "turf" against rivals, most notably the "Jets."[7] There came about a noteworthy philosophical change in the Cobras, however, with the members of the group striving to become more aware of their plight as Afro-Americans; consequently,

TABLE 5.1   Sample totals for the Cobras: Based on following grammatical constraints

gon(na)	Verb + ing	Loc/Adj		NP		Misc.
108	122	134		162		53
		locative	adjective	NP	Det. # NP	
		48	86	126	36	

Total = 578

---

[6] Clarence Robins worked closely with John Lewis in gathering BEV data. Robins was also one of the co-authors of Labov et al., 1968.

[7] The Jets were also studied in Labov's original work and a detailed description of the peer group can be found in Labov et al., 1968.

they began to spout the rhetoric of black awareness and cultural taboos.[8] More generally, these transitions in attitude caused the Cobras to question their outlook on society and several of the interviews contain the theme of "the plight of Black America(ns)." In all, the data contained 578 tokens (i.e., environments where we would anticipate the presence of a copula in other dialects). Table 5.1 shows the breakdown of the totals in relation to the following grammatical constraints.

ANALYTIC PROCEDURE

The first version of the Cedergren–Sankoff program for multivariant analyses was run on the Cobra data in two series of calculations: (*a*) calculations that measured the same constraints as were measured by Labov and Wolfram; (*b*) a series of calculations that introduced new and subdivided constraints. Since Labov's original analysis employed an additive model, and Wolfram's analysis concentrated on white informants, it was felt that the synchronic clarification of BEV copula variation would be enhanced at this time by employing the Cedergren–Sankoff program.[9]

Once having conducted an initial series of calculations on the familiar constraints, it was necessary to repeat the calculations incorporating the following adaptations:

1. Question/non-question: Each token was identified as either a question or non-question and was submitted under this new factor group.
2. Miscellaneous factor for following grammatical constraints: It was necessary to introduce a miscellaneous category for those instances where the arbitrary factors were insufficient. For the most part these were adverbs of manner.
3. The subdivision of __NP: Previously, following NP had been calculated as a single factor. The secondary calculations dividing this factor into:
    (*a*) __NP
    (*b*) __Det. # NP (i.e., *a* and *the*)
4. The separation of __Loc/Adj: Heretofore, the analysis of __Loc/Adj. appeared as a single constraint owing to quantitative confines. The Cedergren–Sankoff program, however, allowed the present separation of these features.

COMPARABLE CALCULATIONS

At first blush, the need for a comparable series of calculations might seem dubious, and cumbersome, but it was felt that a parallel series of calculations would substantiate and/or clarify previous synchronic assessments and show whether the original relations were preserved in a multivariant analysis with extended (i.e., finely divided) constraints. Thus, the first series of calculations was purposely designed to mesh with the previous analyses of Wolfram and Labov, in that identical factors were analyzed. Parenthetically, Cedergren and Sankoff developed their

---

[8] I am using "black rhetoric" here because the Cobras were obviously imitating popular rhetorical styles and as a result would often contradict themselves on a variety of ideological points.

[9] At the 1976 NWAVE conference at Georgetown University, Pascale Rousseau presented advances in the computer program that have not been included in this analysis; however, the revised program is available for general use at this time. She and David Sankoff are most responsible for the many technical improvements in variable rule research.

computer methods—at least in part—by reexamining Labov's 1969 data, and they found that their fit of prediction with observation reliably identified those environments that favored both contraction and deletion.

Table 5.2 shows that, as in Labov, 1969, a preceding pronoun subject heavily favors contraction and somewhat less strongly favors deletion. The phonological effects do not show the reversal for contraction and deletion, but preceding vowels still tend to favor both rules. However, the differential effects on both rules will emerge as the analysis proceeds. The following phonological consonant appears to have an increased effect, but this will diminish in later analyses as well (see Table 5.3). The significant revisions of the original examination concentrate on the following grammatical constraints; these will therefore be of primary concern here.

The percentages from Labov's original research for the Cobras, of full, contracted, and deleted forms of *is* according to the preceding and following grammatical environments are given in Figure 5.1.

TABLE 5.2 Feature weights for the comparable series of calculations for all measured constraints

	Contraction	Deletion
-C __	0.000	0.000
-V __	.396	.239
__ C-	.465	.525
__ V-	0.000	0.000
NP __	0.000	0.000
Pro __	.919	.622
__ gon(na)	1.000	.567
__ Vb + ing	1.000	.375
__ PA/Loc	.336	.868
__ NP	.430	0.000

TABLE 5.3 Feature weights for phonological constraints

		Contraction	Deletion
Labov	-C __	.410	.800
	-V __	.900	.410
Present analysis	-C __	0.000	.061
	-V __	.408	0.000
	__ C-	.522	.322
	__ V-	0.000	0.000

The current contours, based on feature weights from the nonapplications probability model, appear in Figure 5.2. (Labov's illustrated contours are separated with regard to preceding grammatical constraints, whereas the present multivariant analysis does not need to make this kind of separation since all groups are considered simultaneously.) With the exception of the PA/Loc,[10] the orderings from the multivariant analysis are substantially the same with regard to the relative impact of following grammatical constraints on the contraction and deletion rules. Wolfram's analysis of white Southern speakers reflects similar patterns as well:

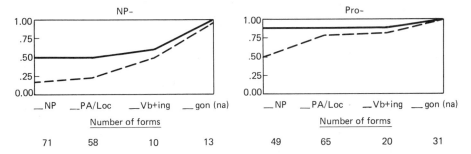

FIGURE 5.1. Percentage of full, contracted, and deleted forms of *is* according to preceding and following environments for the Cobras: ———, percentage contracted; ------, percentage deleted. (From Labov, 1972, p. 92.)

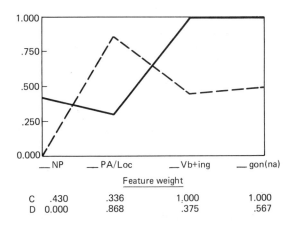

FIGURE 5.2. Probability of full, contracted, and deleted forms of *is* based on feature weights according to following grammatical constraints for the Cobras: ———, φ contracted; ------, φ deleted.

[10] Those who are familiar with previous analyses will immediately recognize that the new implications of the PA/Loc. reversal are not a trivial matter. The situation has changed, or rather, the assessment of the situation has changed, because of a complete analysis. Please recall that previous analyses for the Cobras did not account for all of the available data: "...the data presented here do not exhaust all the material which is available for the Jets and Cobras...[Labov, 1972, p. 91]." The present analysis does exhaust the Cobra data in a multivariant analysis, and the difference that has emerged results from the thorough analysis. It is important, therefore, that the difference illustrated in Figure 5.2 is not construed as a conflict with earlier research.

The patterning of *is*-deletion, although restricted in terms of the proportion of informants who realize the rule and the frequency with which it occurs for these informants, does appear to be a process found among some white Southern dialects. From a qualitative viewpoint, it appears to be a process quite similar to the one observed for VBE [Wolfram, 1974, p. 514].

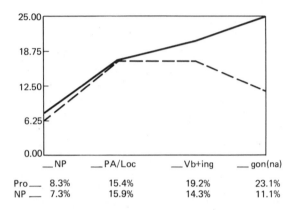

	__ NP	__ PA/Loc	__ Vb+ing	__ gon(na)
Pro __	8.3%	15.4%	19.2%	23.1%
NP __	7.3%	15.9%	14.3%	11.1%

FIGURE 5.3. Percentage of *is* absence in Pro__ and NP__ by following environments for white Southern speakers: ———, Pro__; ------, NP__. (From Wolfram, 1974, p. 514.)

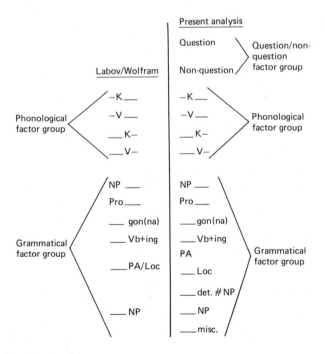

FIGURE 5.4. Factor group revision.

Before shifting the focus to the second series of calculations, we might ask ourselves about the structural similarities and what they mean. First of all, given the increased potential and analytic accountability of the Cedergren–Sankoff program, we see that, by and large, previous assessments were legitimate in their rule orderings. But, additionally, the present confirmation now allows us to look at the nature of each constraint more closely. Thus, leaving aside the factor revisions that we mentioned, the remaining constraints in the second series of calculations were the same (see Figure 5.4).

PHONOLOGICAL CONSTRAINTS

Beginning with preceding phonological constraints, we find the following (see Table 5.3).

In the earlier analysis, the following phonological environment was significant only for adults; here it appears that both contraction and deletion are favored by a following consonant, which indicates the likelihood that an underlying copula is present.

It is important to recall that -C __ factors appear less frequently than do -V __ factors since all relevant pronouns end in vowels. Nevertheless, the comparative findings clearly indicate consistencies with regard to implications for the preceding phonological conditionings: namely, -V __ favors contraction over deletion, whereas the reverse is true for -C __. The difference that is illustrated here, however, would indicate that the phonological constraints are not the strongest constraints with regard to either rule. At the same time, the weighting for -V __ (.408 contraction) is the stronger phonological constraint and this accentuates the comparability with previous assessments.

The preceding phonological factors, in spite of the vocalic appearance as a "slight" constraint are significant because they confirm the preference of a CVC pattern (cf. Labov et al., 1968; Labov, 1969). The maintenance of a CVC pattern is further supported when we consider that much of the evidence of pidgins and creoles has suggested that CVC contours are generally present in contact vernaculars (cf. Hall, 1966). From the standpoint of a more general picture of the phonological conditioning for BEV, consider the case as stated by Labov, 1972 (see Table 5.3): "In any case, the way in which contraction and deletion are opposed with respect to the preceding vowel clearly demonstrates that both contraction and deletion are phonological processes. . . [p. 106]." The present research, although still upholding this position, does not emphasize phonological conditioning in a PRIMARY sense. The point will be examined further when the independence of phonological and grammatical constraints is reviewed, but for the moment it is significant to note that the phonological conditioning is maintained although it does not receive primary emphasis.

THE QUESTION OF WEIGHTINGS

The situation with regard to questions is fairly complex, owing to the phonological, morphological, and syntactic issues that relate to the general class of questions proper and the issues that relate specifically to those questions occurring in copula constructions. From the standpoint of phonology, final *ts* clusters have been shown to have a unique effect on rule application; consequently, *it's*, *that's*, and *what's* are generally omitted in this type of analysis (cf. Labov, 1969; Wolfram, 1974), as they have been here. But given the importance of *what* in the broader context of questions, its omission necessarily limits the extent to which the impact of questions can accurately be assessed with regard to contraction and deletion. Also, considering the exclusive focus on *is* here, the scope of the question factor is further restricted (see Table 5.4).

TABLE 5.4   Feature weights for question constraints

	Question	Nonquestion
Contradiction	1.000	0.000
Deletion	1.000	0.000

GRAMMATICAL CONSTRAINTS

The grammatical arguments surrounding copula variation are by far the most interesting. In the past, it has primarily been the grammatical constraints, and, more specifically, the explanations surrounding various grammatical conditionings, that have lent viable support to both the creole and the English diachronic perspectives. Although the historical alternatives are not of primary importance at this point in the discussion, it is significant to note that the grammatical issues cover a tremendously wide range of diachronic and synchronic territory. This is clearly the case because scholars have been able to construct feasible, yet different, explanations from similar synchronic evidence. With the complexity of grammatical features having been noted, the nature of their conditionings may now be described.

Preceding Grammatical Constraints

Table 5.5 shows that a preceding pronoun favors both rules, with contraction receiving primary emphasis. This is not surprising given the discussion surrounding Pro__:

> it is plain that contraction is heavily favored when the subject is a pronoun. But the effect is much stronger than for other noun phrases ending in vowels. In the case of deletion, it can be seen that the rule operates much more often when a pronoun precedes...[Labov, 1972, pp. 106–7].

A further significant finding here that confirms previous analyses is the replication of the powerful constraint exerted by preceding NP. And, whereas Wolfram and Labov examined the nature of following grammatical conditionings based on separate analyses of the preceding factors, the present analysis has the advantage of being able to identify the overall conditioning. We can therefore see the relative impact of preceding grammatical elements without sacrificing other facets of the analysis.

TABLE 5.5 Effect of preceding NP or Pro on contraction and deletion as shown by feature weights

	NP __	Pro __
Contraction	0.000	.856
Deletion	0.000	.714

Following Grammatical Constraints

Unchanged Factors. The only factors to remain the same in the following grammatical factor group were (*a*) __ *gon(na)* and (*b*) __ verb + *ing*. Both of these factors reflect the same conditioning and rule orderings that have been identified in the past: Following *gon(na)* strongly favors contraction and has a significant effect on deletion; verb + *ing* also favors contraction with a somewhat lesser effect on deletion (see Table 5.6). Stated simply, in the final analysis the relation of __ *gon(na)* and __ verb + *ing* to other constraints remains unchanged when all analyses are considered.

The Subdivision of Following NP. With the complementary factors indicating similar rule orderings, we can now review the implications of the adjusted factors beginning with the following NP. Previous analyses have examined __ NP as a single constraint. The present analysis, however, has subdivided __ NP into two factors.

```
Labov/Wolfram              The present analysis

                                    →——  __ a NP
            ——————→      __ Det. # NP ——→—— __ the NP
 __ NP →——#——————→       __ NP
```

Thus, the implications that have been posited with regard to a following NP can now be reviewed more closely. Consider the rule conditionings that have been suggested thus far (see Figures 5.1, 5.2, and 5.3). As these findings stand, their impact would suggest __ NP as the least favored environment—within the realm of the following grammatical factors—for the application of either rule. With the division of the factor, however, another picture emerges (Table 5.7). We can see, therefore, that it is necessary to subdivide __ NP in the preceding manner because the true nature of the conditioning is camouflaged until this is done. The significance of this separation is further amplified because __ Det. # NP now emerges as a primary factor in the application of both rules. The other side of the coin finds residual __ NP as a low level constraint; in fact, __ NP is the least favored following grammatical factor.

TABLE 5.6   Effect of following *Gon(na)* and
Verb + *ing* on contraction and
deletion feature weights

	__ *Gon(na)*	__ Verb + *ing*
Contraction	1.000	1.000
Deletion	.601	.402

TABLE 5.7   Effect of a following NP or Det. # NP
on contraction and deletion as
shown by feature weights

	__ NP	__ Det. # NP
Contraction	0.000	1.000
Deletion	0.000	.741

Further Confirmation of the Independence of Phonological and Grammatical Conditioning.   At this stage of the discussion, it is beneficial to look back at some of the concerns that have been raised with regard to the independence of phonological and grammatical constraints (cf. Fraser, 1972). In spite of the importance of the various historical options that have been aired, there still remains some confusion—and some justifiable concern—as to the independence of analyzed constraints. We find grammatical criteria and phonological criteria, and numerous questions as to their mutual dependence or independence. The subdivision of our __ NP constraint, however, clearly emphasizes the independence of previously discussed phonological factors, namely, the preference for CVC sequences. The phonological conditioning is clear, but, more than that, the present analysis suggest that grammatical and phonological factors are independent. Turning our attention to grammatical concerns, then, we are again faced with the prospect of an either/or hypothesis: grammar or phonology. The reweighting of the subdivided __ NP constraint, however, would suggest that an either/or approach is insufficient;[11] consider the phonological relations as illustrated here:

$$\longrightarrow a \text{ NP} \qquad \_\ \_\ \_ \text{ Obligatory vocalic status}$$

$$\_ \text{ Det. \# NP} \longrightarrow the \text{ NP} \qquad \_\ \_\ \_ \text{ Obligatory consonantal status}$$

Given the rule-favoring strength of the __ Det. # NP factors (i.e., contraction [1,000], deletion [.741]), we clearly see the overriding impact of the grammatical conditioning. This being the case, the obvious questions shifts to what might be perceived as a conflict between the preference for CVC contours and the grammatical conditioning. The point that is being emphasized here is that NO SUCH CONFLICT EXISTS; rather, these findings suggest that both grammatical and phonological conditionings are operating simultaneously. Undoubtedly, this simul-

---

[11] Traugott (1972, p. 5) has discussed the limits of an either/or perspective with regard to the historical issues before. The new findings presented here tend to reinforce her position.

taneity is selectively conditioned and therefore should not be generalized. Thus, the present analysis, while providing additional insights into the synchronic nature of copula variation, has also confirmed that phonological conditionings and grammatical conditionings are operating simultaneously. It will be necessary to return to this point with regard to Fasold's historical discussion, but for the moment it is significant to note the independence of grammar and phonology—that is, the reconfirmation of their independence and, more importantly, the fact that both condition rule application in selective ways.

The Separation of Locatives and Adjectives

The final grammatical features that must be reviewed are the following locatives and adjectives. Heretofore, PA/Loc. has been measured as a single constraint. The limitation in the past was simply a quantitative barrier. "Because the total number of forms is considerably reduced for each group (even when single and group styles are combined), the following predicate adjectives and locatives are given together [Labov, 1972, p. 92]." Wolfram (1974) also measured locatives and adjectives as a single constraint, stating:

> Although there may be justification for categorizing this set on a different basis (e.g., considering adjectives as verbs, treating locatives as a separate category, etc.), it (i.e., the classification of factors) is considered here in the more traditional classification for the sake of comparability with previous studies [p. 505].

Whereas previous samples may have been considered too small, they are not so rare that their isolated conditionings cannot be accurately assessed at this time.

In the case of locatives, the conditioning is similar to the combined conditionings that have been reported in the past (see Table 5.8). The contraction rule is strong and is also favored over deletion. In addition, the ordering of these rules would strongly suggest an underlying copula, at least in this environment. With adjectives, an unexpected result appears. The rule orderings are emphatically reversed. Reflecting momentarily on the implications of the combined constraints, we see that the true nature of the conditioning was previously obscured. It is of course important to note that previous efforts combined these factors out of procedural necessity; however, with the difference now revealed, we must turn to the more complicated questions of how and why.

TABLE 5.8 Impact of following locative and adjective on contraction and deletion as shown by feature weights

	__ Locative	__ Adjective
Contraction	1.000	.116
Deletion	.682	1.000

For the sake of discussion, let us assume for the moment that the unexpected did not occur: that locatives and adjectives reported similar weightings and by extension, indicated rule orderings as suggested in previous analyses. The situation would merely be one of synchronic clarification. Since the rules are emphatically reversed, however, the historical question of an underlying copula in BEV becomes more complicated and, by extension, requires further diachronic perusal. Now that adjectives have been shown to favor deletion in a rather convincing manner (deletion = 1.000; contraction = .116), the crossover pattern of the rule orderings suggests dialectal influence from at least two sources (see Table 5.8). The implication for adjectives is that deletion must have predated the emergence of contracted forms for this environment.

Based on the illustrated examples, we can see that previous assessments suggest consistent rule orderings with regard to all of the following grammatical constraints (Figures 5.1 and 5.3). Moreover, the historical implications that such an ordering supports would lead one to the conclusion that an underlying copula was a general feature of BEV at an earlier point in history. However, with adjectives favoring deletion over contraction, it is quite possible that a ZERO COPULA did exist in protoforms. This possibility is further reinforced by the relatively slight influence that adjectives have on the contraction rule. This does not imply that we should posit a zero copula in all environments any more than that we should assume an underlying copula was automatically present. Rather, the new locative and adjectival findings would again suggest that phonological and grammatical conditionings are operating independently yet simultaneously, with emphasis, of course, on environmental—and possibly historical—selectivity. The diachronic implications of these findings are unavoidable given the rule reversals that have been identified. It is important to maintain caution in this diachronic regard, and to recognize the limits that such speculation has previously brought to bear. Wolfram (1974) states the case concisely:

> This is the historical question of how BEV and Southern white speech arose, and how the relationship between black and white speech has develcped since the settlement of the United States. In spite of the polemic with which the various historical options have been aired, evidence at this point still tends to be fragmented and anecdotal [p. 522].

SOME HISTORICAL IMPLICATIONS

In this instance, my proposed historical explanation is not based on speculation alone. Recalling the orientation of Fasold's recent discussion, namely, that both grammatical and phonological influences can account for fluctuations in the BEV copula, we can see that his position receives further confirmation based on the final analysis presented here. Let us now consider aspects of Fasold's discussion:

> Proponents of the Creole history of Vernacular Black English often disagree with linguists who have studied the dialect synchronically over the degree to which decreolization has progressed. . . Accepting Labov's analysis of the modern dialect is not tantamount to a denial of the Creole origin hypothesis, but simply to recognize that VBE has reached a late post-Creole stage.

Fasold goes on to outline a "hypothesized development of present tense *be* deletion in Black English." For the purpose of the discussion at hand, his concluding remarks are illuminating:

It is interesting to notice, if I am correct in the historical analysis of *be* forms, that while substantial changes in rules are going on in the background, the surface forms change little. From Stage 3 on, once *da* is relexified as *is*, there continues to be variation between *is* and deletion up to the present day.

As the situation stands now, with Fasold's position reinforced by the present analysis, we would posit that European versus African perspectives on the diachronic origins of BEV are far too simplistic. What is needed is evidence that substantiates a position that further considers both the African and European influence; but for the moment let us consider the linguistic consequence of West Indian contact.

Based on a comparison of two Creole varieties, Holm (1975) examined the grammatical hierarchy of following grammatical constraints. Concentrating on Jamaican (Le Page and De Camp, 1960) and Turner's description of Gullah (1949), Holm found that the syntactic environments where copula deletion were favored differed from the orderings initially identified by Labov. Holm's analysis is illuminating, and the constraint orderings that he has identified are given in Table 5.9.

Holm's research is quite similar to the present analysis because of his quantitative methodology. But more immediately relevant to my purpose is Holm's demonstration of the importance of separating locatives and adjectives. The orderings that Holm has identified tend to confirm the altered grammatical conditionings that have been identified in the present analysis.

TABLE 5.9 Grammatical hierarchy based on percentage of deletion for Jamaican and Gullah

Jamaican	Percentage	Gullah	Percentage
__ Adj.	66	__ *gonna*	88
__ *gonna*	32	__ Adj.	52
__ NP	22	__ V	52
__ V	17	__ Loc.	22
__ Loc.	17	__ NP	11

In an effort to further resolve the issue, let us turn our attention to Bailey's (1966) description of Jamaican Creole English (JCE). Bailey has identified the nature of locatives and adjectives in JCE as follows:

1. Locatives: "the locating verb (V_L) de, 'be' ... MUST be followed by a locative complement or modifier [emphasis my own]."

    (a) *im de a yaad*
        'She is at home.'

    (b) *jan no de ya nou*
        'John is not here now.'

    (c) *wan trii de batamsaid me hous*
        'There is a tree below my house.'

2. Adjectives: The adjectives in JCE operate similarly to those used by the Cobras, that is, the *be* form is absent.

   (a) *di kaafi kuol*   (c) *di bos faas*
        'The coffee is cold.'   'The bus is fast' [pp. 43, 64].
   (b) *di tiicha gud*
        'The teacher is good.'

If we keep in mind the inverse relationship observed in Table 5.9 and how the present assessment differs from the implicit historical perspective presented by Labov (see Figure 5.1), the diachronic aspect of this variation becomes clearer. In the case of locatives, the ___*de* + loc. constructions that Bailey has outlined in JCE are structurally similar to the overriding number of full and contracted forms that have been used by the Cobras. One would necessarily attribute this to an underlying copula, as seen in JCE. Thus, this particular environment in BEV unquestionably reflects structural similarities to JCE (see the relationships presented in Figure 5.5).

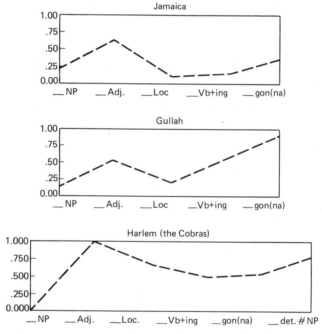

FIGURE 5.5. The impact of following grammatical constraints on deletion in Jamaica, Gullah, and Harlem (the Cobras).

The argument is further strengthened when applied to adjectives because, with the strength of the deletion rule now revealed, related historical concerns must come to the fore. This being the case, the adjectival evidence from JCE, which is structurally similar to the corresponding evidence from the Cobras, lends additional support to the position that there was no copula before adjectives. This also reinforces the creole origin hypothesis. When we consider the overall implications of the preceding investigations, the quantitative confirmation that emerges from the present analysis establishes the creole ancestry of contemporary BEV beyond any doubt.

At this point, however, it is wise to look at the historical implications a little more closely. Although it is necessary to recognize that creole origins have been posited before, it is equally important to recognize that many of these positions were presented prior to concise verification of the historical, empirical, or quantitative facts. The present confirmation, then, stresses the need for this type of validation, especially given the social importance of these historical questions and the availability of new analytic techniques.

CONCLUSION

The historical perspective that is revealed here can be simply stated in spite of the rather elaborate steps that have brought us to this point. It appears that the synchronic status of BEV copula variation has been influenced by West Indian creoles, as well as by SE. Based on the evidence presented, this seems to be the only feasible alternative. Moreover, when all of the structural and phonological facts are weighed, arguments for African versus European origins must again be seen as overly simplistic.

There are unavoidable limitations to the diachronic scope of research on stigmatized languages. This is simply because many of today's stigmatized dialects and languages were the languages of the poor and uneducated classes of yesteryear. The present analysis and discussion attempts to take a step forward with the recognition that new diachronic tools must continually be forged for stigmatized languages. We have justifiably been distracted by the linguistic machinery that seems to operate so quickly, cleanly, and efficiently in more prestigious languages. The question is, are we to let the efficiency of prestigious linguistics dictate the focus, direction, and overall development of these new and special tools?

The fact that BEV should not be viewed in a monogenetic fashion is not surprising considering the wide range of embryonic explanations which have been debated at such length. The difference that I wish to stress focuses on accountability. Based on the needs of linguistics, and for that matter those of all the behavioral sciences, as well as the needs of those who are the object of our scientific investigations, we must continue to strive to maximize the level of accountability before we neglect available data from real world contexts.

It is easy to see how linguists, influenced by a desire to pursue theory, have in large part tried to avoid the descriptive limitations imposed by inductive corpora. However, we must focus our efforts on thorough linguistic descriptions. As long as scholars are willing to dismiss empirical evidence under the banner of "performance" our descriptions will never reflect the complete structure of *langue*. As long as systematic variation exists, and as long as these phenomena are beyond the introspective grasp of the analyst, we must be willing to reestablish the empirical traditions that will expose such phenomena; otherwise, our descriptions cannot possibly represent *langue* in an actual sense.

In the case of BEV, however, the situation is even more complex. The social inequities and problems that were responsible for the initial hubbub about Afro-American research, or lack of it, are still with us today. In fact, these concerns are more vital than ever because many Afro-Americans still suffer from poverty and, by extension, from its social and cultural side effects. The unemployment figures from any urban city in the United States will substantiate my point. Those of us who are concerned with the social consequences of linguistic research are confronted with several decisions. Even when confined to the realm of obligatory empirical research, these decisions cannot be taken lightly. The need to enhance methodologies and theories is clearly desirable whenever and wherever possible, especially considering the subjective tradition within the field.

When one considers the extraneous factors that can influence the impetus and direction of future BEV research, it is important to recognize the unique position in which linguistics finds itself. In the case of BEV, we should make every effort to capitalize on strict linguistic principles to insure that our socially relevant concerns are not distorted by preconceived notions. We have a rare opportunity to make precise statements about an aspect of human behavior. Furthermore, we can hope that such information will benefit native members of the speech community.

REFERENCES

ANSHEN, F. 1969. *Speech variation among Negroes in a small Southern community.* Unpublished doctoral dissertation, New York University.
BAILEY, B. L. 1965. Toward a new perspective in Negro English dialectology. *American Speech*, 40: 171–77.
———. 1966. *Jamaican creole syntax.* London: Cambridge University Press.
BEREITER, C., and ENGELMANN, S. 1966. *Teaching disadvantaged children in the pre-school.* Englewood Cliffs, N.J.: Prentice-Hall.
BLOOMFIELD, L. 1933. *Language.* London: George Allen & Unwin.
Botkin, B. A. 1945. *Lay my burden down: A folk history of slavery.* Chicago: University of Chicago Press.
CEDERGREN, H. J., and SANKOFF, D. 1974. Variable rules: Performance as a statistical reflection of competence. *Language*, 50: 333–55.
DAY, R. 1972. *Patterns of variation in the use of tense, aspect and diathesis in the Hawaiian Creole continuum.* Unpublished doctoral dissertation, University of Hawaii.
FASOLD, R. W. 1969. Tense and the form *be* in Black English. *Language*, 45: 763–76.
———. 1972. Decreolization and autonomous language change. *Florida FL Reporter*, 10: 9–12, 51.
———. 1976. One hundred years from syntax to phonology. Chicago Linguistic Society, University of Chicago.
FERGUSON, C. A. 1971. Absence of copula and the notion of simplicity: A study of normal speech, baby talk, foreigner talk and pidgins. In D. Hymes (ed.), *Pidginization and creolization of languages.* Cambridge: University Press.
FRASER, B. 1972. Optional rules in grammar. *Monograph Series on Languages and Linguistics, Georgetown University*, 25: 1–16.
GRIFFIN, P., GUY, G., and SAG, I. 1973. Variable analysis of variable data. *University of Michigan Papers in Linguistics*, 1.
HALL, R. A., JR. 1966. *Pidgin and creole languages.* Ithaca, N.Y.: Cornell University Press.
HARRIS, Z. 1951. *Methods in structural linguistics.* Chicago: University of Chicago Press.
HOLM, J. 1975. Variability of the copula in Black English and its creole kin. Unpublished manuscript.
HYMES, D. 1962. The ethnography of speaking. In T. Gladwin and W. C. Sturtevant (eds.), *Anthropology and human behavior.* Washington, D.C.: Anthropological Society of Washington.
———. 1974. *Foundations in sociolinguistics.* Philadelphia: University of Pennsylvania Press.
LABOV, W. 1969. Contraction, deletion and inherent variability of the English copula. *Language*, 45: 715–62.
———. 1972. *Language in the inner city.* Philadelphia: University of Pennsylvania Press.
LABOV, W., COHEN, P., ROBINS, C., and LEWIS, J. 1968. *A study of the non-standard English of Negro and Puerto Rican speakers in New York City.* USOE Final Report, Research Project No. 3288.

LAVENDERA, B. 1975. *Linguistic structure and sociolinguistic conditioning in the use of verbal endings in si-clauses (Buenos Aires Spanish)*. Unpublished doctoral dissertation, University of Pennsylvania.

LEGUM, S. E., PFAFF, C., TINNIE, G., and NICHOLAS, M. 1971. *The speech of young black children in Los Angeles*. Technical report 33. Inglewood, California: Southwest Regional Laboratory.

LEPAGE, R., and DECAMP, D. 1960. *Jamaican creole (creole language studies I)*. London: Macmillan.

MITCHELL-KERNAN, C. 1971. *Language behavior in a black urban community*, Language-Behavior Research Laboratory Monographs, 2. Berkeley: University of California.

SANKOFF, G. 1974. A quantitative paradigm for the study of communicative competence. In R. Baumann and J. Sherzer (eds.), *Explorations in the ethnography of speaking*. London: Cambridge University Press.

STEWART, W. A. 1967. Sociolinguistic factors in the history of American Negro dialects. *Florida FL Reporter*, 5: 2, 11, 22, 24, 26.

————. 1969. Historical and structural bases for the recognition of Negro dialect. *Monograph Series on Languages and Linguistics, Georgetown University*, 22, 515–24.

TRAUGOTT, E. C. 1972. Principles in the history of American English—a reply. *Florida FL Reporter*, 10: 5–6, 56.

TRUDGILL, P. J. 1971. The social differentiation of English in Norwich. Unpublished doctoral dissertation, University of Edinburgh.

TURNER, L. 1949. *Africanisms in the Gullah dialect*. Chicago: University of Chicago Press.

WOLFRAM, W. 1969. *A sociolinguistic description of Detroit Negro speech*. Washington, D.C.: Center for Applied Linguistics.

————. 1974. The relationship of white southern speech to vernacular Black English. *Language*, 50: 498–527.

CHRISTINA BRATT PAULSTON

Pronouns of Address in Swedish:
Social Class Semantics
and a Changing System

> *One who has lived soon an entire century must learn to change all her habits, and habits of address surely are not the easiest. What comes simply and naturally in one place is wrong and ill-mannered in another.* (Former servant-girl, informant KU 2849.)

> *Even an ordinary simple worker has today become aware of the fact that he also is a human being, and that the great machinery would not function if he did not play his part. An old conservative postmaster's wife said once to my mother, who was the simple wife of a worker: "I think things now are not the way they should be; the workers' conditions are so good that they dress so well that nowadays one cannot tell the difference between workers and fine folk." This utterance from a woman who believed she belonged to the fine folk my mother never forgot, and I myself have also remembered it.* (Retired railroad worker, informant KU 2768.)[1]

INTRODUCTION

The purpose of this paper is to describe the forms of address in Swedish and the patterning of their usage. When I stated this purpose of my fieldwork in Sweden, a very common reaction was *Det kan du aldrig göra*, 'you'll never do it, it can't be done'. The Swedish address system is in rapid change, and, although Swedes have found difficulties in their address system for the last hundred years, they are sensitive now more than ever to seeming lack of generally accepted rules of usage. Indeed, for some type of encounters the rules are so vague that people may report (I noticed it in my own usage as well) that choice of a particular form of address simply depended on one's mood that day, whether one is feeling cheerful or cranky. Nevertheless, there exists considerably more order than Swedes at present give

From *Language in Society*, Vol. 5, 1976, pp. 359-86. Reprinted with permission of Cambridge University Press and Christina Bratt Paulston.

[1] These quotations and others with a KU number are from the archives of the Nordiska Museet, 'the Nordic (Scandinavian) Museum' which undertook an ethnological investigation on words of address in 1969. The informants are not randomly selected and are not representative of the Swedish population at large as they are especially selected for their ability to express themselves in writing. In reading through the responses from the 290 informants, one is forcibly impressed by their intelligence and power of observation and recall. As a source, say, for investigation of working-class lexicon they would not be valid; for my purposes these informants proved an invaluable source, and I have no doubt as to the validity of the archive data.

themselves and their language credit for. This paper is an attempt to delineate that order.

In Sweden, the Social Democratic party has been continuously in power since 1932 and through its programs for social, economic, and educational reforms has consistently stressed egalitarian relations among all members of society.[2] In spite of this dominant ideology, there remain "strong elements of ascription, elitism, particularism and diffuseness in the Swedish value system" (Lipset, quoted in R.G. Paulston 1968:5). The society is still divided into *Social grupp* 1, 2, and 3, a division into social classes first used in 1911 in connection with bicameral elections. In 1970, social group 1 (the upper class) counted 7.8 per cent of the population, social group 2 (middle class) 34.7 per cent, and social group 3 (working class) 57.5 per cent (*Svenska Dagbladet* 1970:1). Politically induced social structural change does not necessarily result in a change in the cultural value system. Söderberg (1972), a social historian, posits the change in address forms as an indicator of social change with concomitant cultural change. Sweden still remains a country highly stratified in terms of social class but her cultural values are changing and some of the friction between speakers and confusion about usage which stem from the address system can best be understood in terms of the lag between slow cultural change in the wake of rapid social change. The viewpoint from which this paper is written is that linguistic description of the Swedish address system is not possible unless one takes into account the social and historical factors of the society.

METHOD OF DATA COLLECTION

My present data were obtained during a five-month stay in Stockholm, Sweden, in 1973. I was born and grew up in Stockholm and speak a regional dialect of Swedish (Östermalms-stockholmska) which has become stereotyped as Swedish upper-class speech. Methods of data collection included participant-observation and the taking of copious field notes, during and after situations which ranged from a royal dinner in white tie to a coffee clatch in the cafeteria of low-salaried factory workers; structured and unstructured interviews; survey questionnaires; and archive work. I observed the behavior of those I met in my daily life teaching at a branch of the university: students, friends, family members and librarians, bus conductors, salesclerks, the police, hospital personnel, public school personnel, etc.; that is, the public at large such as any working professional Stockholmer would run across. I interviewed many of these people as they crossed my path, from cab drivers to the archbishop. I also systematically interviewed a number of informants in order to get a sampling representative of the various social classes and of the public vs. the private sector. To that purpose I interviewed the rector and teaching staff at the police academy as well as members of the police corps; the personnel manager and management of AB Storstockholms Lokaltrafik (public transportation: buses, streetcars and subway) and observed and talked to innumerable bus drivers; University of Stockholm personnel: students, faculty, staff and administration; Svenska Arbetsgivare Föreningen (Swedish Employers Association, major organ of Swedish private enterprise); management and workers in two factories; and members of the personnel and training sections of three department stores: Nordiska Kompaniet (expensive), Domus (middle), and OBS (inexpensive).

---

[2] The Social Democrats lost the 1978 elections to the center parties.

Special care was taken to corroborate the accuracy of self-report data by firsthand observation. Frequently my own observations were augmented by those of others (friends, family, colleagues, students, informants) after they had been especially instructed in what to observe. In my study of the police, for example, a number of people were simply asked to talk to police officers and to note down how the officers addressed them. I talked to the police myself. I then used my own observations and those of my "assistants" in checking the data obtained in an interview with the instructors at the police academy in order to estimate the reliability of their reported usage. The police instructors' reported data were highly accurate as were most reported data obtained from informants interviewed in depth about the address system of specific groups, organizations, or institutions of which they were members.

Such self-report data, however, are in sharp contradistinction to self-report data on institutional usage from informants who either are not members or who do not have access to all members of an institution. Another way to state this is that internally observed and later reported data tend to be very accurate while externally observed data necessitate more careful double-checking. For example, department store personnel are succinct and accurate on the rules of address usage toward customers; customers are nowhere near as reliable in their self-report on department store sales clerks' address system. Another example is university address usage. Students and the general public will typically generalize that only *du* is now used at the universities, as indeed is officially decreed. This is only partially true, as I shall discuss later and I found that a few 'trick' questions about usage of which I already knew the actual language behavior were helpful in evaluating observational power and reliability of informants. Incorrect information of the type "everyone says *du* at the university" I then considered as data on the discrepancy between perception and actual address behavior, a discrepancy which at present is widespread.

I came to prefer to interview informants in pairs as they would often correct or expound on each other's responses.

When I studied various department stores, I would interview the staff supervisors in a series of two interviews, the first of which partially served to alert them to certain questions and situations. After some weeks I would follow up with a second interview. In the period between the two interviews, the supervisors had watched for and recorded specific speech behaviors (e.g., did customer or clerk initiate form of address?). It became quite clear that their observations (which I collected at the second interview) were as accurate as my own, and deserved to be classified as participant observation data rather than interview reported data.

I mention this technique of "training" (the observation of address forms is a fairly simple operation which does not necessitate any sophisticated linguistic knowledge) some actual members of the group under study for participant observation themselves as it does away with an otherwise insolvable problem. If I am interested in comparing the external system of address behavior of department store staff (i.e., how they speak in the presence of customers) with their internal system (i.e., how they speak among themselves), there is no way for my presence not to cause them to switch to the external system. Study of the internal system necessitates either self-report data or direct observations made by informants with membership in the group under study.

THE FORMS OF ADDRESS

Background

Swedish possesses two second person singular pronouns of address, with the typical distinction in European languages between the familiar, *du*, and the formal *ni*. Because of a reluctance in the past by many Swedes to use *ni*, Swedish also has several other forms of address. In an earlier paper (C.B. Paulston 1975:7), I listed different ways of expressing *What do you want?* and I relist them here with some minor changes:

1.	Vad vill du ha?	'What do you want?' (familiar form)
2.	Vad vill ni ha?	'What do you want?' (formal form)
3.	Vad vill hon ha?	'What do you want?' (third person singular feminine)
4.	Vad vill Christina ha?	'What does Christina want? (in direct address)

5. Vad vill { fru Paulston / Professor / Paulston } ha?   'What does { Mrs. Paulston / Professor / Paulston } want?

6.	Vad vill fröken ha?	'What does the Miss want?' (to unknown female, married or unmarried, a status one can only guess at from the presence or absence of a wedding band)
7.	Vad vill frun ha?	'What does the Mrs. want?' (used only by a female seller in the market place, to unknown female, married or unmarried)
8.	Vad vill professorn ha?	'What does the professor want?'
9.	Vad vill man ha?	'What does one want?'
10.	Vad vill vi ha?	'What do we want?'
11.	Vad får det vara?	'What may it be?'
12.	Vad behagas (det)?	'What is pleased?'
13.	Vad skulle det vara for någonting?	'What would it be?'

To this list should be added one more form: *Vad vill du ha, fröken Lundgren?* This curious usage of informal *du* plus formal title + last name (TLN) is the mode of address between clerks (otherwise on first name terms) in better shops in the presence of a customer. The existence of this usage is frequently denied by Swedes but it occurs in my data both as self-report and in my own observations.[3]

There are strict co-occurrence rules (Ervin-Tripp 1973) of the pronouns with the type of fillers which can occupy the frames in which the pronouns occur. *Du* typically co-occurs with name, usually first name (FN), nickname (NN) or kinship title (KT) but occasionally with last name (LN). *Du* may also occur with no name (Ø). It normally never occurs with T(LN), and hence the discredence of *du* + fröken Lundgren. TØ or TLN co-occurs with *ni* or is used in third person address. The reverse is not true; *ni* may in regional usage co-occur with kinship title (KT), actual or honorary. *Hon* can co-occur with either (T)LN or FN; its use is rural

---

[3] I am grateful to Ulf Hannerz who first pointed it out to me. I am grateful as well for all his other helpful comments.

and disappearing. Although I can remember being so addressed in my youth and there are frequent references to this usage in the archive data (Nordiska Museet 1969), there is not one incidence of it in my 1973 Stockholm data.

All forms in 3 through 13 in the list above represent a relationship between speakers where *du* is not appropriate, i.e. where an expression of "condescension or intimacy," in Brown and Gilman's terms (1960), is not called for. These forms also represent a way of avoiding the use of *ni*, an avoidance of which Swedes are very conscious. In the earlier paper, I speculated that the extreme avoidance of the V-form in address is avoidance of the "linguistic compulsion" of power-coding (as expressed by the *du/ni* choice) in a country which has both social class stratification and social-democratic ideology. This is only partially true, and Haugen was absolutely right when he in a discussion of that paper[4] pointed out the importance of the historical development of *ni*.

The major argument of this paper is that one can describe the Swedish address system adequately only if one recognizes that the social classes have different rules of use due to different "semantics"[5] for the pronouns *du* and *ni*. This difference, I believe, can primarily be accounted for by the historical development of the language and by political ideology. The corollary to that argument is that such different rule systems within a single speech community cannot be discovered, understood, or described by analyzing only the single pronominal forms. Beyond (non)-reciprocity (Brown & Gilman 1960) and dispensation rights (Ervin-Tripp 1973), one needs to consider *inter alia* co-variance of address forms, change of options and the direction of such change, initiation procedures, external versus internal systems of address, but most specifically the particular frames or formulae within which the pronouns occur (Hymes 1974), i.e. with the non-pronominal forms of address with which they do or, just as importantly, do not co-occur. When Swedes discuss their address system, they typically talk about *du*, in and of itself, without looking at the other factors, and this practice is a contributing factor to the confusion and feeling that no rules exist.

Historical Background

Old Swedish had only one singular pronoun of address *du*, used to friend and stranger alike. In the 1600s, under influence of usage at the Byzantine court, says Wellander (1952:1; cf. Brown & Gilman 1960), the plural pronoun *I* came to be used in address to a single person. This pronoun *I* developed into *ni* from the plural suffix *n* of the preceding verb as in *haven I* 'do you have'. During the 1700s the Swedish elite was under strong French influence, and the *du/ni* dichotomy seems to have developed in the upper classes then under influence of French *tu* and *vous*.

The lower classes, especially the peasant class (Sweden remained a primarily rural society much longer than continental Europe) did not adopt this usage but maintained *du* as the mutual form of address to both known and unknown of their equals. To their superiors they used titles which proliferated *ad absurdum*. Americans are familiar with the euphemism of maintenance engineer for janitor but in Sweden such titles were used seriously in direct address; *Herr Mattnedläggaren*

---

[4] Professor Einar Haugen in the discussion following my presentation of the paper at the forty-sixth annual meeting of the Linguistic Society of America, December 30, 1971.

[5] "Semantic" is the term used by Brown and Gilman (1960: 253) to refer to the "covariation between the pronoun used and the objective relationship existing between speaker and addressee."

'Mr. Rug-installer' and *Herr Tågbefälhavaren* 'Mr. Train-commander' occur from the 1930s in my archive data.

It would give a wrong impression to imply that there was no social stratification within the peasant class. At the turn of the century on the large estates, the womenfolk carefully observed social niceties. Informant KU 2525 writes: "At the coffee clatches (by and for the wives of the peasants who worked the estate) the wife of the head gardener was to serve herself first, next the wife of the smith, followed by the coachman's wife." They did not use *du* to each other but *hon*.

The guilds too were careful to maintain the social distance created by skill and age, and apprentice learners were specifically forbidden the use of *du* to their superior fellow workers.

But among full-fledged workers and ordinary peasants *du* was the common form of address, and this peasant *du* survived within the labor class and became a hallmark of membership in the Social Democratic party (many informants say they would address the Prime Minister as *du* because he is a fellow Social Democrat) and the unions. Its semantic now is that of solidarity.

Because of the idiocy and cumbersomeness of the titles, there have been repeated attempts at address reforms during the last hundred years. The first attempts were in the latter part of the 1800s and well in advance of any political ideological change; indeed, members of the royalty were among the co-signers of the public declarations. This movement was referred to as *ni-reformen* and advocated the use of *ni* instead of titles in third person. It failed.

There were further attempts throughout the first half of the twentieth century. Schools and hospitals carried signs which said 'Here we say *ni*'. Many informants comment on a doctor or dentist below such a sign who addressed the nurse as *syster* 'sister, nurse' in third person. I have no evidence which establishes a causal relationship between these reforms and today's practice where the younger generations do not hesitate to use *ni*. But when a people which has over a hundred years been intermittently exposed to editorials and articles in the press on the virtue of *ni* with no result finally changes its address behavior, it makes more sense to look for other causes than the repeatedly ineffectual *ni*-reforms. Whatever other purpose the *ni*-reforms served, they certainly helped to make Swedes conscious of their address system and aware that it often was awkward.

The change toward increased *ni*-usage is becoming obscured by what most accurately can only be described as the *du*-landslide. *Alla säger du nu för tiden* 'all and everyone says *du* nowadays' was the common rejoinder when people heard I was studying the address forms. Although this is far from true, it is a very frequently stated belief, especially among older members of the upper class with whose own usage the increased use of *du* contrasts most sharply.

"*Du* was and is the form of address among the workers," writes a retired railroad worker (KU 2768) who clearly sees the relationship between *du* and the social democratic movement. But in addition to the leftist political parties, organizations such as the Red Cross and the Home Guard with its auxiliaries institutionalized the use of *du* among their members. It is easy to imagine the sense of emergency such organizations must have experienced during the two World Wars. Sweden managed to remain neutral, and the correlation between state of emergency and the T-form is well documented (Brown & Gilman, 1960; Friedrich, 1972; Jonz, 1975). Many informants comment on the formative effect of such experiences.

There certainly was opposition to the use of *du*. Informant KU 2604 writes of the angry speech the rector of his school addressed to the students in 1915 on the "demoralizing tendencies in an evil time." The students, age 16-30, had suggested they be allowed to address each other with *du*.

The earliest attempt at a *du*-reform in the private sector I have come across took place in the early fifties in a department of the Swedish Employers Association. That the director and the janitor were on *du*-terms (+LN) was considered sufficiently newsworthy to be written up in the public press. In those days, however, the janitor delicately changed to Director X in third person in the presence of others outside the department. Not so today. The 1960s saw wide-spread institutionalized *du*-reform, at first in the public institutions like hospitals and universities. Stockholms Spårvägar (public transportation, later Storstockholms Lokaltrafik) 1965-72 carried through a *du*-reform, and my informants directly related this change to membership by management in the Social Democratic party. Around 1968, the public schools began to follow suit, with the vocational schools beginning the trend.

The private sector is also changing, and all factories with which I am familiar have instituted a general use of reciprocal *du* from management to lowest worker. Management's motivation, however, is not the same as that underlying the Social Democratic party. Big business finds it more effective to be on *du* terms with its workers. A case will illustrate. One of the companies whose factory I visited had been in the red five years previously due to faulty management. One of the problems had been poor relations with the union, which had been forced into *underdånig ställnig*, 'subservient obeisant posture'. The then president of the company did not believe in a strong union. On his daily round he reportedly addressed the workers with first name in third person and received a polite TØ, an illustration of the classical non-reciprocal power-relationship, in Brown and Gilman's terms.

The present management had faced the task of having 'to create a climate in which one could exist'. One of their recommendations was general, reciprocal use of *du* throughout the company, and against considerable doubt 'a president is after all a president, not proper (from the workers' side)' the *du*-reform was institutionalized and successful. While I was in Stockholm, a leading journal ran an article on the recovered economic success of the company, and it would be naïve to believe that either success stemmed from egalitarian motives. Swedish management certainly are not ogres, but it makes good capitalistic sense to be on good terms with the labor force, and management clearly conceives the use of *du* as promoting such feelings. It can, however, be argued that the workers' previous unhappiness and subsequent acceptance of the *du*-reform was partially grounded in egalitarian ideology; I am merely arguing that management clearly acted from profit-making motives, and that these coincided with the workers' wishes.

The comments on the *du*-reform by the 60-year-old company physician cannot be laid at any political door: "Listen, it's great; one can reach them so much better." Swedes for whom personal interrelationships tend to be difficult (Garbo's "I vant to be alone" remark is never cited in Sweden, presumably because it is typical of all) feel closer and warmer with the use of *du*. Whatever the reasons—egalitarian, manipulative, or just humanitarian—all agree on the positive aspects of the spreading *du*-usage. Even some 70-year-old upper-class ladies find it agreeable to be addressed as *du* in the street; they say it makes them feel younger.

The change is also observable on an individual level. Many informants comment that their children did not address them as *du* but that their grandchildren do. One informant had sons with an age difference of twenty years; the elder had addressed him with KT in third person; the younger said *du*. There are repeated anecdotes of people who had known each other as youths and not exchanged *du*; on meeting twenty or thirty or forty years later, they either spontaneously used *du* or promptly initiated *du*-usage. The difficulty lies not in demonstrating increased usage of *du* but rather in delineating the new rules which accompany the shift toward *du*, the change in options as context for the specific linguistic expressions.

USES OF *DU*

There are two distinct uses of *du* with two different semantics: intimacy–familiarity and solidarity. The two uses overlap and may well eventually become merged, but at this time the two are distinguishable.

Du + FN

The pattern for intimacy-familiarity use of *du* is distinct in this way: (1) it always co-occurs with FN or KT, and (2) its use among adults is always preceded by the speech act of *lägga bort titlarna* 'putting the titles away' which follows ritualized dispensation rules (Ervin-Tripp 1963).[6] This is an elaborate set of rules as to whose right it is to initiate the use of *du* (primarily from *ni* and/or title-last name (TLN) usage but there are also occurrences from (KT)FN in third person), and worries and misunderstandings about this initiation right occur frequently in the data. The rules, which are found in the Swedish etiquette books, involve the variables of sex, age, and rank in that order of importance. It is always the prerogative of a woman to initiate *du*, with age and rank deciding if the speakers are of the same sex. Age is not necessarily chronological but may involve other factors, such as year of high school matriculation or number of years spent with a company or institution. But note that these are the rules of the educated elite. From the responses to the questionnaire of an ethnological investigation which the Nordic Museum undertook in 1969 on terms of address, it is overwhelmingly clear that for members of social group 2 and especially 3, rank is the all over-ruling factor:

> If an *överordnad* (superior in rank) says *ni* or Fru Angquist, then I address him with the title which is owed him. That person will himself have to suggest if there is to be any change (KU 2411).

Next to rank comes age: 'because he was of middle age, and in that case it was not the lady who should suggest'. The informant was 20 (KU 2854).

More often than not, social group 3 lacks a rule which involves sex as a variable. In my interviews with 18 low-salaried female factory-workers, ten claimed that there was no rule, and eight said that it was a man's prerogative to initiate *du*.

---

[6] Children may use *du* + KT without any initial ritual. They also learn the communicative competence rules much later than the linguistic forms, i.e. the appropriateness of their usage. I am grateful to Aare Mörner for the example of a child's *du* + *vinnan* (from *grevinnan*, 'countess') totally inappropriate in adult speech.

The highly formalized ritual of *dricka du-skål* 'drinking a *du* toast' has now become much simplified although it still can occur. A member of the high nobility writes as follows:

> Now it is much easier to become *du*. I usually propose it as soon as it is practical. I usually say something like: *"Skall vi inte lägga bort titlarna"* 'shan't we put titles away'; it is much easier so (KU 2418).[7]

The act of becoming on *du* terms is called *lägga bort titlarna* ('put the titles away') and so reflects its origin in the higher classes, which had titles. There are other linguistic correlates which help define this speech act: *stå fadder* 'stand godfather' (if such hesitation exists that neither partner can bring themselves to initiate as in the case of a young woman and an old man of high rank, a third party may be brought in to break the ice), *du-broder* 'du-brother.' etc.

Finally, the attitudes of the speakers themselves are clear indications that there are semantics of *du* which vary according to the speaker. They say so. Typical remarks are 'I want to keep *du* only for those I am very close to' versus 'It feels like a relief when that happens' (being addressed by *du*). 'One feels equal' (KU 2920). There are of course exceptions, but in general, intimacy use of *du* is associated with social group 1 usage, and solidarity use of *du* with social group 3. In the Nordic Museum investigation, the last question inquires about the informants' attitudes towards the various reforms of address suggested during the last hundred years in Sweden. Of the 26 responses from members of social group 1, all with only one exception want to keep *ni* and/or titles. Of the 55 responses from social group 3, all with four exceptions wanted general usage of *du* to all people. (Of the four exceptions, three are upwardly socially mobile as measured by occupation or children's occupation.) Social group 2, on the other hand, showed no clear trend: of 50 responses, 29 favored the maintained use of *ni* while 14 were in favor of a *du*-reform, i.e. general use of *du* to everyone. The maintained use of *ni* of course implies an intimacy semantic for *du*.

The fact that two distinct usages of *du* exist, with a tendency to separate along class lines, is not recognized, and there are constant complaints from encounters where the speakers apply different sets of rules with no recognition of the difference. An anecdote will serve to illustrate. Herr and fru (Mr. and Mrs.) Nilsson, members of social group 2 with origin in 3, are caretakers of a farm owned by Lennart B., a member of the Stockholm upper class. The men are approximately of the same age, and because of his social rank, Mr. B. initiated the use of *du* with Mr. Nilsson and the two now freely exchange *du* and FN. But with Fru Nilsson, Mr. B. was stuck. His rules say that a woman initiates *du* no matter what, while

---

[7] The rules for initiating a toast involve the variables of sex and age only. Only a man can initiate a toast with a woman of whatever age, with the older initiating between members of the same sex. A toast is the man's response to a woman's suggested *titelbortläggning* or may be simultaneous with his own *titelbortläggning* to a younger man.

The toast consists of raising the glass to the height equal to the placement of the third button from the top of an officer's dress uniform, eye contact and gracious nod, drinking, raising the glass again, eye contact and second gracious nod with smile. Upper class children learn this ritual early, and my own youngsters have practiced *skåling* (with Coca-Cola) with great delight since they were five.

Indeed, the *du*-dispensation ritual has become much simplified. One of my favorite pieces of data concerns another member of the nobility who initiated *du* with my informant while sharing a urinal with him in the men's room.

Mrs. Nilsson has no such rule. Her rule gives rank precedence and if she does have a rule regarding precedence of sex, it will be that the male initiates. Nor does she use *ni* (see the discussion below), with the result that she addresses Mr. B. as *Direktör B.* in the third person, a practice Mr. B. dislikes intensely.

Mrs. B., on the other hand, who knows perfectly well that Mr. and Mrs. Nilsson would prefer to use *du* with her and that it is up to her to initiate as woman and older, refuses to do so. She does not realize that to Mrs. Nilsson *du* means solidarity, not intimacy, and that it is her rank, not her age which keeps Mrs. Nilsson from initiating. To Mrs. B., the semantic of *du* is strongly one of intimacy, and when pressed by her social-democratic children for reasons of egalitarianism to become *du* with the Nilssons, she will say 'But I don't know them that well.' Mrs. Nilsson is likely to perceive that distance as one of social class rather than as of personal friendship. And certainly neither of them realizes that they don't share the same set of rules.[8]

Upper-class speakers of course think that their rules are the only appropriate ones. But they fully expect the rest of the world not to know these rules since it is only by being one of them (upper class) that one gains access to social niceties. Swedish upper-class children are socialized by stigmatizing their unwanted behavior as lower class: 'Don't drink from a cup without a saucer; that's lower class.' Upper-class speakers expect lower-class speakers not to know their rules, only they don't realize that lower-class behavior also is rule-governed, but rather see it as an absence of rules. Lower-class speakers on the other hand have not spent as much time learning arbitrary rules at a conscious level (see footnote 6 for an example) and are not as likely to realize that their behaviour also is rule-governed. The typical reaction to upper-class speech patterns is that it is 'stuck-up', but lower-class speakers are not likely to question the 'correctness' of upper-class speakers.

Even though the rules for dispensation rights differ between the social classes, it is generally recognized that such rights exist. Consequently people develop strategies for forcing dispensation, for manipulating the other into suggesting *du*. I recognized this dispensation-forcing as a speech act proper much too late in my data collection for careful study but it merits such and in other languages as it is likely to be a universal phenomenon. One informant commented that he would pretend to misspeak and say *du*, and then apologize. He said it never failed that the addressee would ask him to please continue with *du*. Another strategy is constant and repeated use of T + LN (once or twice in each sentence) which marks the address system for attention. This is the strategy Mrs. Nilsson used. A common strategy is some teasing remark like 'Well, you are oldest, I wouldn't dare suggest *du*.' There are bound to be many more such strategies.

Intimacy is not signalled by the use of *du* or by the use of first name but exactly by the combination of *du* + FN. First name by itself does not imply intimacy, and its usage in third person, i.e. repetition of the name instead of the pronoun in direct address, denotes familiarity and often social distance. This usage is disappearing and I have no instances of it in my data from 1973 although I well remember being so addressed, especially in the country from the servants and the local population who had seen me grow up from childhood. Totally gone is the

---

[8] At a visit two years later in 1975, I found that Mrs. B. had indeed initiated *du* with Mrs. Nilsson and thought nothing remarkable of it. If anything is an indicator of socio-cultural change, Mrs. B.'s change of attitude and use of *du* + FN with the caretaker wife is. It would have been not only unthinkable but unimaginable in my childhood.

usage of my grandfather's generation to third person first name among relatives although that may primarily have been between the sexes.

Nor does the use of *du* by itself signal intimacy.

Du + Ø—or Solidarity, yes, Intimacy, no

When the form *I* and titles came into usage, *du* remained within the peasant population as the mutual form of address of equals to both known and unknown, and this manner of address has survived until the present day within the labor class. The semantic of this usage of *du* is one of solidarity, an expression of membership in the same group. It is this usage of *du* which has spread so rapidly and so widely. In 1965, for instance, police officers in patrol cars addressed each other by TLN in third person; today they all use *du*. This increased usage of *du* resulted in a change of available options of address as well as in a change of the frames in which *du* occurs, the latter presumably as a result of the former.

In this use, *du* may co-occur with FN but more frequently with no name (Ø), even when the name is known. The use of first name is often avoided since it is felt to express intimacy. Solidarity use of *du* is now extended to strangers and people with whom one cannot presume an intimate relationship. This development of *du* + Ø reflects the upper-class reciprocal use of *du* which is one of intimacy and which always co-occurs with first name. *Du* by itself, then, expresses solidarity but not intimacy, maintaining a personal but not social distance. By institutional decree, university students now address their professors with *du* as an expression of group membership. Said my Swedish colleague: 'Well, I have gotten used to *du* but when they come and say *Hör du Bengt* (i.e. *du* + FN)—that's going too far.'

My students freely addressed me as *du*, even at guest lectures, but even my regular students *never* referred to me by name. It was of course difficult for them since it meant that they had to have eye contact with me before they could be recognized to speak, lacking a linguistic means by which they could call my attention, since *du* co-occurs with FN but not with T. In the primary and secondary schools such a situation has led to the use of *du* and *fröken*, a combination of the informal pronoun and the formal traditional address of women teachers (originally the title for unmarried daughters of the nobility) which is totally counterintuitive, and I am relieved I can trust my informants by virtue of the fact that I have heard it with my own ears. Other informants, from social groups 2 and 3, have commented on the difficulty of first naming with solidarity *du*. They frequently resort to some kind of made up name or nickname (NN). Swedish last names commonly end in *-son*, 'son of', and there are several occurrences in the data where someone with the name, say, of Valter Danielsson, is addressed as *du* and Daniel in the attempt to avoid the use of *du* + FN.

The development of *du* + Ø is very recent, in all probability only within the last ten, fifteen years. I pointed it out first in my 1971 paper, and Professor Bengt Loman of the University of Lund agreed with me then; he had not been aware of it, which certainly points to recent development. This development of *du* + extreme first name avoidance has resulted, I believe, from the increased use of *du* in relationships which cannot be characterized as intimate. This increased usage is a result of a national policy of social egalitarianism, which in turn has brought about a definite change in the value system. In addition, the alternative options to solidarity *du* have been so cumbersome or considered not acceptable with the result that the linguistic system has supported the pressures of the social system. One is reminded of Labov's "theme that internal, structural pressures and sociolinguistic pressures act in systematic alternation in the mechanism of linguistic change" (Labov 1972: 537).

Solidarity Use of *du*—Individual Usage

The working class has always been very clear on the solidarity function of *du* and clearly sees its relationships to social class; these informants to the ethnological investigation make their points cogently:

> When I began my own company, it happened sometimes that some of my former co-workers would come and take a job; I considered them still as old friends and called them *du*, but it happened sometimes that they did not like this but in a marked manner addressed me as *Herr Andersson*. This was in the twenties when in certain groups it was considered treason against one's class to be on friendly terms with one's "workbuyer" as some used to say. (Retired painter, informant KU 2913.)

> There is a clear line between what we call social group 1 and 3. I heard on one occasion an old woman who claimed that it was not suitable for workers to buy *wienerbröd* 'a type of elegant coffee bread'. It is that kind of mentality one finds when people are classified as "fine folk" and "ordinary folk." The respect for fine folk is still great for many among social group 3. One "degrades" oneself before others who have done well and one really cannot blame them for this. Heard at the hospital how a physician asked a patient of his own age who had been his childhood chum to address him as *du*. The patient who was "only" a worker answered: "It is not proper!" and continued to say "Doctor." A hopeless case. (Retired typesetter, informant KU 2341.)

But attitudes are changing with the younger generations. Within social group 3, such change is often difficult and accompanied by a feeling of conflict. The secretary, born 1936 into a rural family of carpenters and smiths, who wrote the following is typical of the informants:

> And myself, I have also changed my attitude to using *du*—I react with pleased gratitude if I am addressed with *du* by strangers and sex makes no difference. I know that others in my age group can easily feel depressed about this, feel that it is below their dignity to be *duad* by the landlord. I think they seem so small and afraid in their attitude, I am so proud to have changed. I try also myself to say *du* to everyone but meet certain difficulties and feel at times uncertainty. (She comments that she uses *du* to everyone everywhere of her own age but not to older people.) The uncertainty comes when I am struck dumb by respect before a high imposing title and I forsake my good resolutions. I also avoid using *ni*; at a visit to the doctor's office recently, e.g., I said *du* to the nurse but then said *Professorn, Professorn* (T-third person). I want so very much to say *du* to everyone and make no distinction and I get into a conflict when I all the same make a difference between folk and folk on the basis of their social position. (Informant KU 2854.)

The use of solidarity *du* has now spread to members of all social classes, in social group 1 primarily among the younger members who frequently comment that they use it as an expression of their egalitarian ideology. This is very similar to the situation Bates and Benigni (1975) found in Italy. The solidarity *du* is always intended by the addressor to be reciprocal, but there are numerous instances in my observed data that *du* is not returned. Several taxi cab drivers, for instance, who claimed that they virtually always addressed their clients with *du*, carefully avoided any pronoun reference to me, even when I addressed them as *du*. (The use of *ni* by the cab driver would have been insulting in such a situation as it would blatantly have denied my claims to solidarity.) Throughout my conversations with the cab drivers runs a clear awareness on their part of social class, which speech and appearance are used to determine. Generally the informants claimed that they waited to see how they were addressed, meaning they would reciprocate the same address form which in fact they didn't. 'It also depends on how they talk,' said one, 'if they are *bildade*.' *Bildade* roughly corresponds to '*educated*' and is a frequent euphenism for membership in social group 1. This sentiment was echoed by many informants. In other words, although members of social group 1 are increasingly adopting the use of solidarity *du*, this usage is many times met with distrust by members of social group 3 who do not return it, and the result is a condescending *du*, i.e. the non-reciprocal *du* in Brown and Gilman's terms, the very opposite of what was intended.

Although solidarity occurs primarily with social class, there are instances of *du* as an expression of other types of solidarity. When a police chief in a "speech by the coffin" addressed the deceased as *ni*, the editorial commented the following day that he should have used *du* because 'in the face of death we are all alike,' i.e. *du* as an expression of common human frailty and mortality (informant KU 2448).

One informant links these two themes of solidarity in the following folk poem from a church yard:

Att döden han ser inte te personen	Death does not look to the individual
For döden han är demokrat	For Death is a democrat
Så direcktören och fabrikören	So the director and the factory owner
A rätt om di forsmädlitt mot mig le	Even if they scoff at me with a sneer
Sa kanske de få legga breve me.	May end up lying next to me.

(KU 2768)

The archbishop, a man of charisma, told me that, although he in general does not encourage the use of *du*, there exists a group of high school and theology students with whom he works closely, who do address him as *du*. They are profoundly religious and see their work as that of a 'guerilla group' (the archbishop's term) in a profoundly irreligious country. The use of the T-form is common as an expression of religious solidarity (cf. the Quakers) but its usage is almost always institutionalized rather than as here in an individual case.

Solidarity Use of *du*—Institutional Usage

The most widespread use of solidarity *du* occurs in institutionalized usage, *du* as a function of membership in a formal group, such as social institutions of occupation, recreation, organizations, and the like. The decreed use of *du* now occurs in hospitals, factories, universities, offices, clubs, etc. (but not in the military or in the police force). The *du* usage in an institution like the Swedish Employers Association on the immediate surface looks like institutional solidarity *du*, and indeed the receptionist addressed me as *du*, as is their custom, over the telephone. But among its professional members, lawyers by training, reciprocal *du* is always preceded by *titelbortläggning* according to upper-class dispensation rules or disapprovingly commented on as deviant usage when those rules are not adhered to. Nor is there any FN avoidance among the upper-class members, and in fact their usage among themselves retains its intimacy–familiarity function albeit more widely extended than fifteen years ago. But between lawyer and janitor there is a clear change: solidarity *du* with no first name and no initiation rights.

One of the young lawyers commented that in her work at court among her own political group there is automatic use of *du* as distinct from her usage at the Swedish Employers Association, where she begins with *ni* + TLN and proceeds to *titelbortläggning* and *du*. In their individual usage, people will tend toward a perception of *du* either as a function of intimacy–familiarity or of solidarity. In institutionalized usage of *du* this is not so, and upper-class speakers will, as the young lawyer, switch between functions. She exemplifies a system in change as she was brought up with the upper-class intimacy–familiarity semantic of *du*, functions with its rules when they are imposed on her, but has come to prefer solidarity usage of *du*.

One more example to illustrate the switch between the two semantics of *du*. At a visit to the *Kungliga Biblioteket* (Royal Library) to fill out application forms, I was addressed as *du* by the librarian, a woman older than myself. She knew from the forms my occupation as professor and this did not impress her (professors rank very high in the social order in Sweden) sufficiently to avoid *du* + ØN. Her use was clearly that of solidarity *du* to strangers. In the course of the interview of filling out the cards she discovered my Stockholm identity, as it were; she had known my father and for some years lived in the same apartment house as my family. At this point she changed to *ni*. (It is considered the height of rudeness to switch back to *ni* after an initiation ritual to intimacy *du*.) *Du*, at this stage, when I had ceased to be an anonymous stranger, would to her imply an intimacy *du*, and she changed to the mode of address we would mutually employ, had we been introduced in the street.

The University of Stockholm changed to institutional *du* around 1963 and many informants complained that it was difficult, especially for the older secretaries. Within a department, there is now general use of *du* + ØN by all, chairman, students, and secretary. The chairman of linguistics addressed me as *du* with no further ado even though I had addressed him as *ni*. The students all say *du* + ØN to everyone. However, across departments there is considerable uncertainty. The secretaries do not say *du* to professors in other departments without a great deal of caution. Most of inter-departmental contact is by telephone, which makes age difficult to judge, and in institutions with decreed *du*-usage, age especially but not necessarily when paired with rank, is the most important variable in choosing options. The secretaries never initiate address form, and their basic strategy is one of wait and see. They observe the greeting: from an older janitor *goddag* will to them indicate *ni* while *hej* will signal go ahead and use *du*. If the caller introduces himself as Professor X, they respond formally with *ni* or TLN, which is exactly what happened the first time I called the linguistics department. But when I appeared in person and the secretary saw that she was older than I, she changed to *du* + ØN without any hesitation.

Most uncertainty appears in the communication between the academic departments and the bureaucratic non-academic administration with its civil servants. One senses a strain on the feeling of solidarity and there is considerable hesitation and address avoidance from professors and secretaries alike.

Neither do professors automatically address their colleagues in other depart-ments with *du*. Swedish professors can look very old and imposing and to these 'greying men' my informant-professors said they would most certainly not use *du*. Their general policy then is one of address avoidance.

What the students then observe and disseminate to the larger society is the mutual *du* + ØN between student/student and student/professor as well as frequently between professor/professor. They are not likely to notice the address avoidance between professors (avoidance is very difficult to observe) or be party to the administrative communications between departments and even less between departments and the administration. It is easy to understand then that the general perception is that everyone says *du* at the university when in fact they don't.

The solidarity usage of *du* is only extended to members of a group when their social intercourse is a function of group membership. At the Nobel Awards Banquet, a formal dinner at which the king presides and to which only scholars and their spouses (besides the Nobel Foundation officials) are invited, there was a general use of *ni* and titles among the academicians.

Swedish business firms are likely to have international contacts, and many informants commented on the confusion institutional use of *du* resulted in across languages. Swedish secretaries would be *du* with the president of the Danish branch office while he was not on *du* terms with his own secretary of thirty years. Visiting Danes or Germans, who, while colleagues, were on formal terms with each other, would be forced into T-terms with each other. The communicative competence rule for the T-form is so strong for the Swedes that they impose it on the speakers of other languages. It then becomes too awkward to exchange V with a well-known colleague in the same conversation where one exchanges T with a comparative stranger. The rule conflict led to many extraordinary measures, such as granting temporary dispensation to a colleague with the clear understanding that upon return home one resumed formal address. The Swedes, who have long been ridiculed by the Danes (the languages have virtually the same linguistic forms of address) for the awkwardness of their old address system, took great delight in telling these anecdotes.

Deviant Use of *du*

In one sense, the truest expression of solidarity occurs in a state of emergency where class and rank become unimportant in the face of danger and death. There are many types of emergencies but they all share a deviant usage of *du*, i.e. in a given situation, the protagonists would not have exchanged *du* had the state of emergency not been present.

Police and public transportation personnel have long exchanged *du* in situations where their intercourse was the normal result of accidents. My sister reports on unaccustomedly being addressed as *du* by the police as she walked by a bank where a robbery was taking place.

Informant KU 2768 sums it all up:

> During a hospital stay, I had as roommates several people whom I perceived as members of social group 1. Here we said *du* to each other without any *titelbortlägg-ning*, we just simply and naturally said *du* to each other and this with people who I don't think I otherwise would ever have *duad*. It is strange, but in a hospital, on a

ward, one is so to speak in the same boat. The uncertainty perhaps makes one want to feel *gemenskap* 'communion, solidarity' and come closer to the person in the next bed. One is confronted with disease and death and in the face of this, titles have no meaning.

Du is also used to scold. The one of two times I was addressed as *du* by a bus driver was when I unwittingly was using an expired bus pass. Several informants told me they had been similarly scolded for expired passes. *Du* is also used for swearing: *Din djävul* 'you devil' is the only possible form.

Du is typically used deviantly under the influence of alcohol. Occurrence of such usage is frequent in the data. One of my favorite examples concerns the daughter of a pastor whose very life had been threatened by two drunken apprentices who had broken into the manse:

> It had however not gone any further than that the man addressed her as *du*. In spite of the threatening situation, what had most upset fröken Söderblom was the use by the 'murderer' of such a familiar term of address (KU 2341).

Finally, there is dialectal regional usage of *du* where it tends to be the only form used in some provinces, such as Dalarna. All Swedish children know about the Dalmas who addressed the queen: *"Lyft på stjärten, du Landsens Moder..."* ('Lift thy bottom, thou mother of our land, thou art sitting on my mittens'). This usage is deviant only in the sense that it differs from standard Swedish.

USES OF *NI*

While the two semantics of *du* are not recognized at all, the different semantics of *ni* are described in the literature and accounted for by the historical development of the linguistic form. There is, however, considerable confusion in the century-long public debate in the press over the use of the pronoun and, as late as 1963, Rosengren could write: 'The Swedish language still lacks a generally accepted word of address' (1963: 109). He was referring to *ni*. The general uncertainty regarding the semantics of *ni* no doubt has contributed to the recent rapid spread of *du*.

Ni derives from *I*, which was originally the second person plural form. This *I* developed along three different lines.

Ni + (KT) (FN); Peasant *ni*

Among the peasant population, *ni* (with regional variations of *I* and *ji*) became an address of respect reserved for parents, older relatives, and worthy elders within the community. It occurred typically with KT and/or FN and tended to be non-reciprocal with the speaker receiving *du*. This *ni* took the place of *du* as evidenced by the gradual replacement of *ni* by *du* as the children grew up and reached adult status, and also by the fact that *ni* was occasionally refused with 'I'm not so old you'll have to say *ni*' (Ahlgren 1973: 78). This use of *ni* is today rural and rapidly disappearing. I myself have never heard it, but several of my students said they had called their parents by *ni*.

Ni + Ø; Polite and Impolite *ni*

Given this development, it is unclear and curious how *ni* came to be received with such very negative connotations that its usage would be conceived as an insult by parts of the population. A multitude of folk sayings arose as a rejoinder to *ni*: 'Do you think I am lousy?' (meaning that with fleas the addressee would have been plural), '*Ni* the farmer called his mare when he didn't know her name', etc. (Ahlgren 1973: 75, 76). Wellander and Ahlgren account for this development by the fact that *ni* came to be used by the upper classes downward to their inferiors while they expected to be addressed by their titles, and that this non-reciprocity was the cause of the bad reputation of *ni*.

> When the new time came in (1800s) and the *du* of the old *ståndsamhället* 'estate society' by politeness was substituted with the modern *ni*, the mark of social class was transferred from *du* to *ni* which naturally follows with non-reciprocal address forms: he addressed by *ni* got an inferiority complex visavis the titled person (Wellander 1952:7).

But by this argument the earlier non-reciprocal condescending *du* might have been expected to share the same fate. Ahlgren reasons that a downward *ni* would be felt more distancing, more haughty, more arrogant than downward *du* because the inferiors knew that the speaker used *ni* to strangers and *du* to friends: "A downward directed form of address also used between friends has larger possibilities to survive than a downward directed form also used between strangers" (1973: 121). I am not convinced.[9]

It is beyond a doubt that *ni* came to be considered as a rude form of address by parts of the population and in all social classes although by very few in social group 1. In the Nordic Museum questionnaire, only two members (both ministers of the church) from social group 1 objected to the use of *ni* while only two (of 55 responses) from social group 3 were for *ni*. For whatever reasons, people who acquiesced at an endless use of titles, which certainly marked the status relationship, balked at *ni* on the grounds that it was impolite. One of the informants to the Nordic Museum survey from social group 3 writes:

> Already in primary school, our teacher warned us against the use of *ni* as term of address because it was considered as a cussword. He said that in coarse language there was an expression "*Ni* kan kyssa mig där bak" ('*Ni* can kiss me behind'). For this reason he advised us to use *ni* only when we spoke to *bildat folk* 'educated people' so that no misunderstandings would occur (KU 2930).

He had an unusually sensitive teacher. Especially the folkschool teachers show wide variance in their acceptance of *ni*, and many children were categorically taught never to use *ni* while others were taught that it was perfectly acceptable (apparently by teachers of strong egalitarian convictions), and according to many informants such teachings remained with them throughout life.

---

[9] Ahlgren's argument is contradicted by the case in English where the T form disappeared and the V form survived. There is one comment from a Medelpad farmer: "*Ni* from someone of my own age I take as intended: as an insult" (KU 2600) which leads me to speculate. Peasant *ni* was never used to an equal so that its usage in such a case would have been sarcastic just as I might address my husband as Professor Paulston when I think he deals with me as an ignorant student. As upper class usage of *ni* to equals spread, it would not be surprising if such usage was misunderstood by the peasants who themselves would never use *ni* downwards or to equals (see also Haugen 1975).

This considered rudeness of *ni* is no doubt the major reason for the extreme address avoidance and circumlocutions that one finds in Swedish. From my notes on address to customers in department stores I have:

Skall det betalas kontant	'Shall it be paid in cash?'
Vad skall vi ha?	'What shall we have?'
Om damen går...	'If the lady goes'...etc.

with only two occurrences of *ni* (during five months' observation), one by a much older woman and the second, interestingly enough, *after* I had completed my purchase—no need to be polite any more, I suppose.

By necessity, I visited one of the same department stores on December 27, the first day stores were open after the Christmas holidays. The store was crowded, with the majority of customers trying to exchange or return gifts. The clerks gave an impression, say my notes, of cranky sullenness and I heard so many *ni*'s that I lost count. Clearly *ni* is an integral part of Swedish clerks' linguistic competence but in some situations carefully avoided.

In my study of the department stores, I had expected to find a difference in the address systems of the clerks between the expensive and inexpensive store. I found no difference between the three but a lot of difference between the various departments within the store. The clerks in sporting goods, toys, and teenage clothes tended toward solidarity use of *du* + ∅N, but virtually no clerks used *ni*. Their attitude is that *ni* is not polite. The personnel manager of the expensive store (who did address me as *ni*) told me several anecdotes about women customers whose name and title (husband's title in feminine form) were known to the clerk and who had protested at being addressed as *ni* ('I am not *ni* with you'). I suppose after such an episode one is careful to avoid the use of *ni*. From the titles and names cited, like *kunsulinnan Petersson*, I suspect such customers would belong to a class my grandmother would have labelled as *nouveau riche*, i.e. recently upwardly mobile speakers with pretensions to upper class behavior which they knew imperfectly.

Peasant use of *ni* is clearly distinguishable from impolite use of *ni* in that the former always co-occurs with KT and/or FN while the latter never does, but there is no linguistic distinction between polite and impolite use of *ni* + ∅. I have looked very diligently for social settings, scenes, even channels (Hymes 1972) which might mark the meaning of the interaction between linguistic form and social setting. The only vector I have been able to identify is the use of anonymous *ni* to a stranger in public when dressed in street clothes, a usage which is now generally accepted as polite by the younger generation.

The police, for example, freely use *ni* to strangers, but only to those they take to be members of social groups 1 and 2; to members of 3 and to the young they use solidarity *du*. However, the lower ranks do not use *ni* to their own superiors, whom they address with TLN in third person. *Ni* in that situation is considered disrespectful and impolite.

But I can't tell when someone first addresses me as *ni* whether that person considers such usage to be polite or not. The rector of the Police Academy addressed me as Professor Paulston in third person over the telephone, switched to *ni* when he saw me (I was some fifteen years younger than he), and sighed with relief when I initiated *du*. Clearly he does not consider *ni* as impolite but still as less polite than TLN in third person as is reflected in the general usage of the police.

There is, however, no social setting which can inform me that he considers *ni* as less polite than TLN if he had addressed me with *ni* from the beginning; the only clue lies in the direction of his change of address within the formal range.

When a bus driver addresses me with *ni*, I cannot tell whether he considers such usage to be polite or not, without knowing his habitual mode of address. If he usually practices address avoidance or third person address like *damen* and then uses *ni* in a key of irritation (Hymes 1972), his intention is likely to be impolite. But one does not know the habitual modes of strangers and so I cannot distinguish between polite and impolite use of *ni* + Ø and neither can anyone else; it is simply a matter of attitude transmitted through upbringing.

Peculiarly enough, the nominative form is much more avoided than the genitive *ers*, *eders* and the oblique *er*, *eder*. From my notes on bus drivers, whose general tendency was pronoun avoidance, I have the delightful: *Har damen biljett, gå och sätt er bara* 'If the lady has a ticket, just go and sit down' with its mixture of third person + oblique pronoun. Also...*kan gå och sätta er* '...can go and sit down' which must syntactically have been *ni kan gå* but the *ni* was totally inaudible.

To sum up, whether *ni* + Ø is polite or impolite depends entirely on the attitudes of addressor as well as addressee. The no doubt impolite intention of the clerks in the after-Christmas rush will have been decoded (more probably not noticed) as polite usage by habitual upper class *ni*-speakers. Speakers who themselves consider *ni* rude will have been more likely to notice and to decode *ni* as impolite. Often mode of address is not consciously noted and only contributes subliminally to one's impressions. As a glaring example, to my extreme annoyance I never could recall how I addressed the archbishop.

Ni + TLN; Polite *ni*

The third development of *ni* took place in the elite where *du* and *ni* became patterned after French *tu* and *vous* (cf. Russian, Friedrich 1972). Ahlgren writes: "Apparently *ni* during the earlier half of the 1800s has had its strongest support within the aristocracy—where it was perceived as corresponding to French *vous*— and within the peasant class, whereas the growing middle class more often used titles" (1973: 135). Certainly, the spokesmen for the *ni*-reforms advocated during the 1800s and 1900s were all members of the aristocracy and/or the intelligentsia.

In my earlier paper I pointed out that "the free use of *ni* might be said to be a hallmark of address behavior between members of social group 1, who are not on familiar terms with each other" (Paulston 1975: 7). My later work has found no evidence which contradicts this observation, and convincing evidence to support it. The statement needs to be modified to "the free use of *ni* + TLN," since *ni* + ØN to strangers has become fairly common, especially in the intercourse between the public and the many federal institutions like the post office, transportation, communications, etc. Although more formal and definitely class-linked, the use of *ni* + TLN marks the same meaning in personal interrelationship as solidarity *du* + Ø: a maintenance of personal but not social distance. My own address system underwent a drastic change as a result of my findings, and I virtually never use *ni* + TLN any more. When I did, it was invariably with upper-class speakers whom I either disliked or felt to be cool and distant.

Because of the widespread institutional use of *du*, I have fairly few direct observations of reciprocal *ni* + TLN but without exception they all involve members of social group 1. A typical example is the Nobel Awards banquet where the guests addressed each other by *ni* + TLN. Some may, like my own group, have switched to familiarity *du* after proper toasting ceremonies, but those I know of did not. At the banquet I promptly initiated *du* with the professor on my right but the one on my left was much older than I, grey-haired and so distinguished that I hesitated. When I pointed out my dilemma to him, adding teasingly that he could not very well initiate, he delightedly said: *Det är vad du tror* 'That's what you think' and raised his glass in the ritual toast. A younger gentleman across the table then raised his glass and said, 'May I join you?' The three men then prompted the woman across from me to follow my example and initiate *du* with them, which she did. Clearly the men were more than willing to use *du* but the women were reluctant to initiate and so in most groups *ni* + TLN prevailed. But note that the use of *ni* + TLN and the ritual initiation ceremony for switching to *du* were partially a function of the occasion. According to both my partners at table, had I met them at the university they would have addressed me as *du* without further ado.

CHOOSING OPTIONS

Present at the musical soiree which followed the dinner and mingling with the guests were technicians from radio/TV, by official order also dressed in white tie. In my conversation with them, there was mutual use of solidarity *du* + ØN. This episode can be taken to illustrate the ruling principle of all encounters in Swedish in normal situations: the speaker attempts to speak in a fashion he believes will please the addressee (not necessarily consciously so). The sequence followed by the dinner guests of (1) introduction of self which consisted of saying one's first and last name aloud followed by a handshake, (2) use of *ni* + TLN (in order to know which title to use one must either study the place lists carefully before dinner or else find out surreptitiously), (3) initiation ceremony, and (4) use of *du* + FN, I felt would be considered putting on airs by the working-class technicians so I omitted all of that sequence and simply used *du* and no name to them. Certainly I made no such conscious analysis at the time. And certainly one can never be sure that one guesses correctly how the other would like to be addressed; hence all the agony Swedes experience in addressing their fellow man. The following lament from a worker is typical:

> But you can't tell, and you don't want to use titles if they are workers and one doesn't dare use *du* in case they aren't (KU 2932).

He is an older man, and the younger working-class generation is more likely to use *ni* to strangers, which they consider perfectly polite, or practice address avoidance, but note that the criteria for choice of option have not changed. The following comments on why they would choose *du* rather than *ni* are culled from my interviews with young factory workers: 'if he looks kind; age; to "simple" folk; I look at the general style; which social class; those who don't seem arrogant and superior; people I like; not large.' *Ni* is offered to 'older people; in order to be polite; not to irritate someone; to those with snotty manners; and to Östermalms-women.' In other words, social class and age still remain the basic criteria. Rather, what has changed is the situation and the range of options.

Upper-class life is much less formal than twenty years ago when every upper-class family was expected to have at least one servant. That life has disappeared along with the servants. The standard of living has risen enormously and in a country with general good taste it is difficult to tell social class at a glance, as indeed the police complain: 'Now one has to talk to them for a while' (in order to determine social class). With socialized medicine and cultural values which regard corpulence as moral decrepitude and looking youthful as a virtue, age is also difficult to tell. Swedes never lie about their age; they take pride in looking younger than they are, not in *passing* for younger. Social class and age still remain basic criteria but what will count as markers for social class and age has changed, and the range within which they are determined. And with a prevailing egalitarian worldview, there is much less fear of making mistakes.

People do misjudge. The winter 1973, half of the girls and women in Stockholm were wearing loden coats and traditional peasant babushkas (scarves) as was I: no social clue in dress. During the break at the end station, the bus driver approached me and addressed me as *du*. As I answered, he of course noticed my Östermalms-stockholmska. In the five minutes of following chat during which I addressed him as *du*, he scrupulously avoided any pronoun reference. Clearly he must have had (my social rules did not allow me to ask him) the same rule as one of the factory workers quoted above, and did not feel comfortable with using *du* to me any longer after he had revised his judgment of my social class.

Indeed, choice of option can be so delicate a matter that one of the personnel managers of an international business firm, whom I interviewed, uses address choice as a test in hiring salesmen. At the job interview, one was disqualified for greeting the personnel manager with *hej* (marked for *du*) instead of *goddag* (unmarked). Another was disqualified for addressing him as Herr Johansson. The third passed the test; he carefully avoided until he was addressed as *du*, which he unostentatiously reciprocated. On the whole, that is the general rule: Let the other initiate and then reciprocate. Indeed, there is a court ruling on the matter. Engineer T. had been arrested by the police for disturbing the peace (he was drunk). He complained to the court about his treatment and pointed out he had been addressed as *du*. The court cleared the police and acknowledged the recent change in address system, but added that the police had been remiss; they should have waited until they were addressed with *du* or *ni* and then reciprocated—'restrictivity' in the matter of address was essential. (The exception to the reciprocity rule is, as I have discussed, the tendency of some members of social group 3 to avoid the use of *du* in speaking to members of group 1, especially by men to women.)

Obviously, such general strategies strain the rules for dispensation rights to the utmost, as someone must initiate. As a matter of fact, the court's ruling violates the rules of the etiquette books (variables of sex, age, and rank, in that order of importance) as some policemen will be older than their male clients but still cannot initiate. It seems there are two distinct initiation acts.

One is the clearly recognized initiation to *du* by *titelbortläggning*. This is the speech act which follows the dispensation rights discussed above and which vary according to social class. But there is also an initiation act which does not involve dispensation, simply an initiation of choice of option, primarily *ni* + Ø or *du* + Ø, but any form of address is possible. Everyone is aware of the existence of this initiation act, but it is not recognized that its rule occasionally conflicts with those for dispensation rights, another cause of the Swedes' confusion. This initiation act rule says simply that the customer or client initiates. At the hairdresser and the post office, in the bus and the department store, to the police and the bank clerk, the customer is granted choice of option. The exception will be upper class 'patrons', like bank officers and librarians, who will not hesitate to initiate and who tend to use the dispensation rule-variables in choice of option, as will strangers who are not in a client-patron relationship.

At a visit to the Immigration and Naturalization Department of the Federal Police to arrange for my visa, I was puzzled by my irritation at being addressed as *du* by the immigration officer, a woman younger than myself. Puzzled because I had come to prefer to use solidarity *du* and so it made little sense to be irritated at it. But the young woman was breaking every possible rule: no institutional use of *du* existed, I had been addressed as *ni* by others; dispensation rules granted me the initiation (but she also addressed my husband with *du*, which would have been sanctioned by those rules, and I took umbrage at that usage as well). Above all, I was the customer-client and it was my right to initiate choice of option. At the time, I was not able to understand my irritation (especially as I would have initiated *du* + Ø) but the social meaning certainly was clear to me: condescension and reduction to dependent/childhood status, and mine was much the same as the reaction of Engineer T.

The initiation act as distinct from the dispensation act is a recent development, and I was not aware at the time I collected the data that the two did not conform to the same rules. Consequently I did not investigate specifically the parameters of the client-patron relationship, which definitely merits further exploration. I think what is happening is as follows. When the address system was stable, prior to the present change, form of address was fairly predictable: speakers from social group 1 used *ni* or third person to such patrons as police, bank clerks, and sales personnel while members from social group 3 used *du* to patrons from their own social class and *ni*, third person, or avoidance to patrons from social groups 1 and 2. Patrons knew what to expect, and could perfectly well predict and therefore *initiate* address form. Whatever hesitation existed lay only in accurately ascertaining the dispensation rule variables.

There is today no way of predicting form of address between strangers. As a result, patrons from social groups 2 and 3 are developing an "avoid—let the other initiate—then reciprocate" strategy, and the change in choice of options with the present uncertainty in predicting choice is accompanied by new rules, i.e. not a change in rules but additional rules, for who chooses option. Application of the dispensation rules requires some familiarity with the addressee in order to determine sex, age, and rank, in whatever order they are applied. With the rapidly increased use of *du* + Ø between strangers, and clients' fluctuation between this *du* and anonymous *ni*, it makes sense in service relationships to grant the customer the opportunity to miscalculate rather than to offend by one's own faulty estimation of the situation.[10]

It is especially this alternation between anonymous *ni* and solidarity *du* between strangers which lead Swedes to believe that their address system is totally irregular. Anonymous *ni* is being replaced so rapidly by *du* + Ø that an individual's

---

[10] This approach is reflected in the following excerpt from *Trafikhandboken*, Storstockholms *Lokaltrafik* 1974, the manual for employees of the local transportation company: 'Between employees, we usually say *Du* to each other. Avoid, however, saying *du* to customers. Word of address is a personal matter which one ought to agree on. Older persons usually don't like to be addressed as *du*.'

usage will vary day from day depending on his mood that day. When I was cheerful and happy with the world, I would address many more strangers as *du* than when I felt tired and irritated in which case I would use *ni*. I was not aware of this variation in my own usage until several informants commented on the influence of mood on their own usage.

There are, however, certain factors which do influence an individual's alternation so there is not totally free variation. I would never use *du* to somebody much older than I or *ni* to somebody younger. The librarian I overheard at the Royal Library constitutes a perfect example. He was filling out cards for two customers. As upper-class patron, he did not hesitate to initiate, which he did. To the man of his own age, about 30, he said *Vad heter du*? 'What is your name?' while to the reader who was fifteen—twenty years older than he was—he said *Vad är Ert namn*?

The setting of similar transactions may influence choice of pronoun. Many informants commented that they would address the sales clerk in a boutique with *du* but that they would never do so at NK, the expensive department store. Gas station attendants are repeatedly singled out by upper-class informants for their uninhibited address form; although working-class patrons, they frequently initiate *du* + Ø, but they too are sensitive to social class. One amused informant reports that when he drove up in a small car he was addressed with *du* only to be addressed as *ni* later in the day when he returned in a big expensive car. The same informant also reports that the Lutheran minister, who was known to the attendant, in mufti was addressed as *du* but in clerical garb received a polite *Pastorn*, i.e. T-third person.

But individual usage will vary between individuals in the same identical setting, and one cannot predict such usage. My friend, around 40, writes me that the other day two plumbers around 25 came to fix something in her apartment. One of them addressed her as *du*, the other as *ni*. At a cash register in a sports clothes store where I was paying for my purchase, there were two clerks; one addressed me as *du*, the other as *damen*. The *du*-speaker in this case was the younger, and the *du*-usage clearly is spread by the younger generation. But the impossibility of delineating rules of address which will accurately predict choice of address is limited to the interaction of strangers, of *opresenterade* (Andersson et al. 1970) 'people who are not introduced to each other', and all other interactions are clearly rule-governed.

CONCLUSION

The Swedish address system is in a stage of rapid change with an increased use of solidarity *du* + ØN, brought about by the dominant political ideology, and no doubt facilitated by the awkwardness of the previous usage which most Swedes are relieved to escape. Swedes are given to generalizations that (1) today everyone uses *du* and (2) there are no stateable rules for address usage. Neither proposition is true, and I have attempted in this paper to account for those rules. The major argument has been that an adequate description of the Swedish address system is possible only through the recognition that the social classes have different rules due to different semantics of the pronouns *du* and *ni*.

REFERENCES

AHLGREN, P. 1973. Tilltalsordet Ni:s historia, unpublished Phil. Lic. dissertation, University of Uppsala.

ANDERSSON, B., HOLMQUIST, B., LJUNGQUIST, L. and LUND, K. 1970. Om tilltalsskicket i modern Svenska. Unpublished ms. University of Lund.

BATES, E. and BENIGNI, L. 1975. Rules of address in Italy: a sociological survey. *LinS* 4. 271–88.

BECKMAN, N. 1947. Rang och pronomen. *Nysvenska Studier* 27 årgången. 99–112.

BROWN, R. and GILMAN, A. 1960. The pronouns of power and solidarity. In T. Sebeok (ed.) *Style in language*. Cambridge, Mass. The M.I.T. Press. 253–376.

ERVIN-TRIPP, S. 1973. *Language acquisition and communicative choice*. Stanford: Stanford University Press.

FRIEDRICH, P. 1972. Social context and semantic feature: The Russian pronominal usage. In J. Gumperz and D. Hymes (eds.), *Directions in sociolinguistics*. New York: Holt, Rinehart and Winston, 270–300.

HAUGEN, E. 1975. Pronominal address in Icelandic: from you-two to you-all. *LinS* 4. 323–39.

HYMES, D. 1972. Models of the interaction of language and social life. In J. Gumperz and D. Hymes (eds.), *Directions in sociolinguistics*. New York: Holt, Rinehart and Winston. 35–71.

HYMES, D. 1974. *Foundations in sociolinguistics*. Philadelphia: University of Pennsylvania Press.

JONZ, J. 1975. Situated address in the United States Marine Corps. *Anthropological Linguistics* 17. 68–77.

LABOV, W. 1972. On the mechanism of linguistic change. In J. Gumperz and D. Hymes (eds.), *Directions in sociolinguistics*. New York: Holt, Rinehart and Winston, 512–37.

NORDISKA MUSEET 1969. *Etnologiska undersökningen*, Frågelista 194, Tilltalsord, Stockholm.

PAULSTON, C. B. 1975. Language universals and socio-cultural implications in deviant usage: personal questions in Swedish. *Studia Linguistica* XXIX. 1–11. 1–15.

PAULSTON, R. G. 1968. *Educational change in Sweden*. New York: Teachers College Press.

ROSENGREN, K. E. 1963. Ni-reform nit. *Studiekamraten*. 6. 109–112.

SVENSKA DAGBLADET 1970. Sociala structuren lika efter 60 år. August 15, 1970.

SÖDERBERG, T. 1972. *Två sekler svensk medelklass*. Stockholm: Bonniers.

UTHORN, N. 1959. Om *NI* i läroverk och seminar *Modersmålslärarnas Förening*. Arsskrift 1959. Lund: Skånska Central Tryckenet. 113–25.

WELLANDER, E. 1952. Ni eller Du? *Svenska Dagbladet*, August 13, 1952.

WELLANDER, E. 1964. *Språk och Språkvård*. Stockholm: Norstedts.

SUSAN GAL

Peasant Men Can't Get Wives: Language Change and Sex Roles in a Bilingual Community

INTRODUCTION

Differences between men's and women's speech are no longer thought to be characteristic only of "exotic" languages and need no longer be categorical differences in order to be noticed by linguists (cf. Bodine 1975). In accordance with the sociolinguistic assumption that speech differences reflect the social distinctions deemed important by the community of speakers, sexual differentiation of speech is expected to occur whenever a social division exists between the roles of men and women—that is, universally. Further, recent work has shown that linguistic differences between men and women can appear at various levels of grammar: in phonology (Anshen 1969; Sankoff and Cedergren 1971), in syntax and pragmatics (Keenan 1971; Lakoff 1975), in choice of lexical items (Swacker 1975), in choice of language by bilinguals (Rubin 1970; Farber 1974), as well as in patterns of conversational interaction (Zimmerman and West 1975; bibliography in Thorne and Henley 1975).

However, the effects of such sex differences on linguistic *change* have so far been noted only with respect to phonology, where it has been demonstrated that, along with other social correlates of synchronic linguistic diversity such as class and ethnicity, "...the sexual differentiation of speech often plays a major role in the mechanism of linguistic evolution" (Labov 1972:303). The substantive aim of this paper is to describe the way in which the women of a Hungarian-German bilingual town in Austria have contributed to a change in patterns of language choice. The entire community is gradually and systematically changing from stable bilingualism to the use of only one language in all interactions. Sex-linked differences in language choice have influenced the overall community-wide process of change.

In the language usage patterns to be described here, young women are more advanced or further along in the direction of the linguistic change than older people and young men. This is one of the patterns which has been noted in correlational studies of phonological change in urban areas. Most such studies report that women use the newer, advanced forms more frequently than men. Newly introduced forms used mostly by women are sometimes prestigious (Trudgill 1972) and sometimes not (Fasold 1968). In many cases women, as compared to men of the same social

From *Language in Society*, Vol. (7), 1978, pp. 1–16. Reprinted with permission of Cambridge University Press and Susan Gal.

class, use more of the new non-prestigious forms in casual speech, while moving further towards prestige models in formal speech. In other cases women do not lead in the course of linguistic change (reported in Labov 1972).

Although such findings are well documented, adequate explanations of them have not been offered. General statements about the linguistic innovativeness or conservatism of women will not account for the data. Neither Trudgill's (1972) suggestion that women are "linguistically insecure," nor Labov's (1972) allusion to norms of linguistic appropriateness which allow women a wider expressive range than men, can convincingly explain why women are linguistically innovative in some communities and not in others (Nichols 1976). Women's role in language change has rarely been linked to the social position of women in the communities studied and to the related question of what women want to express about themselves in speech. In the present study, men's and women's ways of speaking are viewed as the results of strategic and socially meaningful linguistic choices which systematic-ally link language change to social change: linguistic innovation is a function of speakers' differential involvement in, and evaluation of, social change.

Specifically, in the linguistic repertoire of the bilingual community to be described here, one of the languages has come to symbolize a newly available social status. Young women's language choices can be understood as part of their expression of preference for this newer social identity. The young women of the community are more willing to participate in social change and in the linguistic change which symbolizes it because they are less committed than the men to the traditionally male-dominated system of subsistence agriculture and because they have more to gain than men in embracing the newly available statuses of worker and worker's wife. In order to make this argument in detail several words of background are necessary, first about the community and second about its linguistic repertoire.

THE COMMUNITY

Oberwart (Felsöör) is a town located in the province of Burgenland in eastern Austria. It has belonged to Austria only since 1921 when as part of the post-World War I peace agreements the province was detached from Hungary. The town itself has been a speech island since the 1500s when most of the original Hungarian-speaking population of the region was decimated by the Turkish wars and was replaced by German-speaking (and in some areas Croatian-speaking) settlers. In Oberwart, which was the largest of the five remaining Hungarian-speaking communities, bilingualism in German and Hungarian became common.

During the last thirty years Oberwart has grown from a village of 600 to a town of over 5,000 people because, as the county seat and new commercial center, it has attracted migrants. These new settlers have all been monolingual German speakers, mainly people from neighboring villages, who have been trained in commerce or administration. The bilingual community today constitutes about a fourth of the town's population.

The indigenous bilinguals who will be the focus of this discussion have until recently engaged in subsistence peasant agriculture. Since World War II, however, most of the agriculturalists have become industrial workers or worker-peasants. By 1972 only about one third of the bilingual population was employed exclusively in peasant agriculture.

In short, Oberwart is an example of the familiar post-war process of urbanization and industrialization of the countryside often reported in the literature on the transformation of peasant Europe (e.g. Franklin 1969).

THE LINGUISTIC REPERTOIRE

Bilingual communities provide a particularly salient case of the linguistic heterogeneity which characterizes all communities. In Oberwart the linguistic alternatives available to speakers include not only two easily distinguishable languages but also dialectal differences within each language. These "dialects" are not homogeneous, invariant structures, but rather are best characterized as sets of covarying linguistic variables which have their own appropriate social uses and connotations (c.f. Gumperz 1964; Ervin-Tripp 1972). It is possible for bilingual Oberwarters to move along a continuum from more standard to more local speech in either of their languages (cf. Gal 1976: III).

Of the many functions that code choice has been shown to serve in interaction (Hymes 1967) this paper focuses on just one and on how it is involved in change. As Blom & Gumperz (1972) have argued, alternate codes within a linguistic repertoire are usually each associated with sub-groups in the community and with certain activities. It has been pointed out that a speaker's choice of code in a particular situation is part of that speaker's linguistic presentation of self. The speaker makes the choice as part of a verbal strategy to identify herself or himself with the social categories and activities the code symbolizes. The choice, then, allows the speaker to express solidarity with that category or group of people. It will be argued here that because codes (in this case languages) are associated with social statuses and activities, changes in language choice can be used by speakers to symbolize changes in their own social status or in their attitudes towards the activities the languages symbolize.

THE MEANINGS OF CODES

Although bilingual Oberwarters use both standard and local varieties of German as well as of Hungarian, and although the choice between local and standard features in either language carries meaning in conversation, here we will be concerned only with the symbolically more important alternation between German of any sort (G) and Hungarian of any sort (H).

Today in Oberwart H symbolizes peasant status and is deprecated because peasant status itself is no longer respected. Peasant is used here for a native cultural category that includes all local agriculturalists and carries a negative connotation, at least for young people. Young bilingual workers often say, in Hungarian, that only the old peasants speak Hungarian. There is no contradiction here. The young workers know that they themselves sometimes speak Hungarian and they can report on their language choices accurately. The saying refers not to actual practice but to the association of the Hungarian language with peasant status. All old peasants do speak Hungarian and speak it in more situations than anyone else.

The preferred status for young people is worker, not peasant. The world of work is a totally German-speaking world, and the language itself has come to represent the worker. The peasant parents of young workers often say about their children *Ü má egisz nímët* ('He/she is totally German already').[1] This is not a reference to citizenship, nor to linguistic abilities. Oberwarters consider themselves Austrians, not Germans, and even young people are considered bilingual, often using Hungarian in interactions with elders. The phrase indicates the strong symbolic relationship between the young people's status as workers and the language which they use at work.

German also represents the money and prestige available to those who are employed, but not available to peasants. German therefore carries more prestige than Hungarian. The children of a monolingual German speaker and a bilingual speaker never learn Hungarian, regardless of which parent is bilingual. In addition, while in previous generations the ability simply to speak both German and Hungarian was the goal of the Oberwarters, today there is a premium not just on speaking German, but on speaking it without any interference from Hungarian. Parents often boast that in their children's German speech *Nëm vág bele e madzsar* ('The Hungarian doesn't cut into it'). That is, passing as a monolingual German speaker is now the aim of young bilingual Oberwarters.

Such general statements about symbolic associations between languages, social statuses and the evaluations of those statuses do not in themselves predict language choice in particular situations. For instance, although H is negatively evaluated by young people it is nevertheless used by them in a number of interactions where, for various reasons, they choose to present themselves as peasants. Besides the values associated with languages, the three factors which must be known in order to predict choices and to describe the changes in these choices are the speaker's age and sex and the nature of the social network in which that speaker habitually interacts.

HOW DO LANGUAGE CHOICE PATTERNS CHANGE?

In any interaction between bilingual Oberwarters a choice must be made between G and H. While in most situations one or the other language is chosen, there are some interactions in which both appear to be equally appropriate. In such interactions it is impossible to predict which language will be used by which speaker and both are often used within one short exchange. Gumperz (1976) has called this conversational code-switching. When both languages may appropriately be used, Oberwarters say they are speaking *ehodzsan dzsün* ('as it comes'). A description of language choice in such situations must include such variation and in this sense is comparable to the rule conflicts described for syntactic change by Bickerton (1973).

In predicting an individual's choice between the three possibilities—G, H, or both—the habitual role-relationship between participants in the interaction proved to be the most important factor. Other aspects of the situation such as locale, purpose or occasion were largely irrelevant. Therefore, specification of the identity of the interlocutor was sufficient to define the social situation for the purposes of the present analysis.

We can think of informants as being ranked along a vertical axis and social situations being arranged along a horizontal axis, as in Tables 1 and 2. Note that all

---

[1] The orthography is a modified version of Imre (1971) and of the Hungarian dialect atlas.

speakers listed in these tables are bilingual. The information is drawn from a language usage questionnaire which was constructed on the basis of native categories of interlocutors and linguistic resources. Similar scales based on systematic observation of language choice were also constructed. There was a high degree of agreement between observed usage and the questionnaire results (average agreement for men 86%, for women 90%). That is, the questionnaire results were corroborated by direct observation of language choice.

The language choices of a particular informant in all situations are indicated in the rows of Tables 1 and 2 and the choices of all informants in a particular situation are indicated in the columns. The choices of Oberwarters, arranged in this way, form a nearly perfect implicational scale. Note that for all speakers there is at least one situation in which they use only H. For almost all speakers there are some situations in which they use both G and H and some in which they use only G. Further, for any speaker there are no bilingual interlocutors with whom she or he speaks both G and H unless there are some, listed to the left of that interlocutor, with whom the speaker uses H. With few exceptions, if G is used with an interlocutor then only G is used to interlocutors listed to the right of that, and GH or

TABLE 1. Language choice pattern of women

Infor- mant	Age	1	2	3	4	5	6	7	8	9	10	11
		\multicolumn{11}{Social situations (identity of participant)}										
A	14	H	GH		G	G	G			G		G
B	15	H	GH		G	G	G			G		G
C	25	H	GH	GH	GH	G	G	G	G	G		G
D	27	H	H		GH	G	G			G		G
E	17	H	H		H	GH	G			G		G
F	39	H	H		H	GH	GH			G		G
G	23	H	H		H	GH	H		GH	G		G
H	40	H	H		H	GH		GH	G	G		G
I	52	H	H	H	GH	H		GH	G	G	G	G
J	40	H	H	H	H	H	H	GH	GH	GH		G
K	35	H	H	H	H	H	H	H	GH	H		G
L	61	H	H		H	H	H	H	GH	H		G
M	50	H	H	H	H	H	H	H	H	H		G
N	60	H	H	H	H	H	H	H	H	H	GH	G
O	54	H	H		H	H	H	H	H	H	GH	H
P	63	H	H	H	H	H	H	H	H	H	GH	H
Q	64	H	H	H	H	H	H	H	H	H	H	H
R	59	H	H	H	H	H	H	H	H	H	H	H

No. of informants = 18   Scalability = 95.4%

1 = to god
2 = grandparents and their generation
3 = bilingual clients in black market
4 = parents and their generation
5 = friends and age-mate neighbors
6 = brothers and sisters

7 = spouse
8 = children and their generation
9 = bilingual government officials
10 = grandchildren and their generation
11 = doctors

G = German, H = Hungarian, GH = both German and Hungarian.

TABLE 2. Language choice pattern of men

Infor-mant	Age	Social situations (identity of participant)										
		1	2	3	4	5	6	7	8	9	10	11
A	17	H	GH		G	G	G			G		G
B	25	H	H		GH	G	G			G		G
C	42		H		GH	G	G	G	G	G		G
D	20	H	H	H	H	GH	G	G	G	G		G
E	22	H	H		H	GH	GH			G		G
F	62	H	H	H	H	H	H	GH	GH	GH	G	G
G	63	H	H		H	H	H	H		GH		G
H	64	H	H	H	H	H	H	H	GH	GH		G
I	43	H	H		H	H	H	H	G	H		G
J	41	H	H	H	H	H	H	H	GH	H		H
K	54	H	H		H	H	H	H	H	H		G
L	61	H	H		H	H	H	H	H	G	GH	G
M	74	H	H		H	H	H	H	H	H	GH	H
N	58	G	H		H	H	H	H	H	H	H	H

No. of informants = 14   Scalability = 95.2%

1 = to god
2 = grandparents and their generation
3 = bilingual clients in black market
4 = parents and their generation
5 = friends and age-mate neighbors
6 = brothers and sisters

7 = spouse
8 = children and their generation
9 = bilingual government officials
10 = grandchildren and their generation
11 = doctors

G = German, H = Hungarian, GH = both German and Hungarian.

H are used with those listed to the left. The occurrence of any of the three linguistic categories in a cell implies the occurrence of particular others in the cells to the left and right.

In addition, looking at the columns instead of the rows in Tables 1 and 2, and considering not one speaker at a time but the group of speakers as a whole, we see that if a speaker high on the list uses both G and H in a particular situation, then speakers lower down can be expected to use H or both in that situation. But if the speaker at the top of the list uses H, then all others use H in that situation as well. The presence of any one of the three linguistic categories in a cell restricts which of the three may occur in the cells above and below that one. When one speaker's choice of language in a particular situation is known it also gives information about the possibilities open to those lower on the list and those higher on the list. The closer an informant is to the top of the list the more situations there are in which he or she uses G. The closer to the bottom, the more H he or she uses. Tables 1 and 2 have scalabilities of 95.4% and 95.2% respectively, showing that there are only a few exceptions to these generalizations.[2]

Given this, it is worth considering the factors that determine the place of a speaker on the scale. Two factors determine the degree to which a person uses H as

---

[2] "Scalability" is the proportion of cells that fit the scale model. Inapplicable cells (those left empty in Tables 1 and 2) were omitted from the denominator.

opposed to G: the person's age and her or his social network. Because historical evidence (cf. Imre 1973; Kovács 1942:73-6) shows that present-day age differences are not due to age-grading of language choice, we can take age (apparent time) as a surrogate for repeated sampling over real time (cf. Labov 1965 for details of this strategy).

Social network is defined here as all the people (contacts) an individual spoke to in the course of a unit of time. The average amount of time for all informants was seven days. Each of these network contacts was assigned to one of two categories: (a) those who lived in households which owned either pigs or cows, (b) those who lived in households which owned neither pigs nor cows. Oberwarters themselves define those who own cows and pigs as peasants. The peasantness of a person's network, expressed as the percentage of contacts who fit into category (a) is, in effect, a measure of that person's social involvement with the category of persons with which the use of H is associated.

The more peasants the individual has in her or his social network the greater the number of social situations in which that individual uses H. In fact, in most cases a *person's own status*, whether peasant, worker or some gradation in between, *was not as accurate a predictor of his or her choices as the status of the person's social contacts*. These results lend support to the notion that social networks are instrumental in constraining speakers' linguistic presentation of self (Gumperz 1964; Labov 1973).

The three-way relationship between language choices, age, and peasantness of social network can be demonstrated by ranking informants on each of the measures and then correlating the rankings with each other. Table 3 shows the correlations for this sample of informants. All are significant at the 0.01 level. Note that this group of informants was not formally selected as a representative sample of the bilingual community, but rather was chosen to represent the entire range of the two variables—age and social network—so that conclusions could be drawn about the effect of each variable on changing language choices. In order to distinguish the effects on language choice of time on the one hand and the effects of changing social networks on the other, both old people who had never been totally involved in peasant agriculture and young people who were very much involved were included in the sample.

TABLE 3. Correlations between language choice and age, language choice and peasantness of network*

	All informants	Women	Men
Language choice and age	0.82	0.93	0.69
Language choice and peasantness of network	0.78	0.74	0.78
	N = 32	N = 18	N = 14

* Spearman rank correlation coefficients all significant at the 0.01 level.

On the basis of the rank correlations the following brief outline of the synchronic pattern of language choice can be drawn. For the sample as a whole, the more peasants in one's social network the more likely it is that one will use H in a large number of situations. The older one is the more likely it is that one will use H in a large number of situations. Young people who interact only with workers use the least H, older people who interact mostly with peasants use the most H. Older people who associate mostly with workers are closer in their language choices to people much younger than themselves, while very young people who associated mostly with peasants use more H than others their own age.

Because historical evidence rules out the possibility of age-grading and because the sample allows one to disentangle the effects of time and that of networks, it is possible to hypothesize the following process of change. Changes in language choices occur situation by situation. The rule for one situation is always first categorical for the old form (H), then variable (GH), before it is categorical for the new form (G). As speakers' networks become less and less peasant they use H in fewer and fewer situations. And, in a parallel but separate process, as time passes new generations use H in fewer and fewer situations regardless of the content of their social networks.

DIFFERENCES BETWEEN MEN AND WOMEN

The implicational scales describing choices seem to indicate no differences between men and women. Both men and women show the same kinds of implicational relationships in the same ordered list of situations. However, the rank correlations of language choice, age, and peasantness of network, summarized in Table 3, present a more complicated picture. Here the issue is whether age and social networks are equally well correlated with language choice for men and women. In fact they are not: for men the correlation between social network and language choice is about the same as the correlation between age and language choice (0.78 and 0.69 respectively). For women age alone is more closely correlated with language choice (0.93) than is the social network measure (0.74). This difference between men and women is significant at the 0.05 level.

In short there is a difference between men and women in the way each is going through the process of change in language choice. If we distinguish three twenty-year generations, separate the men from the women and those with very peasant networks from those with nonpeasant networks, it is possible to illustrate the process at work. Informants' networks ranged from 13% peasant contacts to 94% peasant contacts. This continuum was divided into two parts. All those scoring at or above the median were put in the peasant network category in Figure 1, all those scoring below the median were in the nonpeasant network category.

Figure 1 illustrates the fact that for men there is a very regular pattern in the correlations. From the oldest to the youngest generation use of G increases, but for each generation this increase is greatest for those whose social networks include a majority of nonpeasants. Among the men the youngest group as a whole uses less H than any of the others. But those young men with heavily peasant networks do use more H. Regardless of the negative evaluations, for these young men expression of peasant identity is still preferred for many situations.

For women the process is different. First we find that in the oldest generation this sample includes not one person with a nonpeasant network. This is not a sampling error but reflects the limited range of activities, and therefore of social contacts, open to women before World War II. In the middle generation the women's pattern matches that of men exactly. Many women of the generation reaching

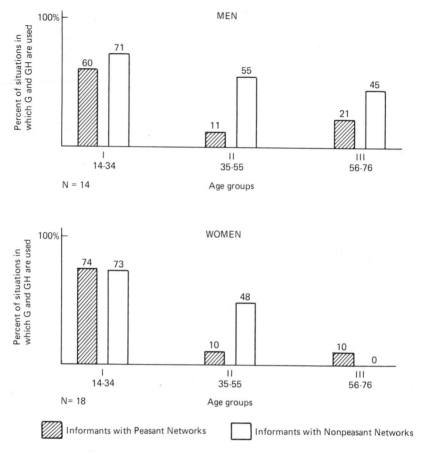

FIGURE 1. Percentage of G and GH language choices of informants with peasant and nonpeasant social networks in three age groups

maturity during and after World War II left the peasant home, if only temporarily, to work in inns, factories and shops. Often they remained in contact with those they befriended. As with the men, those who have heavily peasant networks use more H than those who do not.

The youngest generation of women differs both from the older women and from the men. First, these youngest women use more G and less H than anyone else in the community, including the youngest men. In addition, for these women, *peasantness of social network makes no difference in language choice.* Young women with peasant networks use Hungarian as rarely as young women with nonpeasant networks. Recall that for all the men, including the youngest, peasantness of network did make a difference since it was associated with more use of H.

To understand these differences it is necessary to go back to the activities from which the languages derive their meanings and evaluations. For the most recent generation of women, peasant life is a much less attractive choice that it is for men. Now that other opportunities are open to these young women, they reject peasant life as a viable alternative. It will be argued here that their language choices are part of this rejection.

There are some young men who, despite a general preference for industrial and commercial employment, want to take over family farms. Some of these young men have the newly developing attitude that farming can be an occupation, a 'Beruf', like any other. These are men whose families own enough land to make agriculture if not as lucrative as wage work at least a satisfactory livelihood. In contrast, young women, since World War II, have not been willing to take over the family farm when this opportunity is offered to them. More importantly, they specifically state that they do not want to marry peasant men. The life of a peasant wife is seen by Oberwart young women as particularly demeaning and difficult when compared to the other choices which have recently become available to them.

Let us compare the choices open to Oberwart young men and women as they see them. For men the life possibilities are (a) to be an industrial or construction worker (usually a commuter coming home only on weekends), (b) to be a peasant-worker, holding two full-times jobs, and (3) to be a full-time agriculturalist. This last is felt by Oberwart men to have the advantage of independence—no orders from strangers—and the disadvantage of lack of cash and prestige. But it is generally agreed that while agricultural work was once more grueling and difficult than factory and construction work, this is no longer the case. Although peasant men still work longer hours than those in industry, machines such as the tractor and the combine make men's farm work highly mechanized and considerably less difficult than it once was.

For women the life possibilities depend mainly on whom they marry. The peasant wife typically spends the day doing farm work: milking, feeding pigs, hoeing, planting and harvesting potatoes and a few other rootcrops. Her evenings are spent doing housework. Industriousness is traditionally considered a young peasant wife's most valuable quality.

There are machines now available which lighten the work of the peasant wife considerably, including the washing machine, the electric stove and the silo (which eliminates the need for rootcrops as cattle feed). But in peasant households the male labor saving machines are always acquired before any of the ones which lighten women's work. For instance the silo, which is perhaps the most substantial work saver for the peasant wife, is never built before a combine is purchased, and the combine itself is among the last and most expensive of the machines acquired. In this Oberwart exemplifies the pattern all over Europe, where, for instance, the German small peasant's wife in 1964 averaged over the year seventeen more work hours per week than her husband (Franklin 1969:37-44). In addition, although peasant life in Oberwart is less male-dominated than, for instance, in the Balkans (compare Denich 1975 with Fél and Hofer 1969:113-14), nevertheless for the peasant wife the independence which is said to compensate the peasant man for his work is not freely available. In fact, being a young peasant wife often means living under the authority of a mother-in-law who supervises the kitchen and women's farm work generally.

In marked contrast, marriage to a worker involves only household tasks and upkeep of a kitchen garden. Wives of workers are sometimes employed as maids or salespersons, but mostly they hold part-time jobs or are not employed at all. Because of the increased access to money, because agricultural equipment is not needed and because some of the women themselves contribute part of the money, electric stoves and washing machines are among the first appliances bought by working married couples, thereby further lightening the wife's work load. Peasant wives work far more than peasant men. Peasant men work more hours than worker men. Workers' wives, especially if not employed, often work fewer hours than their husbands.

This contrast is not lost on young Oberwart women. When discussing life choices they especially dwell on the dirtyness and heaviness of peasant work. Rejection of the use of local Hungarian, the symbol of peasant status, can be seen as part of the rejection, by young women, of peasant status and life generally. They do not want to be peasants; they do not present themselves as peasants in speech.

Mothers of marriageable daughters specifically advise them against marriage to peasants. Oberwarters agree that 'Paraszt legin nëm kap nüöt' (Peasant lads can't get women). For instance, in reference to a particular young couple an old man remarked: *Az e Trüumfba jár, az fog neki tehen szart lapáni? Abbu má paraszt nëm lesz, az má zicher!* ('She works at the [local bra factory], *she*'s going to shovel cow manure for him? She'll never be a peasant, that's for sure.') Although the young men themselves are usually also reluctant to become peasants, for those who nevertheless choose family agriculture as their livelihood, the anti-peasant attitudes of the community's young women present a problem.

If in recent years Oberwart young women have not wanted to marry peasant men, and if they have acted on this preference, then Oberwart peasant men must have found wives elsewhere. The town's marriage records should provide evidence for the difference in attitudes between young men and young women.

TABLE 4. **Endogamous marriages of all bilingual Oberwarters and bilingual male peasant Oberwarters**

	% Endogamous marriages of all marriages	% Endogamous marriages of male peasants
1911-40	71%	87%
1941-60	65	54
1961-72	32	0

Source: Marriage Register, City of Oberwart.

The general trend in Oberwart in the post-war years has been away from the traditional village endogamy and towards exogamy. For instance, Table 4 shows that between 1911 and 1940, 71% of the marriages of bilinguals in Oberwart were endogamous. Between 1961 and 1972 only 32% were. But for the bilingual peasant men of Oberwart the figures are different. As Table 4 indicates, between 1911 and 1940 a larger percentage of peasant men married endogamously than all bilingual Oberwarters (87%). Between 1941 and 1960, however, this was reversed. Finally, by 1961-72, when 32% of all bilingual Oberwarters married endogamously, not one peasant man married endogamously. Those peasant men who did marry during those years found wives in the neighbouring small German monolingual villages where being a peasant wife has not been negatively valued. In short, the marriage records provide evidence that young Oberwart women's stated attitudes towards peasant men have been translated into action. The effect of this is discussed below.

CONCLUSION

There are two ways, one direct and one indirect, in which the attitudes and choices of young bilingual women are changing the language usage pattern in this community. Directly, the young women, even those with heavily peasant networks refuse, in most situations, to present themselves as peasants by using H. This contrasts with the language choices of older women and has the general effect that more German is used in more interactions in the community. It also contrasts with the choices of young men, who use Hungarian in more interactions than the young women and who are constrained by the peasantness of their social networks so that those with heavily peasant networks choose local Hungarian in more interactions than those with nonpeasant networks.

Indirectly, young women's marriage preferences are also having a linguistic effect. They refuse to marry local peasant men, preferring workers instead. As a result, exactly that small group of young men most likely to be using Hungarian in many situations, that is the ones engaged in peasant agriculture, are the ones who have married German monolingual women with the greatest frequency in the last decade or so. Because the children of marriages between monolingual German speakers and bilingual Hungarian-German speakers in Oberwart rarely if ever learn Hungarian, in an indirect way the present generation of young women is limiting the language possibilities of the next generation.

In exploring the reasons for the difference between young men's and young women's language choices, evidence was presented showing that in their stated attitudes and their marriage choices the women evaluate peasant life more negatively than the men and reject the social identity of peasant wife. The women of Oberwart feel they have more to gain than men by embracing the new opportunities of industrial employment. Also, considering the male-dominated nature of East European peasant communities generally and the lives of Oberwart women in particular, women have less to lose in rejecting the traditional peasant roles and values.

This paper has argued that women's language choices and their linguistic innovativeness in this community are the linguistic expressions of women's greater participation in social change. The linguistic pattern is best understood by considering the social meanings of the available languages and the strategic choices and evaluations which men and women make concerning the ways of life symbolized by those languages.

REFERENCES

ANSHEN, F. 1969.   Speech variation among Negros in a small southern community. Unpublished Ph.D. dissertation. New York University.

BICKERTON, D. 1973.   The nature of a creole continuum. *Language* 44:640-69.

BODINE, A. 1975.   Sex differentiation in language. In S. Thorne and N. Henley (eds.). *Language and sex: Difference and dominance*, Rowley, Massachusetts: Newbury House.

BLOM, J.P. and GUMPERZ, J.J. 1974.   Social meaning in linguistic structures: Code-switching in Norway. In J.J. Gumperz and D. Hymes (eds.), *Directions in sociolinguistics*. New York: Holt, Rinehart and Winston.

DENICH, B. 1974.   Sex and power in the Balkans. In M.S. Rosaldo and L. Lamphere (eds.), *Woman, culture and society*. Stanford: Stanford University Press.

ERVIN-TRIPP, S. 1972. On sociolinguistic rules: Alternation and co-occurrence. In J.J. Gumperz and D. Hymes (eds.), *Directions in sociolinguistics*. New York: Holt, Rinehart and Winston.

FASOLD, R. 1968. A sociolinguistic study of the pronunciation of three vowels in Detroit speech. Washington, D.C.: Center for Applied Linguistics. Mimeo.

FARBER, A. 1974. Women's language use in Comalapa, Guatemala. Paper presented at the 73rd AAA Meetings, Mexico City.

FÉL, E. and HOFER, T. 1969. *Proper peasants*. Chicago: Aldine.

FRANKLIN, S. H. 1969. *The European peasantry*. London: Methuen.

GAL, S. 1976. *Language change and its social determinants in a bilingual community*. Ann Arbor, Michigan: University Microfilms.

GUMPERZ, J. J. 1964. Linguistic and social interaction in two communities. *American Anthropologist* 66 (6). Part II, 137-54.

————. 1970. Verbal strategies in multilingual communication. Language Behavior Research Laboratory Working Paper # 36, Berkeley: University of California.

————. 1976. The sociolinguistic significance of conversational code-switching. Ms.

HYMES, D. 1967. Models of the interaction of language and social setting. *Journal of Social Issues* 23 (2), 8-28.

IMRE, S. 1971. A felsööri nyelvjárás (The Oberwart dialect). *Nyelvtudományi Értekezések* 72. Budapest.

————. 1973. Az ausztriai (burgenlandi) magyar szorványok (The Hungarian minority group in Austria). In *Népi Kultura—Népi Társadalom* (Folk Culture—Folk Society), Budapest: Akadémiai Kiadó.

KEENAN, E. 1974. Norm-makers, norm-breakers: Uses of speech by men and women in a Malagasy community. In R. Bauman and J. Sherzer (eds.), *Explorations in the ethnography of speaking*. London: Cambridge University Press.

KOVÁCS, M. 1942. A felsööri magyar népsziget (The Hungarian folk-island of Oberwart). Budapest: Sylvester-Nyomda.

LABOV, W. 1972. *Sociolinguistic patterns*. Philadelphia: University of Pennsylvania Press.

————. 1973. The linguistic consequences of being a lame. *LinS* 2, 81-115.

LAKOFF, R. 1973. Language and women's place. *LinS* 2, 45-80.

NICHOLS, P. 1976. Black women in the rural south: Conservative and innovative. Paper presented to the conference on the Sociology of the Languages of American Women. Las Cruces, New Mexico.

RUBIN, J. 1970. Bilingual usage in Paraguay. In J. Fishman (ed.), *Readings in the sociology of language*. The Hague: Mouton.

SANKOFF, G. and CEDERGREN. H. 1971. Some results of a sociolinguistic study of Montreal French. In R. Darnell (ed.), *Linguistic diversity in Canadian society*. Edmonton: Linguistic Research.

SWACKER, M. 1975. The sex of the speaker as a sociolinguistic variable. In B. Thorne and N. Henley (eds.), *Language and sex: Difference and dominance*. Rowley, Massachusetts: Newbury House Publishers, Inc.

THORNE, B. and HENLEY, N. (eds.). 1975. *Language and sex: Difference and dominance*. Rowley, Massachusetts: Newbury House Publishers, Inc.

TRUDGILL, P. 1972. Sex, covert prestige and linguistic change in the urban British English of Norwich. *LinS* 1, 179-95.

ZIMMERMAN, D. and WEST, C. 1975. Sex roles, interruptions and silences in conversation. In B. Thorne and N. Henley (eds.), *Language and sex: Difference and dominance*. Rowley, Massachusetts: Newbury House Publishers, Inc.

GILLIAN SANKOFF and SUZANNE LABERGE

On the Acquisition of Native Speakers
by a Language

1. BACKGROUND OF TOK PISIN

New Guinea Tok Pisin[1] is considered to be a descendant of the widespread South
Pacific pidgin known in the nineteenth century as Beach-la-Mar (Churchill 1911)[2]
and to have gained a foothold in New Britain, the location of the German capital of
New Guinea at one period, by the 1880s (Salisbury 1967; Laycock 1970b). The
extreme linguistic diversity of New Guinea, with approximately seven hundred
languages for its population of two and one half million, gave Tok Pisin a selective
advantage in the colonial situation. It was, in fact, very rapidly adopted as a *lingua
franca* among New Guineans having no other language in common and suddenly
finding themselves in a number of new situations where communication was
necessary: as laborers on plantations, crews on coastal vessels, domestic servants
and other employees of government officers, and a host of other situations created
by the colonial system. Most students of Tok Pisin maintain that from its beginning,
it has been used primarily for communication among New Guineans rather than for
communication between New Guineans and Europeans.

This very useful *lingua franca* function of Tok Pisin has been the principal
reason for the way it has spread and flourished, presently numbering more than a
half million speakers, more than double the number of New Guineans having any
other language in common (Laycock 1970a: X; Table 5-2, p. 123). An important
reason why Tok Pisin has had a selective advantage over the other languages with
which one might say it has been in competition (the approximately seven hundred
Papuan and Austronesian languages, German, Japanese, English) may be that it is
easier to learn as a second language. Like other pidgin languages, it has been, up to
the present, nobody's native language, but rather a second language for all its
speakers—a language relatively easy to learn because, also like other pidgin
languages, it had in comparison with natural languages a relatively limited
vocabulary, relatively few grammatical categories, and a relative lack of grammatic-

Reprinted from *Kivung* 6 (1973): 32-47, with permission of Gillian Sankoff and Suzanne Laberge.

[1] The standard source on the language has for many years been the work of Hall (1943, 1952,
1955a, 1955b), who used the term Neo-Melanesian, as did Mihalic (1957). Wurm (1971b) and Laycock
(1970a) speak of New Guinea Pidgin; Mihalic (1971) and Brash (1971) of Melanesian Pidgin.

[2] Churchill's book is based on a number of late nineteenth-century and early twentieth-century
publications citing examples of the Beach-la-Mar "jargon." Despite the unevenness of his sources,
examination of the many sentences compiled by Churchill reveals an unexpectedly close relationship
with Tok Pisin, a large number of the words and usages being still current in the language. It should be
noted that there was also some input to Tok Pisin from the speech of returned laborers from the
Queensland sugar fields, and for further historical details cf. Laycock (1970b) and Salisbury (1967).

al complexity. This "relative ease of learning" contention is based not on the experience of native speakers of English in learning Tok Pisin, but on reports by many Papuans and New Guineans who have learned it as adolescents or adults.

2. PIDGINIZATION VERSUS CREOLIZATION

Hymes (1971) has recently proposed that pidginization as a process involves reduction and simplification of language structure that can be directly related to the reduction of linguistic (communicative) function. Thus the kinds of simplifications mentioned above generally appear to be introduced in the interests of facilitating communication in a limited range of communication situations. That is, the pidgin is not used by anyone for the whole range of communication situations in which he/she participates: everyone has his/her native language to fall back on. This relationship between functional (communicative) and structural (grammatical) aspects can be characterized as follows:

> *Invariance in form*, rather than allomorphic variation; *invariant relation between form and grammatical function*, rather than derivational and inflectional declensional and conjugational variation; *largely monomorphemic words*, rather than inflected and derived words; *reliance on overt word order*; all have in common that they minimize the knowledge a speaker must have, and the speed with which he must decode, to know what in fact has grammatically happened. (Hymes 1971:73)

Hymes goes on to say that, conversely, creolization as a process involves expansion and complication of language structure, again directly related to the expansion of functions of the language. Using the traditional definition of a creole as a pidgin which has acquired native speakers, Labov (ms., 1971) has also recently argued that creolization involves concomitant complication of structure, because pidgins do not seem to be grammatically adequate to function as natural languages, i.e., languages with native speakers. He says:

> Full competence in a pidgin grammar is still less than competence in one's native grammar. . .; we have objective evidence that pidgins do not provide all of the features which native speakers seem to demand in a language. When pidgins acquire native speakers, they change.

The goal of our research on Tok Pisin was not only to study the structure of the language as it is presently spoken in New Guinea but also to systematically investigate its contexts of use, including the range of competence displayed by different speakers. As such, it was important for us to make a series of recordings of Tok Pisin as it is actually used, over a wide range of communication situations. We hoped to discover systematic patterning of variation with respect to grammar and use, which would indicate the directions of linguistic change in the light of changes in usage.

3. PRESENT DAY USE OF TOK PISIN

During the last twenty years or so, Tok Pisin has undergone an impressive widening of its social and communicative functions. It has acquired the status of one of New

Guinea's three official languages, and has been since 1964, the date of the inception of the first House of Assembly, the predominant language used in parliamentary debates. It has acquired two new channels other than the verbal. First, it has become a language of literacy, and is used in a host of newspapers, information bulletins, and the like. Second, it is the dominant radio language, though there are broadcasts in other languages as well. More important still, it has acquired a generation of native speakers. These people are the ever more numerous urbanites, more specifically, the children who have grown up in one of New Guinea's urban communities. Their parents may be from different areas, having no language in common except Tok Pisin, which is used as the household language. Even if the parents do have a native language in common, children growing up in towns frequently have little more than a partial and passive command of it. Parents commonly say: "The children only understand simple commands like when we tell them to go and get something, and they never answer us in our own language, but only in Tok Pisin." On the basis of observations we made during June-August 1971 (principally in Lae, but also in Wewak and Port Moresby), it appears that the native speakers of Tok Pisin are, by and large, under twenty years of age, and that their numbers are growing very rapidly.

4. NATIVE SPEAKERS (CREOLIZATION) AND LINGUISTIC CHANGE

The fact that Tok Pisin is presently undergoing creolization (or depidginization)[3] enables us to examine the ways in which the social and communicative functions of a language may be related to its structure. We thus attempted to discover in what respects the Tok Pisin spoken by this new generation of native speakers is different from that spoken by their (nonnative speaker) parents, in order to understand the kinds of changes that are taking place in the grammar of the language as it becomes a creole (i.e., a natural language). We hypothesized that native speakers in general tend to have little patience with or respect for a language with few grammatical categories, limited lexicon, virtually no morphophonemic reduction rules, insufficient redundancy, and little opportunity for stylistic maneuver. (These are of course *relative* characteristics; cf. also Kay and Sankoff 1973. The fact that Tok Pisin has been widely and extensively used in a great variety of communicative situations for several generations is sufficient explanation for its considerable stylistic resources, as clearly evidenced by Brash (1971), by the numerous literary works produced in the past five or six years, and by listening to any fluent Tok Pisin-speaking politician. Our goal was to investigate what particular aspects of grammar appear to be changing in the language as spoken by native speakers.)

There is a great range of competence in Tok Pisin among speakers who have acquired it at different ages and different historical periods, and who use it for different communicative purposes: the newly arrived migrant in town (who at first may speak little and halting Pisin); the ex-*luluai* or *tultul*[4] in villages long used to government patrols, who may have learned their Pisin as plantation laborers in German times; the young generation of town-born children, for whom it may be a

---

[3] The terms "creolization" and "depidginization" are used here synonymously.

[4] Government-appointed "headman" and "interpreter" respectively, under the earlier system of administration. These officials have been replaced by a system of elected Local Government Councils.

first language. Though we made recordings of all these and many more, we concentrated on families in which Tok Pisin is used as the normal language in the home. The parents were all fluent speakers of Tok Pisin, people who had lived in town for many years and who had for a long time spoken Tok Pisin rather than their native language. In looking for differences between their speech and that of their children, for whom Tok Pisin is a native language, it may be too much to expect, after only one incomplete generation, discrete, qualitative differences. Though more obvious differences might easily be found by comparing, say, new immigrants with the urban children, we wanted to specifically examine differences between *fluent* second-language speakers (the parents) and first-generation native speakers (the children). In making some preliminary comparisons, we have observed a number of tendencies which may represent ongoing changes in the language.

The children speak with much greater speed and fluency, involving a number of morphophonemic reductions as well as a reduction in the number of syllables characteristically receiving primary stress. Whereas an adult will say, for the sentence "I am going home,"

(1)   Mi gó loṅg háus;

a child will often say:

(2)   Mi gò háus;

three syllables rather than four, with one primary stress rather than two.

The particular phenomenon we examine in this chapter is related to a further generalization of Labov's. He says (ms., 1971:29):

> It is not at all obvious that a pidgin will develop obligatory tense markers when it becomes a native language. Yet this has happened in case after case. . . . When pidgins become creoles, the system of optional adverbs gives way to an obligatory tense marker next to the verb.

After examining a corpus of tapes and transcriptions of second-language speakers of Tok Pisin collected by Gillian Sankoff during the 1960s, Labov suggested that the adverb *bai* is presently shifting to the status of a future marker. This, he said, is evidenced by:

1.   its reduction from *baimbai* to *bai* (a change which has almost gone to completion, *baimbai* being rare in current usage);

2.   its loss of obligatory stress;

3.   its occurrence with adverbs having a future meaning, e.g.,

(3)   *klostu bai i dai* 'soon he will die';
(4)   *bihain bai i kambek gen* 'later it will come back again'

4.   its apparent tendency to be placed next to the main verb, after the subject, rather than at the beginning of the sentence or in presubject position.

We will deal with these four points in the light of our corpus of native and nonnative speakers, in order to see whether the usage of *bai* by the two generations of speakers indicates change in its grammatical function. The corpus on which the present discussion is based consists of 395 examples of *bai* in the speech of eighteen people: nine children and adolescents, between the ages of five and seventeen, and nine adults, parents of seven of the children, and between the ages of approximately twenty-five and forty-five. The children include four boys and five girls; the adults, four men and five women. Recordings were made of mealtime conversations among families, children's play, gossip, and storytelling (including the recounting of events), and our examples are drawn from all these sources.

4.1. *Baimbai* > *bai* in Historical Perspective

Among 395 cases, involving several hours of taped speech of various kinds, we found only five instances of *baimbai*, pronounced [bə'mbai] or [bə'bai]. These five cases occurred in the speech of three of the nine adults in our sample; there were no instances in the speech of any of the nine children.

Though *baimbai* is very infrequent in the ordinary conversational speech of the adults we observed, and nonexistent in the usage of the children, it is still used regularly within the speech community in some contexts, notably in radio

TABLE 10-1. Children and adults in the sample: Adults are parents of children with corresponding second initials.

		Approx. age	No. of cases
Children:	J.M.	5	20
	C.W.	6	15
	S.D.	8	47
	W.D.	11	12
	P.T.	11	21
	L.X.	11	12
	J.B.	12	25
	J.P.	15	20
	L.Z.	17	20
Total			192
Adults:	Mrs. M.	25-30	22
	Mr. W.	40	21
	Mrs. W.	25-30	20
	Mr. D.	35	20
	Mrs. D.	35	24
	Mr. T.	45	20
	Mrs. T.	30	24
	Mr. X.	40	20
	Mrs. Z.	35	32
Total			203
Grand Total			395

broadcasts. Though it appears to be disappearing today, *baimbai* (< English 'by and by') was most probably the original form. Exactly when the reduction process from *baimbai* to *bai* was initiated is very unclear from the existing documentation. Churchill (1911) contains no mention of *bai*, nor does Mihalic (1957), for over a decade the most reliable and respected source. Both of these do, however, list *baimbai*, as does Murphy (1966:59), noted as "*adv.*, afterwards, later, in time, then (future)." Murphy, however, also lists *bai*, noted as "*conj.*, then, after, that, in order that, in consequence, so that." By 1971 (p. 63), Mihalic had added *bai*, listed with *baimbai* as being derived from English 'by and by', and having the same range of meanings (though for the 'in order to' meaning, the only example cited is that of *bai*).

Though it would seem logical that *bai* is the result of a reduction of *baimbai* (involving deletion of the first, rather than second syllable), the two forms appear to have existed side by side for a long time. Ann Chowning (personal communication) reports that in areas of New Britain in the 1950s, *bai* was the exclusively used form, with *baimbai* appearing later as a novel introduction. We hope that further research into historical sources will help to shed light on this problem.

It is clear that for our subjects the change has already taken place, *baimbai* having virtually disappeared from ordinary conversation. Whether it can be said that *bai* has in fact become the regular "future" marker will depend, however, on a more detailed study of time relations in the verb system as a whole. *Laik*, for example, is frequently mentioned in the literature (Murphy 1966; Mihalic 1971; Laycock 1970a) as an auxiliary indicating immediate future. Though we have not examined *laik* in any detail, we find its occurrence to be very frequent in our sample, in many cases carrying the "immediate future" meaning, as in the following example from our corpus:

> (5) . . . nait, em i no inap kaikai, em *bai* pilei long graun igo igo igo nait tru nau, *bai* em i *laik* slip *bai* em *bai* kaikai.
> '. . . at night he didn't eat, he would play in the dirt right up until the middle of the night, until he would be about to go to sleep, then he would eat.' (S.D.)

The speaker employs a complicated tense structure in this story, using unmarked forms (not shown in this extract) for single completed actions in the past, *bai* to indicate habitual actions in the past, and *bai* with *laik* to indicate habitual being about to do something in the past. *Ken* has also been mentioned (Wurm 1971b; Laycock 1970a) as an indicator of future time; however, its use as a future marker by Lae area residents we recorded (including people from many parts of Papua New Guinea) was not sufficiently frequent for the type of quantitative analysis which follows.

4.2 Stress

Our data on *bai* indicate that it never receives primary stress. Transcribing the stress pattern for all sentences containing *bai*, we found that we could, however, distinguish three stress levels: secondary stress, where *bai* receives full syllabic weight, analogous to stressed syllables in nouns or pronouns; tertiary stress, where *bai* still retains syllabic weight, with stress equivalent to "unstressed" syllables in nouns or adjectives, or to most prepositions. The fourth stress level involves a reduction of the vowel nucleus to [ə], or even its disappearance, so that *bai* is barely if at all distinguishable as a syllable. Examples of each of these levels appear as examples 6, 7, and 8 below:

         ³   ²   ²   ¹   ² ²   ¹
(6) Em *bai* yu kam, *bai* yu dai. (Mrs. T.) 'You come; you'll die.'

         ³ ²   ³   ³ ³ ¹ ²
(7) Ating *bai* klostu belo. (Mrs. D.) 'It must be nearly noon.'

         ² ³   ⁴ ³   ³   ¹ ³   ⁴   ² ³   ³
(8) Suga bilong mi klostu *bai* [bə] finis nau. (C.W.) 'My sugar cane is nearly finished now.'

A tabulation of the number of cases in which *bai* receives each of the three stress levels indicates that the children show a definite tendency to place less stress on *bai* that do the adults. Figures presented in Table 10-2 show that whereas adult usage is almost evenly split between levels 3 and 2, level 2 predominating slightly, children are twice as likely to use level 3 for *bai* as level 2. Children also show a significant tendency to reduce *bai* to [bə] (level 4), a phenomenon virtually absent among the adults.

Considering the data individually we can see from the plot in Figure 10-1 that the results of Table 10-2 are not simply an artifact of aggregating the data. There is a definite slope from left to right, and from lower to higher percentages, indicating that nonnative speakers (the adults) show a much greater tendency to stress *bai* than do native speakers (the children). The use of minimal stress (level 4) was used only twice by adults (two speakers), whereas five of the nine children used it a total of twenty times.

The data on stress support the hypothesis that the grammatical function of *bai* is changing from that of an adverb to that of a tense marker, as we would expect the latter to carry less stress. As a marker, however, we might also expect *bai* to show another characteristic of markers, i.e., to exhibit high redundancy.

4.3 Redundancy

We found numerous examples of *bai* being used in sentences containing either adverbs of time such as *klostu* 'soon' (cf. examples 7 and 8 above), *bihain* 'later', and *nau* 'right now' (including immediate future), or other indications of future time. In these cases, *bai* is not semantically necessary, future meaning already being present in the adverb or adverbial phrase.

TABLE 10-2. **Differential stress on *bai* for adults and children.**

Stress level	Children	Adults
2	29.1%	51.7%
3	60.4%	47.3%
4	10.4%	1.0%
Total cases	192	203

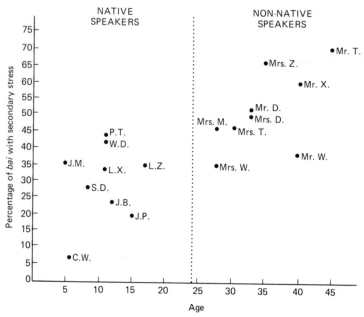

FIGURE 10-1. Percentage of cases of *bai* showing secondary stress for nine children and nine adults.

The redundant character of *bai* is also evident where it is used many times within a single sentence (as an alternative to the earlier system of marking a sentence, or even a longer segment, only once, usually at the beginning, for time, and using any following verbs in their invariant stem forms). The redundant, obligatory character of *bai* can be seen in the following quotation:

(9) Pes pikinini ia *bai* yu go wok long,—*bai* yu stap ia na *bai* yu stap long banis kau bilong mi na *bai* taim mi dai *bai* yu lukautim na yu save wokim susu na *bai* yu givim long, wonem ia, stua, na *bai* ol i baim. (Mr. D.) 'You, first son, will go and work in,—you'll remain here and you'll just stay on my cattle farm and when I die you'll look after it, and you'll be doing the milking and you'll send it to the, uh, store, and they will buy it.'

In this extract, every verb except *wokim* (qualified by the auxiliary *save*, meaning 'keep on doing') carries the marker *bai*. Application of the *bai* marker to every verb in compound sentences was extremely regular for all subjects studied, both adults and children, there being very few exceptions to this rule.

Dependent clauses in conditional constructions also appear to take *bai* obligatorily,[5] whether the independent clause contains *sapos* 'if' or not, as in examples 10 and 11.

(10) Sapos yu no lusim mi, *bai* mi kikim yu nau. (J.P.) 'If you don't let me go, I'll kick you.'

(11) Givim man i kaikai, em *bai* i dai. (Mr. T.) 'If you give it to somebody to eat, he'll die.'

[5] *Bai* indeed has broader functions than simply marking the future, as evidenced in example 6 above. An analysis of the whole tense-aspect system might show that it could be analyzed as an irrealis marker (cf. Bickerton 1975).

Bai seems to be redundant and obligatory for both adults and children in the present sample, and we detected no significant differences in usage with respect to these characteristics. It is probable that the older generation of speakers, people in their sixties, do use *bai* less frequently, and we plan to examine our corpus of older speakers for this phenomenon.

4.4   Position of *bai* in the Sentence

(Baim)bai functioning as an adverb of time was free to occupy many positions in the sentence. It appears, however, that the clause-initial position has traditionally been favored. Mihalic (1957:43) puts *baimbai* (glossed as 'in the future' or 'after a while') in a list of adverbs "to be found only at the beginning of a sentence." His 1971 edition modifies the position, putting it in a list of adverbs "found usually at the beginning of a sentence." If we interpret Mihalic's statement to include clause-initial as well as sentence-initial position, we find that all of the eleven examples of *baimbai* cited by Churchill (1911:37) are of this type.

What is crucial in the switch to a marker function, however, is the position of *(baim)bai* with respect not to the sentence but to the verb. Here there appear to be three principal alternatives:

   i.   *bai* + NP + VP (NP = any noun phrase other than a pronoun)
   ii. *bai* + pronoun + VP
  iii. *bai* + VP

verbs normally being preceded by the predicate marker *i*. Of the eleven examples given by Churchill, four are of the first type. In our corpus, however, the frequency of this type is very low, as shown in Table 10-3. Cases where *bai* is separated from the verb phrase by more than a pronoun form only 5.9 percent of the total number of classifiable cases, twenty-two in all.

TABLE 10-3.   Occurrences of *bai* in different positions.

	No. of cases
bai + NP + VP	22
bai + pronoun + VP	199
⎧ NP ⎫	
⎨ pronoun ⎬ + *bai* + VP	151
⎩ ø ⎭	
Total	372*

* The twenty-three remaining cases were un-classifiable due to hesitations occurring after *bai*.

Looking at the data in detail, we can observe strong and consistent patterns of ordering with respect to the various pronouns and to the type of noun phrase involved. Table 10-4 indicates that virtually all the pronouns display a marked tendency to occur immediately adjacent to the verb phrase, with *bai* preceding the pronoun. This is the case for *mi, yu, ol, yumi, yu(tu)pela,* and *mi(tu)pela.* Of the fifteen cases where *bai* was interposed between one of these pronouns and the verb phrase, eleven were found in the speech of children. *Em* is the only pronoun which tends to precede *bai,*[6] as do noun phrases.

TABLE 10-4. Order of *bai* with respect to various types of subject NP.

Subject NP	Order of *bai*	
	bai + {NP / Pro} + VP	{NP / Pro / ø} + *bai* + VP
mi	78	7
yu	52	1
ol	31	1
{ {mi / yu} ⟨tu⟩pela / yumi }	22	6
Subtotal	183	15
em	11	47
NP	22	36*
ø subj.	—	53
Subtotal	33	136
Total	216	151

* Five of these cases also contain a *bai* preceding the noun phrase of the pattern *bai* + NP + *bai* + VP.

TABLE 10-5. Ordering of *bai* by number of phonological words in the subject NP.

NP =	Order of *bai*			Total
	bai + NP	NP + *bai*	*bai* + NP + *bai*	
1 word	8	9	—	17
2 words	7	7	—	14
3 words	1	7	2	10
4 words	1	6	—	7
5[+] words	—	2	3	5
Total	17	31	5	53

[6] The status of *em* as a pronoun that behaves similarly to the others is already dubious on other grounds. Its optional character permits its frequent omission, which accounts for the majority of ø-subject sentences in Table 10-4.

Table 10-5 indicates that the number of phonological words in the subject noun phrase has an influence on the position of *bai*. In effect, *bai* rarely precedes a noun phrase longer than two phonological words, and when it does, the speaker frequently inserts another *bai* immediately before the verb phrase. Noun phrases composed of one or two phonological words are almost equally likely to precede or follow *bai*; longer noun phrases almost always precede *bai*.

Table 10-6 adds further clarification, showing that the relationships of Table 10-5 can perhaps be better understood in terms of grammatical conditioning. Noun phrases consisting of a single noun, a noun plus modifier, or a pronoun plus modifier can be either preceded or followed by *bai* but more complex noun phrases are always followed by *bai*. It is interesting to note that subject noun phrases consisting of possessives (structures containing *bilong*) behave in the same way as subject noun phrases consisting of embeddings (i.e., containing surface verbs). Neither of these constructions occurs with a single preceding *bai*.

No significant differences with respect to the ordering of *bai* can be observed between the children and the adults. All speakers appear to share a rule that categorically inserts *bai* in immediate pre-VP position in the case of complex subject noun phrases, and which operates with a probability of approximately 0.5 in the case of other nonpronominal subject noun phrases.

TABLE 10-6. Ordering of *bai* by grammatical structure of subject NP.

	Order of *bai*			
Structure of NP	*bai* + NP	NP + *bai*	*bai* + NP + *bai*	Total
$\left\{ \begin{array}{l} \text{mod.} + \text{Pro} \\ \langle\text{mod.}\rangle + \text{N} \end{array} \right\}$	15	16	1	32
$\left\{ \begin{array}{l} \text{mod.} + \text{Pro} \\ \langle\text{mod.}\rangle + \text{N} \end{array} \right\}$ + adv.	2	1	1	4
$\left\{ \begin{array}{l} \text{N} \\ \text{Pro} \end{array} \right\}$ + *bilong* + $\left\{ \begin{array}{l} \text{N} \\ \text{Pro} \end{array} \right\}$	—	8	2	10
$\left\{ \begin{array}{l} \text{N} \\ \text{Pro} \end{array} \right\}$ + embedding	—	6	1	7
Total	17	31	5	53

CONCLUSION

That *bai* has been undergoing a transition to the status of a future marker is supported by historical data indicating the anteriority of *baimbai*, with subsequent reduction through [bə′mbai] and [bə′bai] to *bai* ([bai] and [ba]), a process now almost gone to completion. A continuation of this process has led to further reduction (as is clear from the children in our sample) to [bə]. *Bai* has become a highly redundant, obligatory marker for fluent present-day speakers. The marker status of *bai* for the children in our sample is also indicated by the reduced stress it receives in their speech, compared with adult speech. A shift in the position of *bai* with respect to the verb also appears to have taken place in the past, though fluent second language speakers now show no difference from native speakers in this regard. Further work on the behavior of various kinds of embeddings[7] that clearly affect the *bai*-movement rule for all fluent present-day speakers, may also help to clarify the history of this change.

It is obvious that change in the status of *bai* was well under way prior to the existence of a large number of native speakers: native speakers appear to be carrying further tendencies which were already present in the language. We are not arguing that the presence of native speakers creates sudden and dramatic changes in a language, but rather that their presence may be one factor in influencing directions in language change.

Further, we feel that evidence presented here supported the argument that Tok Pisin is proving and will continue to prove adequate to handle whatever communicative demands are put on it, and that as these demands increase, the available linguistic resources will also increase, as they have clearly done in the past and continue to do in the present. *Olsem mitupela i bin suim yupela long dispela liklik toktok.*

REFERENCES

BICKERTON, DEREK. 1975. *Dynamics of a Creole System.* Cambridge: Cambridge University Press.

BRASH, ELTON. 1971. Tok pilai, tok piksa na tok bokis. *Kivung* 4:1-10.

CHURCHILL, WILLIAM. 1911. Beach-la-mar, the jargon or trade speech of the Western Pacific. Carnegie Institution of Washington, Publication no. 164.

DeCAMP, DAVID and IAN HANCOCK. 1974. *Pidgins and Creoles: current trends and prospects.* Washington, D.C.: Georgetown University Press.

HALL, ROBERT A., JR. 1943. Melanesian pidgin English: grammar, texts, vocabulary. Baltimore: Linguistic Society of America.

———. 1952. The vocabulary of Melanesian pidgin. *American Speech* 18:192-99.

———. 1955a. Innovations in Melanesian pidgin (Neo-Melanesian.) *Oceania* 26, no. 2:91-109.

———. 1955b. *Hands off Pidgin English.* Sydney: Pacific Publications.

HYMES, DELL (ed.). 1971. *Introduction to Part III, Pidginization and Creolization of Languages.* Cambridge: Cambridge University Press.

KAY, PAUL and GILLIAN SANKOFF. 1974. A language-universals approach to pidgins and creoles. In DeCamp and Hancock (eds.), 1974, 61-72.

LABOV, WILLIAM. 1971. Methodology. In W.O. Dingwall (ed.), *A survey of linguistic science.* Linguistics Program, University of Maryland, 412-97.

———. 1971. On the Adequacy of Natural Languages: I: The Development of Tense. Ms.

LAYCOCK, D.C. 1970a. Materials in New Guinea pidgin (coastal and lowlands). *Pacific Linguistics* D-5.

———. 1970b. Pidgin English in New Guinea. In W.S. Ramson (ed.), English transported: essays on Australasian English. Canberra: Australian National University Press, 102-22.

MIHALIC, REV. F. 1957. *Grammar and dictionary of Neo-Melanesian.* The Mission Press, Westmead, New South Wales, Australia.

———. 1971. *The Jacaranda dictionary and grammar of Melanesian Pidgin.* Port Moresby: Jacaranda Press.

MURPHY, JOHN. 1966. *The book of Pidgin English.* Revised edition, Brisbane: W.R. Smith and Paterson Pty. Ltd.

SALISBURY, RICHARD. 1967. Pidgin's respectable past. *New Guinea* 2 (2):44-48.

WURM, S.A. 1971. New Guinea highlands pidgin: course material. *Pacific Linguistics,* D-3.

---

[7] E.g., relatives.